dun & bradstreet

Industry & Financial Consulting Services

INDUSTRY NORMS
AND KEY BUSINESS RATIOS

**One Year
Desk-Top Edition
SIC #0100-8999**

ISBN 978-1-63053-497-4

To obtain reprint permission, please send your correspondence to

Mergent Inc.
444 Madison Avenue Suite 502
New York, NY 10022
Telephone: 800.342.5647
www.mergentbusinesspress.com

Manufactured in the United States of America.

CONTENTS

INDUSTRY NORMS AND KEY BUSINESS RATIOS

APPENDIX - SIC Numbers Appearing in This Directory

The Desk-Top Edition of The D&B Industry Norms and Key Business Ratios is made possible through over one million financial statements in the D&B Financial Information Base. This file consists of U.S. corporations, partnerships and proprietorships both public and privately owned, in all size ranges, and includes over 800 different lines of business as defined by the U.S. Standard Industrial Classification (SIC) code numbers. Our data is collected weekly, maintained daily, and constantly edited and updated. All of these factors combine to make this financial information unequaled anywhere for scope and timeliness*.

It should be noted that only general data is supplied in the Desk-Top Edition. However, for more detailed asset/geographical breakdowns of this data, an expanded set of Industry Norms and Key Business Ratios are also published by D&B for the Corporate Marketplace in the following five segments:

1. **Agriculture, Mining, Construction/ Transportation/Communication/Utilities**
2. **Manufacturing**
3. **Wholesaling**
4. **Retailing**
5. **Finance/Real Estate/Services**

All five segments are available in two other formats. The formats are as follows:

1. **Industry Norms and Key Business Ratios, Three Year Edition.**
   Directories and electronic file versions available.

2. **Industry Norms and Key Business Ratios, One Year Edition.**
   Directories and electronic file versions available.

Note that the Industry Norms contain "typical" balance sheets and income statements, and "common-size" financial figures, <u>as well as Key Business Ratios</u>. The Key Business Ratios books contain fourteen indicators of performance.

*To provide the most current information available, fiscal years January 1 - December 31 were utilized to calculate the Norms.

INDUSTRY NORM FORMAT

At the top of each industry norm will be identifying information: SIC code number and short title. Beside the year date, in parenthesis, is the number of companies in the sample. The "typical" balance-sheet figures are in the first column and the "common-size" balance-sheet figures are in the second. The respective income statements begin with the item "Net Sales", and the respective Key Business Ratios begin with the item "Ratios." The latter are further broken down, or refined, into the median, and the upper quartile and lower quartile.

THE COMMON - SIZE FINANCIAL STATEMENT

The common-size balance-sheet and income statement present each item of the financial statement as a percentage of its respective aggregate total. Common-size percentages are computed for all statement items of all the individual companies used in the industry sample. An average for each statement item is then determined and presented as the industry norm.

This enables the analyst to examine the current composition of assets, liabilities and sales of a particular industry.

THE TYPICAL FINANCIAL STATEMENT

The typical balance-sheet figures are the result of translating the common-size percentages into dollar figures. They permit, for example, a quick check of the relative size of assets and liabilities between one's own company and that company's own line of business.

After the common-size percentages have been computed for the particular sample, the actual financial statements are then sequenced by both *total assets* and *total sales*, with the median, or mid-point figure in both these groups serving as the "typical" amount. We then compute the typical balance-sheet and income statement dollar figures by multiplying the common-size percentages for each statement item by their respective total amounts.

(For example, if the median total assets for an SIC category are $669,599, and the common-size figure for cash is 9.2 percent, then by multiplying the two we derive a cash figure of $61,603 for the typical balance sheet.)

KEY BUSINESS RATIOS

The Fourteen Key Business Ratios are broken down into median figures, with upper and lower quartiles, giving the analyst an even more refined set of figures to work with. These ratios cover all those critical areas of business performance with indicators of solvency, efficiency and profitability.

They provide a profound and well-documented insight into all aspects for everyone interested in the financial workings of business—business executives and managers, credit executives, bankers, lenders, investors, academicians and students.

In the ratio tables appearing in this book, the figures are broken down into the median—which is the midpoint of all companies in the sample—and the upper quartile and lower quartile—which are mid-points of the upper and lower halves.

Upper quartile figures are not always the highest numerical value, nor are lower quartile figures always the lowest numerical value. The quartile listings reflect *judgmental ranking*, thus the upper quartile represents the best condition in any given ratio and is not necessarily the highest numerical value. (For example, see the items Total Liabilities-to-Net Worth or Collection Period, where a lower numerical value represents a better condition.)

Each of the fourteen ratios is calculated individually for every concern in the sample. These individual figures are then sequenced for each ratio according to condition (best to worst), and the figure that falls in the middle of this series becomes the median (or mid-point) for that ratio in that line of business. The figure halfway between the median and the best condition of the series becomes the upper quartile; and the number halfway between the median and the least favorable condition of the series is the lower quartile.

In a statistical sense, each median is considered the *typical* ratio figure for a concern in a given category.

SOLVENCY RATIOS

Quick Ratio

Cash + Accounts Receivable
Current Liabilities

The Quick Ratio is computed by dividing cash plus accounts receivable by total current liabilities. Current liabilities are all the liabilities that fall due within one year. This ratio reveals the protection afforded short-term creditors in cash or near-cash assets. It shows the number of dollars of liquid assets available to cover each dollar of current debt. Any time this ratio is as much as 1 to 1 (1.0) the business is said to be in a liquid condition. The larger the ratio the greater the liquidity.

Current Ratio

Current Assets
Current Liabilities

Total current assets are divided by total current liabilities. Current assets include cash, accounts and notes receivable (less reserves for bad debts), advances on inventories, merchandise inventories and marketable securities. This ratio measures the degree to which current assets cover current liabilities. The higher the ratio the more assurance exists that the retirement of current liabilities can be made. The current ratio measures the margin of safety available to cover any possible shrinkage in the value of current assets. Normally a ratio of 2 to 1 (2.0) or better is considered good.

Current Liabilities to Net Worth

Current Liabilities
Net Worth

Current Liabilities to Net Worth is derived by dividing current liabilities by net worth. This contrasts the funds that creditors temporarily are risking with the funds permanently invested by the owners. The smaller the net worth and the larger the liabilities, the less security for the creditors. Care should be exercised when selling any firm with current liabilities exceeding two-thirds (66.6 percent) of net worth.

Current Liabilities to Inventory

Current Liabilities
Inventory

Dividing current liabilities by inventory yields another indication of the extent to which the business relies on funds from disposal of unsold inventories to meet its debts. This ratio combines with Net Sales to Inventory to indicate how management controls inventory. It is possible to have decreasing liquidity while maintaining consistent sales-to-inventory ratios. Large increases in sales with corresponding increases in inventory levels can cause an inappropriate rise in current liabilities if growth isn't made wisely.

Total Liabilities to Net Worth

Total Liabilities
Net Worth

Obtained by dividing total current plus long-term and deferred liabilities by net worth. The effect of long-term (funded) debt on a business can be determined by comparing this ratio with Current Liabilities to Net Worth. The difference will pinpoint the relative size of long-term debt, which, if sizable, can burden a firm with substantial interest charges. In general, total liabilities shouldn't exceed net worth (100 percent) since in such cases creditors have more at stake than owners.

Fixed Assets to Net Worth

Fixed Assets
Net Worth

Fixed assets are divided by net worth. The proportion of net worth that consists of fixed assets will vary greatly from industry to industry but generally a smaller proportion is desirable. A high ratio is unfavorable because heavy investment in fixed assets indicates that either the concern has a low net working capital and is overtrading or has utilized large funded debt to supplement working capital. Also, the larger the fixed assets, the bigger the annual depreciation charge that must be deducted from the income statement. Normally, fixed assets above 75 percent of net worth indicate possible over-investment and should be examined with care.

EFFICIENCY RATIOS

Collection Period

> Accounts Receivable
> Sales   x 365

Accounts receivable are divided by sales and then multiplied by 365 days to obtain this figure. The quality of the receivables of a company can be determined by this relationship when compared with selling terms and industry norms. In some industries where credit sales are not the normal way of doing business, the percentage of cash sales should be taken into consideration. Generally, where most sales are for credit, any collection period more than one-third over normal selling terms (40.0 for 30-day terms) is indicative of some slow-turning receivables. When comparing the collection period of one concern with that of another, allowances should be made for possible variations in selling terms.

Sales to Inventory

> Annual Net Sales
> Inventory

Obtained by dividing annual net sales by inventory. Inventory control is a prime management objective since poor controls allow inventory to become costly to store, obsolete or insufficient to meet demands. The sales-to-inventory relationship is a guide to the rapidity at which merchandise is being moved and the effect on the flow of funds into the business. This ratio varies widely between lines of business and a company's figure is only meaningful when compared with industry norms. Individual figures that are outside either the upper or lower quartiles for a given industry should be examined with care. Although low figures are usually the biggest problem, as they indicate excessively high inventories, extremely high turnovers might reflect insufficient merchandise to meet customer demand and result in lost sales.

Asset to Sales

> Total Assets
> Net Sales

Assets to sales is calculated by dividing total assets by annual net sales. This ratio ties in sales and the total investment that is used to generate those sales. While figures vary greatly from in-

dustry to industry, by comparing a company's ratio with industry norms it can be determined whether a firm is overtrading (handling an excessive volume of sales in relation to investment) or undertrading (not generating sufficient sales to warrant the assets invested). Abnormally low percentages (above the upper quartile) can indicate overtrading which may lead to financial difficulties if not corrected. Extremely high percentages (below the lower quartile) can be the result of overly conservative or poor sales management, indicating a more aggressive sales policy may need to be followed.

Sales to Net Working Capital

> Sales
> Net Working Capital

Net sales are divided by net working capital (net working capital is current assets minus current liabilities.). This relationship indicates whether a company is overtrading or conversely carrying more liquid assets than needed for its volume. Each industry can vary substantially and it is necessary to compare a company with its peers to see if it is either overtrading on its available funds or being overly conservative. Companies with substantial sales gains often reach a level where their working capital becomes strained. Even if they maintain an adequate total investment for the volume being generated (Assets to Sales), that investment may be so centered in fixed assets or other noncurrent items that it will be difficult to continue meeting all current obligations without additional investment or reducing sales.

Accounts Payable to Sales

> Accounts Payable
> Annual Net Sales

Computed by dividing accounts payable by annual net sales. This ratio measures how the company is paying its suppliers in relation to the volume being transacted. An increasing percentage, or one larger than the industry norm, indicates the firm may be using suppliers to help finance operations. This ratio is especially important to short-term creditors since a high percentage could indicate potential problems in paying vendors.

PROFITABILITY RATIOS

Return on Sales (Profit Margin)

> Net Profit After Taxes
> Annual Net Sales

Obtained by dividing net profit after taxes by annual net sales. This reveals the profits earned per dollar of sales and therefore measures the efficiency of the operation. Return must be adequate for the firm to be able to achieve satisfactory profits for its owners. This ratio is an indicator of the firm's ability to withstand adverse conditions such as falling prices, rising costs and declining sales.

Return on Assets

> Net Profit After Taxes
> Total Assets

Net profit after taxes divided by total assets. This ratio is the key indicator of profitability for a firm. It matches operating profits with the assets available to earn a return. Companies efficiently using their assets will have a relatively high return while less well-run businesses will be relatively low.

Return on Net Worth (Return on Equity)

> Net Profit After Taxes
> Net Worth

Obtained by dividing net profit after tax by net worth. This ratio is used to analyze the ability of the firm's management to realize an adequate return on the capital invested by the owners of the firm. Tendency is to look increasingly to this ratio as a final criterion of profitability. Generally, a relationship of at least 10 percent is regarded as a desirable objective for providing dividends plus funds for future growth.

Using Industry Norms for Financial Analysis

The principal purpose of financial analysis is to identify irregularities that require explanations to completely understand an industry's or company's current status and future potential. These irregularities can be identified by comparing the industry norms with the figures of specific companies (*comparative analysis*). D&B's Industry Norms are specifically formatted to accommodate this analysis.

Relative Position

Common-size and typical balance sheets provide an excellent picture of the makeup of the industry's assets and liabilities. Are assets concentrated in inventories or accounts receivable? Are payables to the trade or bank loans more important as a method for financing operations? The answers to these and other important questions are clearly shown by the Industry Norms, its common-size balance sheet approach and is then further crystallized by the typical balance sheets.

Financial Ratio Trends

Key Business Ratio changes indicate trends in the important *relationships* between key financial items, such as the relationship between Net Profits and Net Sales (a common indicator of profitability). Ratios that reflect short and long-term liquidity, efficiency in managing assets and controlling debt, and different measures of profitability are all included in the Key Business Ratios sections of the Industry Norms.

Comparative Analysis

Comparing a company with its peers is a reliable method for evaluating financial status. The key to this technique is the composition of the peer group and the timeliness of the data. The D&B Industry Norms are unique in scope of sample size and in level of detail.

Sample Size

The number of firms in the sample must be representative or they will be unduly influenced by irregular figures from relatively few companies. The more than one million companies used as a basis for the Industry Norms allow for more than adequate sample sizes in most cases.

Key Business Ratios Analysis

Valuable insights into an industry's performance can be obtained by equating two related statement items in the form of a financial ratio. For really effective ratio analysis, the items compared must be meaningful and the comparison should reflect the combined effort of two potentially diverse trends. While dozens of different ratios can be computed from financial statements, the fourteen included in the Industry Norms and Key Business Ratio books are those most commonly used and were rated as the most significant as shown in a survey of financial analysts. Many of the other ratios in existence are variations on these fourteen.

The fourteen Key Business Ratios are categorized into three major groups:

Solvency, or liquidity, measurements are significant in evaluating a company's ability to meet short and long-term obligations. These figures are of prime interest to credit managers of commercial companies and financial institutions.

Efficiency ratios indicate how effectively a company uses and controls its assets. This is critical information for evaluating how a company is managed. Studying these ratios is useful for credit, marketing and investment purposes.

Profitability ratios show how successfully a business is earning a return to its owners. Those interested in mergers and acquisitions consider this key data for selecting candidates.

Recent research efforts have revealed that the use of financial analysis (via Industry Norms) is very useful in several functional areas. To follow are only a few of the more widely used applications of this unique data.

Credit

Industry Norm data has proven to be an invaluable tool in determining minimum acceptable standards for risk. The credit worthiness of an existing or potential account is immediately visible by ranking its solvency status and comparing its solvency trends to that of the industry. Short term solvency gauges, such as the quick and current ratios, are ideal indicators when evaluating an account. Balance sheet comparisons supplement this qualification by allowing a comparison of the make-up of current assets and liability items. Moreover, leverage ratios such as current liability to net worth and total liability to net worth provide valuable benchmarks to spot potential problem accounts while profitability and collection period figures provide cash flow comparisons for an overall evaluation of accounts.

In addition to evaluating individual accounts against industry standards, internal credit polices also benefit from Industry Norm data. Are receivables growing at an excessive rate as compared to the industry? If so, how does your firm's collections stack up to the industry?

Finance

Here exists a unique opportunity for financial executives to rank their firm, or their firm's subsidiaries and divisions, against its peers. Determine the efficiency of management via ratio quartile breakdowns which provides you the opportunity to pinpoint your firm's profitability position versus the industry. For example, are returns on sales and gross profit margins comparatively low thereby indicating that pricing per unit may be too low or that the cost of goods is unnecessarily high?

In much the same way, matching the firm's growth and efficiency trends to that of the industry reveals conditions which prove to be vital in projecting budgets. If asset expansion exceeds the industry standard while asset utilization (as indicated by the asset to sales ratio) is sub par, should growth be slowed?

Investment executives have also utilized this diverse information when identifying optimal investment opportunities. By uncovering which industries exhibit the strongest sales growth while maintaining adequate returns, risk is minimized.

Corporate Planning

Corporate plans, competitive strategies and merger/acquisition decisions dictate a comprehensive analysis of the industry in question. Industry Norm data provides invaluable information in scrutinizing the performance of today's highly competitive, and sometimes unstable, markets. Does the liquidity of an industry provide a sufficient cushion to endure the recent record-high interest levels or is it too volatile to risk an entry? Are the profitability and equity statuses of an acquisition candidate among the best in the industry thereby qualifying it as an ideal acquisition target?

Industry Norm data provides these all-important benchmarks for setting strategic goals and measuring overall corporate performance.

Marketing and Sales

Attaining an in-depth knowledge of a potential or existing customer base is a key factor when developing successful marketing strategies and sales projections. Industry Norm data provides a competitive edge when determining market potential and market candidates. Identify those industries that meet or exceed your qualifications and take it one step further by focusing in on the specific region or size category that exhibits the greatest potential. For example, isolate the industries which have experienced the strongest growth trends in sales and inventory turnover and then fine tune marketing and sales strategies by identifying the particular *segment* which is the most attractive (such as firms with assets of $1 million or more).

You can also utilize this information from a different perspective by examining the industries of existing accounts. If an account's industry shows signs of faltering profitability and stagnating sales, should precautionary measures be taken? Will the next sale be profitable for your company or will it be written-off? Industry Norm data assist in answering these and many other important questions.

FINAL NOTE

The SIC categories in this directory reflect those appearing in the 1987 edition of the Standard Industrial Classification Manual

The D&B Financial Information Base includes over one million U.S. companies and is the most extensive and complete source of financial information of its kind. This compilation of data should be regarded only as a source of financial information, to be used in conjunction with other sources of data, when performing financial analysis. When utilizing these figures, remember:

· Because of the size of this database, and in order to facilitate the many calculations and rankings, many of the very large group samples have been randomly reduced.

· On the other hand, some of the samples from our file are very small, and, therefore, may not present a true picture of an entire line of business. In these small groups there is a chance that a few extreme variations might have an undue influence on the overall figures in a particular category.

· The companies composing our database are organized by principal line of business without consideration for multiple-operation functions.

· Within the primary SIC numbers, no allowance has been made for differing accounting methods, terms of sale, or fiscal-year closing date, all of which might have had an effect on the composite data.

· Therefore, D&B advises users that the Industry Norms and Key Business Ratios be used as yardsticks and not as absolutes.

SIC 01 — AGRICULTURL CROPS (NO BREAKDOWN) 2014 (76 Establishments)

	$	%
Cash	741,582	12.1
Accounts Receivable	931,574	15.2
Notes Receivable	79,674	1.3
Inventory	802,870	13.1
Other Current	612,878	10.0
Total Current	**3,168,578**	**51.7**
Fixed Assets	2,506,670	40.9
Other Non-current	453,529	7.4
Total Assets	**6,128,777**	**100.0**
Accounts Payable	2,770,207	45.2
Bank Loans	42,901	0.7
Notes Payable	631,264	10.3
Other Current	8,451,584	137.9
Total Current	**11,895,956**	**194.1**
Other Long Term	1,213,498	19.8
Deferred Credits	73,545	1.2
Net Worth	(7,054,222)	(115.1)
Total Liab & Net Worth	**6,128,777**	**100.0**
Net Sales	9,414,404	100.0
Gross Profit	2,965,537	31.5
Net Profit After Tax	423,648	4.5
Working Capital	(8,727,378)	—

RATIOS	UQ	MED	LQ
SOLVENCY			
Quick Ratio (times)	2.0	0.8	0.2
Current Ratio (times)	5.2	1.6	1.0
Curr Liab To Nw (%)	7.9	45.7	114.0
Curr Liab To Inv (%)	90.9	183.8	547.5
Total Liab To Nw (%)	18.4	77.1	172.5
Fixed Assets To Nw (%)	37.0	60.7	110.1
EFFICIENCY			
Coll Period (days)	16.4	28.1	41.3
Sales To Inv (times)	37.0	14.8	4.5
Assets To Sales (%)	28.0	65.1	135.9
Sales To Nwc (times)	16.7	7.0	3.2
Acct Pay To Sales (%)	2.7	5.7	9.4
PROFITABILITY			
Return On Sales (%)	8.4	2.3	0.2
Return On Assets (%)	15.9	4.4	(0.4)
Return On Nw (%)	30.4	13.0	2.0

SIC 0181 — ORNMNTL NURS PRDCTS (NO BREAKDOWN) 2014 (15 Establishments)

	$	%
Cash	1,043,641	29.2
Accounts Receivable	214,447	6.0
Notes Receivable	21,445	0.6
Inventory	729,119	20.4
Other Current	450,337	12.6
Total Current	**2,458,989**	**68.8**
Fixed Assets	936,417	26.2
Other Non-current	178,706	5.0
Total Assets	**3,574,112**	**100.0**
Accounts Payable	343,115	9.6
Bank Loans	0	0.0
Notes Payable	10,722	0.3
Other Current	443,190	12.4
Total Current	**797,027**	**22.3**
Other Long Term	814,898	22.8
Deferred Credits	0	0.0
Net Worth	1,962,187	54.9
Total Liab & Net Worth	**3,574,112**	**100.0**
Net Sales	7,105,590	100.0
Gross Profit	2,536,696	35.7
Net Profit After Tax	468,969	6.6
Working Capital	1,661,962	—

RATIOS	UQ	MED	LQ
SOLVENCY			
Quick Ratio (times)	4.9	1.8	0.9
Current Ratio (times)	5.7	3.9	1.8
Curr Liab To Nw (%)	6.6	38.6	59.0
Curr Liab To Inv (%)	33.5	82.8	560.6
Total Liab To Nw (%)	19.3	62.7	103.6
Fixed Assets To Nw (%)	37.0	51.0	64.0
EFFICIENCY			
Coll Period (days)	6.2	20.3	40.5
Sales To Inv (times)	51.8	13.4	5.1
Assets To Sales (%)	30.5	50.3	67.3
Sales To Nwc (times)	9.8	6.6	4.6
Acct Pay To Sales (%)	2.7	4.1	8.9
PROFITABILITY			
Return On Sales (%)	14.0	4.7	0.9
Return On Assets (%)	24.9	9.7	2.5
Return On Nw (%)	33.8	12.5	4.5

SIC 0191 — GEN FARMS, PRIM CROP (NO BREAKDOWN) 2014 (15 Establishments)

	$	%
Cash	263,294	9.0
Accounts Receivable	105,318	3.6
Notes Receivable	157,977	5.4
Inventory	289,624	9.9
Other Current	444,674	15.2
Total Current	**1,260,887**	**43.1**
Fixed Assets	1,430,565	48.9
Other Non-current	234,039	8.0
Total Assets	**2,925,491**	**100.0**
Accounts Payable	1,845,985	63.1
Bank Loans	0	0.0
Notes Payable	1,056,102	36.1
Other Current	7,223,037	246.9
Total Current	**10,125,124**	**346.1**
Other Long Term	207,710	7.1
Deferred Credits	155,051	5.3
Net Worth	(7,562,394)	(258.5)
Total Liab & Net Worth	**2,925,491**	**100.0**
Net Sales	1,780,579	100.0
Gross Profit	267,087	15.0
Net Profit After Tax	(3,561)	(0.2)
Working Capital	(8,864,237)	—

RATIOS	UQ	MED	LQ
SOLVENCY			
Quick Ratio (times)	0.6	0.2	0.1
Current Ratio (times)	4.0	1.2	0.4
Curr Liab To Nw (%)	4.9	17.1	63.0
Curr Liab To Inv (%)	78.2	146.0	198.4
Total Liab To Nw (%)	13.1	50.9	134.1
Fixed Assets To Nw (%)	61.6	97.8	127.5
EFFICIENCY			
Coll Period (days)	16.6	19.0	45.7
Sales To Inv (times)	15.0	5.9	3.9
Assets To Sales (%)	72.7	164.3	172.5
Sales To Nwc (times)	18.0	11.5	2.9
Acct Pay To Sales (%)	3.5	5.7	43.0
PROFITABILITY			
Return On Sales (%)	3.9	2.2	(191.5)
Return On Assets (%)	6.9	(3.4)	(90.4)
Return On Nw (%)	13.0	4.7	(45.8)

SIC 02 — AGRICULTURAL PRD LVSK (NO BREAKDOWN) 2014 (18 Establishments)

	$	%
Cash	1,405,718	10.7
Accounts Receivable	840,803	6.4
Notes Receivable	0	0.0
Inventory	2,614,372	19.9
Other Current	499,226	3.8
Total Current	**5,360,119**	**40.8**
Fixed Assets	6,266,610	47.7
Other Non-current	1,510,818	11.5
Total Assets	**13,137,547**	**100.0**
Accounts Payable	354,714	2.7
Bank Loans	65,688	0.5
Notes Payable	643,740	4.9
Other Current	1,865,531	14.2
Total Current	**2,929,673**	**22.3**
Other Long Term	1,786,706	13.6
Deferred Credits	26,275	0.2
Net Worth	8,394,893	63.9
Total Liab & Net Worth	**13,137,547**	**100.0**
Net Sales	25,963,532	100.0
Gross Profit	9,554,580	36.8
Net Profit After Tax	2,544,426	9.8
Working Capital	2,430,446	—

RATIOS	UQ	MED	LQ
SOLVENCY			
Quick Ratio (times)	5.4	0.8	0.3
Current Ratio (times)	11.9	2.2	1.6
Curr Liab To Nw (%)	3.1	16.4	56.7
Curr Liab To Inv (%)	54.7	80.2	181.0
Total Liab To Nw (%)	3.2	38.2	80.5
Fixed Assets To Nw (%)	48.7	65.0	83.3
EFFICIENCY			
Coll Period (days)	3.5	15.2	22.3
Sales To Inv (times)	12.2	7.2	4.3
Assets To Sales (%)	40.0	50.6	86.7
Sales To Nwc (times)	9.9	6.4	4.4
Acct Pay To Sales (%)	1.0	1.6	2.7
PROFITABILITY			
Return On Sales (%)	12.6	9.4	4.4
Return On Assets (%)	20.7	15.3	8.6
Return On Nw (%)	33.2	20.3	11.9

SIC 07 AGRICULTURAL SERVICES
(NO BREAKDOWN)
2014 (121 Establishments)

	$	%
Cash	504,439	18.0
Accounts Receivable	658,574	23.5
Notes Receivable	11,210	0.4
Inventory	263,429	9.4
Other Current	215,788	7.7
Total Current	**1,653,440**	**59.0**
Fixed Assets	922,003	32.9
Other Non-current	226,998	8.1
Total Assets	**2,802,441**	**100.0**
Accounts Payable	322,281	11.5
Bank Loans	11,210	0.4
Notes Payable	56,049	2.0
Other Current	661,375	23.6
Total Current	**1,050,915**	**37.5**
Other Long Term	532,464	19.0
Deferred Credits	0	0.0
Net Worth	1,219,062	43.5
Total Liab & Net Worth	**2,802,441**	**100.0**
Net Sales	6,578,500	100.0
Gross Profit	2,315,632	35.2
Net Profit After Tax	407,867	6.2
Working Capital	602,525	---

RATIOS	UQ	MED	LQ
SOLVENCY			
Quick Ratio (times)	2.4	1.2	0.6
Current Ratio (times)	3.3	1.5	1.2
Curr Liab To Nw (%)	19.0	66.8	134.8
Curr Liab To Inv (%)	163.9	356.5	999.9
Total Liab To Nw (%)	36.3	103.5	190.1
Fixed Assets To Nw (%)	35.2	59.5	93.7
EFFICIENCY			
Coll Period (days)	14.5	31.6	58.2
Sales To Inv (times)	67.6	25.9	12.0
Assets To Sales (%)	29.9	42.6	69.4
Sales To Nwc (times)	20.8	9.2	5.4
Acct Pay To Sales (%)	1.6	4.2	8.3
PROFITABILITY			
Return On Sales (%)	7.4	2.6	0.3
Return On Assets (%)	13.8	6.2	0.6
Return On Nw (%)	34.3	15.2	2.9

SIC 0723 CROP PREP SVCS,MRKT
(NO BREAKDOWN)
2014 (32 Establishments)

	$	%
Cash	1,831,180	14.3
Accounts Receivable	2,458,648	19.2
Notes Receivable	38,416	0.3
Inventory	1,959,235	15.3
Other Current	1,318,962	10.3
Total Current	**7,606,441**	**59.4**
Fixed Assets	4,545,937	35.5
Other Non-current	653,078	5.1
Total Assets	**12,805,456**	**100.0**
Accounts Payable	1,997,651	15.6
Bank Loans	0	0.0
Notes Payable	230,498	1.8
Other Current	3,124,532	24.4
Total Current	**5,352,681**	**41.8**
Other Long Term	1,997,651	15.6
Deferred Credits	12,805	0.1
Net Worth	5,442,319	42.5
Total Liab & Net Worth	**12,805,456**	**100.0**
Net Sales	23,846,287	100.0
Gross Profit	6,462,344	27.1
Net Profit After Tax	930,005	3.9
Working Capital	2,253,760	---

RATIOS	UQ	MED	LQ
SOLVENCY			
Quick Ratio (times)	1.3	0.9	0.5
Current Ratio (times)	1.6	1.3	1.2
Curr Liab To Nw (%)	46.0	100.8	169.1
Curr Liab To Inv (%)	154.0	283.4	818.3
Total Liab To Nw (%)	73.7	145.9	221.8
Fixed Assets To Nw (%)	52.3	86.1	97.0
EFFICIENCY			
Coll Period (days)	10.6	30.5	44.9
Sales To Inv (times)	54.7	22.4	12.4
Assets To Sales (%)	30.0	53.7	82.0
Sales To Nwc (times)	24.9	9.7	7.6
Acct Pay To Sales (%)	1.4	5.1	11.9
PROFITABILITY			
Return On Sales (%)	4.9	1.4	0.3
Return On Assets (%)	10.0	3.6	0.5
Return On Nw (%)	20.9	10.9	2.8

SIC 0781 LNDSCPE CNSLNG,PLNG
(NO BREAKDOWN)
2014 (22 Establishments)

	$	%
Cash	120,418	14.2
Accounts Receivable	308,676	36.4
Notes Receivable	848	0.1
Inventory	55,969	6.6
Other Current	50,880	6.0
Total Current	**536,791**	**63.3**
Fixed Assets	214,547	25.3
Other Non-current	96,673	11.4
Total Assets	**848,011**	**100.0**
Accounts Payable	100,065	11.8
Bank Loans	18,656	2.2
Notes Payable	5,936	0.7
Other Current	312,917	36.9
Total Current	**437,574**	**51.6**
Other Long Term	133,985	15.8
Deferred Credits	0	0.0
Net Worth	276,452	32.6
Total Liab & Net Worth	**848,011**	**100.0**
Net Sales	2,323,318	100.0
Gross Profit	968,824	41.7
Net Profit After Tax	185,865	8.0
Working Capital	99,217	---

RATIOS	UQ	MED	LQ
SOLVENCY			
Quick Ratio (times)	1.7	1.2	0.6
Current Ratio (times)	2.0	1.4	0.9
Curr Liab To Nw (%)	47.3	107.7	185.5
Curr Liab To Inv (%)	140.3	273.3	420.6
Total Liab To Nw (%)	81.0	125.4	238.6
Fixed Assets To Nw (%)	16.1	40.9	82.4
EFFICIENCY			
Coll Period (days)	20.8	59.2	102.2
Sales To Inv (times)	23.3	18.4	12.5
Assets To Sales (%)	28.6	36.5	52.7
Sales To Nwc (times)	17.6	9.6	7.2
Acct Pay To Sales (%)	3.2	5.7	8.4
PROFITABILITY			
Return On Sales (%)	12.3	5.7	2.2
Return On Assets (%)	40.7	13.3	5.6
Return On Nw (%)	76.4	35.3	15.1

SIC 0782 LAWN GARDEN SVCS
(NO BREAKDOWN)
2014 (34 Establishments)

	$	%
Cash	405,171	25.2
Accounts Receivable	458,229	28.5
Notes Receivable	0	0.0
Inventory	86,822	5.4
Other Current	67,529	4.2
Total Current	**1,017,751**	**63.3**
Fixed Assets	585,247	36.4
Other Non-current	4,824	0.3
Total Assets	**1,607,822**	**100.0**
Accounts Payable	186,507	11.6
Bank Loans	0	0.0
Notes Payable	54,666	3.4
Other Current	258,860	16.1
Total Current	**500,033**	**31.1**
Other Long Term	270,114	16.8
Deferred Credits	0	0.0
Net Worth	837,675	52.1
Total Liab & Net Worth	**1,607,822**	**100.0**
Net Sales	4,154,579	100.0
Gross Profit	1,641,059	39.5
Net Profit After Tax	116,328	2.8
Working Capital	517,718	---

RATIOS	UQ	MED	LQ
SOLVENCY			
Quick Ratio (times)	4.8	1.5	0.7
Current Ratio (times)	5.0	1.8	1.2
Curr Liab To Nw (%)	18.6	59.4	95.3
Curr Liab To Inv (%)	290.7	829.7	999.9
Total Liab To Nw (%)	20.8	68.2	167.7
Fixed Assets To Nw (%)	15.3	43.0	88.8
EFFICIENCY			
Coll Period (days)	17.2	32.9	45.6
Sales To Inv (times)	297.3	63.7	25.8
Assets To Sales (%)	27.9	38.7	52.8
Sales To Nwc (times)	13.5	8.3	4.7
Acct Pay To Sales (%)	1.6	2.9	6.4
PROFITABILITY			
Return On Sales (%)	6.1	2.3	0.2
Return On Assets (%)	12.8	6.2	0.6
Return On Nw (%)	30.8	13.7	0.7

	SIC 08 FORESTRY (NO BREAKDOWN) 2014 (10 Establishments) $	%	SIC 10 METAL MINING (NO BREAKDOWN) 2014 (68 Establishments) $	%	SIC 1041 GOLD ORES (NO BREAKDOWN) 2014 (36 Establishments) $	%	SIC 1081 METAL MINING SVCS (NO BREAKDOWN) 2014 (14 Establishments) $	%
Cash	1,988,990	20.0	496,428	24.7	327,488	30.9	168,924	20.4
Accounts Receivable	367,963	3.7	44,216	2.2	30,735	2.9	19,045	2.3
Notes Receivable	0	0.0	0	0.0	0	0.0	0	0.0
Inventory	328,183	3.3	60,295	3.0	21,197	2.0	10,765	1.3
Other Current	606,642	6.1	217,062	10.8	108,102	10.2	167,268	20.2
Total Current	**3,291,778**	**33.1**	**818,001**	**40.7**	**487,522**	**46.0**	**366,002**	**44.2**
Fixed Assets	4,753,686	47.8	671,283	33.4	278,736	26.3	299,757	36.2
Other Non-current	1,899,486	19.1	520,546	25.9	293,573	27.7	162,300	19.6
Total Assets	**9,944,950**	**100.0**	**2,009,830**	**100.0**	**1,059,831**	**100.0**	**828,059**	**100.0**
Accounts Payable	288,404	2.9	5,279,823	262.7	2,219,286	209.4	2,880,817	347.9
Bank Loans	0	0.0	0	0.0	0	0.0	0	0.0
Notes Payable	29,835	0.3	956,679	47.6	695,249	65.6	452,120	54.6
Other Current	1,998,934	20.1	4,952,222	246.4	1,395,798	131.7	5,191,930	627.0
Total Current	**2,317,173**	**23.3**	**11,188,724**	**556.7**	**4,310,333**	**406.7**	**8,524,867**	**29.5**
Other Long Term	7,876,401	79.2	395,936	19.7	152,615	14.4	211,155	25.5
Deferred Credits	0	0.0	20,098	1.0	0	0.0	24,842	3.0
Net Worth	(248,624)	(2.5)	(9,594,928)	(477.4)	(3,403,117)	(321.1)	(7,932,805)	(958.0)
Total Liab & Net Worth	**9,944,950**	**100.0**	**2,009,830**	**100.0**	**1,059,831**	**100.0**	**828,059**	**100.0**
Net Sales	5,829,396	100.0	493,694	100.0	297,038	100.0	82,814	100.0
Gross Profit	2,728,157	46.8	83,928	17.0	63,269	21.3	22,857	27.6
Net Profit After Tax	1,241,661	21.3	(12,836)	(2.6)	25,842	8.7	0	0.0
Working Capital	974,605	---	(10,370,723)	---	(3,822,811)	---	(8,158,865)	---

RATIOS	UQ	MED	LQ	UQ	MED	LQ	UQ	MED	LQ	UQ	MED	LQ
SOLVENCY												
Quick Ratio (times)	3.6	2.1	0.4	1.9	0.3	0.0	1.9	0.2	0.0	0.3	0.1	0.0
Current Ratio (times)	7.6	2.3	1.3	2.6	0.4	0.1	3.0	0.4	0.1	0.5	0.2	0.0
Curr Liab To Nw (%)	6.0	6.2	32.1	6.5	16.7	29.7	6.1	16.8	29.7	3.7	11.4	27.5
Curr Liab To Inv (%)	140.8	167.6	229.3	138.3	284.8	999.9	191.7	896.3	999.9	289.7	999.9	999.9
Total Liab To Nw (%)	17.5	55.3	105.4	18.0	51.9	148.7	6.1	28.3	90.4	21.0	35.2	74.4
Fixed Assets To Nw (%)	27.7	63.2	202.5	30.4	88.7	129.3	32.6	61.7	124.6	21.4	64.3	116.4
EFFICIENCY												
Coll Period (days)	5.1	5.8	14.2	4.6	25.2	84.0	4.6	24.5	84.0	222.7	222.7	222.7
Sales To Inv (times)	19.8	19.3	7.3	14.8	5.9	0.9	14.8	9.0	2.3	5.1	3.0	0.9
Assets To Sales (%)	64.4	170.6	231.9	274.3	407.1	999.9	314.5	356.8	633.7	190.5	999.9	999.9
Sales To Nwc (times)	11.4	3.8	2.8	3.5	1.5	0.2	3.9	2.2	2.2	1.0	1.0	1.0
Acct Pay To Sales (%)	1.2	1.5	2.6	8.6	28.1	697.4	7.0	15.7	90.2	7.4	876.7	999.9
PROFITABILITY												
Return On Sales (%)	36.4	14.8	4.1	(3.5)	)149.1	(999.9)	4.1	(167.2)	(229.4)	(122.7)	)999.9	(999.9)
Return On Assets (%)	25.3	9.0	3.7	(13.9)	)70.4	(173.0)	(13.8)	)75.0	(252.0)	(102.4)	)125.4	(355.6)
Return On Nw (%)	39.9	14.0	7.3	(8.7)	)42.3	(135.3)	(0.2)	)38.7	(135.3)	(67.4)	)129.4	(202.8)

SIC 13 — OIL,GAS EXTRACTION (NO BREAKDOWN) 2014 (200 Establishments)

	$	%
Cash	22,067,735	14.9
Accounts Receivable	10,959,815	7.4
Notes Receivable	148,106	0.1
Inventory	2,369,690	1.6
Other Current	12,737,081	8.6
Total Current	**48,282,427**	**32.6**
Fixed Assets	81,161,872	54.8
Other Non-current	18,661,306	12.6
Total Assets	**148,105,605**	**100.0**
Accounts Payable	78,347,865	52.9
Bank Loans	296,211	0.2
Notes Payable	87,530,413	59.1
Other Current	235,487,912	159.0
Total Current	**401,662,401**	**271.2**
Other Long Term	51,096,434	34.5
Deferred Credits	296,211	0.2
Net Worth	(304,949,441)	(205.9)
Total Liab & Net Worth	**148,105,605**	**100.0**
Net Sales	53,084,446	100.0
Gross Profit	23,675,663	44.6
Net Profit After Tax	1,061,689	2.0
Working Capital	(353,379,974)	---

RATIOS	UQ	MED	LQ
SOLVENCY			
Quick Ratio (times)	1.3	0.6	0.2
Current Ratio (times)	1.8	1.1	0.5
Curr Liab To Nw (%)	13.7	26.6	50.7
Curr Liab To Inv (%)	326.6	999.9	999.9
Total Liab To Nw (%)	60.1	108.8	158.6
Fixed Assets To Nw (%)	73.1	137.5	190.6
EFFICIENCY			
Coll Period (days)	31.8	47.5	71.2
Sales To Inv (times)	92.3	34.4	16.0
Assets To Sales (%)	149.7	279.0	426.0
Sales To Nwc (times)	13.2	5.8	3.2
Acct Pay To Sales (%)	4.9	13.4	32.4
PROFITABILITY			
Return On Sales (%)	18.3	4.1	(40.0)
Return On Assets (%)	6.2	(0.2)	(33.6)
Return On Nw (%)	15.6	6.2	(16.2)

SIC 1311 — CRUDE PTRLM,NAT GAS (NO BREAKDOWN) 2014 (115 Establishments)

	$	%
Cash	56,143,643	14.6
Accounts Receivable	17,304,548	4.5
Notes Receivable	384,546	0.1
Inventory	4,614,546	1.2
Other Current	26,533,639	6.9
Total Current	**104,980,922**	**27.3**
Fixed Assets	233,034,573	60.6
Other Non-current	46,530,005	12.1
Total Assets	**384,545,500**	**100.0**
Accounts Payable	276,872,760	72.0
Bank Loans	0	0.0
Notes Payable	344,552,768	89.6
Other Current	462,608,237	120.3
Total Current	**84,033,765**	**281.9**
Other Long Term	122,670,014	31.9
Deferred Credits	769,091	0.2
Net Worth	(822,927,370)	(214.0)
Total Liab & Net Worth	**384,545,500**	**100.0**
Net Sales	114,040,777	100.0
Gross Profit	72,643,975	63.7
Net Profit After Tax	1,482,530	1.3
Working Capital	(979,052,843)	---

RATIOS	UQ	MED	LQ
SOLVENCY			
Quick Ratio (times)	1.0	0.5	0.2
Current Ratio (times)	1.7	1.0	0.4
Curr Liab To Nw (%)	15.1	26.5	45.9
Curr Liab To Inv (%)	838.6	999.9	999.9
Total Liab To Nw (%)	68.3	114.8	162.9
Fixed Assets To Nw (%)	112.1	158.3	216.1
EFFICIENCY			
Coll Period (days)	27.4	43.8	69.9
Sales To Inv (times)	123.4	39.1	20.2
Assets To Sales (%)	232.4	337.2	477.0
Sales To Nwc (times)	16.5	6.1	2.6
Acct Pay To Sales (%)	6.7	16.7	42.1
PROFITABILITY			
Return On Sales (%)	20.8	2.9	(51.6)
Return On Assets (%)	5.6	(0.5)	(26.9)
Return On Nw (%)	13.7	6.1	(17.2)

SIC 1382 — OIL GAS EXPLOR SVCS (NO BREAKDOWN) 2014 (29 Establishments)

	$	%
Cash	8,423,035	23.3
Accounts Receivable	1,301,413	3.6
Notes Receivable	0	0.0
Inventory	36,150	0.1
Other Current	5,964,810	16.5
Total Current	**15,725,408**	**43.5**
Fixed Assets	15,038,551	41.6
Other Non-current	5,386,405	14.9
Total Assets	**36,150,364**	**100.0**
Accounts Payable	21,979,421	60.8
Bank Loans	0	0.0
Notes Payable	16,918,370	46.8
Other Current	213,612,502	590.9
Total Current	**252,510,293**	**698.5**
Other Long Term	10,483,605	29.0
Deferred Credits	36,150	0.1
Net Worth	(226,879,684)	(627.6)
Total Liab & Net Worth	**36,150,364**	**100.0**
Net Sales	10,733,481	100.0
Gross Profit	5,012,536	46.7
Net Profit After Tax	2,146,696	20.0
Working Capital	(236,784,885)	---

RATIOS	UQ	MED	LQ
SOLVENCY			
Quick Ratio (times)	0.8	0.3	0.0
Current Ratio (times)	1.5	0.6	0.1
Curr Liab To Nw (%)	11.5	32.1	100.3
Curr Liab To Inv (%)	320.7	999.9	999.9
Total Liab To Nw (%)	26.6	93.9	143.8
Fixed Assets To Nw (%)	26.8	72.6	144.7
EFFICIENCY			
Coll Period (days)	43.8	47.8	65.3
Sales To Inv (times)	336.2	206.9	77.6
Assets To Sales (%)	213.1	336.8	441.5
Sales To Nwc (times)	14.8	6.4	3.0
Acct Pay To Sales (%)	6.4	15.0	26.0
PROFITABILITY			
Return On Sales (%)	27.1	8.0	(70.8)
Return On Assets (%)	4.9	(33.7)	(157.3)
Return On Nw (%)	14.1	5.3	(31.1)

SIC 1389 — OIL GAS FLD SVC,NEC (NO BREAKDOWN) 2014 (36 Establishments)

	$	%
Cash	4,021,441	13.3
Accounts Receivable	5,442,552	18.0
Notes Receivable	0	0.0
Inventory	1,179,220	3.9
Other Current	2,781,749	9.2
Total Current	**13,424,962**	**44.4**
Fixed Assets	12,729,525	42.1
Other Non-current	4,081,915	13.5
Total Assets	**30,236,402**	**100.0**
Accounts Payable	3,144,586	10.4
Bank Loans	241,891	0.8
Notes Payable	332,600	1.1
Other Current	5,230,898	17.3
Total Current	**8,949,975**	**29.6**
Other Long Term	11,399,124	37.7
Deferred Credits	90,709	0.3
Net Worth	9,796,594	32.4
Total Liab & Net Worth	**30,236,402**	**100.0**
Net Sales	31,139,446	100.0
Gross Profit	9,279,555	29.8
Net Profit After Tax	(373,673)	(1.2)
Working Capital	4,474,987	---

RATIOS	UQ	MED	LQ
SOLVENCY			
Quick Ratio (times)	2.1	1.3	0.6
Current Ratio (times)	3.3	1.8	1.2
Curr Liab To Nw (%)	16.3	29.5	68.3
Curr Liab To Inv (%)	137.8	242.4	960.0
Total Liab To Nw (%)	52.2	96.8	138.5
Fixed Assets To Nw (%)	45.3	78.8	138.5
EFFICIENCY			
Coll Period (days)	38.7	49.6	73.9
Sales To Inv (times)	37.4	15.9	8.2
Assets To Sales (%)	63.2	97.1	163.5
Sales To Nwc (times)	8.3	4.9	3.3
Acct Pay To Sales (%)	2.3	5.3	12.2
PROFITABILITY			
Return On Sales (%)	10.5	4.2	(6.7)
Return On Assets (%)	12.3	4.4	(6.4)
Return On Nw (%)	24.3	10.0	(4.5)

SIC 14 NONMETALLIC MINERALS
(NO BREAKDOWN)
2014 (43 Establishments)

	$	%
Cash	1,879,607	19.5
Accounts Receivable	886,789	9.2
Notes Receivable	173,502	1.8
Inventory	963,901	10.0
Other Current	616,897	6.4
Total Current	**4,520,696**	**46.9**
Fixed Assets	3,518,239	36.5
Other Non-current	1,600,076	16.6
Total Assets	**9,639,011**	**100.0**
Accounts Payable	11,354,755	117.8
Bank Loans	9,639	0.1
Notes Payable	3,682,102	38.2
Other Current	1,522,964	15.8
Total Current	**16,569,460**	**171.9**
Other Long Term	2,168,777	22.5
Deferred Credits	19,278	0.2
Net Worth	(9,118,504)	(94.6)
Total Liab & Net Worth	**9,639,011**	**100.0**
Net Sales	6,802,407	100.0
Gross Profit	1,782,231	26.2
Net Profit After Tax	258,491	3.8
Working Capital	(12,048,764)	---

RATIOS	UQ	MED	LQ
SOLVENCY			
Quick Ratio (times)	2.8	1.6	0.8
Current Ratio (times)	4.6	3.0	1.6
Curr Liab To Nw (%)	7.6	20.9	43.6
Curr Liab To Inv (%)	85.7	142.4	206.9
Total Liab To Nw (%)	17.2	51.6	110.2
Fixed Assets To Nw (%)	34.6	68.9	107.2
EFFICIENCY			
Coll Period (days)	26.7	46.7	58.6
Sales To Inv (times)	11.6	9.2	4.7
Assets To Sales (%)	102.3	141.7	227.4
Sales To Nwc (times)	4.7	3.0	1.9
Acct Pay To Sales (%)	3.2	5.1	7.6
PROFITABILITY			
Return On Sales (%)	13.2	3.5	(0.1)
Return On Assets (%)	10.6	2.0	(3.5)
Return On Nw (%)	20.3	4.4	0.9

SIC 1422 CRUSHED BRKN LMSTNE
(NO BREAKDOWN)
2014 (16 Establishments)

	$	%
Cash	1,630,168	16.3
Accounts Receivable	1,000,103	10.0
Notes Receivable	0	0.0
Inventory	1,540,158	15.4
Other Current	650,067	6.5
Total Current	**4,820,496**	**48.2**
Fixed Assets	4,110,423	41.1
Other Non-current	1,070,110	10.7
Total Assets	**10,001,029**	**100.0**
Accounts Payable	290,030	2.9
Bank Loans	30,003	0.3
Notes Payable	90,009	0.9
Other Current	1,830,188	18.3
Total Current	**2,240,230**	**22.4**
Other Long Term	1,590,164	15.9
Deferred Credits	20,002	0.2
Net Worth	6,150,633	61.5
Total Liab & Net Worth	**10,001,029**	**100.0**
Net Sales	7,038,022	100.0
Gross Profit	1,984,722	28.2
Net Profit After Tax	429,319	6.1
Working Capital	2,580,266	---

RATIOS	UQ	MED	LQ
SOLVENCY			
Quick Ratio (times)	2.7	1.6	1.0
Current Ratio (times)	6.2	2.4	2.1
Curr Liab To Nw (%)	9.1	11.9	32.5
Curr Liab To Inv (%)	79.8	105.3	188.2
Total Liab To Nw (%)	16.2	26.8	62.1
Fixed Assets To Nw (%)	33.9	63.5	73.5
EFFICIENCY			
Coll Period (days)	25.6	32.9	44.9
Sales To Inv (times)	9.9	6.6	2.7
Assets To Sales (%)	102.0	142.1	162.9
Sales To Nwc (times)	5.3	2.8	1.5
Acct Pay To Sales (%)	1.7	3.5	4.8
PROFITABILITY			
Return On Sales (%)	11.7	6.8	(0.1)
Return On Assets (%)	10.6	2.5	0.2
Return On Nw (%)	17.7	6.6	1.3

SIC 1442 CNSTR SAND,GRAVEL
(NO BREAKDOWN)
2014 (11 Establishments)

	$	%
Cash	1,304,526	16.1
Accounts Receivable	899,393	11.1
Notes Receivable	550,980	6.8
Inventory	478,056	5.9
Other Current	372,721	4.6
Total Current	**3,605,676**	**44.5**
Fixed Assets	2,771,104	34.2
Other Non-current	1,725,863	21.3
Total Assets	**8,102,643**	**100.0**
Accounts Payable	397,030	4.9
Bank Loans	0	0.0
Notes Payable	8,103	0.1
Other Current	964,214	11.9
Total Current	**1,369,347**	**16.9**
Other Long Term	1,272,115	15.7
Deferred Credits	0	0.0
Net Worth	5,461,181	67.4
Total Liab & Net Worth	**8,102,643**	**100.0**
Net Sales	6,961,034	100.0
Gross Profit	2,116,154	30.4
Net Profit After Tax	153,143	2.2
Working Capital	2,236,329	---

RATIOS	UQ	MED	LQ
SOLVENCY			
Quick Ratio (times)	38.0	1.1	0.5
Current Ratio (times)	51.4	2.2	1.0
Curr Liab To Nw (%)	2.2	29.5	58.8
Curr Liab To Inv (%)	144.3	222.0	372.9
Total Liab To Nw (%)	4.0	67.2	127.9
Fixed Assets To Nw (%)	20.0	56.5	126.8
EFFICIENCY			
Coll Period (days)	26.7	66.8	93.4
Sales To Inv (times)	14.2	11.0	6.8
Assets To Sales (%)	111.4	116.4	225.3
Sales To Nwc (times)	6.2	3.8	1.7
Acct Pay To Sales (%)	4.2	6.4	12.8
PROFITABILITY			
Return On Sales (%)	13.4	3.5	1.7
Return On Assets (%)	11.5	3.1	1.8
Return On Nw (%)	16.5	4.4	3.0

SIC 15 GEN'L BLDG CONTRS
(NO BREAKDOWN)
2014 (1090 Establishments)

	$	%
Cash	1,019,567	25.5
Accounts Receivable	1,463,379	36.6
Notes Receivable	11,995	0.3
Inventory	103,956	2.6
Other Current	747,683	18.7
Total Current	**3,346,580**	**83.7**
Fixed Assets	419,822	10.5
Other Non-current	231,901	5.8
Total Assets	**3,998,303**	**100.0**
Accounts Payable	1,419,398	35.5
Bank Loans	3,998	0.1
Notes Payable	31,986	0.8
Other Current	615,739	15.4
Total Current	**2,071,121**	**51.8**
Other Long Term	223,905	5.6
Deferred Credits	3,998	0.1
Net Worth	1,699,279	42.5
Total Liab & Net Worth	**3,998,303**	**100.0**
Net Sales	11,970,967	100.0
Gross Profit	1,867,471	15.6
Net Profit After Tax	323,216	2.7
Working Capital	1,275,459	---

RATIOS	UQ	MED	LQ
SOLVENCY			
Quick Ratio (times)	1.9	1.3	0.9
Current Ratio (times)	2.5	1.6	1.3
Curr Liab To Nw (%)	51.7	120.8	259.4
Curr Liab To Inv (%)	329.1	999.9	999.9
Total Liab To Nw (%)	59.9	134.7	277.1
Fixed Assets To Nw (%)	6.4	15.5	33.7
EFFICIENCY			
Coll Period (days)	30.7	48.0	71.5
Sales To Inv (times)	875.6	208.5	24.6
Assets To Sales (%)	24.7	33.4	47.5
Sales To Nwc (times)	17.9	9.7	5.1
Acct Pay To Sales (%)	4.4	8.3	13.6
PROFITABILITY			
Return On Sales (%)	4.6	1.7	0.4
Return On Assets (%)	12.0	4.8	1.1
Return On Nw (%)	32.5	13.7	3.1

SIC 1521 SNGL-FAM HSNG CNSTR (NO BREAKDOWN) 2014 (111 Establishments)
SIC 1522 RSDNTL CNSTR, NEC (NO BREAKDOWN) 2014 (54 Establishments)
SIC 1531 OPERATIVE BUILDERS (NO BREAKDOWN) 2014 (16 Establishments)
SIC 1541 INDL BLDNGS, WRHSES (NO BREAKDOWN) 2014 (193 Establishments)

	SIC 1521 $	SIC 1521 %	SIC 1522 $	SIC 1522 %	SIC 1531 $	SIC 1531 %	SIC 1541 $	SIC 1541 %
Cash	393,272	24.1	729,952	21.4	6,056,056	14.4	1,061,357	25.2
Accounts Receivable	337,789	20.7	1,224,546	35.9	9,252,307	22.0	1,549,918	36.8
Notes Receivable	16,318	1.0	6,822	0.2	0	0.0	4,212	0.1
Inventory	189,293	11.6	64,809	1.9	11,691,552	27.8	42,117	1.0
Other Current	290,466	17.8	760,651	22.3	5,551,385	13.2	817,077	19.4
Total Current	**1,227,138**	**75.2**	**2,786,780**	**81.7**	**32,551,300**	**77.4**	**3,474,681**	**82.5**
Fixed Assets	252,934	15.5	405,908	11.9	6,434,559	15.3	492,773	11.7
Other Non-current	151,761	9.3	218,304	6.4	3,070,084	7.3	244,281	5.8
Total Assets	**1,631,833**	**100.0**	**3,410,992**	**100.0**	**42,055,943**	**100.0**	**4,211,735**	**100.0**
Accounts Payable	212,138	13.0	972,133	28.5	7,738,294	18.4	1,099,263	26.1
Bank Loans	8,159	0.5	3,411	0.1	0	0.0	0	0.0
Notes Payable	21,214	1.3	64,809	1.9	2,985,972	7.1	21,059	0.5
Other Current	567,878	34.8	726,541	21.3	15,728,922	37.4	880,252	20.9
Total Current	**809,389**	**49.6**	**1,766,894**	**51.8**	**26,453,188**	**62.9**	**2,000,574**	**47.5**
Other Long Term	223,561	13.7	276,290	8.1	2,481,301	5.9	176,893	4.2
Deferred Credits	3,264	0.2	0	0.0	0	0.0	4,212	0.1
Net Worth	595,619	36.5	1,367,808	40.1	13,121,454	31.2	2,030,056	48.2
Total Liab & Net Worth	**1,631,833**	**100.0**	**3,410,992**	**100.0**	**42,055,943**	**100.0**	**4,211,735**	**100.0**
Net Sales	4,249,565	100.0	11,369,973	100.0	28,628,961	100.0	11,897,556	100.0
Gross Profit	1,019,896	24.0	1,841,936	16.2	6,556,032	22.9	1,903,609	16.0
Net Profit After Tax	110,489	2.6	375,209	3.3	2,204,430	7.7	428,312	3.6
Working Capital	417,749	---	1,019,886	---	6,098,112	---	1,474,107	---

RATIOS	1521 UQ	1521 MED	1521 LQ	1522 UQ	1522 MED	1522 LQ	1531 UQ	1531 MED	1531 LQ	1541 UQ	1541 MED	1541 LQ
SOLVENCY												
Quick Ratio (times)	1.9	1.2	0.5	1.6	1.2	0.8	1.4	0.4	0.1	2.2	1.3	0.9
Current Ratio (times)	3.1	1.7	1.2	2.4	1.5	1.3	1.9	1.6	1.3	3.0	1.7	1.3
Curr Liab To Nw (%)	20.8	86.3	183.4	61.0	135.5	3216	98.6	149.0	179.1	32.9	103.4	226.5
Curr Liab To Inv (%)	103.8	315.2	968.9	272.1	999.9	999.9	71.5	82.1	91.0	435.9	999.9	999.9
Total Liab To Nw (%)	29.3	99.6	225.9	82.4	154.0	348.3	98.6	157.2	214.4	40.3	115.5	260.6
Fixed Assets To Nw (%)	7.1	20.9	47.6	4.4	17.8	54.2	5.7	8.3	18.9	6.5	14.2	32.9
EFFICIENCY												
Coll Period (days)	6.6	26.3	53.1	20.8	44.6	59.9	4.4	11.3	46.5	36.2	59.7	77.1
Sales To Inv (times)	141.0	21.3	5.5	999.9	220.0	48.0	1.8	1.0	0.9	734.5	219.4	42.2
Assets To Sales (%)	21.6	38.4	58.9	20.2	30.0	36.9	33.1	146.9	195.1	28.4	35.4	49.9
Sales To Nwc (times)	21.9	6.3	4.2	22.9	12.1	6.4	9.3	2.5	1.6	14.6	9.4	4.7
Acct Pay To Sales (%)	2.0	4.5	8.8	3.0	7.9	10.2	4.0	5.9	10.4	4.7	8.6	13.7
PROFITABILITY												
Return On Sales (%)	6.1	3.2	0.3	5.9	2.3	0.8	6.6	5.1	1.8	4.3	2.0	0.5
Return On Assets (%)	17.8	6.3	1.0	21.5	8.6	2.9	5.2	3.1	1.6	11.0	4.8	1.2
Return On Nw (%)	33.1	15.1	3.9	58.6	26.6	9.3	27.1	10.4	4.9	31.0	11.6	3.1

	SIC 1542 NONRESID CONSTR.NEC (NO BREAKDOWN) 2014 (716 Establishments)		SIC 16 HEAVY CONSTR CONTRS (NO BREAKDOWN) 2014 (523 Establishments)		SIC 1611 HIGHWAY,ST CONSTR (NO BREAKDOWN) 2014 (182 Establishments)		SIC 1622 BRDGE,TNNEL,ELV HGY (NO BREAKDOWN) 2014 (40 Establishments)	
	$	%	$	%	$	%	$	%
Cash	1,106,967	26.3	1,122,876	22.1	1,080,084	20.6	1,957,668	30.0
Accounts Receivable	1,658,346	39.4	1,376,921	27.1	1,415,644	27.0	1,155,024	17.7
Notes Receivable	8,418	0.2	15,243	0.3	15,729	0.3	13,051	0.2
Inventory	46,299	1.1	111,780	2.2	146,808	2.8	137,037	2.1
Other Current	782,875	18.6	741,809	14.6	692,093	13.2	1,246,381	19.1
Total Current	**3,602,905**	**85.6**	**3,368,629**	**66.3**	**3,350,358**	**63.9**	**4,509,161**	**69.1**
Fixed Assets	387,228	9.2	1,407,406	27.7	1,525,750	29.1	1,553,083	23.8
Other Non-current	218,868	5.2	304,854	6.0	367,018	7.0	463,315	7.1
Total Assets	**4,209,001**	**100.0**	**5,080,889**	**100.0**	**5,243,126**	**100.0**	**6,525,559**	**100.0**
Accounts Payable	1,788,825	42.5	624,949	12.3	702,579	13.4	828,746	12.7
Bank Loans	4,209	0.1	30,485	0.6	26,216	0.5	0	0.0
Notes Payable	25,254	0.6	55,890	1.1	57,674	1.1	26,102	0.4
Other Current	412,483	9.8	899,318	17.7	891,331	17.0	1,089,769	16.7
Total Current	**2,230,771**	**53.0**	**1,610,642**	**31.7**	**1,677,800**	**32.0**	**1,944,617**	**29.8**
Other Long Term	197,823	4.7	721,486	14.2	849,387	16.2	776,541	11.9
Deferred Credits	4,209	0.1	5,081	0.1	0	0.0	13,051	0.2
Net Worth	1,776,198	42.2	2,743,680	54.0	2,715,939	51.8	3,791,350	58.1
Total Liab & Net Worth	**4,209,001**	**100.0**	**5,080,889**	**100.0**	**5,243,126**	**100.0**	**6,525,559**	**100.0**
Net Sales	12,871,563	100.0	10,719,175	100.0	11,472,923	100.0	12,921,899	100.0
Gross Profit	1,776,276	13.8	2,143,835	20.0	1,915,978	16.7	1,666,925	12.9
Net Profit After Tax	308,918	2.4	439,486	4.1	401,552	3.5	155,063	1.2
Working Capital	1,372,134	---	1,757,987	---	1,672,558	---	2,564,544	---

RATIOS	UQ	MED	LQ	UQ	MED	LQ	UQ	MED	LQ	UQ	MED	LQ
SOLVENCY												
Quick Ratio (times)	1.9	1.3	1.0	2.8	1.5	1.1	2.5	1.5	1.1	2.4	1.6	1.0
Current Ratio (times)	2.3	1.6	1.3	3.6	2.1	1.5	3.2	2.0	1.5	3.6	2.5	1.6
Curr Liab To Nw (%)	58.8	130.8	262.9	23.8	46.9	98.1	24.0	51.0	100.2	24.6	50.9	92.9
Curr Liab To Inv (%)	999.9	999.9	999.9	315.6	866.6	999.9	233.5	602.6	999.9	315.1	731.0	999.9
Total Liab To Nw (%)	67.7	142.9	285.5	33.0	74.8	150.0	35.8	79.1	144.8	31.7	71.2	138.3
Fixed Assets To Nw (%)	6.4	15.2	31.4	20.8	47.0	82.9	21.8	50.7	80.7	22.9	39.2	69.9
EFFICIENCY												
Coll Period (days)	32.3	49.3	72.1	29.9	49.6	70.5	26.7	42.0	63.9	24.3	35.8	50.1
Sales To Inv (times)	999.9	328.2	97.0	2013	73.0	30.2	262.0	55.3	24.5	148.2	63.3	43.8
Assets To Sales (%)	24.3	32.7	44.9	34.7	47.4	64.7	33.0	45.7	60.3	38.2	50.5	58.3
Sales To Nwc (times)	18.2	10.3	5.6	11.7	6.7	3.8	12.0	7.3	4.1	11.8	6.5	4.3
Acct Pay To Sales (%)	5.0	9.1	14.1	2.4	4.8	8.7	2.5	4.8	8.4	2.6	5.5	11.1
PROFITABILITY												
Return On Sales (%)	4.2	1.5	0.3	7.9	2.9	0.6	6.4	2.5	0.3	2.8	1.7	(0.8)
Return On Assets (%)	11.6	4.3	1.0	16.2	6.0	1.1	13.8	5.5	0.8	7.9	2.9	(1.9)
Return On Nw (%)	30.9	13.1	2.6	32.3	13.1	2.1	24.9	11.7	1.5	15.0	5.3	(4.4)

SIC 1623 WTER,SWER,UTIL LNES (NO BREAKDOWN) 2014 (179 Establishments)

	$	%
Cash	941,110	21.8
Accounts Receivable	1,286,472	29.8
Notes Receivable	17,268	0.4
Inventory	60,438	1.4
Other Current	638,920	14.8
Total Current	**2,944,208**	**68.2**
Fixed Assets	1,174,229	27.2
Other Non-current	198,583	4.6
Total Assets	**4,317,020**	**100.0**
Accounts Payable	479,189	11.1
Bank Loans	34,536	0.8
Notes Payable	51,804	1.2
Other Current	755,479	17.5
Total Current	**1,321,008**	**30.6**
Other Long Term	561,213	13.0
Deferred Credits	4,317	0.1
Net Worth	2,430,482	56.3
Total Liab & Net Worth	**4,317,020**	**100.0**
Net Sales	9,185,149	100.0
Gross Profit	2,057,473	22.4
Net Profit After Tax	505,183	5.5
Working Capital	1,623,200	---

RATIOS	UQ	MED	LQ
SOLVENCY			
Quick Ratio (times)	2.9	1.6	1.1
Current Ratio (times)	3.6	2.3	1.5
Curr Liab To Nw (%)	22.2	46.9	85.7
Curr Liab To Inv (%)	489.3	999.9	999.9
Total Liab To Nw (%)	31.4	71.3	144.2
Fixed Assets To Nw (%)	19.9	47.3	90.5
EFFICIENCY			
Coll Period (days)	37.6	54.4	77.4
Sales To Inv (times)	203.9	102.7	36.5
Assets To Sales (%)	35.6	47.0	61.8
Sales To Nwc (times)	11.7	6.8	4.0
Acct Pay To Sales (%)	2.4	4.8	7.9
PROFITABILITY			
Return On Sales (%)	9.9	4.3	1.3
Return On Assets (%)	23.8	9.4	2.4
Return On Nw (%)	43.6	21.0	4.3

SIC 1629 HEAVY CONSTR,NEC (NO BREAKDOWN) 2014 (122 Establishments)

	$	%
Cash	1,199,536	22.1
Accounts Receivable	1,432,930	26.4
Notes Receivable	10,856	0.2
Inventory	130,266	2.4
Other Current	814,165	15.0
Total Current	**3,587,753**	**66.1**
Fixed Assets	1,498,063	27.6
Other Non-current	341,950	6.3
Total Assets	**5,427,766**	**100.0**
Accounts Payable	667,615	12.3
Bank Loans	32,567	0.6
Notes Payable	59,705	1.1
Other Current	1,052,987	19.4
Total Current	**1,812,874**	**33.4**
Other Long Term	754,459	13.9
Deferred Credits	5,428	0.1
Net Worth	2,855,005	52.6
Total Liab & Net Worth	**5,427,766**	**100.0**
Net Sales	10,338,602	100.0
Gross Profit	2,450,249	23.7
Net Profit After Tax	403,205	3.9
Working Capital	1,774,879	---

RATIOS	UQ	MED	LQ
Quick Ratio (times)	3.1	1.5	0.9
Current Ratio (times)	4.0	2.2	1.5
Curr Liab To Nw (%)	21.3	46.0	109.8
Curr Liab To Inv (%)	426.9	999.9	999.9
Total Liab To Nw (%)	34.6	77.2	172.3
Fixed Assets To Nw (%)	19.1	41.6	80.1
Coll Period (days)	32.1	53.7	74.5
Sales To Inv (times)	220.2	71.2	34.5
Assets To Sales (%)	37.0	52.5	78.5
Sales To Nwc (times)	11.7	6.0	3.4
Acct Pay To Sales (%)	1.8	4.9	9.1
Return On Sales (%)	8.1	2.8	0.2
Return On Assets (%)	13.8	5.3	0.5
Return On Nw (%)	27.5	10.0	1.6

SIC 17 SPECIAL TRADE CONTRS (NO BREAKDOWN) 2014 (2005 Establishments)

	$	%
Cash	482,826	20.4
Accounts Receivable	946,717	40.0
Notes Receivable	4,734	0.2
Inventory	127,807	5.4
Other Current	328,984	13.9
Total Current	**1,891,068**	**79.9**
Fixed Assets	364,486	15.4
Other Non-current	111,239	4.7
Total Assets	**2,366,793**	**100.0**
Accounts Payable	345,552	14.6
Bank Loans	9,467	0.4
Notes Payable	35,502	1.5
Other Current	553,829	23.4
Total Current	**944,350**	**39.9**
Other Long Term	196,444	8.3
Deferred Credits	2,367	0.1
Net Worth	1,223,632	51.7
Total Liab & Net Worth	**2,366,793**	**100.0**
Net Sales	6,502,179	100.0
Gross Profit	1,762,091	27.1
Net Profit After Tax	273,092	4.2
Working Capital	946,718	---

RATIOS	UQ	MED	LQ
Quick Ratio (times)	3.1	1.7	1.1
Current Ratio (times)	3.9	2.3	1.5
Curr Liab To Nw (%)	25.7	59.0	123.3
Curr Liab To Inv (%)	242.6	716.7	999.9
Total Liab To Nw (%)	31.1	75.1	151.5
Fixed Assets To Nw (%)	8.9	19.9	41.6
Coll Period (days)	37.2	58.0	78.5
Sales To Inv (times)	201.7	62.6	24.6
Assets To Sales (%)	27.9	36.4	48.4
Sales To Nwc (times)	10.6	6.3	4.0
Acct Pay To Sales (%)	2.5	4.6	7.5
Return On Sales (%)	6.9	2.8	0.7
Return On Assets (%)	18.7	7.5	2.0
Return On Nw (%)	35.9	14.5	3.9

SIC 1711 PLBNG,HTNG,AIR-COND (NO BREAKDOWN) 2014 (492 Establishments)

	$	%
Cash	474,404	21.1
Accounts Receivable	924,076	41.1
Notes Receivable	4,497	0.2
Inventory	146,143	6.5
Other Current	283,293	12.6
Total Current	**1,832,413**	**81.5**
Fixed Assets	292,287	13.0
Other Non-current	123,660	5.5
Total Assets	**2,248,360**	**100.0**
Accounts Payable	379,973	16.9
Bank Loans	4,497	0.2
Notes Payable	24,732	1.1
Other Current	505,881	22.5
Total Current	**915,083**	**40.7**
Other Long Term	173,124	7.7
Deferred Credits	2,248	0.1
Net Worth	1,157,905	51.5
Total Liab & Net Worth	**2,248,360**	**100.0**
Net Sales	6,593,431	100.0
Gross Profit	1,819,787	27.6
Net Profit After Tax	243,957	3.7
Working Capital	917,330	---

RATIOS	UQ	MED	LQ
Quick Ratio (times)	2.6	1.6	1.1
Current Ratio (times)	3.4	2.1	1.5
Curr Liab To Nw (%)	32.3	67.1	138.7
Curr Liab To Inv (%)	266.1	725.6	999.9
Total Liab To Nw (%)	38.8	80.3	159.1
Fixed Assets To Nw (%)	9.2	19.0	38.9
Coll Period (days)	32.5	52.8	76.3
Sales To Inv (times)	165.2	61.5	24.1
Assets To Sales (%)	26.5	34.1	44.2
Sales To Nwc (times)	11.0	7.1	4.5
Acct Pay To Sales (%)	2.9	4.8	7.6
Return On Sales (%)	6.0	2.3	0.6
Return On Assets (%)	17.2	6.8	2.0
Return On Nw (%)	36.7	13.7	3.6

	SIC 1721 PNTNG,PAPER HANGING (NO BREAKDOWN) 2014 (73 Establishments)		SIC 1731 ELECTRICAL WORK (NO BREAKDOWN) 2014 (574 Establishments)		SIC 1741 MSNRY,OTHER STNWRK (NO BREAKDOWN) 2014 (50 Establishments)		SIC 1742 PLSTRNG,DWALL,INSUL (NO BREAKDOWN) 2014 (66 Establishments)	
	$	%	$	%	$	%	$	%
Cash	476,058	22.2	587,951	22.0	402,268	17.4	460,851	19.6
Accounts Receivable	883,495	41.2	1,103,745	41.3	1,065,778	46.1	1,058,077	45.0
Notes Receivable	8,578	0.4	2,673	0.1	11,559	0.5	11,756	0.5
Inventory	23,588	1.1	136,298	5.1	57,797	2.5	84,646	3.6
Other Current	257,328	12.0	371,477	13.9	372,213	16.1	355,045	15.1
Total Current	**1,649,047**	**76.9**	**2,202,144**	**82.4**	**1,909,615**	**82.6**	**1,970,375**	**83.8**
Fixed Assets	392,426	18.3	358,116	13.4	309,792	13.4	232,777	9.9
Other Non-current	102,932	4.8	112,245	4.2	92,476	4.0	148,131	6.3
Total Assets	**2,144,405**	**100.0**	**2,672,505**	**100.0**	**2,311,883**	**100.0**	**2,351,283**	**100.0**
Accounts Payable	233,740	10.9	379,496	14.2	321,352	13.9	268,046	11.4
Bank Loans	34,310	1.6	16,035	0.6	6,936	0.3	16,459	0.7
Notes Payable	51,466	2.4	40,088	1.5	46,238	2.0	47,026	2.0
Other Current	512,513	23.9	569,243	21.3	654,262	28.3	524,336	22.3
Total Current	**832,029**	**38.8**	**1,004,862**	**37.6**	**1,028,788**	**44.5**	**855,867**	**36.4**
Other Long Term	160,831	7.5	213,800	8.0	143,337	6.2	126,969	5.4
Deferred Credits	2,144	0.1	0	0.0	0	0.0	0	0.0
Net Worth	1,149,401	53.6	1,453,843	54.4	1,139,758	49.3	1,368,447	58.2
Total Liab & Net Worth	**2,144,405**	**100.0**	**2,672,505**	**100.0**	**2,311,883**	**100.0**	**2,351,283**	**100.0**
Net Sales	5,584,388	100.0	7,423,625	100.0	6,231,491	100.0	6,337,690	100.0
Gross Profit	1,725,576	30.9	1,937,566	26.1	1,476,863	23.7	1,419,643	22.4
Net Profit After Tax	346,232	6.2	289,521	3.9	199,408	3.2	234,495	3.7
Working Capital	817,018	—	1,197,282	—	880,827	—	1,114,508	—

RATIOS	UQ	MED	LQ	UQ	MED	LQ	UQ	MED	LQ	UQ	MED	LQ
SOLVENCY												
Quick Ratio (times)	4.5	2.4	1.3	3.0	1.8	1.1	2.5	1.7	1.0	4.0	1.9	1.2
Current Ratio (times)	4.9	2.8	1.6	3.8	2.3	1.6	3.4	2.1	1.3	4.8	2.6	1.6
Curr Liab To Nw (%)	19.2	45.7	87.6	26.4	61.2	122.8	30.1	82.1	130.7	23.0	55.0	107.4
Curr Liab To Inv (%)	635.8	942.0	999.9	257.8	915.7	999.9	363.0	953.1	999.9	225.7	676.1	999.9
Total Liab To Nw (%)	25.8	54.5	130.1	29.9	74.3	148.3	32.7	97.7	148.9	26.2	60.4	125.9
Fixed Assets To Nw (%)	12.9	23.7	37.7	8.4	17.2	34.5	7.0	21.9	48.0	6.4	12.3	27.1
EFFICIENCY												
Coll Period (days)	39.5	58.4	81.8	40.9	61.3	80.7	47.1	63.9	87.8	43.1	62.4	85.8
Sales To Inv (times)	313.4	93.2	41.7	284.0	83.3	33.4	62.2	38.5	24.2	575.4	45.2	21.4
Assets To Sales (%)	31.3	38.4	48.2	28.6	36.0	47.1	28.5	37.1	49.2	28.2	37.1	49.8
Sales To Nwc (times)	9.9	5.7	3.7	10.2	6.0	3.9	9.6	5.9	3.8	9.3	5.2	3.2
Acct Pay To Sales (%)	1.5	2.9	4.7	2.9	4.9	7.3	2.0	4.5	6.5	1.7	3.3	5.9
PROFITABILITY												
Return On Sales (%)	10.0	4.4	1.1	6.4	2.7	0.6	6.8	3.0	0.8	6.9	2.5	0.6
Return On Assets (%)	24.8	9.2	3.2	16.6	6.6	1.9	18.3	7.0	1.3	19.8	6.2	1.9
Return On Nw (%)	39.3	15.8	3.9	33.6	14.5	4.1	42.1	17.2	2.9	31.6	12.2	2.3

SIC 1743 TRZ,TILE,MRBL,MSAIC
(NO BREAKDOWN)
2014 (13 Establishments)

	$	%
Cash	403,057	18.3
Accounts Receivable	1,310,486	59.5
Notes Receivable	0	0.0
Inventory	6,607	0.3
Other Current	229,061	10.4
Total Current	**1,949,211**	**88.5**
Fixed Assets	138,757	6.3
Other Non-current	114,530	5.2
Total Assets	**2,202,498**	**100.0**
Accounts Payable	222,452	10.1
Bank Loans	57,265	2.6
Notes Payable	8,810	0.4
Other Current	455,917	20.7
Total Current	**744,444**	**33.8**
Other Long Term	158,580	7.2
Deferred Credits	0	0.0
Net Worth	1,299,474	59.0
Total Liab & Net Worth	**2,202,498**	**100.0**
Net Sales	5,968,829	100.0
Gross Profit	1,510,114	25.3
Net Profit After Tax	244,722	4.1
Working Capital	1,204,767	—

RATIOS	UQ	MED	LQ
SOLVENCY			
Quick Ratio (times)	3.4	2.3	1.9
Current Ratio (times)	3.9	2.7	2.0
Curr Liab To Nw (%)	35.8	50.1	93.6
Curr Liab To Inv (%)	999.9	999.9	999.9
Total Liab To Nw (%)	47.5	67.0	101.2
Fixed Assets To Nw (%)	9.0	12.5	15.5
EFFICIENCY			
Coll Period (days)	59.9	79.4	90.2
Sales To Inv (times)	515.4	293.4	205.5
Assets To Sales (%)	30.8	36.9	49.2
Sales To Nwc (times)	7.2	4.8	3.8
Acct Pay To Sales (%)	1.2	4.5	7.0
PROFITABILITY			
Return On Sales (%)	6.1	4.5	2.3
Return On Assets (%)	14.2	11.1	5.6
Return On Nw (%)	33.3	16.3	9.2

SIC 1751 CARPENTRY WORK
(NO BREAKDOWN)
2014 (26 Establishments)

	$	%
Cash	366,025	21.8
Accounts Receivable	673,284	40.1
Notes Receivable	10,074	0.6
Inventory	122,568	7.3
Other Current	216,592	12.9
Total Current	**1,388,543**	**82.7**
Fixed Assets	208,197	12.4
Other Non-current	82,272	4.9
Total Assets	**1,679,012**	**100.0**
Accounts Payable	251,852	15.0
Bank Loans	15,111	0.9
Notes Payable	8,395	0.5
Other Current	347,555	20.7
Total Current	**622,913**	**37.1**
Other Long Term	397,926	23.7
Deferred Credits	0	0.0
Net Worth	658,173	39.2
Total Liab & Net Worth	**1,679,012**	**100.0**
Net Sales	4,810,923	100.0
Gross Profit	1,419,222	29.5
Net Profit After Tax	221,302	4.6
Working Capital	765,630	—

RATIOS	UQ	MED	LQ
SOLVENCY			
Quick Ratio (times)	2.9	1.6	0.9
Current Ratio (times)	3.9	2.1	1.6
Curr Liab To Nw (%)	39.8	93.1	162.6
Curr Liab To Inv (%)	110.4	221.4	939.1
Total Liab To Nw (%)	43.7	111.4	228.7
Fixed Assets To Nw (%)	7.5	14.7	43.4
EFFICIENCY			
Coll Period (days)	32.5	50.4	79.2
Sales To Inv (times)	65.3	37.8	22.1
Assets To Sales (%)	24.5	34.9	43.0
Sales To Nwc (times)	10.3	7.2	4.7
Acct Pay To Sales (%)	1.3	3.7	7.2
PROFITABILITY			
Return On Sales (%)	5.8	3.2	1.2
Return On Assets (%)	25.8	11.2	2.9
Return On Nw (%)	49.9	17.8	7.5

SIC 1752 FLR LAYING WORK.NEC
(NO BREAKDOWN)
2014 (59 Establishments)

	$	%
Cash	255,279	16.2
Accounts Receivable	679,168	43.1
Notes Receivable	0	0.0
Inventory	159,155	10.1
Other Current	255,279	16.2
Total Current	**1,348,881**	**85.6**
Fixed Assets	170,186	10.8
Other Non-current	56,729	3.6
Total Assets	**1,575,796**	**100.0**
Accounts Payable	222,187	14.1
Bank Loans	12,606	0.8
Notes Payable	29,940	1.9
Other Current	404,980	25.7
Total Current	**669,713**	**42.5**
Other Long Term	59,881	3.8
Deferred Credits	0	0.0
Net Worth	846,202	53.7
Total Liab & Net Worth	**1,575,796**	**100.0**
Net Sales	4,689,869	100.0
Gross Profit	1,195,917	25.5
Net Profit After Tax	206,354	4.4
Working Capital	679,168	—

RATIOS	UQ	MED	LQ
SOLVENCY			
Quick Ratio (times)	3.7	1.4	0.8
Current Ratio (times)	4.9	2.2	1.4
Curr Liab To Nw (%)	22.6	70.4	205.1
Curr Liab To Inv (%)	164.3	305.5	999.9
Total Liab To Nw (%)	25.3	80.4	218.1
Fixed Assets To Nw (%)	6.4	13.5	25.7
EFFICIENCY			
Coll Period (days)	38.9	57.3	81.4
Sales To Inv (times)	144.6	29.9	17.8
Assets To Sales (%)	26.3	33.6	40.4
Sales To Nwc (times)	9.9	6.6	4.1
Acct Pay To Sales (%)	1.8	3.9	6.3
PROFITABILITY			
Return On Sales (%)	7.7	3.0	0.5
Return On Assets (%)	19.0	8.1	2.7
Return On Nw (%)	39.9	20.5	5.0

SIC 1761 RRNF.SDNG.SHT MTLWK
(NO BREAKDOWN)
2014 (175 Establishments)

	$	%
Cash	498,035	20.7
Accounts Receivable	950,356	39.5
Notes Receivable	2,406	0.1
Inventory	137,140	5.7
Other Current	404,202	16.8
Total Current	**1,992,139**	**82.8**
Fixed Assets	324,805	13.5
Other Non-current	89,021	3.7
Total Assets	**2,405,965**	**100.0**
Accounts Payable	380,142	15.8
Bank Loans	4,812	0.2
Notes Payable	38,495	1.6
Other Current	457,134	19.0
Total Current	**880,583**	**36.6**
Other Long Term	149,170	6.2
Deferred Credits	0	0.0
Net Worth	1,376,212	57.2
Total Liab & Net Worth	**2,405,965**	**100.0**
Net Sales	6,973,812	100.0
Gross Profit	1,868,982	26.8
Net Profit After Tax	278,952	4.0
Working Capital	1,111,556	—

RATIOS	UQ	MED	LQ
SOLVENCY			
Quick Ratio (times)	3.1	1.7	1.1
Current Ratio (times)	4.2	2.4	1.6
Curr Liab To Nw (%)	27.2	56.5	115.9
Curr Liab To Inv (%)	285.9	850.5	999.9
Total Liab To Nw (%)	29.1	66.2	128.1
Fixed Assets To Nw (%)	10.3	20.8	37.0
EFFICIENCY			
Coll Period (days)	40.5	56.2	71.5
Sales To Inv (times)	119.2	64.3	26.2
Assets To Sales (%)	27.6	34.5	45.7
Sales To Nwc (times)	9.5	6.2	4.0
Acct Pay To Sales (%)	2.6	5.0	8.1
PROFITABILITY			
Return On Sales (%)	7.3	2.9	0.8
Return On Assets (%)	21.5	7.5	2.3
Return On Nw (%)	39.4	17.1	4.5

	SIC 1771 CONCRETE WORK (NO BREAKDOWN) 2014 (92 Establishments) $	%	SIC 1781 WATER WELL DRILLING (NO BREAKDOWN) 2014 (13 Establishments) $	%	SIC 1791 STRUCT STEEL ERCTN (NO BREAKDOWN) 2014 (26 Establishments) $	%	SIC 1793 GLASS,GLAZING WORK (NO BREAKDOWN) 2014 (41 Establishments) $	%
Cash	501,173	20.4	366,801	13.4	513,213	16.9	294,701	20.5
Accounts Receivable	899,163	36.6	470,819	17.2	1,272,405	41.9	688,594	47.9
Notes Receivable	2,457	0.1	0	0.0	0	0.0	0	0.0
Inventory	51,591	2.1	270,995	9.9	85,029	2.8	84,816	5.9
Other Current	309,548	12.6	339,428	12.4	522,324	17.2	178,259	12.4
Total Current	**1,763,932**	**71.8**	**1,448,043**	**52.9**	**2,392,971**	**78.8**	**1,246,370**	**86.7**
Fixed Assets	555,221	22.6	1,059,343	38.7	586,096	19.3	125,068	8.7
Other Non-current	137,577	5.6	229,935	8.4	57,698	1.9	66,128	4.6
Total Assets	**2,456,730**	**100.0**	**2,737,321**	**100.0**	**3,036,765**	**100.0**	**1,437,566**	**100.0**
Accounts Payable	452,038	18.4	183,401	6.7	674,162	22.2	173,945	12.1
Bank Loans	4,913	0.2	0	0.0	0	0.0	8,625	0.6
Notes Payable	39,308	1.6	62,958	2.3	30,368	1.0	23,001	1.6
Other Current	1,022,000	41.6	339,428	12.4	704,529	23.2	281,764	19.6
Total Current	**1,518,259**	**61.8**	**585,787**	**21.4**	**1,409,059**	**46.4**	**487,335**	**33.9**
Other Long Term	270,240	11.0	476,294	17.4	242,941	8.0	31,626	2.2
Deferred Credits	0	0.0	2,737	0.1	0	0.0	0	0.0
Net Worth	668,231	27.2	1,672,503	61.1	1,384,765	45.6	918,605	63.9
Total Liab & Net Worth	**2,456,730**	**100.0**	**2,737,321**	**100.0**	**3,036,765**	**100.0**	**1,437,566**	**100.0**
Net Sales	7,162,478	100.0	5,155,030	100.0	7,213,219	100.0	3,949,357	100.0
Gross Profit	1,718,995	24.0	1,572,284	30.5	1,601,335	22.2	1,038,681	26.3
Net Profit After Tax	272,174	3.8	350,542	6.8	79,345	1.1	146,126	3.7
Working Capital	245,673	---	862,256	---	983,912	---	759,035	---

RATIOS	UQ	MED	LQ	UQ	MED	LQ	UQ	MED	LQ	UQ	MED	LQ
SOLVENCY												
Quick Ratio (times)	3.0	1.6	1.0	3.1	1.2	0.7	1.8	1.3	0.9	3.5	2.5	1.6
Current Ratio (times)	3.7	2.4	1.5	4.4	2.9	1.6	2.2	1.6	1.2	4.8	2.9	1.9
Curr Liab To Nw (%)	26.0	55.0	113.5	8.9	40.0	66.8	52.0	125.1	215.3	22.8	37.4	97.3
Curr Liab To Inv (%)	298.3	999.9	999.9	93.2	227.2	833.9	638.5	999.9	999.9	203.2	596.7	999.9
Total Liab To Nw (%)	31.9	77.6	140.0	8.9	56.3	106.4	63.6	143.7	294.3	28.9	47.1	97.3
Fixed Assets To Nw (%)	11.2	28.9	58.2	18.0	65.7	115.0	15.1	39.4	82.6	6.3	9.1	20.9
EFFICIENCY												
Coll Period (days)	31.4	55.0	75.8	29.6	48.6	49.6	48.6	68.6	86.9	43.4	63.7	77.8
Sales To Inv (times)	408.7	95.2	33.4	46.9	19.3	10.7	385.2	76.7	25.2	166.4	50.4	27.7
Assets To Sales (%)	26.9	34.3	48.0	43.9	53.1	66.9	34.0	42.1	62.4	28.8	36.4	43.6
Sales To Nwc (times)	11.5	6.9	3.4	7.1	5.2	4.0	14.8	8.5	4.4	8.7	5.6	4.0
Acct Pay To Sales (%)	3.7	6.2	8.5	0.5	2.5	6.8	3.0	6.9	14.2	1.6	3.2	5.8
PROFITABILITY												
Return On Sales (%)	7.0	2.7	0.7	11.6	5.7	0.1	3.7	2.6	0.0	6.0	2.5	0.4
Return On Assets (%)	18.5	7.5	1.6	24.6	12.6	0.1	13.7	4.1	0.0	13.9	7.0	1.2
Return On Nw (%)	35.8	15.7	3.1	30.7	18.4	0.1	40.0	12.5	0.0	26.1	10.4	2.5

	SIC 1794 EXCAVATION WORK (NO BREAKDOWN) 2014 (93 Establishments)		SIC 1795 WRCKNG,DMLTN WORK (NO BREAKDOWN) 2014 (23 Establishments)		SIC 1796 INSTL BLDG EQPT,NEC (NO BREAKDOWN) 2014 (29 Establishments)		SIC 1799 SPCL TRD CNTRS,NEC (NO BREAKDOWN) 2014 (160 Establishments)	
	$	%	$	%	$	%	$	%
Cash	605,059	18.0	1,096,373	18.9	879,544	15.1	286,723	17.3
Accounts Receivable	850,445	25.3	2,076,727	35.8	2,137,701	36.7	604,936	36.5
Notes Receivable	6,723	0.2	0	0.0	11,650	0.2	1,657	0.1
Inventory	53,783	1.6	145,023	2.5	384,437	6.6	139,218	8.4
Other Current	447,072	13.3	817,929	14.1	1,194,083	20.5	245,289	14.8
Total Current	**1,963,082**	**58.4**	**4,136,052**	**71.3**	**4,607,415**	**79.1**	**1,277,823**	**77.1**
Fixed Assets	1,200,034	35.7	1,566,247	27.0	966,916	16.6	296,667	17.9
Other Non-current	198,325	5.9	98,615	1.7	250,467	4.3	82,868	5.0
Total Assets	**3,361,441**	**100.0**	**5,800,914**	**100.0**	**5,824,798**	**100.0**	**1,657,358**	**100.0**
Accounts Payable	309,253	9.2	771,522	13.3	803,822	13.8	197,226	11.9
Bank Loans	3,361	0.1	17,403	0.3	0	0.0	1,657	0.1
Notes Payable	60,506	1.8	232,037	4.0	116,496	2.0	31,490	1.9
Other Current	594,975	17.7	1,316,806	22.7	1,840,636	31.6	497,207	30.0
Total Current	**968,095**	**28.8**	**2,337,768**	**40.3**	**2,760,954**	**47.4**	**727,580**	**43.9**
Other Long Term	514,301	15.3	962,952	16.6	407,736	7.0	169,051	10.2
Deferred Credits	3,361	0.1	0	0.0	0	0.0	1,657	0.1
Net Worth	1,875,684	55.8	2,500,194	43.1	2,656,108	45.6	759,070	45.8
Total Liab & Net Worth	**3,361,441**	**100.0**	**5,800,914**	**100.0**	**5,824,798**	**100.0**	**1,657,358**	**100.0**
Net Sales	5,697,358	100.0	14,148,571	100.0	11,985,181	100.0	4,540,707	100.0
Gross Profit	1,424,340	25.0	3,565,440	25.2	3,859,228	32.2	1,534,759	33.8
Net Profit After Tax	347,539	6.1	919,657	6.5	191,763	1.6	286,065	6.3
Working Capital	994,987	—	1,798,284	—	1,846,461	—	550,243	—

RATIOS	UQ	MED	LQ	UQ	MED	LQ	UQ	MED	LQ	UQ	MED	LQ
SOLVENCY												
Quick Ratio (times)	3.5	1.6	1.2	2.7	1.4	0.9	3.3	1.6	0.7	3.6	1.8	1.0
Current Ratio (times)	4.5	2.2	1.5	3.8	1.6	1.2	4.3	2.2	1.4	5.2	2.5	1.5
Curr Liab To Nw (%)	16.6	38.1	80.4	30.5	76.0	309.6	20.2	63.5	133.6	18.0	47.4	106.9
Curr Liab To Inv (%)	298.4	759.3	999.9	241.4	817.8	999.9	150.2	611.5	999.9	128.1	314.5	999.9
Total Liab To Nw (%)	23.7	68.1	141.0	45.6	138.5	325.9	35.9	86.4	193.7	24.3	62.1	137.2
Fixed Assets To Nw (%)	37.3	55.8	90.8	27.0	58.4	134.7	4.5	16.0	45.0	8.7	21.4	50.6
EFFICIENCY												
Coll Period (days)	26.3	57.3	81.8	45.5	57.7	82.3	32.1	59.1	81.8	31.8	54.4	72.3
Sales To Inv (times)	162.2	61.4	35.6	889.5	260.5	21.3	152.5	43.9	13.6	136.5	37.2	14.9
Assets To Sales (%)	43.2	59.0	69.7	32.0	41.0	57.2	35.8	48.6	85.2	27.5	36.5	48.7
Sales To Nwc (times)	11.0	6.5	3.5	18.3	8.1	5.1	8.1	5.5	2.7	11.4	6.2	4.3
Acct Pay To Sales (%)	1.8	3.9	8.3	2.1	3.5	8.5	2.4	4.4	10.2	1.8	3.9	6.4
PROFITABILITY												
Return On Sales (%)	10.5	4.0	1.0	8.9	6.4	1.0	6.2	3.3	0.2	9.1	3.3	1.1
Return On Assets (%)	16.3	8.5	2.1	18.9	11.3	3.0	12.1	4.9	0.4	23.6	9.4	2.5
Return On Nw (%)	26.3	13.7	4.0	81.2	17.8	6.4	39.7	10.9	3.0	40.7	18.3	4.0

	SIC 20 FOOD,KINDRED PRODUCT (NO BREAKDOWN) 2014 (235 Establishments)		SIC 2023 DRY CNDNSD EVAP PROD (NO BREAKDOWN) 2014 (11 Establishments)		SIC 2033 CANNED FRTS,VGTBLS (NO BREAKDOWN) 2014 (10 Establishments)		SIC 2048 PREPARED FEEDS, NEC (NO BREAKDOWN) 2014 (13 Establishments)	
	$	%	$	%	$	%	$	%
Cash	2,186,985	12.8	13,880,947	15.1	6,760,939	3.6	1,644,483	15.8
Accounts Receivable	3,075,447	18.0	14,248,654	15.5	24,602,307	13.1	2,081,624	20.0
Notes Receivable	34,172	0.2	0	0.0	563,412	0.3	31,224	0.3
Inventory	4,015,167	23.5	13,421,313	14.6	72,867,902	38.8	2,758,152	26.5
Other Current	905,548	5.3	17,925,728	19.5	11,268,232	6.0	187,348	1.8
Total Current	**10,217,319**	**59.8**	**59,476,642**	**64.7**	**116,062,792**	**61.8**	**6,702,831**	**64.4**
Fixed Assets	4,305,626	25.2	19,764,263	21.5	47,702,183	25.4	2,383,460	22.9
Other Non-current	2,562,873	15.0	12,685,898	13.8	24,038,896	12.8	1,321,831	12.7
Total Assets	**17,085,818**	**100.0**	**91,926,803**	**100.0**	**187,803,871**	**100.0**	**10,408,122**	**100.0**
Accounts Payable	6,765,984	39.6	90,915,608	98.9	10,704,821	5.7	1,769,381	17.0
Bank Loans	187,944	1.1	0	0.0	2,441,450	1.3	114,489	1.1
Notes Payable	2,972,932	17.4	275,780	0.3	563,412	0.3	145,714	1.4
Other Current	9,516,801	55.7	651,485,253	708.7	40,941,243	21.8	1,342,648	12.9
Total Current	**19,443,661**	**113.8**	**742,676,641**	**807.9**	**54,650,926**	**29.1**	**3,372,232**	**32.4**
Other Long Term	3,895,567	22.8	48,169,645	52.4	47,138,772	25.1	2,196,113	21.1
Deferred Credits	153,772	0.9	0	0.0	0	0.0	0	0.0
Net Worth	(6,407,182)	(37.5)	(698,919,483)	(760.3)	86,014,173	45.8	4,839,777	46.5
Total Liab & Net Worth	**17,085,818**	**100.0**	**91,926,803**	**100.0**	**187,803,871**	**100.0**	**10,408,122**	**100.0**
Net Sales	33,567,422	100.0	181,673,524	100.0	303,398,822	100.0	24,781,243	100.0
Gross Profit	10,070,227	30.0	56,137,119	30.9	50,667,603	16.7	4,881,905	19.7
Net Profit After Tax	1,577,669	4.7	11,082,085	6.1	19,114,126	6.3	1,040,812	4.2
Working Capital	(9,226,342)	---	(683,199,999)	---	61,411,866	---	3,330,599	---

RATIOS	UQ	MED	LQ	UQ	MED	LQ	UQ	MED	LQ	UQ	MED	LQ
SOLVENCY												
Quick Ratio (times)	1.7	0.9	0.5	1.1	0.8	0.4	0.8	0.6	0.5	1.9	1.1	0.7
Current Ratio (times)	3.5	2.0	1.2	2.0	1.2	0.9	3.8	2.2	1.9	3.4	1.7	1.4
Curr Liab To Nw (%)	23.3	45.9	100.5	36.6	96.4	206.7	30.4	44.3	127.2	24.3	71.2	164.9
Curr Liab To Inv (%)	65.4	130.2	234.4	132.4	204.3	282.3	40.4	61.7	108.7	70.3	132.6	186.0
Total Liab To Nw (%)	38.3	86.1	198.6	70.1	114.2	323.5	55.2	103.3	442.5	44.5	125.8	287.3
Fixed Assets To Nw (%)	24.3	48.5	85.4	33.4	68.6	130.3	28.7	58.9	135.3	32.6	48.5	114.9
EFFICIENCY												
Coll Period (days)	19.4	28.5	40.2	17.2	25.2	31.8	24.3	35.3	38.7	12.8	17.4	29.9
Sales To Inv (times)	21.3	10.0	6.3	16.3	8.7	7.9	19.3	3.2	2.6	32.6	17.0	7.6
Assets To Sales (%)	32.0	50.9	89.6	27.6	50.6	85.6	57.4	61.9	78.1	27.4	42.0	49.0
Sales To Nwc (times)	15.5	6.8	3.7	30.9	7.7	4.7	11.2	5.1	3.2	22.7	12.3	5.0
Acct Pay To Sales (%)	2.6	4.9	9.3	1.4	4.8	11.1	2.0	3.7	6.7	2.4	4.0	6.3
PROFITABILITY												
Return On Sales (%)	8.4	3.7	0.7	8.4	6.5	0.7	10.3	4.1	1.0	6.2	2.7	0.4
Return On Assets (%)	13.6	6.8	1.9	17.7	5.5	(9.2)	9.7	6.5	3.8	14.5	5.2	2.5
Return On Nw (%)	31.9	13.5	6.6	49.5	25.6	8.6	13.7	12.0	9.5	39.7	17.8	9.6

SIC 2051 BRD,CKE,RLTD PRDCTS (NO BREAKDOWN) 2014 (11 Establishments)

	$	%
Cash	365,376	16.1
Accounts Receivable	719,406	31.7
Notes Receivable	59,005	2.6
Inventory	426,651	18.8
Other Current	59,005	2.6
Total Current	**1,629,443**	**71.8**
Fixed Assets	462,961	20.4
Other Non-current	177,015	7.8
Total Assets	**2,269,419**	**100.0**
Accounts Payable	701,250	30.9
Bank Loans	56,735	2.5
Notes Payable	0	0.0
Other Current	549,200	24.2
Total Current	**1,307,185**	**57.6**
Other Long Term	615,013	27.1
Deferred Credits	0	0.0
Net Worth	347,221	15.3
Total Liab & Net Worth	**2,269,419**	**100.0**
Net Sales	6,856,251	100.0
Gross Profit	2,132,294	31.1
Net Profit After Tax	0	0.0
Working Capital	322,258	—

RATIOS	UQ	MED	LQ
SOLVENCY			
Quick Ratio (times)	2.3	1.5	0.7
Current Ratio (times)	4.2	2.0	1.2
Curr Liab To Nw (%)	12.2	95.1	204.7
Curr Liab To Inv (%)	67.6	235.6	582.9
Total Liab To Nw (%)	12.2	185.8	412.3
Fixed Assets To Nw (%)	14.8	21.3	87.0
EFFICIENCY			
Coll Period (days)	12.3	29.2	43.9
Sales To Inv (times)	30.1	26.0	23.1
Assets To Sales (%)	18.7	33.1	46.0
Sales To Nwc (times)	13.8	7.0	3.7
Acct Pay To Sales (%)	1.8	2.4	4.5
PROFITABILITY			
Return On Sales (%)	7.1	2.7	0.4
Return On Assets (%)	10.3	8.7	1.1
Return On Nw (%)	41.2	22.3	16.4

SIC 2086 BOTL,CND SFT DRNKS (NO BREAKDOWN) 2014 (20 Establishments)

	$	%
Cash	1,055,516	17.5
Accounts Receivable	1,230,430	20.4
Notes Receivable	0	0.0
Inventory	784,098	13.0
Other Current	343,797	5.7
Total Current	**3,413,841**	**56.6**
Fixed Assets	1,230,430	20.4
Other Non-current	1,387,251	23.0
Total Assets	**6,031,522**	**100.0**
Accounts Payable	7,690,191	127.5
Bank Loans	0	0.0
Notes Payable	6,032	0.1
Other Current	144,756	2.4
Total Current	**7,840,979**	**130.0**
Other Long Term	1,248,525	20.7
Deferred Credits	102,536	1.7
Net Worth	(3,160,518)	(52.4)
Total Liab & Net Worth	**6,031,522**	**100.0**
Net Sales	12,135,859	100.0
Gross Profit	4,041,241	33.3
Net Profit After Tax	(97,087)	(0.8)
Working Capital	(4,427,138)	—

RATIOS	UQ	MED	LQ
SOLVENCY			
Quick Ratio (times)	2.0	1.0	0.6
Current Ratio (times)	4.0	1.6	1.2
Curr Liab To Nw (%)	26.2	60.8	192.8
Curr Liab To Inv (%)	109.7	203.8	452.4
Total Liab To Nw (%)	30.1	109.8	477.4
Fixed Assets To Nw (%)	16.2	56.0	132.3
EFFICIENCY			
Coll Period (days)	25.9	33.1	48.9
Sales To Inv (times)	30.0	22.3	14.1
Assets To Sales (%)	34.6	49.7	87.4
Sales To Nwc (times)	21.7	8.2	4.6
Acct Pay To Sales (%)	4.2	7.1	16.5
PROFITABILITY			
Return On Sales (%)	7.4	2.2	(0.8)
Return On Assets (%)	12.3	5.7	(2.2)
Return On Nw (%)	31.9	13.5	0.2

SIC 2099 FOOD PRPRTNS,NEC (NO BREAKDOWN) 2014 (24 Establishments)

	$	%
Cash	1,085,087	10.7
Accounts Receivable	1,602,278	15.8
Notes Receivable	10,141	0.1
Inventory	2,291,866	22.6
Other Current	841,703	8.3
Total Current	**5,831,075**	**57.5**
Fixed Assets	2,433,840	24.0
Other Non-current	1,876,085	18.5
Total Assets	**10,141,000**	**100.0**
Accounts Payable	1,470,445	14.5
Bank Loans	0	0.0
Notes Payable	294,089	2.9
Other Current	1,622,560	16.0
Total Current	**3,387,094**	**33.4**
Other Long Term	1,622,560	16.0
Deferred Credits	750,434	7.4
Net Worth	4,380,912	43.2
Total Liab & Net Worth	**10,141,000**	**100.0**
Net Sales	24,916,462	100.0
Gross Profit	9,418,423	37.8
Net Profit After Tax	2,242,482	9.0
Working Capital	2,443,981	—

RATIOS	UQ	MED	LQ
SOLVENCY			
Quick Ratio (times)	1.2	0.9	0.5
Current Ratio (times)	3.0	1.7	1.3
Curr Liab To Nw (%)	26.7	47.7	82.7
Curr Liab To Inv (%)	84.5	171.2	285.5
Total Liab To Nw (%)	49.5	80.4	144.0
Fixed Assets To Nw (%)	16.5	41.6	77.3
EFFICIENCY			
Coll Period (days)	15.3	21.2	31.0
Sales To Inv (times)	28.4	11.3	7.1
Assets To Sales (%)	24.2	40.7	59.5
Sales To Nwc (times)	16.5	9.0	5.2
Acct Pay To Sales (%)	3.3	5.2	8.8
PROFITABILITY			
Return On Sales (%)	10.2	4.3	2.6
Return On Assets (%)	15.3	12.0	7.1
Return On Nw (%)	43.8	22.7	11.9

SIC 22 TEXTILE MILL PDTS (NO BREAKDOWN) 2014 (31 Establishments)

	$	%
Cash	828,365	8.1
Accounts Receivable	2,658,949	26.0
Notes Receivable	0	0.0
Inventory	2,863,484	28.0
Other Current	685,190	6.7
Total Current	**7,035,988**	**68.8**
Fixed Assets	2,208,973	21.6
Other Non-current	981,766	9.6
Total Assets	**10,226,727**	**100.0**
Accounts Payable	1,912,398	18.7
Bank Loans	0	0.0
Notes Payable	10,227	0.1
Other Current	2,270,333	22.2
Total Current	**4,192,958**	**41.0**
Other Long Term	2,014,665	19.7
Deferred Credits	0	0.0
Net Worth	4,019,104	39.3
Total Liab & Net Worth	**10,226,727**	**100.0**
Net Sales	23,295,506	100.0
Gross Profit	6,033,536	25.9
Net Profit After Tax	861,934	3.7
Working Capital	2,843,030	—

RATIOS	UQ	MED	LQ
SOLVENCY			
Quick Ratio (times)	2.0	1.2	0.7
Current Ratio (times)	3.3	2.5	1.8
Curr Liab To Nw (%)	28.4	46.9	76.7
Curr Liab To Inv (%)	58.5	101.1	168.9
Total Liab To Nw (%)	31.4	70.2	152.8
Fixed Assets To Nw (%)	11.4	29.4	54.5
EFFICIENCY			
Coll Period (days)	27.9	47.0	56.1
Sales To Inv (times)	14.8	6.7	5.0
Assets To Sales (%)	28.0	43.9	71.1
Sales To Nwc (times)	7.0	4.9	4.2
Acct Pay To Sales (%)	4.8	7.5	9.9
PROFITABILITY			
Return On Sales (%)	6.1	3.1	1.0
Return On Assets (%)	14.7	6.4	2.1
Return On Nw (%)	18.4	10.3	8.1

	SIC 23 APPAREL,RELATED PDTS (NO BREAKDOWN) 2014 (90 Establishments)		SIC 24 LUMBER,WOOD PRODUCTS (NO BREAKDOWN) 2014 (125 Establishments)		SIC 2421 SAWML PLNG,MLL,GNRL (NO BREAKDOWN) 2014 (24 Establishments)		SIC 2431 MILLWORK (NO BREAKDOWN) 2014 (25 Establishments)	
	$	%	$	%	$	%	$	%
Cash	809,716	14.7	421,218	16.6	570,839	14.1	265,256	20.5
Accounts Receivable	1,156,737	21.0	512,567	20.2	566,790	14.0	300,192	23.2
Notes Receivable	16,525	0.3	10,150	0.4	24,291	0.6	3,882	0.3
Inventory	1,845,270	33.5	596,303	23.5	1,218,599	30.1	317,013	24.5
Other Current	418,628	7.6	129,411	5.1	117,406	2.9	62,109	4.8
Total Current	**4,246,876**	**77.1**	**1,669,649**	**65.8**	**2,497,925**	**61.7**	**948,452**	**73.3**
Fixed Assets	655,484	11.9	695,264	27.4	1,299,569	32.1	232,908	18.0
Other Non-current	605,910	11.0	172,547	6.8	251,007	6.2	112,572	8.7
Total Assets	**5,508,270**	**100.0**	**2,537,460**	**100.0**	**4,048,501**	**100.0**	**1,293,932**	**100.0**
Accounts Payable	4,340,517	78.8	200,459	7.9	299,589	7.4	135,863	10.5
Bank Loans	22,033	0.4	20,300	0.8	0	0.0	1,294	0.1
Notes Payable	71,608	1.3	53,287	2.1	101,213	2.5	7,764	0.6
Other Current	1,316,476	23.9	428,830	16.9	999,979	24.7	200,559	15.5
Total Current	**5,750,634**	**104.4**	**702,876**	**27.7**	**1,400,781**	**34.6**	**345,480**	**26.7**
Other Long Term	1,063,096	19.3	342,558	13.5	514,160	12.7	190,208	14.7
Deferred Credits	16,525	0.3	2,537	0.1	0	0.0	0	0.0
Net Worth	(1,321,985)	(24.0)	1,489,489	58.7	2,133,560	52.7	758,244	58.6
Total Liab & Net Worth	**5,508,270**	**100.0**	**2,537,460**	**100.0**	**4,048,501**	**100.0**	**1,293,932**	**100.0**
Net Sales	9,924,811	100.0	5,887,378	100.0	7,281,477	100.0	3,423,101	100.0
Gross Profit	3,821,052	38.5	1,554,268	26.4	2,111,628	29.0	688,043	20.1
Net Profit After Tax	238,195	2.4	176,621	3.0	509,703	7.0	61,616	1.8
Working Capital	(1,503,758)	---	966,773	---	1,097,144	---	602,972	---

RATIOS	UQ	MED	LQ	UQ	MED	LQ	UQ	MED	LQ	UQ	MED	LQ
SOLVENCY												
Quick Ratio (times)	2.3	1.3	0.6	4.6	1.4	0.8	2.7	1.1	0.6	5.4	2.3	1.0
Current Ratio (times)	4.6	2.6	1.7	6.9	2.9	1.7	5.3	2.9	1.6	10.8	4.6	1.9
Curr Liab To Nw (%)	23.7	51.7	119.5	11.0	31.5	58.4	12.1	25.1	44.7	7.5	22.9	73.7
Curr Liab To Inv (%)	58.4	93.0	148.1	42.1	91.8	167.8	20.3	73.0	148.0	33.6	74.6	127.9
Total Liab To Nw (%)	28.9	86.7	176.0	13.3	42.1	94.6	19.0	54.5	77.2	10.2	22.9	145.6
Fixed Assets To Nw (%)	7.4	17.0	32.2	12.9	39.1	83.5	18.2	47.2	98.2	12.7	23.0	54.8
EFFICIENCY												
Coll Period (days)	23.6	34.5	55.5	15.0	25.2	41.3	9.1	20.1	30.2	23.8	43.4	48.0
Sales To Inv (times)	11.0	6.4	4.2	16.9	10.1	5.7	12.6	6.2	4.6	28.9	12.7	8.5
Assets To Sales (%)	37.9	55.5	71.6	31.3	43.1	66.5	38.4	55.6	66.0	28.7	37.8	59.5
Sales To Nwc (times)	6.4	4.2	2.5	10.0	5.3	3.3	7.7	4.9	3.1	8.9	5.0	3.3
Acct Pay To Sales (%)	2.5	5.1	10.2	1.4	2.7	5.0	0.8	2.4	4.5	2.0	4.1	6.0
PROFITABILITY												
Return On Sales (%)	6.2	3.1	0.1	6.8	3.3	0.9	11.5	3.9	1.4	6.6	1.9	0.9
Return On Assets (%)	12.4	7.2	0.1	17.3	8.1	1.4	23.6	7.5	1.9	14.4	7.1	1.6
Return On Nw (%)	23.8	13.5	2.7	32.2	13.6	3.4	34.4	25.7	3.7	27.2	14.7	4.4

SIC 2434 WOOD KTCHN CABINETS (NO BREAKDOWN) 2014 (10 Establishments)
SIC 25 FURNITURE,FIXTURES (NO BREAKDOWN) 2014 (82 Establishments)
SIC 2512 UPHLSTRD HSHLD FURN (NO BREAKDOWN) 2014 (14 Establishments)
SIC 2515 MATTRESSES,BDSPRNGS (NO BREAKDOWN) 2014 (10 Establishments)

	2434 $	2434 %	25 $	25 %	2512 $	2512 %	2515 $	2515 %
Cash	142,280	18.4	549,239	16.5	505,184	11.0	523,467	19.2
Accounts Receivable	279,921	36.2	808,880	24.3	964,442	21.0	485,298	17.8
Notes Receivable	4,640	0.6	3,329	0.1	4,593	0.1	2,726	0.1
Inventory	95,111	12.3	902,084	27.1	1,726,810	37.6	913,341	33.5
Other Current	57,995	7.5	169,765	5.1	349,036	7.6	81,793	3.0
Total Current	**579,947**	**75.0**	**2,433,297**	**73.1**	**3,550,065**	**77.3**	**2,006,625**	**73.6**
Fixed Assets	150,786	19.5	629,129	18.9	629,184	13.7	452,581	16.6
Other Non-current	42,530	5.5	266,297	8.0	413,332	9.0	267,186	9.8
Total Assets	**773,263**	**100.0**	**3,328,723**	**100.0**	**4,592,581**	**100.0**	**2,726,392**	**100.0**
Accounts Payable	75,780	9.8	426,077	12.8	578,665	12.6	283,545	10.4
Bank Loans	0	0.0	46,602	1.4	0	0.0	0	0.0
Notes Payable	24,744	3.2	49,931	1.5	18,370	0.4	16,358	0.6
Other Current	203,368	26.3	752,291	22.6	684,295	14.9	684,325	25.1
Total Current	**303,892**	**39.3**	**1,274,901**	**38.3**	**1,281,330**	**27.9**	**984,228**	**36.1**
Other Long Term	187,903	24.3	492,651	14.8	247,999	5.4	515,288	18.9
Deferred Credits	0	0.0	36,616	1.1	0	0.0	0	0.0
Net Worth	281,468	36.4	1,524,555	45.8	3,063,252	66.7	1,226,876	45.0
Total Liab & Net Worth	**773,263**	**100.0**	**3,328,723**	**100.0**	**4,592,581**	**100.0**	**2,726,392**	**100.0**
Net Sales	1,909,291	100.0	7,514,047	100.0	9,587,852	100.0	4,903,583	100.0
Gross Profit	754,170	39.5	2,404,495	32.0	2,253,145	23.5	1,770,193	36.1
Net Profit After Tax	168,018	8.8	187,851	2.5	335,575	3.5	161,818	3.3
Working Capital	276,055	--	1,158,396	--	2,268,735	--	1,022,397	--

RATIOS	2434 UQ	MED	LQ	25 UQ	MED	LQ	2512 UQ	MED	LQ	2515 UQ	MED	LQ
SOLVENCY												
Quick Ratio (times)	2.5	1.1	0.8	2.5	1.1	0.6	3.6	1.6	0.9	3.9	0.8	0.3
Current Ratio (times)	3.4	2.4	1.4	4.3	2.1	1.4	10.8	3.8	1.5	5.0	2.9	1.4
Curr Liab To Nw (%)	28.0	43.2	133.5	20.5	49.4	119.0	7.4	26.9	83.9	29.1	41.5	85.9
Curr Liab To Inv (%)	211.7	270.0	301.2	53.8	115.3	218.2	20.3	74.4	113.9	52.8	170.2	223.2
Total Liab To Nw (%)	28.7	82.9	342.3	29.8	72.4	176.0	20.2	38.1	87.0	29.1	41.5	171.9
Fixed Assets To Nw (%)	4.2	19.0	70.0	11.1	24.1	56.2	10.3	20.9	30.9	9.0	34.1	113.0
EFFICIENCY												
Coll Period (days)	26.3	44.5	59.9	19.7	34.3	49.3	28.0	32.9	43.8	13.2	20.7	38.7
Sales To Inv (times)	50.0	21.6	10.1	17.4	9.7	5.6	11.2	9.2	5.4	14.3	7.8	4.1
Assets To Sales (%)	32.6	40.5	45.4	28.7	44.3	63.4	37.1	47.9	53.1	29.3	55.6	79.0
Sales To Nwc (times)	7.2	5.1	3.7	12.4	6.4	3.0	8.5	3.8	2.8	8.6	4.6	4.1
Acct Pay To Sales (%)	2.5	2.9	4.0	2.3	4.1	7.6	2.3	3.3	5.0	2.2	2.8	6.7
PROFITABILITY												
Return On Sales (%)	10.6	7.8	5.8	4.6	3.1	1.0	4.5	3.4	1.1	7.1	1.9	(0.2)
Return On Assets (%)	31.7	18.3	10.7	11.3	5.3	2.0	8.2	7.1	4.4	21.0	2.8	(2.4)
Return On Nw (%)	85.1	43.8	25.9	35.0	10.6	5.7	15.7	9.0	7.4	44.3	35.0	6.0

	SIC 2541 WD PARTNS.FXTRS (NO BREAKDOWN) 2014 (19 Establishments)		SIC 26 PAPER,ALLIED PDTS (NO BREAKDOWN) 2014 (79 Establishments)		SIC 2653 CRRGTD SLD FBR BXS (NO BREAKDOWN) 2014 (15 Establishments)		SIC 2673 BAGS:PLSTC,LMND,CTD (NO BREAKDOWN) 2014 (10 Establishments)	
	$	%	$	%	$	%	$	%
Cash	241,101	18.8	859,157	8.5	644,480	7.9	218,414	6.2
Accounts Receivable	445,011	34.7	2,264,131	22.4	1,762,122	21.6	940,591	26.7
Notes Receivable	1,282	0.1	0	0.0	0	0.0	0	0.0
Inventory	237,254	18.5	2,213,592	21.9	1,811,069	22.2	965,251	27.4
Other Current	51,299	4.0	495,278	4.9	530,268	6.5	253,643	7.2
Total Current	**975,947**	**76.1**	**5,832,158**	**57.7**	**4,747,939**	**58.2**	**2,377,899**	**67.5**
Fixed Assets	287,269	22.4	3,022,210	29.9	2,659,498	32.6	803,202	22.8
Other Non-current	19,237	1.5	1,253,358	12.4	750,533	9.2	341,713	9.7
Total Assets	**1,282,453**	**100.0**	**10,107,726**	**100.0**	**8,157,970**	**100.0**	**3,522,814**	**100.0**
Accounts Payable	194,933	15.2	1,233,143	12.2	1,125,800	13.8	535,468	15.2
Bank Loans	67,970	5.3	10,108	0.1	0	0.0	0	0.0
Notes Payable	15,389	1.2	141,508	1.4	0	0.0	0	0.0
Other Current	316,766	24.7	1,394,866	13.8	1,835,543	22.5	521,376	14.8
Total Current	**595,058**	**46.4**	**2,779,625**	**27.5**	**2,961,343**	**36.3**	**1,056,844**	**30.0**
Other Long Term	130,810	10.2	2,587,577	25.6	1,419,486	17.4	644,675	18.3
Deferred Credits	0	0.0	50,539	0.5	106,054	1.3	0	0.0
Net Worth	556,585	43.4	4,689,985	46.4	3,671,087	45.0	1,821,295	51.7
Total Liab & Net Worth	**1,282,453**	**100.0**	**10,107,726**	**100.0**	**8,157,970**	**100.0**	**3,522,814**	**100.0**
Net Sales	4,032,871	100.0	20,712,553	100.0	22,048,568	100.0	10,839,428	100.0
Gross Profit	1,201,796	29.8	5,033,150	24.3	4,630,199	21.0	2,753,215	25.4
Net Profit After Tax	108,888	2.7	973,490	4.7	573,263	2.6	585,329	5.4
Working Capital	380,889	---	3,052,533	---	1,786,596	---	1,321,055	---

RATIOS	UQ	MED	LQ	UQ	MED	LQ	UQ	MED	LQ	UQ	MED	LQ
SOLVENCY												
Quick Ratio (times)	2.2	1.3	0.8	1.9	1.1	0.8	1.5	1.0	0.6	1.8	1.1	0.8
Current Ratio (times)	2.8	2.1	1.7	4.0	2.3	1.6	3.0	2.0	1.3	2.7	2.2	1.6
Curr Liab To Nw (%)	45.5	66.3	117.7	22.9	39.1	71.9	25.4	42.7	143.0	28.4	55.4	148.3
Curr Liab To Inv (%)	87.7	188.5	732.0	79.0	118.3	229.7	104.0	135.5	217.5	92.2	149.2	244.6
Total Liab To Nw (%)	66.3	84.0	180.1	32.6	108.8	223.7	53.8	115.5	199.8	59.4	106.7	161.0
Fixed Assets To Nw (%)	15.9	19.7	59.1	19.7	63.9	106.4	25.9	64.6	106.4	19.7	24.8	103.5
EFFICIENCY												
Coll Period (days)	10.6	37.3	69.0	28.8	36.1	47.5	27.1	31.0	39.7	23.8	28.8	37.1
Sales To Inv (times)	73.2	18.6	9.3	16.2	10.3	7.7	16.0	11.1	8.8	15.4	11.4	9.9
Assets To Sales (%)	22.8	31.8	35.7	29.9	48.8	86.4	26.2	37.0	65.2	22.1	32.5	64.4
Sales To Nwc (times)	10.8	7.1	5.9	13.0	7.3	4.8	14.0	10.6	7.1	13.2	9.8	6.9
Acct Pay To Sales (%)	2.3	4.0	6.7	3.3	5.6	8.8	3.0	5.6	9.3	2.6	4.3	6.3
PROFITABILITY												
Return On Sales (%)	5.1	3.1	1.2	5.8	3.0	0.5	5.2	1.5	0.7	3.9	2.1	0.4
Return On Assets (%)	21.8	8.5	3.6	10.0	5.3	1.1	7.6	4.4	1.0	8.4	3.6	1.8
Return On Nw (%)	39.0	17.1	6.7	23.6	11.8	5.9	20.2	12.2	2.6	24.2	9.5	3.4

Balance Sheet / Income

	SIC 2679 CNVTD PPR PRDTS,NEC (NO BREAKDOWN) 2014 (13 Establishments) $	%	SIC 27 PRINTING,PUBLISHING (NO BREAKDOWN) 2014 (159 Establishments) $	%	SIC 2711 NEWSPAPERS (NO BREAKDOWN) 2014 (13 Establishments) $	%	SIC 2731 BOOK PUBLISHING (NO BREAKDOWN) 2014 (21 Establishments) $	%
Cash	819,040	17.2	568,922	16.3	66,620,581	22.3	1,192,508	24.0
Accounts Receivable	976,182	20.5	781,832	22.4	30,770,941	10.3	929,162	18.7
Notes Receivable	0	0.0	3,490	0.1	0	0.0	0	0.0
Inventory	1,233,323	25.9	408,367	11.7	3,286,217	1.1	1,073,257	21.6
Other Current	171,427	3.6	244,323	7.0	35,550,893	11.9	486,940	9.8
Total Current	**3,199,972**	**67.2**	**2,006,934**	**57.5**	**136,228,632**	**45.6**	**3,681,867**	**74.1**
Fixed Assets	1,133,323	23.8	903,993	25.9	72,296,774	24.2	511,785	10.3
Other Non-current	428,568	9.0	579,393	16.6	90,221,594	30.2	775,130	15.6
Total Assets	**4,761,863**	**100.0**	**3,490,320**	**100.0**	**298,747,000**	**100.0**	**4,968,782**	**100.0**
Accounts Payable	466,663	9.8	488,645	14.0	11,352,386	3.8	1,778,824	35.8
Bank Loans	19,047	0.4	20,942	0.6	0	0.0	0	0.0
Notes Payable	61,904	1.3	76,787	2.2	896,241	0.3	19,875	0.4
Other Current	590,471	12.4	666,651	19.1	44,513,303	14.9	1,947,763	39.2
Total Current	**1,138,085**	**23.9**	**1,253,025**	**35.9**	**56,761,930**	**19.0**	**3,746,462**	**75.4**
Other Long Term	623,804	13.1	698,064	20.0	95,897,787	32.1	342,846	6.9
Deferred Credits	14,286	0.3	6,981	0.2	298,747	0.1	0	0.0
Net Worth	2,985,688	62.7	1,532,250	43.9	145,788,536	48.8	879,474	17.7
Total Liab & Net Worth	**4,761,863**	**100.0**	**3,490,320**	**100.0**	**298,747,000**	**100.0**	**4,968,782**	**100.0**
Net Sales	10,153,226	100.0	6,038,616	100.0	236,163,636	100.0	4,782,273	100.0
Gross Profit	2,345,395	23.1	2,608,682	43.2	129,653,836	54.9	3,089,348	64.6
Net Profit After Tax	385,823	3.8	271,738	4.5	18,656,927	7.9	473,445	9.9
Working Capital	2,061,887	—	753,909	—	79,466,702	—	(64,595)	—

RATIOS

	SIC 2679 UQ	MED	LQ	SIC 27 UQ	MED	LQ	SIC 2711 UQ	MED	LQ	SIC 2731 UQ	MED	LQ
SOLVENCY												
Quick Ratio (times)	3.9	2.2	1.4	2.8	1.3	0.8	2.1	1.0	0.9	2.8	1.0	0.7
Current Ratio (times)	7.5	3.9	2.2	4.4	2.0	1.2	2.7	2.0	1.2	7.1	1.9	1.3
Curr Liab To Nw (%)	10.9	21.0	51.2	16.1	37.8	70.4	18.8	35.0	63.1	8.1	31.0	73.3
Curr Liab To Inv (%)	38.0	100.2	127.2	110.9	230.7	896.0	983.9	999.9	999.9	69.1	110.9	285.0
Total Liab To Nw (%)	27.7	34.2	86.1	22.6	60.1	159.0	21.3	79.5	179.1	9.9	40.8	92.0
Fixed Assets To Nw (%)	12.2	39.1	95.8	11.8	37.2	80.3	23.2	47.5	91.2	2.2	6.1	16.0
EFFICIENCY												
Coll Period (days)	29.0	33.6	44.9	28.5	39.8	56.9	39.4	46.0	52.6	35.8	67.4	90.2
Sales To Inv (times)	15.1	8.9	5.5	62.0	27.3	9.4	105.5	82.6	55.7	7.4	3.8	3.0
Assets To Sales (%)	25.9	46.9	52.6	37.2	57.8	94.6	97.0	126.5	189.4	81.3	103.9	132.0
Sales To Nwc (times)	8.4	6.1	4.0	11.5	6.1	3.4	15.7	4.4	2.6	5.0	1.6	1.4
Acct Pay To Sales (%)	1.9	4.0	10.3	2.6	4.1	7.0	2.5	4.1	4.6	1.8	5.0	8.0
PROFITABILITY												
Return On Sales (%)	4.1	3.0	2.8	5.8	2.7	0.4	11.1	1.5	0.4	9.0	4.4	2.0
Return On Assets (%)	13.6	7.6	6.1	11.1	4.5	1.0	8.2	1.5	(0.1)	7.0	3.6	0.8
Return On Nw (%)	29.5	15.3	11.2	19.7	9.0	1.8	73.6	2.5	(0.7)	13.6	8.2	3.2

	SIC 2752 COMMRCL PRTNG,LITH (NO BREAKDOWN) 2014 (60 Establishments) $	%	SIC 2759 COMMRCL PRTNG,NEC (NO BREAKDOWN) 2014 (26 Establishments) $	%	SIC 28 CHEMICALS,ALLIED PDT (NO BREAKDOWN) 2014 (562 Establishments) $	%	SIC 2819 IND INORG CHEM,NEC (NO BREAKDOWN) 2014 (16 Establishments) $	%
Cash	413,800	16.0	232,473	10.1	18,653,375	32.5	53,227,227	11.4
Accounts Receivable	708,632	27.4	621,462	27.0	5,108,155	8.9	55,561,755	11.9
Notes Receivable	2,586	0.1	11,509	0.5	57,395	0.1	0	0.0
Inventory	225,004	8.7	455,739	19.8	5,624,710	9.8	72,837,258	15.6
Other Current	142,244	5.5	80,558	3.5	8,551,855	14.9	33,150,290	7.1
Total Current	**1,492,266**	**57.7**	**1,401,741**	**60.9**	**37,995,490**	**66.2**	**214,776,530**	**46.0**
Fixed Assets	863,807	33.4	699,720	30.4	8,953,620	15.6	126,998,296	27.2
Other Non-current	230,176	8.9	200,249	8.7	10,445,890	18.2	125,130,674	26.8
Total Assets	**2,586,249**	**100.0**	**2,301,710**	**100.0**	**57,395,000**	**100.0**	**466,905,500**	**100.0**
Accounts Payable	367,247	14.2	230,171	10.0	57,222,815	99.7	565,889,466	121.2
Bank Loans	23,276	0.9	36,827	1.6	57,395	0.1	0	0.0
Notes Payable	49,139	1.9	96,672	4.2	16,988,920	29.6	28,014,330	6.0
Other Current	372,420	14.4	400,498	17.4	21,982,285	38.3	325,900,039	69.8
Total Current	**812,082**	**31.4**	**764,168**	**33.2**	**96,251,415**	**167.7**	**919,803,835**	**197.0**
Other Long Term	475,870	18.4	483,359	21.0	12,052,950	21.0	149,876,665	32.1
Deferred Credits	2,586	0.1	2,302	0.1	1,492,270	2.6	1,400,717	0.3
Net Worth	1,295,711	50.1	1,051,881	45.7	(52,401,635)	(91.3)	(604,175,717)	(129.4)
Total Liab & Net Worth	**2,586,249**	**100.0**	**2,301,710**	**100.0**	**57,395,000**	**100.0**	**466,905,500**	**100.0**
Net Sales	5,760,020	100.0	5,871,709	100.0	40,533,192	100.0	355,602,056	100.0
Gross Profit	2,246,408	39.0	2,160,789	36.8	18,321,003	45.2	112,725,852	31.7
Net Profit After Tax	213,121	3.7	176,151	3.0	283,732	0.7	13,868,480	3.9
Working Capital	680,184	---	637,573	---	(58,255,925)	---	(705,027,305)	---

RATIOS	UQ	MED	LQ	UQ	MED	LQ	UQ	MED	LQ	UQ	MED	LQ
SOLVENCY												
Quick Ratio (times)	3.4	2.1	1.0	2.4	1.0	0.7	4.0	1.5	0.7	1.7	1.1	0.7
Current Ratio (times)	4.9	2.8	1.4	2.9	1.7	1.4	6.8	3.1	1.6	3.4	2.1	1.4
Curr Liab To Nw (%)	15.5	24.5	57.7	42.4	53.1	79.8	11.4	26.2	59.7	18.6	43.5	119.6
Curr Liab To Inv (%)	172.0	236.7	691.6	147.8	196.9	520.0	100.7	191.3	421.3	88.7	139.8	284.9
Total Liab To Nw (%)	21.2	42.1	122.8	48.2	89.2	214.2	18.7	58.8	164.3	69.6	170.1	305.2
Fixed Assets To Nw (%)	24.3	49.0	94.7	21.9	64.4	109.5	2.3	19.1	58.8	35.5	54.8	146.9
EFFICIENCY												
Coll Period (days)	27.8	38.7	52.2	27.6	35.3	47.3	27.7	46.0	66.8	43.1	53.3	61.7
Sales To Inv (times)	73.5	33.7	17.4	62.0	15.3	10.6	14.4	8.0	5.2	7.0	5.7	4.6
Assets To Sales (%)	31.4	44.9	61.0	24.9	39.2	50.2	64.2	141.6	356.5	98.0	131.3	212.8
Sales To Nwc (times)	9.4	6.1	3.6	13.4	10.7	7.0	5.4	2.5	0.7	6.3	4.3	2.6
Acct Pay To Sales (%)	2.8	4.3	5.8	2.5	4.1	6.8	4.6	8.3	23.7	7.2	8.8	11.1
PROFITABILITY												
Return On Sales (%)	4.8	2.7	0.6	4.4	2.9	0.6	8.1	1.0	(129.0)	9.0	1.8	(19.4)
Return On Assets (%)	16.5	6.7	1.4	13.3	7.8	1.4	5.7	(9.6)	(56.5)	6.9	1.4	(22.6)
Return On Nw (%)	21.8	9.4	2.2	24.3	14.7	5.6	15.5	(1.4)	(55.9)	14.8	11.8	(20.6)

Balance Sheet

	SIC 2833 MEDCNLS,BOTANICALS (NO BREAKDOWN) 2014 (10 Establishments)		SIC 2834 PHRMCTCL PREPRTNS (NO BREAKDOWN) 2014 (270 Establishments)		SIC 2835 DGNOSTIC SUBSTANCES (NO BREAKDOWN) 2014 (22 Establishments)		SIC 2836 BIOL PRD,EXC DGNSTC (NO BREAKDOWN) 2014 (41 Establishments)	
	$	%	$	%	$	%	$	%
Cash	11,889,792	28.8	28,440,720	46.2	8,570,580	31.9	25,228,728	39.2
Accounts Receivable	3,344,004	8.1	2,647,080	4.3	3,170,309	11.8	3,861,540	6.0
Notes Receivable	0	0.0	61,560	0.1	0	0.0	64,359	0.1
Inventory	6,357,736	15.4	2,770,200	4.5	1,907,559	7.1	3,217,950	5.0
Other Current	2,931,164	7.1	11,881,080	19.3	5,077,866	18.9	16,282,827	25.3
Total Current	**24,522,696**	**59.4**	**45,800,640**	**74.4**	**18,726,314**	**69.7**	**48,655,404**	**75.6**
Fixed Assets	6,316,452	15.3	4,247,640	6.9	2,874,771	10.7	6,178,464	9.6
Other Non-current	10,444,852	25.3	11,511,720	18.7	5,265,937	19.6	9,525,132	14.8
Total Assets	**41,284,000**	**100.0**	**61,560,000**	**100.0**	**26,867,022**	**100.0**	**64,359,000**	**100.0**
Accounts Payable	43,389,484	105.1	51,956,640	84.4	17,463,564	65.0	135,733,131	210.9
Bank Loans	0	0.0	123,120	0.2	0	0.0	0	0.0
Notes Payable	660,544	1.6	2,954,880	4.8	44,464,921	165.5	1,544,616	2.4
Other Current	40,417,036	97.9	55,280,880	89.8	23,804,182	88.6	51,487,200	80.0
Total Current	**84,467,064**	**204.6**	**110,315,520**	**179.2**	**85,732,667**	**319.1**	**188,764,947**	**293.3**
Other Long Term	26,504,328	64.2	25,793,640	41.9	8,758,649	32.6	13,257,954	20.6
Deferred Credits	0	0.0	2,708,640	4.4	53,734	0.2	965,385	1.5
Net Worth	(69,687,392)	(168.8)	(77,257,800)	(125.5)	(67,678,028)	(251.9)	(138,629,286)	(215.4)
Total Liab & Net Worth	**41,284,000**	**100.0**	**61,560,000**	**100.0**	**26,867,022**	**100.0**	**64,359,000**	**100.0**
Net Sales	48,341,920	100.0	20,616,209	100.0	16,605,082	100.0	31,876,672	100.0
Gross Profit	26,249,663	54.3	12,575,887	61.0	10,295,151	62.0	21,134,234	66.3
Net Profit After Tax	(3,867,354)	(8.0)	(989,578)	(4.8)	(1,477,852)	(8.9)	1,370,697	4.3
Working Capital	(59,944,368)	---	(64,514,880)	---	(67,006,353)	---	(140,109,543)	---

RATIOS

	UQ	MED	LQ	UQ	MED	LQ	UQ	MED	LQ	UQ	MED	LQ
SOLVENCY												
Quick Ratio (times)	1.8	0.8	0.3	6.4	2.0	0.9	4.8	2.3	1.3	4.0	2.5	0.9
Current Ratio (times)	3.9	2.8	0.4	9.6	4.6	1.7	7.6	5.5	2.5	9.1	3.9	3.1
Curr Liab To Nw (%)	17.3	22.6	57.3	9.4	19.6	47.4	8.2	13.7	18.1	9.6	24.4	40.8
Curr Liab To Inv (%)	53.1	80.4	523.5	183.6	411.2	999.9	63.0	145.3	203.7	97.6	277.3	616.1
Total Liab To Nw (%)	33.4	45.4	169.0	15.5	40.3	117.2	12.7	20.9	84.3	11.7	32.4	117.7
Fixed Assets To Nw (%)	20.8	46.3	56.7	0.8	3.1	18.1	8.9	14.5	20.1	1.7	10.6	21.9
EFFICIENCY												
Coll Period (days)	13.5	22.7	37.8	29.2	55.9	79.9	46.8	56.6	71.2	43.4	57.1	100.0
Sales To Inv (times)	15.1	5.9	3.8	16.6	8.0	4.5	9.2	7.4	6.7	18.9	7.6	5.5
Assets To Sales (%)	50.3	85.4	128.6	159.9	298.6	999.9	87.5	161.8	317.9	149.7	201.9	999.9
Sales To Nwc (times)	3.9	3.7	3.2	2.1	0.7	0.2	2.3	1.8	0.8	1.0	0.8	0.2
Acct Pay To Sales (%)	7.0	7.9	24.7	6.1	15.9	63.8	3.5	6.8	20.7	3.8	16.9	40.4
PROFITABILITY												
Return On Sales (%)	3.1	(1.1)	(33.8)	5.1	(81.6)	(648.9)	7.6	(26.6)	(76.3)	13.2	(26.6)	(470.5)
Return On Assets (%)	3.8	(1.4)	(292.5)	(5.5)	(41.7)	(85.6)	5.2	(26.9)	(49.6)	2.3	(26.9)	(67.6)
Return On Nw (%)	7.7	(0.9)	(10.3)	(1.6)	(43.9)	(99.3)	9.2	(14.9)	(38.9)	9.0	(14.9)	(57.8)

Balance Sheet

	SIC 2842 POLISHES,SANT GOODS (NO BREAKDOWN) 2014 (14 Establishments) $	%	SIC 2844 TOILET PREPARATIONS (NO BREAKDOWN) 2014 (23 Establishments) $	%	SIC 2851 PAINTS,ALLIED PRDTS (NO BREAKDOWN) 2014 (17 Establishments) $	%	SIC 2869 IND ORG CHEM. NEC (NO BREAKDOWN) 2014 (42 Establishments) $	%
Cash	950,304	18.4	5,078,051	14.5	870,971	17.8	20,593,767	21.4
Accounts Receivable	929,645	18.0	4,902,945	14.0	822,040	16.8	6,158,883	6.4
Notes Receivable	0	0.0	0	0.0	0	0.0	577,395	0.6
Inventory	1,001,951	19.4	6,794,081	19.4	1,076,481	22.0	7,506,139	7.8
Other Current	779,869	15.1	4,202,525	12.0	249,547	5.1	5,485,256	5.7
Total Current	**3,661,769**	**70.9**	**20,977,602**	**59.9**	**3,019,039**	**61.7**	**40,321,440**	**41.9**
Fixed Assets	800,528	15.5	4,412,651	12.6	841,612	17.2	41,861,161	43.5
Other Non-current	702,399	13.6	9,630,785	27.5	1,032,443	21.1	14,049,953	14.6
Total Assets	**5,164,696**	**100.0**	**35,021,038**	**100.0**	**4,893,094**	**100.0**	**96,232,554**	**100.0**
Accounts Payable	1,916,102	37.1	4,517,714	12.9	23,780,437	486.0	25,309,162	26.3
Bank Loans	0	0.0	105,063	0.3	0	0.0	0	0.0
Notes Payable	2,969,700	57.5	490,295	1.4	8,347,618	170.6	9,527,023	9.9
Other Current	1,606,221	31.1	17,895,750	51.1	(24,514,401)	(501.0)	64,764,508	67.3
Total Current	**6,492,023**	**125.7**	**23,008,822**	**65.7**	**7,613,654**	**155.6**	**99,600,693**	**103.5**
Other Long Term	531,964	10.3	13,553,142	38.7	1,081,374	22.1	30,698,185	31.9
Deferred Credits	0	0.0	0	0.0	9,786	0.2	481,163	0.5
Net Worth	(1,859,291)	(36.0)	(1,540,926)	(4.4)	(3,811,720)	(77.9)	(34,547,487)	(35.9)
Total Liab & Net Worth	**5,164,696**	**100.0**	**35,021,038**	**100.0**	**4,893,094**	**100.0**	**96,232,554**	**100.0**
Net Sales	12,180,887	100.0	38,654,567	100.0	8,251,423	100.0	165,632,623	100.0
Gross Profit	5,091,611	41.8	21,723,867	56.2	2,879,747	34.9	37,929,871	22.9
Net Profit After Tax	816,119	6.7	1,198,292	3.1	214,537	2.6	3,147,020	1.9
Working Capital	(2,830,254)	---	(2,031,220)	---	(4,594,615)	---	(59,279,253)	---

Ratios

RATIOS	SIC 2842 UQ	MED	LQ	SIC 2844 UQ	MED	LQ	SIC 2851 UQ	MED	LQ	SIC 2869 UQ	MED	LQ
SOLVENCY												
Quick Ratio (times)	2.6	1.2	0.5	1.6	0.9	0.6	2.4	1.3	0.7	2.7	1.2	0.6
Current Ratio (times)	6.5	2.9	1.1	3.5	2.0	1.4	3.2	2.5	1.7	3.3	2.2	1.1
Curr Liab To Nw (%)	14.9	32.7	111.0	22.5	48.2	101.1	17.7	38.3	64.8	11.7	23.4	42.1
Curr Liab To Inv (%)	50.5	111.8	319.8	83.6	158.9	291.2	66.6	106.2	166.9	108.5	192.5	414.4
Total Liab To Nw (%)	17.5	53.7	158.8	30.8	76.2	184.8	17.7	57.4	234.0	20.9	42.6	128.3
Fixed Assets To Nw (%)	10.6	26.7	120.4	8.6	31.9	49.3	7.7	26.6	58.7	56.9	70.5	120.5
EFFICIENCY												
Coll Period (days)	29.4	39.8	44.4	28.1	44.9	54.8	25.6	48.2	67.5	5.1	11.3	39.8
Sales To Inv (times)	20.5	9.0	5.4	10.9	5.9	3.4	9.3	8.0	6.7	32.8	18.3	9.2
Assets To Sales (%)	32.7	42.4	73.5	67.2	90.6	133.0	37.6	59.3	114.5	48.5	58.1	159.1
Sales To Nwc (times)	10.1	4.7	2.8	5.5	3.6	2.3	6.8	4.8	4.1	11.3	8.1	2.9
Acct Pay To Sales (%)	3.8	4.5	7.7	4.4	7.9	9.8	2.8	7.2	12.0	2.6	5.0	11.9
PROFITABILITY												
Return On Sales (%)	10.5	5.6	2.2	9.3	2.4	(11.2)	7.3	2.0	0.1	15.5	5.8	(31.1)
Return On Assets (%)	14.3	8.8	2.4	12.2	2.1	(14.6)	7.8	4.5	(1.1)	28.9	6.1	(37.6)
Return On Nw (%)	63.3	15.3	6.4	18.5	7.5	(32.6)	34.2	7.0	4.7	47.5	20.9	(9.7)

	SIC 2899 CHEM PRPRTNS, NEC (NO BREAKDOWN) 2014 (17 Establishments) $	%	SIC 30 RUBBER & PLASTICS (NO BREAKDOWN) 2014 (149 Establishments) $	%	SIC 3069 FBRTD RBBR PRDS.NEC (NO BREAKDOWN) 2014 (20 Establishments) $	%	SIC 3089 PLSTCS PRODUCTS.NEC (NO BREAKDOWN) 2014 (82 Establishments) $	%
Cash	1,178,779	11.5	956,325	16.0	595,988	21.8	860,601	14.3
Accounts Receivable	2,224,305	21.7	1,285,062	21.5	579,585	21.2	1,354,092	22.5
Notes Receivable	10,250	0.1	5,977	0.1	0	0.0	6,018	0.1
Inventory	1,834,795	17.9	1,440,465	24.1	579,585	21.2	1,420,292	23.6
Other Current	1,578,539	15.4	239,082	4.0	128,493	4.7	234,709	3.9
Total Current	**6,826,668**	**66.6**	**3,926,911**	**65.7**	**1,883,651**	**68.9**	**3,875,712**	**64.4**
Fixed Assets	2,070,551	20.2	1,446,442	24.2	593,254	21.7	1,504,547	25.0
Other Non-current	1,353,033	13.2	603,680	10.1	256,986	9.4	637,927	10.6
Total Assets	**10,250,252**	**100.0**	**5,977,033**	**100.0**	**2,733,891**	**100.0**	**6,018,186**	**100.0**
Accounts Payable	1,086,527	10.6	1,906,674	31.9	333,535	12.2	2,912,802	48.4
Bank Loans	0	0.0	5,977	0.1	0	0.0	12,036	0.2
Notes Payable	102,503	1.0	101,610	1.7	82,017	3.0	126,382	2.1
Other Current	2,183,303	21.3	3,831,277	64.1	995,136	36.4	4,724,276	78.5
Total Current	**3,372,333**	**32.9**	**5,845,538**	**97.8**	**1,410,688**	**51.6**	**7,775,496**	**129.2**
Other Long Term	2,747,067	26.8	1,075,866	18.0	349,938	12.8	1,173,546	19.5
Deferred Credits	41,001	0.4	11,954	0.2	0	0.0	18,055	0.3
Net Worth	4,089,851	39.9	(956,325)	(16.0)	973,265	35.6	(2,948,911)	(49.0)
Total Liab & Net Worth	**10,250,252**	**100.0**	**5,977,033**	**100.0**	**2,733,891**	**100.0**	**6,018,186**	**100.0**
Net Sales	14,436,975	100.0	11,835,709	100.0	6,021,786	100.0	11,708,533	100.0
Gross Profit	6,077,966	42.1	3,408,684	28.8	2,137,734	35.5	3,336,932	28.5
Net Profit After Tax	(332,050)	(2.3)	591,785	5.0	355,285	5.9	737,638	6.3
Working Capital	3,454,335	—	(1,918,627)	—	472,963	—	(3,899,784)	—

RATIOS	UQ	MED	LQ	UQ	MED	LQ	UQ	MED	LQ	UQ	MED	LQ
SOLVENCY												
Quick Ratio (times)	2.0	1.1	0.7	2.7	1.5	0.8	4.7	2.1	0.9	2.3	1.3	0.7
Current Ratio (times)	4.1	2.3	1.7	5.0	2.5	1.7	5.7	4.1	1.3	4.7	2.3	1.6
Curr Liab To Nw (%)	19.2	35.7	48.5	15.8	38.1	66.2	12.0	19.4	44.3	15.8	42.3	69.7
Curr Liab To Inv (%)	111.0	210.0	342.8	61.0	117.9	187.5	37.5	139.1	202.3	61.5	126.9	223.7
Total Liab To Nw (%)	24.5	74.8	173.9	21.2	54.6	147.2	12.9	19.4	74.6	30.0	71.5	147.2
Fixed Assets To Nw (%)	19.7	48.7	84.8	21.8	39.3	63.2	17.7	28.6	50.4	25.8	41.7	67.7
EFFICIENCY												
Coll Period (days)	42.2	52.8	67.0	31.2	42.0	56.4	31.0	38.0	46.0	31.4	48.6	58.4
Sales To Inv (times)	13.1	8.7	6.6	13.8	8.2	5.9	21.9	9.5	7.0	14.2	8.2	5.9
Assets To Sales (%)	48.5	71.0	141.6	36.7	50.5	73.6	36.4	45.4	92.3	36.7	51.4	78.5
Sales To Nwc (times)	6.6	3.1	1.9	7.4	4.8	3.3	5.7	3.5	2.7	7.2	4.8	3.4
Acct Pay To Sales (%)	3.4	7.2	11.0	2.9	4.9	7.3	1.3	2.6	3.8	3.4	5.2	7.7
PROFITABILITY												
Return On Sales (%)	3.8	1.6	(11.4)	8.9	4.0	1.5	8.8	4.6	1.0	11.0	4.6	2.1
Return On Assets (%)	4.9	2.2	(27.1)	15.6	7.5	2.1	18.5	7.7	2.6	16.7	7.7	2.3
Return On Nw (%)	12.7	5.8	2.7	29.2	12.9	6.7	31.9	12.6	8.7	30.7	15.8	8.0

	SIC 31 LEATHER,LEATHER PDTS (NO BREAKDOWN) 2014 (16 Establishments) $	%	SIC 32 STONE CLAY,GLASS PDT (NO BREAKDOWN) 2014 (79 Establishments) $	%	SIC 3272 CONCRETE PRDCTS,NEC (NO BREAKDOWN) 2014 (20 Establishments) $	%	SIC 3273 READY-MIX CONCRETE (NO BREAKDOWN) 2014 (13 Establishments) $	%
Cash	395,527	14.5	1,252,067	15.6	1,228,169	14.1	805,244	23.0
Accounts Receivable	586,471	21.5	1,565,084	19.5	2,125,342	24.4	696,711	19.9
Notes Receivable	0	0.0	8,026	0.1	8,710	0.1	8,710	0.0
Inventory	834,699	30.6	1,139,702	14.2	1,202,037	13.8	185,556	5.3
Other Current	240,044	8.8	634,061	7.9	992,987	11.4	66,520	1.9
Total Current	**2,056,741**	**75.4**	**4,598,940**	**57.3**	**5,557,245**	**63.8**	**1,754,031**	**50.1**
Fixed Assets	300,055	11.0	2,488,083	31.0	2,264,708	26.0	1,116,838	31.9
Other Non-current	370,977	13.6	939,050	11.7	888,463	10.2	630,190	18.0
Total Assets	**2,727,773**	**100.0**	**8,026,073**	**100.0**	**8,710,416**	**100.0**	**3,501,059**	**100.0**
Accounts Payable	256,411	9.4	642,086	8.0	609,729	7.0	339,603	9.7
Bank Loans	0	0.0	16,052	0.2	43,552	0.5	0	0.0
Notes Payable	0	0.0	48,156	0.6	26,131	0.3	24,507	0.7
Other Current	540,099	19.8	882,868	11.0	1,202,038	13.8	238,072	6.8
Total Current	**796,510**	**29.2**	**1,589,162**	**19.8**	**1,881,450**	**21.6**	**602,182**	**17.2**
Other Long Term	182,761	6.7	2,142,962	26.7	1,184,616	13.6	647,696	18.5
Deferred Credits	0	0.0	16,052	0.2	0	0.0	17,505	0.5
Net Worth	1,748,502	64.1	4,277,897	53.3	5,644,350	64.8	2,233,676	63.8
Total Liab & Net Worth	**2,727,773**	**100.0**	**8,026,073**	**100.0**	**8,710,416**	**100.0**	**3,501,059**	**100.0**
Net Sales	3,993,811	100.0	13,135,962	100.0	13,118,096	100.0	7,339,746	100.0
Gross Profit	1,429,784	35.8	4,334,867	33.0	4,407,680	33.6	1,981,731	27.0
Net Profit After Tax	343,468	8.6	906,381	6.9	787,086	6.0	264,231	3.6
Working Capital	1,260,231	---	3,009,778	---	3,675,795	---	1,151,849	---

RATIOS	UQ	MED	LQ	UQ	MED	LQ	UQ	MED	LQ	UQ	MED	LQ
SOLVENCY												
Quick Ratio (times)	2.0	1.4	1.0	3.1	2.0	1.2	3.5	2.6	1.4	3.3	2.6	1.5
Current Ratio (times)	4.2	2.8	2.1	4.9	3.2	2.0	5.5	4.1	2.3	3.8	3.1	1.8
Curr Liab To Nw (%)	21.4	37.8	73.3	12.9	25.3	44.3	13.5	22.9	44.9	16.6	26.8	33.8
Curr Liab To Inv (%)	44.2	110.6	173.1	59.0	166.6	324.5	102.4	134.6	269.2	226.9	517.3	999.9
Total Liab To Nw (%)	31.2	49.2	91.3	22.3	38.8	108.7	22.9	32.8	75.8	34.5	42.0	89.7
Fixed Assets To Nw (%)	6.3	10.8	29.5	27.3	48.9	82.0	26.0	41.3	73.8	38.5	47.8	62.1
EFFICIENCY												
Coll Period (days)	20.5	39.4	68.6	28.8	39.8	48.9	33.6	41.6	70.1	27.0	32.5	43.4
Sales To Inv (times)	9.3	5.8	3.8	34.6	12.9	7.0	20.1	10.1	5.8	93.4	61.4	29.7
Assets To Sales (%)	43.4	68.3	77.4	41.6	61.1	97.4	48.5	66.4	86.9	36.0	47.7	61.1
Sales To Nwc (times)	4.8	3.9	2.9	8.4	4.5	3.0	7.0	3.8	2.8	11.3	5.9	4.2
Acct Pay To Sales (%)	3.3	5.3	6.3	2.8	4.5	6.9	3.0	4.6	5.7	3.1	4.3	6.2
PROFITABILITY												
Return On Sales (%)	11.0	7.0	2.7	9.8	5.3	1.8	15.8	5.3	2.0	4.1	2.1	0.0
Return On Assets (%)	15.1	10.3	5.3	20.3	7.2	2.0	22.4	6.3	1.8	8.7	4.3	0.1
Return On Nw (%)	27.7	15.9	10.1	30.5	14.6	5.9	30.5	15.7	5.7	20.3	5.9	0.1

	SIC 33 PRIMARY METAL INDS (NO BREAKDOWN) 2014 (106 Establishments) $	%	SIC 3312 BLST FRNCS,STL MLLS (NO BREAKDOWN) 2014 (20 Establishments) $	%	SIC 3357 NFER WRDRWNG,INSUL (NO BREAKDOWN) 2014 (10 Establishments) $	%	SIC 34 FABRICATED METAL PDT (NO BREAKDOWN) 2014 (470 Establishments) $	%
Cash	2,500,589	11.9	44,273,417	10.3	861,683	11.8	735,523	16.4
Accounts Receivable	4,559,897	21.7	85,108,122	19.8	2,453,606	33.6	1,166,073	26.0
Notes Receivable	147,093	0.7	0	0.0	0	0.0	8,970	0.2
Inventory	4,538,884	21.6	76,511,342	17.8	2,300,255	31.5	838,675	18.7
Other Current	1,218,775	5.8	14,614,526	3.4	314,003	4.3	367,761	8.2
Total Current	**12,965,238**	**61.7**	**220,507,407**	**51.3**	**5,929,547**	**81.2**	**3,117,002**	**69.5**
Fixed Assets	5,673,605	27.0	158,610,591	36.9	861,683	11.8	977,707	21.8
Other Non-current	2,374,508	11.3	50,721,002	11.8	511,168	7.0	390,186	8.7
Total Assets	**21,013,351**	**100.0**	**429,839,000**	**100.0**	**7,302,398**	**100.0**	**4,484,895**	**100.0**
Accounts Payable	3,004,909	14.3	38,685,510	9.0	1,102,662	15.1	1,161,588	25.9
Bank Loans	126,080	0.6	0	0.0	153,350	2.1	17,940	0.4
Notes Payable	3,614,296	17.2	0	0.0	43,814	0.6	183,881	4.1
Other Current	4,664,965	22.2	75,651,664	17.6	1,182,989	16.2	825,220	18.4
Total Current	**11,410,250**	**54.3**	**114,337,174**	**26.6**	**2,482,815**	**34.0**	**2,188,629**	**48.8**
Other Long Term	4,265,710	20.3	122,504,115	28.5	890,893	12.2	713,098	15.9
Deferred Credits	0	0.0	0	0.0	0	0.0	13,455	0.3
Net Worth	5,337,391	25.4	192,997,711	44.9	3,928,690	53.8	1,569,713	35.0
Total Liab & Net Worth	**21,013,351**	**100.0**	**429,839,000**	**100.0**	**7,302,398**	**100.0**	**4,484,895**	**100.0**
Net Sales	30,676,425	100.0	559,686,198	100.0	12,924,598	100.0	8,351,760	100.0
Gross Profit	7,270,313	23.7	88,430,419	15.8	3,528,415	27.3	2,513,880	30.1
Net Profit After Tax	1,257,733	4.1	12,872,783	2.3	400,663	3.1	367,477	4.4
Working Capital	1,554,988	---	106,170,233	---	3,446,732	---	928,373	---

RATIOS	UQ	MED	LQ	UQ	MED	LQ	UQ	MED	LQ	UQ	MED	LQ
SOLVENCY												
Quick Ratio (times)	2.1	1.4	0.9	1.8	1.2	0.8	1.9	1.4	1.1	3.3	1.6	0.9
Current Ratio (times)	4.4	2.7	2.0	3.0	2.8	1.8	4.2	2.5	1.8	5.6	2.7	1.6
Curr Liab To Nw (%)	18.0	35.3	71.3	26.0	36.9	51.1	30.7	68.9	103.2	14.3	34.3	82.9
Curr Liab To Inv (%)	56.3	96.4	149.7	65.2	95.7	145.2	53.1	92.0	136.8	58.1	126.2	331.6
Total Liab To Nw (%)	42.7	71.6	153.2	50.1	98.4	161.5	40.0	98.6	216.1	19.1	55.2	129.0
Fixed Assets To Nw (%)	17.4	46.8	92.1	56.6	81.2	109.3	6.1	35.8	39.2	14.3	32.1	61.7
EFFICIENCY												
Coll Period (days)	35.2	47.7	59.7	35.8	49.1	54.0	33.6	59.9	64.6	32.9	45.3	61.0
Sales To Inv (times)	12.0	7.6	5.0	7.7	5.7	5.0	12.5	8.8	4.5	24.0	10.5	5.8
Assets To Sales (%)	49.2	68.5	105.7	55.5	76.8	140.7	49.1	56.5	84.4	38.3	53.7	73.9
Sales To Nwc (times)	6.1	4.1	2.8	6.1	4.9	3.5	5.4	4.1	2.8	9.2	4.8	2.9
Acct Pay To Sales (%)	4.0	6.5	10.8	5.6	10.3	12.2	6.0	7.7	10.3	2.2	3.9	7.8
PROFITABILITY												
Return On Sales (%)	6.0	3.3	1.3	4.2	1.6	0.2	5.1	3.2	1.9	7.9	3.4	1.0
Return On Assets (%)	10.1	4.7	1.3	5.2	3.1	0.1	6.5	4.4	2.3	13.5	5.9	1.9
Return On Nw (%)	21.7	8.8	2.7	9.5	5.9	1.2	17.0	7.5	6.7	25.4	12.3	3.8

	SIC 3433 HTNG EQPT.EXC ELEC (NO BREAKDOWN) 2014 (13 Establishments) $	%	SIC 3441 FBRCTED STRCTRL MTL (NO BREAKDOWN) 2014 (95 Establishments) $	%	SIC 3442 MTL DOORS.SASH.TRIM (NO BREAKDOWN) 2014 (15 Establishments) $	%	SIC 3443 FBRCT PLT WK BLR SH (NO BREAKDOWN) 2014 (44 Establishments) $	%
Cash	1,213,282	15.0	518,914	14.2	783,212	21.7	857,510	18.4
Accounts Receivable	2,345,678	29.0	1,268,050	34.7	757,947	21.0	1,071,887	23.0
Notes Receivable	0	0.0	21,926	0.6	36,093	1.0	0	0.0
Inventory	1,075,776	13.3	507,951	13.9	613,576	17.0	824,887	17.7
Other Current	1,245,636	15.4	347,160	9.5	407,846	11.3	326,227	7.0
Total Current	**5,880,372**	**72.7**	**2,664,001**	**72.9**	**2,598,674**	**72.0**	**3,080,511**	**66.1**
Fixed Assets	978,714	12.1	767,408	21.0	573,874	15.9	960,038	20.6
Other Non-current	1,229,459	15.2	222,913	6.1	436,722	12.1	619,830	13.3
Total Assets	**8,088,545**	**100.0**	**3,654,322**	**100.0**	**3,609,270**	**100.0**	**4,660,379**	**100.0**
Accounts Payable	44,923,779	555.4	456,790	12.5	314,006	8.7	442,736	9.5
Bank Loans	0	0.0	18,272	0.5	0	0.0	23,302	0.5
Notes Payable	9,584,926	118.5	36,543	1.0	61,358	1.7	74,566	1.6
Other Current	(46,897,384)	(579.8)	3,917,433	107.2	757,947	21.0	922,755	19.8
Total Current	**7,611,321**	**94.1**	**4,429,038**	**121.2**	**1,133,311**	**31.4**	**1,463,359**	**31.4**
Other Long Term	622,818	7.7	391,012	10.7	306,788	8.5	610,510	13.1
Deferred Credits	0	0.0	18,272	0.5	0	0.0	0	0.0
Net Worth	(145,594)	(1.8)	(1,184,000)	(32.4)	2,169,171	60.1	2,586,510	55.5
Total Liab & Net Worth	**8,088,545**	**100.0**	**3,654,322**	**100.0**	**3,609,270**	**100.0**	**4,660,379**	**100.0**
Net Sales	16,307,550	100.0	7,677,147	100.0	6,287,927	100.0	9,120,115	100.0
Gross Profit	4,941,188	30.3	2,019,090	26.3	2,068,728	32.9	2,471,551	27.1
Net Profit After Tax	(309,843)	(1.9)	199,606	2.6	176,062	2.8	437,766	4.8
Working Capital	(1,730,949)	---	(1,765,037)	---	1,465,363	---	1,617,152	---

RATIOS	3433 UQ	MED	LQ	3441 UQ	MED	LQ	3442 UQ	MED	LQ	3443 UQ	MED	LQ
SOLVENCY												
Quick Ratio (times)	2.4	1.1	0.5	2.6	1.5	0.9	3.6	1.1	0.8	2.5	1.1	0.9
Current Ratio (times)	3.1	1.5	0.8	4.4	2.0	1.5	5.9	2.5	1.8	4.2	2.2	1.4
Curr Liab To Nw (%)	26.9	52.0	150.4	21.9	49.7	102.0	12.3	57.6	108.6	17.9	56.1	83.3
Curr Liab To Inv (%)	53.9	171.1	807.4	106.9	281.9	602.2	42.6	110.0	346.9	86.5	179.7	403.3
Total Liab To Nw (%)	26.9	87.9	138.4	32.5	77.1	131.4	12.8	66.6	222.6	22.7	63.0	134.1
Fixed Assets To Nw (%)	19.7	23.3	54.8	15.3	35.5	56.3	16.0	34.6	69.7	13.2	33.3	72.7
EFFICIENCY												
Coll Period (days)	41.5	60.2	82.4	32.3	55.3	79.8	33.3	48.6	61.2	32.5	46.9	55.9
Sales To Inv (times)	18.3	9.6	5.4	61.7	19.5	8.6	18.3	10.9	8.4	23.8	11.8	6.6
Assets To Sales (%)	38.5	49.6	70.5	33.4	47.6	61.6	41.3	57.4	89.8	44.3	51.1	68.9
Sales To Nwc (times)	10.9	4.5	2.5	9.5	5.8	3.7	10.0	4.1	3.1	9.9	4.7	3.4
Acct Pay To Sales (%)	3.6	11.1	24.5	2.9	4.7	8.6	2.4	3.5	5.4	2.5	3.8	6.5
PROFITABILITY												
Return On Sales (%)	9.9	6.2	(43.2)	5.5	2.7	0.7	6.3	2.4	1.0	9.3	2.4	0.3
Return On Assets (%)	29.8	14.6	(21.1)	12.7	4.6	1.1	14.6	3.7	2.4	13.1	5.0	1.2
Return On Nw (%)	30.2	26.2	11.0	26.1	10.2	2.9	40.6	7.1	3.3	29.6	11.0	2.3

	SIC 3444 SHEET METALWORK (NO BREAKDOWN) 2014 (52 Establishments) $	%	SIC 3446 ARCHTCTRL METALWORK (NO BREAKDOWN) 2014 (10 Establishments) $	%	SIC 3448 PREFBRCTD MTL BLDGS (NO BREAKDOWN) 2014 (12 Establishments) $	%	SIC 3451 SCREW MACHINE PRDTS (NO BREAKDOWN) 2014 (16 Establishments) $	%
Cash	677,200	18.1	849,412	27.1	1,552,106	13.1	558,272	17.2
Accounts Receivable	969,031	25.9	1,028,071	32.8	2,381,475	20.1	662,136	20.4
Notes Receivable	7,483	0.2	0	0.0	71,089	0.6	3,246	0.1
Inventory	669,717	17.9	197,465	6.3	2,452,564	20.7	1,035,400	31.9
Other Current	310,539	8.3	667,620	21.3	1,931,246	16.3	58,424	1.8
Total Current	**2,633,970**	**70.4**	**2,742,568**	**87.5**	**8,388,480**	**70.8**	**2,317,478**	**71.4**
Fixed Assets	830,598	22.2	385,527	12.3	2,085,272	17.6	746,526	23.0
Other Non-current	276,866	7.4	6,268	0.2	1,374,383	11.6	181,763	5.6
Total Assets	**3,741,434**	**100.0**	**3,134,363**	**100.0**	**11,848,135**	**100.0**	**3,245,767**	**100.0**
Accounts Payable	463,938	12.4	294,630	9.4	1,220,358	10.3	227,204	7.0
Bank Loans	11,224	0.3	0	0.0	0	0.0	0	0.0
Notes Payable	26,190	0.7	0	0.0	94,785	0.8	16,229	0.5
Other Current	512,577	13.7	561,051	17.9	2,630,286	22.2	473,882	14.6
Total Current	**1,013,929**	**27.1**	**855,681**	**27.3**	**3,945,429**	**33.3**	**717,315**	**22.1**
Other Long Term	355,436	9.5	260,152	8.3	1,113,725	9.4	366,771	11.3
Deferred Credits	0	0.0	0	0.0	11,848	0.1	9,737	0.3
Net Worth	2,372,069	63.4	2,018,530	64.4	6,777,133	57.2	2,151,944	66.3
Total Liab & Net Worth	**3,741,434**	**100.0**	**3,134,363**	**100.0**	**11,848,135**	**100.0**	**3,245,767**	**100.0**
Net Sales	8,887,017	100.0	5,339,630	100.0	22,567,876	100.0	6,021,831	100.0
Gross Profit	2,523,913	28.4	1,687,323	31.6	5,190,611	23.0	1,541,589	25.6
Net Profit After Tax	373,255	4.2	256,302	4.8	677,036	3.0	283,026	4.7
Working Capital	1,620,041	---	1,886,887	---	4,443,051	---	1,600,163	---

RATIOS	UQ	MED	LQ	UQ	MED	LQ	UQ	MED	LQ	UQ	MED	LQ
SOLVENCY												
Quick Ratio (times)	3.7	1.8	1.1	4.9	2.1	1.8	2.1	0.9	0.6	2.5	1.7	1.1
Current Ratio (times)	9.0	2.8	1.9	6.0	2.8	2.1	4.5	1.8	1.4	5.1	3.4	1.9
Curr Liab To Nw (%)	10.7	30.1	63.0	18.2	46.2	88.2	20.8	66.9	123.8	15.3	34.1	46.8
Curr Liab To Inv (%)	61.6	132.3	280.3	114.7	460.6	999.9	112.7	186.9	610.4	43.4	72.3	98.3
Total Liab To Nw (%)	13.3	42.4	103.1	18.2	46.9	88.2	29.5	90.8	184.6	19.2	63.7	92.1
Fixed Assets To Nw (%)	14.3	31.3	57.1	10.8	14.2	32.1	21.5	35.2	67.6	15.6	27.9	54.9
EFFICIENCY												
Coll Period (days)	27.4	39.1	54.0	61.9	82.5	106.1	19.0	28.8	40.7	35.4	40.5	45.6
Sales To Inv (times)	30.2	13.5	9.1	459.4	15.4	13.5	19.9	12.2	10.4	8.4	7.4	4.4
Assets To Sales (%)	30.1	42.1	63.6	31.2	58.7	71.4	39.1	52.5	55.4	48.7	53.9	66.9
Sales To Nwc (times)	10.0	6.0	2.9	5.0	4.3	1.9	16.6	9.9	3.2	5.4	4.6	2.5
Acct Pay To Sales (%)	1.4	3.8	6.1	2.2	3.9	4.1	2.8	3.8	6.2	1.4	3.4	5.5
PROFITABILITY												
Return On Sales (%)	9.6	2.4	0.6	7.4	2.7	1.1	4.8	1.4	1.0	7.8	3.6	1.2
Return On Assets (%)	17.2	5.7	2.3	11.8	7.7	3.7	6.5	4.3	2.0	14.8	6.7	2.4
Return On Nw (%)	36.9	10.0	3.8	14.4	12.6	8.2	13.8	5.3	2.8	29.3	10.3	3.5

SIC 3452 BLTS,NUTS,RVTS,WSHR (NO BREAKDOWN) 2014 (13 Establishments)

	$	%
Cash	527,976	5.1
Accounts Receivable	1,728,863	16.7
Notes Receivable	0	0.0
Inventory	3,074,685	29.7
Other Current	952,428	9.2
Total Current	**6,283,952**	**60.7**
Fixed Assets	3,447,374	33.3
Other Non-current	621,149	6.0
Total Assets	**10,352,475**	**100.0**
Accounts Payable	683,263	6.6
Bank Loans	0	0.0
Notes Payable	82,820	0.8
Other Current	766,083	7.4
Total Current	**1,532,166**	**14.8**
Other Long Term	1,966,971	19.0
Deferred Credits	0	0.0
Net Worth	6,853,338	66.2
Total Liab & Net Worth	**10,352,475**	**100.0**
Net Sales	15,428,428	100.0
Gross Profit	4,505,101	29.2
Net Profit After Tax	555,423	3.6
Working Capital	4,751,786	---

RATIOS	UQ	MED	LQ
SOLVENCY			
Quick Ratio (times)	3.0	1.9	0.9
Current Ratio (times)	8.5	4.1	3.1
Curr Liab To Nw (%)	8.2	21.5	33.1
Curr Liab To Inv (%)	18.7	37.4	78.3
Total Liab To Nw (%)	21.5	54.3	113.1
Fixed Assets To Nw (%)	16.8	41.4	58.7
EFFICIENCY			
Coll Period (days)	39.3	42.7	49.5
Sales To Inv (times)	8.2	4.5	3.1
Assets To Sales (%)	53.4	67.1	79.7
Sales To Nwc (times)	5.4	2.8	2.2
Acct Pay To Sales (%)	1.7	3.8	5.8
PROFITABILITY			
Return On Sales (%)	5.3	3.9	2.3
Return On Assets (%)	11.0	6.2	3.9
Return On Nw (%)	13.9	9.4	7.6

SIC 3469 METAL STAMPINGS,NEC (NO BREAKDOWN) 2014 (29 Establishments)

	$	%
Cash	664,925	15.5
Accounts Receivable	982,374	22.9
Notes Receivable	4,290	0.1
Inventory	943,765	22.0
Other Current	398,955	9.3
Total Current	**2,994,309**	**69.8**
Fixed Assets	1,059,591	24.7
Other Non-current	235,941	5.5
Total Assets	**4,289,841**	**100.0**
Accounts Payable	424,694	9.9
Bank Loans	8,580	0.2
Notes Payable	17,159	0.4
Other Current	1,051,011	24.5
Total Current	**1,501,444**	**35.0**
Other Long Term	767,882	17.9
Deferred Credits	8,580	0.2
Net Worth	2,011,935	46.9
Total Liab & Net Worth	**4,289,841**	**100.0**
Net Sales	8,974,563	100.0
Gross Profit	2,764,165	30.8
Net Profit After Tax	26,924	0.3
Working Capital	1,492,865	---

RATIOS	UQ	MED	LQ
SOLVENCY			
Quick Ratio (times)	3.0	1.2	0.6
Current Ratio (times)	5.5	2.5	1.4
Curr Liab To Nw (%)	17.1	34.5	90.0
Curr Liab To Inv (%)	63.4	110.7	308.7
Total Liab To Nw (%)	24.0	51.0	164.8
Fixed Assets To Nw (%)	17.7	40.2	67.5
EFFICIENCY			
Coll Period (days)	31.8	40.7	50.7
Sales To Inv (times)	28.1	9.5	5.4
Assets To Sales (%)	38.0	47.8	66.1
Sales To Nwc (times)	9.6	7.1	3.1
Acct Pay To Sales (%)	2.6	4.7	8.3
PROFITABILITY			
Return On Sales (%)	5.1	1.7	0.6
Return On Assets (%)	8.2	4.3	1.0
Return On Nw (%)	14.4	9.6	1.9

SIC 3471 PLATING,POLISHING (NO BREAKDOWN) 2014 (18 Establishments)

	$	%
Cash	795,662	28.9
Accounts Receivable	718,573	26.1
Notes Receivable	8,259	0.3
Inventory	137,658	5.0
Other Current	209,240	7.6
Total Current	**1,869,392**	**67.9**
Fixed Assets	759,871	27.6
Other Non-current	123,892	4.5
Total Assets	**2,753,155**	**100.0**
Accounts Payable	132,151	4.8
Bank Loans	5,506	0.2
Notes Payable	19,272	0.7
Other Current	289,082	10.5
Total Current	**446,011**	**16.2**
Other Long Term	250,537	9.1
Deferred Credits	35,791	1.3
Net Worth	2,020,816	73.4
Total Liab & Net Worth	**2,753,155**	**100.0**
Net Sales	5,517,345	100.0
Gross Profit	2,206,938	40.0
Net Profit After Tax	281,385	5.1
Working Capital	1,423,381	---

RATIOS	UQ	MED	LQ
SOLVENCY			
Quick Ratio (times)	15.2	4.8	2.0
Current Ratio (times)	18.3	5.7	2.7
Curr Liab To Nw (%)	4.1	14.1	28.4
Curr Liab To Inv (%)	46.8	173.4	415.6
Total Liab To Nw (%)	4.1	22.4	36.5
Fixed Assets To Nw (%)	12.7	27.5	62.0
EFFICIENCY			
Coll Period (days)	43.3	49.6	58.8
Sales To Inv (times)	43.7	30.2	24.2
Assets To Sales (%)	45.6	49.9	66.6
Sales To Nwc (times)	5.2	4.7	2.7
Acct Pay To Sales (%)	0.8	1.9	3.8
PROFITABILITY			
Return On Sales (%)	8.3	5.8	1.3
Return On Assets (%)	15.9	6.0	2.4
Return On Nw (%)	21.2	12.3	5.7

SIC 3479 MTL CTNG,ALLD SVCS (NO BREAKDOWN) 2014 (18 Establishments)

	$	%
Cash	538,943	15.7
Accounts Receivable	1,074,453	31.3
Notes Receivable	0	0.0
Inventory	387,902	11.3
Other Current	140,742	4.1
Total Current	**2,142,040**	**62.4**
Fixed Assets	947,441	27.6
Other Non-current	343,276	10.0
Total Assets	**3,432,757**	**100.0**
Accounts Payable	267,755	7.8
Bank Loans	13,731	0.4
Notes Payable	3,433	0.1
Other Current	545,808	15.9
Total Current	**830,727**	**24.2**
Other Long Term	638,493	18.6
Deferred Credits	54,924	1.6
Net Worth	1,908,613	55.6
Total Liab & Net Worth	**3,432,757**	**100.0**
Net Sales	5,808,387	100.0
Gross Profit	2,253,654	38.8
Net Profit After Tax	638,923	11.0
Working Capital	1,311,313	---

RATIOS	UQ	MED	LQ
SOLVENCY			
Quick Ratio (times)	5.0	1.8	1.2
Current Ratio (times)	6.3	2.7	1.6
Curr Liab To Nw (%)	13.4	46.3	79.1
Curr Liab To Inv (%)	101.6	151.1	314.3
Total Liab To Nw (%)	24.9	102.0	226.4
Fixed Assets To Nw (%)	15.6	41.8	90.8
EFFICIENCY			
Coll Period (days)	40.7	50.1	62.4
Sales To Inv (times)	18.5	13.4	9.5
Assets To Sales (%)	33.8	59.1	94.9
Sales To Nwc (times)	14.1	4.2	2.5
Acct Pay To Sales (%)	1.8	2.6	5.5
PROFITABILITY			
Return On Sales (%)	17.4	4.8	0.1
Return On Assets (%)	27.6	5.9	0.5
Return On Nw (%)	36.0	6.4	1.1

Balance Sheet

	SIC 3496 MISC FBRCTD WRE PRD (NO BREAKDOWN) 2014 (20 Establishments) $	%	SIC 3498 FBRCTD PIPE.FITTNGS (NO BREAKDOWN) 2014 (12 Establishments) $	%	SIC 3499 FBRCTD MTL PRDS.NEC (NO BREAKDOWN) 2014 (20 Establishments) $	%	SIC 35 MACHINERY EX ELECTRL (NO BREAKDOWN) 2014 (631 Establishments) $	%
Cash	608,767	16.8	1,438,688	13.2	370,166	13.7	929,218	18.3
Accounts Receivable	862,421	23.8	1,863,756	17.1	772,756	28.6	1,127,248	22.2
Notes Receivable	0	0.0	0	0.0	0	0.0	15,233	0.3
Inventory	1,090,708	30.1	2,441,411	22.4	553,899	20.5	1,010,461	19.9
Other Current	119,580	3.3	1,111,713	10.2	113,481	4.2	426,526	8.4
Total Current	**2,681,476**	**74.0**	**6,855,568**	**62.9**	**1,810,302**	**67.0**	**3,508,686**	**69.1**
Fixed Assets	677,616	18.7	3,302,444	30.3	694,400	25.7	990,150	19.5
Other Non-current	264,524	7.3	741,143	6.8	197,242	7.3	578,857	11.4
Total Assets	**3,623,616**	**100.0**	**10,899,155**	**100.0**	**2,701,944**	**100.0**	**5,077,693**	**100.0**
Accounts Payable	344,244	9.5	806,537	7.4	435,013	16.1	1,203,413	23.7
Bank Loans	79,720	2.2	0	0.0	29,721	1.1	40,622	0.8
Notes Payable	0	0.0	43,597	0.4	8,106	0.3	167,564	3.3
Other Current	409,468	11.3	1,297,000	11.9	691,698	25.6	1,178,024	23.2
Total Current	**833,432**	**23.0**	**2,147,134**	**19.7**	**1,164,538**	**43.1**	**2,589,623**	**51.0**
Other Long Term	344,243	9.5	861,033	7.9	370,166	13.7	1,254,190	24.7
Deferred Credits	7,247	0.2	0	0.0	0	0.0	20,311	0.4
Net Worth	2,438,694	67.3	7,890,988	72.4	1,167,240	43.2	1,213,569	23.9
Total Liab & Net Worth	**3,623,616**	**100.0**	**10,899,155**	**100.0**	**2,701,944**	**100.0**	**5,077,693**	**100.0**
Net Sales	7,517,876	100.0	17,056,581	100.0	4,939,569	100.0	8,243,008	100.0
Gross Profit	2,247,845	29.9	4,298,258	25.2	2,074,619	42.0	2,934,511	35.6
Net Profit After Tax	421,001	5.6	733,433	4.3	360,589	7.3	321,477	3.9
Working Capital	1,848,044	---	4,708,434	---	645,764	---	919,063	---

RATIOS

	SIC 3496 UQ	MED	LQ	SIC 3498 UQ	MED	LQ	SIC 3499 UQ	MED	LQ	SIC 35 UQ	MED	LQ
SOLVENCY												
Quick Ratio (times)	8.8	1.7	0.9	5.8	2.9	1.1	2.0	1.1	0.7	3.0	1.5	0.8
Current Ratio (times)	13.0	3.9	2.3	9.6	6.5	1.7	3.2	1.9	1.2	4.9	2.7	1.6
Curr Liab To Nw (%)	5.8	27.0	99.0	7.0	14.1	31.1	21.1	39.9	106.0	16.9	38.7	77.6
Curr Liab To Inv (%)	24.2	42.3	88.2	30.1	35.9	580.9	92.6	191.0	339.0	66.7	140.4	321.7
Total Liab To Nw (%)	8.0	36.2	107.0	8.8	22.0	69.9	26.9	76.7	147.1	25.1	63.2	136.4
Fixed Assets To Nw (%)	11.1	18.2	55.6	26.6	55.4	64.7	19.5	47.5	83.7	11.5	28.4	56.5
EFFICIENCY												
Coll Period (days)	31.0	38.2	45.6	38.4	54.0	57.5	30.3	42.7	53.7	33.2	47.5	65.2
Sales To Inv (times)	8.3	5.9	4.3	98.0	8.0	4.5	24.8	9.8	6.1	20.1	8.9	5.3
Assets To Sales (%)	37.7	48.2	68.9	49.3	63.9	94.7	24.5	54.7	95.1	40.5	61.6	95.3
Sales To Nwc (times)	5.7	3.6	3.0	11.5	3.2	2.1	11.7	6.0	3.4	6.4	4.1	2.6
Acct Pay To Sales (%)	1.3	3.2	5.4	1.3	2.3	6.3	2.6	5.4	9.2	2.3	4.7	8.6
PROFITABILITY												
Return On Sales (%)	10.7	3.4	1.8	8.1	4.2	1.5	9.4	4.1	1.0	8.7	3.8	0.4
Return On Assets (%)	14.6	8.1	4.1	12.1	8.7	2.9	13.6	7.3	1.6	14.2	6.1	0.8
Return On Nw (%)	17.8	10.7	4.8	19.0	12.3	4.3	25.7	14.9	7.5	27.0	12.6	3.1

	SIC 3523 FARM MCHNRY,EQPMT (NO BREAKDOWN) 2014 (28 Establishments)		SIC 3531 CONSTR MACHINERY (NO BREAKDOWN) 2014 (21 Establishments)		SIC 3533 OIL,GAS FLD MCHNRY (NO BREAKDOWN) 2014 (22 Establishments)		SIC 3535 CNVYRS,CNVYNG EQPMT (NO BREAKDOWN) 2014 (14 Establishments)	
	$	%	$	%	$	%	$	%
Cash	1,736,426	20.7	760,576	12.1	4,703,469	20.2	783,906	25.0
Accounts Receivable	1,140,840	13.6	911,434	14.5	5,402,004	23.2	990,858	31.6
Notes Receivable	16,777	0.2	157,144	2.5	0	0.0	0	0.0
Inventory	2,759,827	32.9	1,923,440	30.6	3,399,537	14.6	517,378	16.5
Other Current	511,702	6.1	427,431	6.8	1,723,053	7.4	304,156	9.7
Total Current	**6,165,572**	**73.5**	**4,180,025**	**66.5**	**15,228,063**	**65.4**	**2,596,298**	**82.8**
Fixed Assets	1,577,044	18.8	1,056,006	16.8	3,888,512	16.7	351,190	11.2
Other Non-current	645,917	7.7	1,049,721	16.7	4,167,925	17.9	188,137	6.0
Total Assets	**8,388,533**	**100.0**	**6,285,752**	**100.0**	**23,284,500**	**100.0**	**3,135,625**	**100.0**
Accounts Payable	553,643	6.6	697,718	11.1	2,701,002	11.6	482,886	15.4
Bank Loans	0	0.0	119,429	1.9	0	0.0	0	0.0
Notes Payable	260,045	3.1	25,143	0.4	23,285	0.1	0	0.0
Other Current	1,518,324	18.1	1,992,584	31.7	6,053,970	26.0	642,803	20.5
Total Current	**2,332,012**	**27.8**	**2,834,874**	**45.1**	**8,778,257**	**37.7**	**1,125,689**	**35.9**
Other Long Term	981,459	11.7	1,112,578	17.7	3,702,234	15.9	181,867	5.8
Deferred Credits	0	0.0	0	0.0	23,285	0.1	21,949	0.7
Net Worth	5,075,062	60.5	2,338,300	37.2	10,780,724	46.3	1,806,120	57.6
Total Liab & Net Worth	**8,388,533**	**100.0**	**6,285,752**	**100.0**	**23,284,500**	**100.0**	**3,135,625**	**100.0**
Net Sales	13,231,125	100.0	8,131,633	100.0	25,447,541	100.0	7,158,961	100.0
Gross Profit	3,625,328	27.4	2,472,016	30.4	10,051,779	39.5	2,720,405	38.0
Net Profit After Tax	1,137,877	8.6	414,713	5.1	1,883,118	7.4	672,942	9.4
Working Capital	3,833,560	---	1,345,151	---	6,449,806	---	1,470,609	---

RATIOS	UQ	MED	LQ	UQ	MED	LQ	UQ	MED	LQ	UQ	MED	LQ
SOLVENCY												
Quick Ratio (times)	2.7	1.8	0.5	2.0	1.0	0.5	4.4	1.4	0.7	2.7	1.7	1.1
Current Ratio (times)	5.1	3.6	2.5	4.0	2.6	1.4	6.1	2.5	1.6	3.7	2.4	1.9
Curr Liab To Nw (%)	20.1	26.5	60.2	24.5	42.4	79.1	11.5	21.7	47.8	30.5	62.2	87.1
Curr Liab To Inv (%)	38.6	43.8	136.2	41.5	88.7	199.4	69.1	148.5	636.7	104.4	158.9	429.6
Total Liab To Nw (%)	20.3	37.6	105.6	32.9	74.3	184.0	16.4	56.6	91.4	31.5	63.6	112.2
Fixed Assets To Nw (%)	12.7	27.9	49.2	18.3	31.3	48.5	13.2	24.8	47.0	5.6	23.6	38.6
EFFICIENCY												
Coll Period (days)	19.4	31.6	45.6	13.7	33.2	49.5	51.3	74.8	84.2	36.3	62.4	71.6
Sales To Inv (times)	8.3	5.5	4.8	7.8	4.8	3.1	16.4	9.0	4.2	32.9	14.7	9.9
Assets To Sales (%)	55.2	63.4	85.2	39.7	77.3	124.2	45.5	91.5	127.7	34.5	43.8	65.5
Sales To Nwc (times)	5.7	3.0	2.5	4.9	3.8	3.0	4.8	3.1	2.4	5.8	4.5	3.7
Acct Pay To Sales (%)	1.8	3.4	5.7	3.2	5.4	8.7	3.5	6.9	13.1	2.9	3.7	12.5
PROFITABILITY												
Return On Sales (%)	9.9	6.1	3.3	7.7	3.3	0.3	11.7	8.2	(1.0)	16.4	8.8	2.8
Return On Assets (%)	17.9	9.5	5.5	5.4	3.7	1.0	20.4	7.8	(1.1)	39.1	20.7	5.8
Return On Nw (%)	32.3	20.4	10.0	23.1	11.8	3.0	35.5	15.5	9.2	80.1	53.3	18.3

	SIC 3541 MACH TLS,MTL CTTNG (NO BREAKDOWN) 2014 (11 Establishments)		SIC 3544 SPCL DIES,TLS,FXTRS (NO BREAKDOWN) 2014 (46 Establishments)		SIC 3545 MACHINE TOOL,ACCS (NO BREAKDOWN) 2014 (23 Establishments)		SIC 3549 MTLWRKNG MCHNRY,NEC (NO BREAKDOWN) 2014 (13 Establishments)	
	$	%	$	%	$	%	$	%
Cash	1,489,909	10.4	409,695	19.4	402,461	15.3	582,765	12.0
Accounts Receivable	3,581,512	25.0	511,063	24.2	523,462	19.9	1,014,983	20.9
Notes Receivable	0	0.0	4,224	0.2	5,261	0.2	4,856	0.1
Inventory	3,939,663	27.5	291,433	13.8	597,115	22.7	1,398,637	28.8
Other Current	1,360,975	9.5	202,736	9.6	320,916	12.2	577,910	11.9
Total Current	**10,372,059**	**72.4**	**1,419,151**	**67.2**	**1,849,215**	**70.3**	**3,579,151**	**73.7**
Fixed Assets	3,223,361	22.5	538,517	25.5	555,028	21.1	985,845	20.3
Other Non-current	730,629	5.1	154,164	7.3	226,220	8.6	291,383	6.0
Total Assets	**14,326,049**	**100.0**	**2,111,832**	**100.0**	**2,630,463**	**100.0**	**4,856,379**	**100.0**
Accounts Payable	1,432,605	10.0	152,052	7.2	205,176	7.8	621,617	12.8
Bank Loans	0	0.0	27,454	1.3	0	0.0	82,558	1.7
Notes Payable	0	0.0	27,454	1.3	63,131	2.4	247,675	5.1
Other Current	3,896,685	27.2	371,682	17.6	239,372	9.1	1,087,829	22.4
Total Current	**5,329,290**	**37.2**	**578,642**	**27.4**	**507,679**	**19.3**	**2,039,679**	**42.0**
Other Long Term	2,077,277	14.5	268,202	12.7	460,331	17.5	922,712	19.0
Deferred Credits	0	0.0	2,112	0.1	0	0.0	19,426	0.4
Net Worth	6,919,482	48.3	1,262,876	59.8	1,662,453	63.2	1,874,562	38.6
Total Liab & Net Worth	**14,326,049**	**100.0**	**2,111,832**	**100.0**	**2,630,463**	**100.0**	**4,856,379**	**100.0**
Net Sales	19,760,068	100.0	3,910,800	100.0	5,178,077	100.0	8,093,965	100.0
Gross Profit	6,026,821	30.5	1,271,010	32.5	1,848,573	35.7	2,282,498	28.2
Net Profit After Tax	869,443	4.4	164,254	4.2	378,000	7.3	48,564	0.6
Working Capital	5,042,769	---	840,509	---	1,341,536	---	1,539,472	---

RATIOS	UQ	MED	LQ	UQ	MED	LQ	UQ	MED	LQ	UQ	MED	LQ
SOLVENCY												
Quick Ratio (times)	4.3	1.6	1.3	3.5	2.1	0.9	3.6	2.2	1.8	1.6	0.9	0.3
Current Ratio (times)	13.3	3.0	2.7	6.1	3.0	1.5	7.7	4.1	3.0	3.4	2.0	1.5
Curr Liab To Nw (%)	5.7	29.4	41.5	10.6	39.0	75.9	13.3	26.2	41.4	27.4	70.5	232.9
Curr Liab To Inv (%)	41.7	81.4	332.0	85.8	183.7	333.4	31.0	84.2	128.3	79.6	161.7	363.6
Total Liab To Nw (%)	8.1	71.9	113.5	19.7	54.7	94.8	26.1	47.2	85.8	28.4	136.2	310.1
Fixed Assets To Nw (%)	16.6	29.1	66.1	18.5	37.2	74.4	12.7	33.5	70.6	17.2	37.9	111.1
EFFICIENCY												
Coll Period (days)	46.0	61.5	86.9	36.9	46.9	66.7	26.3	44.5	59.5	23.7	29.6	63.9
Sales To Inv (times)	11.3	5.7	2.8	37.7	19.0	9.8	14.3	11.1	4.6	20.6	6.3	3.3
Assets To Sales (%)	65.8	72.5	136.5	41.0	54.0	71.1	37.2	50.8	65.6	45.5	60.0	74.3
Sales To Nwc (times)	5.4	2.3	1.6	9.2	5.3	3.3	5.6	3.9	2.8	6.2	4.4	2.6
Acct Pay To Sales (%)	2.1	3.3	8.2	1.3	2.7	5.6	1.0	4.0	5.8	3.0	4.1	6.7
PROFITABILITY												
Return On Sales (%)	13.0	2.7	(0.2)	8.4	3.9	1.1	8.6	4.7	2.2	3.7		0.1
Return On Assets (%)	15.2	5.9	(0.3)	13.8	7.9	2.7	18.4	7.1	3.5	9.8		0.4
Return On Nw (%)	23.6	16.1	1.4	24.5	13.9	5.7	40.0	22.6	5.3	38.2	18.8	(2.8)

SIC 3556 FOOD PRDCTS MCHNRY (NO BREAKDOWN) 2014 (12 Establishments)

	$	%
Cash	586,715	5.5
Accounts Receivable	2,698,888	25.3
Notes Receivable	0	0.0
Inventory	3,050,917	28.6
Other Current	1,056,087	9.9
Total Current	**7,392,607**	**69.3**
Fixed Assets	2,176,179	20.4
Other Non-current	1,098,756	10.3
Total Assets	**10,667,542**	**100.0**
Accounts Payable	1,760,144	16.5
Bank Loans	85,340	0.8
Notes Payable	170,681	1.6
Other Current	3,744,308	35.1
Total Current	**5,760,473**	**54.0**
Other Long Term	1,290,772	12.1
Deferred Credits	0	0.0
Net Worth	3,616,297	33.9
Total Liab & Net Worth	**10,667,542**	**100.0**
Net Sales	20,673,531	100.0
Gross Profit	5,974,650	28.9
Net Profit After Tax	454,818	2.2
Working Capital	1,632,134	---

RATIOS	UQ	MED	LQ
SOLVENCY			
Quick Ratio (times)	0.9	0.5	0.3
Current Ratio (times)	1.8	1.3	1.0
Curr Liab To Nw (%)	118.6	187.6	445.9
Curr Liab To Inv (%)	84.8	180.0	511.7
Total Liab To Nw (%)	125.9	248.8	485.1
Fixed Assets To Nw (%)	32.5	63.2	111.8
EFFICIENCY			
Coll Period (days)	36.3	38.7	54.6
Sales To Inv (times)	15.4	8.3	5.0
Assets To Sales (%)	35.0	51.6	73.5
Sales To Nwc (times)	24.3	8.7	4.8
Acct Pay To Sales (%)	5.2	7.9	8.0
PROFITABILITY			
Return On Sales (%)	4.0	1.9	0.0
Return On Assets (%)	7.7	3.1	0.1
Return On Nw (%)	24.6	13.8	1.5

SIC 3559 SPEC IND MCHNRY,NEC (NO BREAKDOWN) 2014 (28 Establishments)

	$	%
Cash	4,791,021	23.2
Accounts Receivable	4,088,889	19.8
Notes Receivable	227,160	1.1
Inventory	4,006,285	19.4
Other Current	2,292,257	11.1
Total Current	**15,405,612**	**74.6**
Fixed Assets	2,870,483	13.9
Other Non-current	2,374,859	11.5
Total Assets	**20,650,954**	**100.0**
Accounts Payable	4,254,097	20.6
Bank Loans	206,510	1.0
Notes Payable	1,135,802	5.5
Other Current	9,003,815	43.6
Total Current	**14,600,224**	**70.7**
Other Long Term	1,239,058	6.0
Deferred Credits	0	0.0
Net Worth	4,811,672	23.3
Total Liab & Net Worth	**20,650,954**	**100.0**
Net Sales	21,899,209	100.0
Gross Profit	7,861,816	35.9
Net Profit After Tax	0	0.0
Working Capital	805,388	---

RATIOS	UQ	MED	LQ
Quick Ratio	2.2	1.5	1.1
Current Ratio	3.5	2.9	2.1
Curr Liab To Nw	22.8	35.9	51.4
Curr Liab To Inv	92.0	133.9	213.6
Total Liab To Nw	34.1	53.3	64.8
Fixed Assets To Nw	7.8	10.8	24.0
Coll Period	50.0	63.2	85.3
Sales To Inv	10.2	5.8	4.1
Assets To Sales	65.3	94.3	162.8
Sales To Nwc	3.7	2.2	1.6
Acct Pay To Sales	4.7	6.7	11.6
Return On Sales	10.2	5.0	(8.8)
Return On Assets	8.1	4.1	(4.9)
Return On Nw	14.9	7.3	(2.1)

SIC 3569 GNRL IND MCHNRY,NEC (NO BREAKDOWN) 2014 (21 Establishments)

	$	%
Cash	844,156	15.8
Accounts Receivable	1,479,944	27.7
Notes Receivable	10,686	0.2
Inventory	924,297	17.3
Other Current	614,416	11.5
Total Current	**3,873,499**	**72.5**
Fixed Assets	758,671	14.2
Other Non-current	710,587	13.3
Total Assets	**5,342,757**	**100.0**
Accounts Payable	646,474	12.1
Bank Loans	96,170	1.8
Notes Payable	42,742	0.8
Other Current	1,800,508	33.7
Total Current	**2,585,894**	**48.4**
Other Long Term	299,195	5.6
Deferred Credits	0	0.0
Net Worth	2,457,668	46.0
Total Liab & Net Worth	**5,342,757**	**100.0**
Net Sales	12,087,686	100.0
Gross Profit	3,928,498	32.5
Net Profit After Tax	(157,140)	(1.3)
Working Capital	1,287,605	---

RATIOS	UQ	MED	LQ
Quick Ratio	1.8	1.3	0.8
Current Ratio	3.8	2.1	1.3
Curr Liab To Nw	26.8	53.4	113.9
Curr Liab To Inv	99.4	204.9	476.6
Total Liab To Nw	27.2	62.8	145.7
Fixed Assets To Nw	12.1	32.5	42.5
Coll Period	24.1	46.7	73.0
Sales To Inv	33.4	11.5	6.9
Assets To Sales	33.3	44.2	88.6
Sales To Nwc	13.1	5.0	2.0
Acct Pay To Sales	4.7	5.9	10.3
Return On Sales	6.8	2.1	0.0
Return On Assets	9.4	5.6	0.1
Return On Nw	22.2	9.7	1.5

SIC 3571 ELECTRNC COMPUTERS (NO BREAKDOWN) 2014 (15 Establishments)

	$	%
Cash	2,350,325	21.4
Accounts Receivable	2,932,415	26.7
Notes Receivable	21,966	0.2
Inventory	1,735,287	15.8
Other Current	1,054,351	9.6
Total Current	**8,094,344**	**73.7**
Fixed Assets	1,164,180	10.6
Other Non-current	1,724,304	15.7
Total Assets	**10,982,828**	**100.0**
Accounts Payable	2,207,548	20.1
Bank Loans	0	0.0
Notes Payable	54,914	0.5
Other Current	2,273,446	20.7
Total Current	**4,535,908**	**41.3**
Other Long Term	878,626	8.0
Deferred Credits	87,863	0.8
Net Worth	5,480,431	49.9
Total Liab & Net Worth	**10,982,828**	**100.0**
Net Sales	20,115,070	100.0
Gross Profit	7,362,116	36.6
Net Profit After Tax	1,206,904	6.0
Working Capital	3,558,436	---

RATIOS	UQ	MED	LQ
Quick Ratio	2.1	1.1	0.9
Current Ratio	3.0	2.0	1.3
Curr Liab To Nw	28.8	59.8	161.2
Curr Liab To Inv	123.7	258.5	681.8
Total Liab To Nw	43.5	72.3	278.8
Fixed Assets To Nw	7.7	15.6	27.8
Coll Period	39.1	53.0	82.5
Sales To Inv	44.3	10.8	5.3
Assets To Sales	31.7	54.6	114.6
Sales To Nwc	6.0	4.3	2.1
Acct Pay To Sales	4.4	9.3	10.5
Return On Sales	9.7	5.3	2.7
Return On Assets	10.7	7.8	5.5
Return On Nw	31.0	14.5	9.7

	SIC 3572 COMPTR STRGE DVCES (NO BREAKDOWN) 2014 (15 Establishments)		SIC 3577 CMPTR PRPRL EQP,NEC (NO BREAKDOWN) 2014 (41 Establishments)		SIC 3585 RRFGRTN,HTNG EQPMT (NO BREAKDOWN) 2014 (21 Establishments)		SIC 3589 SVC IND MCHNRY,NEC (NO BREAKDOWN) 2014 (24 Establishments)	
	$	%	$	%	$	%	$	%
Cash	12,850,838	28.6	22,844,080	26.6	1,666,484	14.1	483,190	20.6
Accounts Receivable	11,502,848	25.6	14,341,960	16.7	2,848,388	24.1	595,778	25.4
Notes Receivable	0	0.0	0	0.0	23,638	0.2	9,382	0.4
Inventory	5,616,625	12.5	10,820,880	12.6	3,427,521	29.0	452,697	19.3
Other Current	4,313,568	9.6	14,170,200	16.5	567,314	4.8	302,580	12.9
Total Current	**34,283,879**	**76.3**	**62,177,120**	**72.4**	**8,533,345**	**72.2**	**1,843,627**	**78.6**
Fixed Assets	4,268,635	9.5	6,269,240	7.3	1,902,865	16.1	387,021	16.5
Other Non-current	6,380,486	14.2	17,433,640	20.3	1,382,828	11.7	114,934	4.9
Total Assets	**44,933,000**	**100.0**	**85,880,000**	**100.0**	**11,819,038**	**100.0**	**2,345,582**	**100.0**
Accounts Payable	232,034,012	516.4	8,072,720	9.4	1,453,742	12.3	534,793	22.8
Bank Loans	0	0.0	0	0.0	330,933	2.8	4,691	0.2
Notes Payable	3,594,640	8.0	0	0.0	47,276	0.4	182,955	7.8
Other Current	(47,988,444)	(106.8)	16,317,200	19.0	1,536,475	13.0	3,014,073	128.5
Total Current	**187,640,208**	**417.6**	**24,389,920**	**28.4**	**3,368,426**	**28.5**	**3,736,512**	**159.3**
Other Long Term	8,627,136	19.2	20,439,440	23.8	2,682,921	22.7	558,249	23.8
Deferred Credits	1,258,124	2.8	2,404,640	2.8	11,819	0.1	0	0.0
Net Worth	(152,592,468)	(339.6)	38,646,000	45.0	5,755,872	48.7	(1,949,179)	(83.1)
Total Liab & Net Worth	**44,933,000**	**100.0**	**85,880,000**	**100.0**	**11,819,038**	**100.0**	**2,345,582**	**100.0**
Net Sales	41,954,248	100.0	86,485,398	100.0	20,342,578	100.0	4,037,146	100.0
Gross Profit	16,655,836	39.7	46,183,203	53.4	5,675,579	27.9	1,501,818	37.2
Net Profit After Tax	(1,594,261)	(3.8)	(2,248,620)	(2.6)	549,250	2.7	40,371	1.0
Working Capital	(153,356,329)	---	37,787,200	---	5,164,919	---	(1,892,885)	---

RATIOS	UQ	MED	LQ	UQ	MED	LQ	UQ	MED	LQ	UQ	MED	LQ
SOLVENCY												
Quick Ratio (times)	1.4	1.1	0.8	2.6	2.0	1.0	2.3	1.2	0.7	3.0	1.2	0.3
Current Ratio (times)	2.4	1.8	1.1	4.4	2.9	1.9	4.9	2.4	1.5	5.3	2.0	0.8
Curr Liab To Nw (%)	40.0	52.2	87.6	22.8	36.3	66.9	24.0	51.5	116.7	13.7	36.6	88.1
Curr Liab To Inv (%)	309.7	399.2	992.5	123.6	285.6	677.1	51.5	117.7	178.6	75.5	233.4	399.7
Total Liab To Nw (%)	57.7	83.8	121.9	31.3	65.4	117.5	29.4	142.5	211.9	24.7	55.8	94.5
Fixed Assets To Nw (%)	9.6	11.1	16.0	5.8	10.4	15.4	7.2	23.1	52.8	11.4	27.6	31.5
EFFICIENCY												
Coll Period (days)	43.8	48.6	65.7	40.6	53.1	62.6	34.3	46.0	56.2	20.4	41.4	65.3
Sales To Inv (times)	35.5	16.3	9.2	29.8	11.4	5.4	9.1	7.4	5.8	16.7	10.2	4.3
Assets To Sales (%)	55.2	107.1	145.8	56.6	99.3	152.0	43.7	58.1	73.0	31.2	58.1	88.3
Sales To Nwc (times)	5.1	3.1	1.9	4.3	2.5	1.5	9.5	4.9	3.2	7.7	4.1	2.6
Acct Pay To Sales (%)	6.1	7.9	13.0	2.7	5.8	10.2	3.2	7.6	11.3	2.9	5.0	11.7
PROFITABILITY												
Return On Sales (%)	10.1	0.2	(8.6)	4.9	1.6	(6.6)	7.8	3.8	0.1	5.7	2.5	(2.8)
Return On Assets (%)	6.8	0.5	(25.6)	5.3	0.8	(6.8)	11.7	7.1	0.2	14.2	5.9	(2.9)
Return On Nw (%)	15.4	6.5	(22.5)	9.3	4.3	(8.7)	26.5	12.9	0.2	29.6	17.0	6.2

	SIC 3599 IND MACHINERY.NEC (NO BREAKDOWN) 2014 (164 Establishments) $	%	SIC 36 ELECTRICAL EQUIPMENT (NO BREAKDOWN) 2014 (498 Establishments) $	%	SIC 3613 SWTCHGR,BRD APPRTUS (NO BREAKDOWN) 2014 (10 Establishments) $	%	SIC 3621 MOTORS.GENERATORS (NO BREAKDOWN) 2014 (21 Establishments) $	%
Cash	409,087	19.5	4,804,822	19.7	987,586	17.1	1,493,632	21.9
Accounts Receivable	520,275	24.8	4,560,922	18.7	1,807,687	31.3	893,451	13.1
Notes Receivable	8,392	0.4	48,780	0.2	11,551	0.2	0	0.0
Inventory	335,661	16.0	4,853,602	19.9	906,731	15.7	1,473,171	21.6
Other Current	119,580	5.7	2,390,215	9.8	768,124	13.3	518,339	7.6
Total Current	**1,392,995**	**66.4**	**16,658,341**	**68.3**	**4,481,679**	**77.6**	**4,378,593**	**64.2**
Fixed Assets	574,820	27.4	3,438,984	14.1	675,717	11.7	1,452,711	21.3
Other Non-current	130,069	6.2	4,292,633	17.6	617,963	10.7	988,934	14.5
Total Assets	**2,097,884**	**100.0**	**24,389,958**	**100.0**	**5,775,359**	**100.0**	**6,820,238**	**100.0**
Accounts Payable	165,733	7.9	5,219,451	21.4	444,703	7.7	1,616,396	23.7
Bank Loans	25,175	1.2	48,780	0.2	0	0.0	0	0.0
Notes Payable	16,783	0.8	1,390,228	5.7	202,138	3.5	477,417	7.0
Other Current	325,172	15.5	18,950,997	77.7	1,085,767	18.8	6,697,474	98.2
Total Current	**532,863**	**25.4**	**25,609,456**	**105.0**	**1,732,608**	**30.0**	**8,791,287**	**128.9**
Other Long Term	350,346	16.7	7,414,547	30.4	427,376	7.4	3,771,592	55.3
Deferred Credits	0	0.0	121,950	0.5	11,551	0.2	6,820	0.1
Net Worth	1,214,675	57.9	(8,755,995)	(35.9)	3,603,824	62.4	(5,749,461)	(84.3)
Total Liab & Net Worth	**2,097,884**	**100.0**	**24,389,958**	**100.0**	**5,775,359**	**100.0**	**6,820,238**	**100.0**
Net Sales	3,935,992	100.0	26,310,634	100.0	12,527,894	100.0	8,080,851	100.0
Gross Profit	1,440,573	36.6	9,024,547	34.3	3,307,364	26.4	1,616,170	20.0
Net Profit After Tax	204,672	5.2	26,311	0.1	751,674	6.0	(258,587)	(3.2)
Working Capital	860,132	---	(8,951,115)	---	2,749,071	---	(4,412,694)	---

RATIOS	UQ	MED	LQ	UQ	MED	LQ	UQ	MED	LQ	UQ	MED	LQ
SOLVENCY												
Quick Ratio (times)	4.9	2.0	1.0	2.5	1.4	0.8	2.1	1.7	1.3	1.5	1.0	0.6
Current Ratio (times)	6.5	3.2	1.8	4.8	2.5	1.6	4.3	2.7	1.8	3.0	1.8	1.0
Curr Liab To Nw (%)	12.5	31.2	70.6	16.4	36.0	75.2	26.8	42.2	78.8	30.9	57.5	87.3
Curr Liab To Inv (%)	67.2	138.0	437.6	80.5	145.8	290.8	110.4	329.5	549.8	79.4	130.9	461.2
Total Liab To Nw (%)	17.4	49.4	130.8	21.9	63.6	136.7	36.6	55.5	79.4	36.1	117.0	183.2
Fixed Assets To Nw (%)	20.0	45.1	70.8	7.5	19.7	40.2	10.8	11.8	21.8	12.0	27.2	46.6
EFFICIENCY												
Coll Period (days)	33.6	44.6	56.9	36.7	51.1	67.2	31.4	52.4	79.9	38.2	47.5	52.6
Sales To Inv (times)	40.8	12.8	7.0	10.5	6.8	4.4	41.1	13.6	8.7	10.4	6.0	4.3
Assets To Sales (%)	37.0	53.3	70.6	53.4	92.7	140.3	43.2	46.1	49.9	54.1	84.4	159.6
Sales To Nwc (times)	6.6	4.4	3.1	5.2	3.1	1.7	6.3	3.8	3.4	6.3	4.5	2.4
Acct Pay To Sales (%)	1.6	2.7	5.3	4.2	7.2	12.7	3.1	3.3	4.9	5.6	8.8	18.0
PROFITABILITY												
Return On Sales (%)	7.5	3.4	0.5	7.6	2.2	(6.3)	10.4	5.4	1.2	9.4	2.7	(2.4)
Return On Assets (%)	15.4	6.4	1.7	8.5	2.5	(7.2)	21.7	7.7	2.5	8.8	2.0	(28.1)
Return On Nw (%)	28.1	11.6	2.9	17.1	6.2	(5.2)	38.9	11.5	3.3	24.8	16.1	(4.8)

	SIC 3625 RELAYS,IND CONTROLS (NO BREAKDOWN) 2014 (22 Establishments) $	%	SIC 3643 CUR-CRRYNG WRNG DVC (NO BREAKDOWN) 2014 (11 Establishments) $	%	SIC 3651 HSHLD AUDIO,VDEO EQ (NO BREAKDOWN) 2014 (16 Establishments) $	%	SIC 3661 TLPHNE,TLGPH APPTUS (NO BREAKDOWN) 2014 (26 Establishments) $	%
Cash	581,614	17.9	510,172	8.8	3,310,276	27.1	22,599,010	17.3
Accounts Receivable	968,274	29.8	1,750,816	30.2	1,734,536	14.2	26,648,544	20.4
Notes Receivable	0	0.0	63,771	1.1	61,075	0.5	130,630	0.1
Inventory	594,611	18.3	1,750,816	30.2	3,285,845	26.9	19,071,997	14.6
Other Current	269,687	8.3	249,288	4.3	952,773	7.8	19,855,778	15.2
Total Current	**2,414,186**	**74.3**	**4,324,863**	**74.6**	**9,344,505**	**76.5**	**88,305,959**	**67.6**
Fixed Assets	344,420	10.6	881,205	15.2	1,465,805	12.0	13,324,272	10.2
Other Non-current	490,635	15.1	591,336	10.2	1,404,729	11.5	28,999,886	22.2
Total Assets	**3,249,241**	**100.0**	**5,797,404**	**100.0**	**12,215,039**	**100.0**	**130,630,117**	**100.0**
Accounts Payable	347,669	10.7	852,218	14.7	3,383,566	27.7	13,977,423	10.7
Bank Loans	22,745	0.7	0	0.0	0	0.0	0	0.0
Notes Payable	9,748	0.3	5,797	0.1	97,720	0.8	1,306,301	1.0
Other Current	620,604	19.1	492,780	8.5	9,674,311	79.2	23,905,311	18.3
Total Current	**1,000,766**	**30.8**	**1,350,795**	**23.3**	**13,155,597**	**107.7**	**39,189,035**	**30.0**
Other Long Term	581,614	17.9	915,990	15.8	1,832,256	15.0	26,779,174	20.5
Deferred Credits	0	0.0	5,797	0.1	0	0.0	914,411	0.7
Net Worth	1,666,861	51.3	3,524,822	60.8	(2,772,814)	(22.7)	63,747,497	48.8
Total Liab & Net Worth	**3,249,241**	**100.0**	**5,797,404**	**100.0**	**12,215,039**	**100.0**	**130,630,117**	**100.0**
Net Sales	5,092,854	100.0	12,334,902	100.0	15,326,272	100.0	144,183,352	100.0
Gross Profit	2,021,863	39.7	3,490,777	28.3	5,686,047	37.1	59,115,174	41.0
Net Profit After Tax	259,736	5.1	715,424	5.8	(168,589)	(1.1)	(5,046,417)	(3.5)
Working Capital	1,413,420	--	2,974,068	--	(3,811,092)	--	49,116,924	--

RATIOS	UQ	MED	LQ	UQ	MED	LQ	UQ	MED	LQ	UQ	MED	LQ
SOLVENCY												
Quick Ratio (times)	2.9	1.5	1.0	3.0	2.2	1.1	3.0	1.0	0.6	2.1	1.4	0.8
Current Ratio (times)	5.1	2.3	1.6	5.8	3.6	2.6	5.1	1.8	1.2	5.2	2.5	1.5
Curr Liab To Nw (%)	13.4	55.9	72.3	20.5	28.6	79.6	23.3	43.7	215.9	15.1	36.2	59.8
Curr Liab To Inv (%)	76.3	143.9	349.3	41.7	64.6	150.4	109.2	178.1	218.6	101.2	150.1	370.2
Total Liab To Nw (%)	36.6	65.7	165.9	25.5	45.8	145.0	43.7	61.7	216.2	16.6	45.3	85.8
Fixed Assets To Nw (%)	7.0	13.2	34.4	6.9	29.2	58.4	15.1	24.3	58.8	3.8	10.9	20.2
EFFICIENCY												
Coll Period (days)	35.0	56.1	67.5	38.5	50.7	54.2	13.5	38.2	63.5	42.3	57.7	71.9
Sales To Inv (times)	14.9	9.8	6.1	9.9	7.7	6.0	11.2	6.3	4.8	13.4	9.1	5.5
Assets To Sales (%)	38.9	63.8	75.7	35.5	47.0	68.4	39.0	79.7	156.3	74.3	90.6	129.4
Sales To Nwc (times)	6.3	4.0	3.0	7.3	4.2	3.8	6.2	3.1	2.2	5.7	2.5	1.8
Acct Pay To Sales (%)	2.3	7.0	8.0	3.0	4.5	6.7	4.9	8.4	14.1	5.6	8.5	9.6
PROFITABILITY												
Return On Sales (%)	10.2	6.0	1.7	8.5	6.1	1.6	6.6	2.5	(41.8)	3.1	0.6	(5.3)
Return On Assets (%)	14.4	9.0	1.9	15.4	9.7	5.4	9.8	3.7	(20.8)	3.1	1.6	(3.5)
Return On Nw (%)	31.1	16.2	7.2	28.0	19.7	7.0	27.1	11.6	1.7	6.9	2.6	(4.8)

	SIC 3663 RDIO.TV CMMNCTNS EQ (NO BREAKDOWN) 2014 (43 Establishments) $	%	SIC 3669 CMMNCTNS EQPMNT.NEC (NO BREAKDOWN) 2014 (23 Establishments) $	%	SIC 3672 PRINTED CIRCT BRDS (NO BREAKDOWN) 2014 (29 Establishments) $	%	SIC 3674 SMCNDCTRS.RLTD DVCS (NO BREAKDOWN) 2014 (113 Establishments) $	%
Cash	4,882,329	21.1	2,485,621	19.1	15,148,332	14.6	52,337,222	21.8
Accounts Receivable	3,378,294	14.6	3,032,197	23.3	28,947,840	27.9	31,210,270	13.0
Notes Receivable	69,417	0.3	156,165	1.2	0	0.0	240,079	0.1
Inventory	4,581,522	19.8	1,782,880	13.7	22,307,476	21.5	28,329,322	11.8
Other Current	2,452,734	10.6	1,678,769	12.9	6,329,098	6.1	39,132,877	16.3
Total Current	**15,364,296**	**66.4**	**9,135,632**	**70.2**	**72,732,746**	**70.1**	**151,249,770**	**63.0**
Fixed Assets	1,758,564	7.6	1,561,647	12.0	24,486,345	23.6	37,692,403	15.7
Other Non-current	6,016,140	26.0	2,316,442	17.8	6,536,609	6.3	51,136,827	21.3
Total Assets	**23,139,000**	**100.0**	**13,013,721**	**100.0**	**103,755,700**	**100.0**	**240,079,000**	**100.0**
Accounts Payable	4,650,939	20.1	2,342,470	18.0	21,269,919	20.5	45,855,089	19.1
Bank Loans	300,807	1.3	0	0.0	0	0.0	0	0.0
Notes Payable	92,556	0.4	182,192	1.4	2,178,870	2.1	45,374,931	18.9
Other Current	10,412,550	45.0	3,539,732	27.2	15,978,377	15.4	401,172,009	167.1
Total Current	**15,456,852**	**66.8**	**6,064,394**	**46.6**	**39,427,166**	**38.0**	**492,402,029**	**205.1**
Other Long Term	8,260,623	35.7	2,810,964	21.6	14,940,821	14.4	98,672,469	41.1
Deferred Credits	300,807	1.3	143,151	1.1	0	0.0	720,237	0.3
Net Worth	(879,282)	(3.8)	3,995,212	30.7	49,387,713	47.6	(351,715,735)	(146.5)
Total Liab & Net Worth	**23,139,000**	**100.0**	**13,013,721**	**100.0**	**103,755,700**	**100.0**	**240,079,000**	**100.0**
Net Sales	18,600,482	100.0	15,274,320	100.0	155,322,904	100.0	177,968,125	100.0
Gross Profit	7,570,396	40.7	5,697,321	37.3	37,277,497	24.0	69,941,473	39.3
Net Profit After Tax	(353,409)	(1.9)	15,274	0.1	2,019,198	1.3	(3,381,394)	(1.9)
Working Capital	(92,556)	---	3,071,238	---	33,305,580	---	(341,152,259)	---

RATIOS	UQ	MED	LQ	UQ	MED	LQ	UQ	MED	LQ	UQ	MED	LQ
SOLVENCY												
Quick Ratio (times)	3.3	1.3	0.6	2.1	1.4	0.9	1.9	1.2	0.9	2.5	1.5	1.0
Current Ratio (times)	4.9	2.6	1.6	4.0	2.1	1.6	2.9	2.0	1.4	5.4	3.2	1.9
Curr Liab To Nw (%)	12.5	28.4	59.6	22.6	41.3	74.9	37.8	66.8	136.3	13.5	20.8	42.1
Curr Liab To Inv (%)	88.7	153.3	652.2	74.5	193.4	670.6	104.1	178.1	284.0	101.3	169.0	299.1
Total Liab To Nw (%)	18.2	64.0	145.2	45.0	63.0	146.6	63.6	121.3	197.9	18.6	40.4	83.0
Fixed Assets To Nw (%)	3.6	7.4	22.0	5.1	13.2	28.7	14.8	53.5	88.3	8.7	19.2	40.6
EFFICIENCY												
Coll Period (days)	30.3	56.9	84.3	24.1	57.0	72.3	47.5	57.1	69.6	36.1	49.6	65.3
Sales To Inv (times)	10.9	5.4	2.2	21.9	11.2	5.6	10.3	9.1	6.5	10.4	7.2	5.4
Assets To Sales (%)	76.0	124.4	205.3	46.9	85.2	159.3	53.6	66.8	117.4	96.3	134.9	190.5
Sales To Nwc (times)	3.3	2.5	1.1	7.2	3.7	2.2	6.6	4.5	2.9	3.5	2.1	1.2
Acct Pay To Sales (%)	4.6	7.3	22.1	2.7	6.6	9.7	5.1	10.9	16.4	5.0	7.9	12.6
PROFITABILITY												
Return On Sales (%)	6.7	2.3	(22.7)	6.4	2.6	(26.4)	3.5	1.2	(0.8)	8.5	2.1	(12.7)
Return On Assets (%)	4.9	0.0	(22.1)	12.0	3.4	(18.4)	5.7	1.8	(1.1)	6.6	1.4	(11.6)
Return On Nw (%)	11.8	3.5	(10.0)	21.7	7.9	(7.4)	12.7	5.3	(1.3)	10.0	2.4	(12.8)

Balance Sheet (Dollars and Percent)

	SIC 3679 ELEC COMPONENTS,NEC (NO BREAKDOWN) 2014 (47 Establishments) $	%	SIC 3691 STORAGE BATTERIES (NO BREAKDOWN) 2014 (11 Establishments) $	%	SIC 3699 ELEC EQPT,SPPLS,NEC (NO BREAKDOWN) 2014 (35 Establishments) $	%	SIC 37 TRANSPORTATION EQPT (NO BREAKDOWN) 2014 (202 Establishments) $	%
Cash	1,319,136	20.8	23,049,846	26.3	995,598	23.6	3,016,025	14.7
Accounts Receivable	1,395,240	22.0	16,038,486	18.3	873,258	20.7	3,241,714	15.8
Notes Receivable	0	0.0	0	0.0	0	0.0	123,103	0.6
Inventory	1,604,526	25.3	14,285,646	16.3	991,379	23.5	5,006,191	24.4
Other Current	291,732	4.6	3,505,680	4.0	295,305	7.0	1,374,651	6.7
Total Current	**4,610,634**	**72.7**	**56,879,658**	**64.9**	**3,155,540**	**74.8**	**12,761,684**	**62.2**
Fixed Assets	957,642	15.1	14,811,498	16.9	472,487	11.2	4,370,159	21.3
Other Non-current	773,724	12.2	15,950,844	18.2	590,609	14.0	3,385,334	16.5
Total Assets	**6,342,000**	**100.0**	**87,642,000**	**100.0**	**4,218,636**	**100.0**	**20,517,177**	**100.0**
Accounts Payable	1,769,418	27.9	14,723,856	16.8	1,569,333	37.2	4,698,434	22.9
Bank Loans	12,684	0.2	0	0.0	0	0.0	41,034	0.2
Notes Payable	31,710	0.5	350,568	0.4	185,620	4.4	3,734,126	18.2
Other Current	2,853,900	45.0	45,924,408	52.4	1,708,547	40.5	5,354,983	26.1
Total Current	**4,667,712**	**73.6**	**60,998,832**	**69.6**	**3,463,500**	**82.1**	**13,828,577**	**67.4**
Other Long Term	761,040	12.0	16,038,486	18.3	2,311,813	54.8	6,688,600	32.6
Deferred Credits	12,684	0.2	0	0.0	92,810	2.2	20,517	0.1
Net Worth	900,564	14.2	10,604,682	12.1	(1,649,487)	(39.1)	(20,517)	(0.1)
Total Liab & Net Worth	**6,342,000**	**100.0**	**87,642,000**	**100.0**	**4,218,636**	**100.0**	**20,517,177**	**100.0**
Net Sales	12,266,925	100.0	67,886,909	100.0	4,006,302	100.0	30,760,385	100.0
Gross Profit	3,937,683	32.1	10,115,149	14.9	1,622,552	40.5	7,813,138	25.4
Net Profit After Tax	61,335	0.5	2,987,024	4.4	120,189	3.0	1,168,895	3.8
Working Capital	(57,078)	---	(4,119,174)	---	(307,960)	---	(1,066,893)	---

RATIOS

	3679 UQ	3679 MED	3679 LQ	3691 UQ	3691 MED	3691 LQ	3699 UQ	3699 MED	3699 LQ	37 UQ	37 MED	37 LQ
SOLVENCY												
Quick Ratio (times)	2.8	1.5	0.8	2.0	1.1	0.9	3.1	1.7	1.1	1.7	1.0	0.5
Current Ratio (times)	4.7	2.6	1.5	2.6	2.0	1.6	5.4	2.5	1.6	3.2	2.1	1.4
Curr Liab To Nw (%)	21.6	42.7	72.8	24.5	44.4	59.9	12.3	31.9	87.5	23.8	48.2	101.3
Curr Liab To Inv (%)	77.2	118.4	173.9	122.6	213.4	332.5	78.4	150.2	543.6	62.1	116.1	247.1
Total Liab To Nw (%)	21.6	70.4	129.0	35.2	71.4	131.4	16.0	37.6	136.1	39.4	96.5	195.6
Fixed Assets To Nw (%)	7.6	18.1	49.8	11.7	29.7	31.9	6.1	18.2	29.0	17.6	36.8	77.0
EFFICIENCY												
Coll Period (days)	36.9	56.3	62.4	48.6	61.7	83.2	46.7	59.9	74.1	19.4	39.8	54.6
Sales To Inv (times)	9.8	6.3	4.8	8.0	7.0	5.8	8.2	5.6	3.1	10.9	6.5	4.3
Assets To Sales (%)	34.0	51.7	93.1	82.5	129.1	205.6	61.0	105.3	142.7	43.1	66.7	108.5
Sales To Nwc (times)	7.5	4.0	2.6	7.0	3.7	1.5	4.9	2.8	1.5	6.9	4.8	3.0
Acct Pay To Sales (%)	3.7	6.4	11.4	8.0	9.4	17.6	2.2	4.8	8.7	3.4	5.9	9.9
PROFITABILITY												
Return On Sales (%)	8.2	2.9	0.1	5.8	(3.2)	(252.9)	8.0	2.2	(19.8)	7.7	4.0	0.9
Return On Assets (%)	13.2	5.4	(2.9)	5.7	(2.4)	(57.3)	8.3	2.3	(23.5)	10.5	5.5	1.3
Return On Nw (%)	29.2	9.8	3.9	27.1	8.5	(36.7)	13.9	6.5	(5.6)	24.3	13.6	4.2

SIC 3711 MTR VHCL,CAR BODIES
(NO BREAKDOWN)
2014 (19 Establishments)

	$	%
Cash	22,209,609	9.3
Accounts Receivable	23,642,487	9.9
Notes Receivable	238,813	0.1
Inventory	69,255,770	29.0
Other Current	17,910,975	7.5
Total Current	**133,257,654**	**55.8**
Fixed Assets	51,105,982	21.4
Other Non-current	54,449,364	22.8
Total Assets	**238,813,000**	**100.0**
Accounts Payable	37,254,828	15.6
Bank Loans	1,910,504	0.8
Notes Payable	5,492,699	2.3
Other Current	61,374,941	25.7
Total Current	**106,032,972**	**44.4**
Other Long Term	58,270,372	24.4
Deferred Credits	1,194,065	0.5
Net Worth	73,315,591	30.7
Total Liab & Net Worth	**238,813,000**	**100.0**
Net Sales	333,072,524	100.0
Gross Profit	49,294,734	14.8
Net Profit After Tax	(1,998,435)	(0.6)
Working Capital	27,224,682	---

RATIOS	UQ	MED	LQ
SOLVENCY			
Quick Ratio (times)	1.0	0.4	0.3
Current Ratio (times)	1.9	1.5	1.1
Curr Liab To Nw (%)	36.7	69.6	192.3
Curr Liab To Inv (%)	92.3	126.2	289.7
Total Liab To Nw (%)	71.8	148.5	235.8
Fixed Assets To Nw (%)	18.8	29.9	78.9
EFFICIENCY			
Coll Period (days)	11.3	25.6	44.2
Sales To Inv (times)	8.2	5.8	1.7
Assets To Sales (%)	47.0	71.7	133.2
Sales To Nwc (times)	11.9	6.2	4.4
Acct Pay To Sales (%)	4.9	7.1	20.0
PROFITABILITY			
Return On Sales (%)	5.9	0.2	(7.3)
Return On Assets (%)	8.2	0.4	(6.4)
Return On Nw (%)	18.6	4.0	(4.9)

SIC 3713 TRUCK,BUS BODIES
(NO BREAKDOWN)
2014 (12 Establishments)

	$	%
Cash	913,873	11.2
Accounts Receivable	1,117,863	13.7
Notes Receivable	8,160	0.1
Inventory	3,361,747	41.2
Other Current	179,510	2.2
Total Current	**5,581,153**	**68.4**
Fixed Assets	1,207,618	14.8
Other Non-current	1,370,810	16.8
Total Assets	**8,159,581**	**100.0**
Accounts Payable	783,320	9.6
Bank Loans	0	0.0
Notes Payable	293,745	3.6
Other Current	962,830	11.8
Total Current	**2,039,895**	**25.0**
Other Long Term	1,542,161	18.9
Deferred Credits	0	0.0
Net Worth	4,577,525	56.1
Total Liab & Net Worth	**8,159,581**	**100.0**
Net Sales	18,931,742	100.0
Gross Profit	3,483,441	18.4
Net Profit After Tax	757,270	4.0
Working Capital	3,541,258	---

RATIOS	UQ	MED	LQ
SOLVENCY			
Quick Ratio (times)	1.4	0.9	0.5
Current Ratio (times)	3.9	2.9	2.5
Curr Liab To Nw (%)	23.5	42.3	79.5
Curr Liab To Inv (%)	38.9	43.3	84.9
Total Liab To Nw (%)	32.7	50.3	202.0
Fixed Assets To Nw (%)	12.0	24.7	50.2
EFFICIENCY			
Coll Period (days)	10.6	19.0	29.9
Sales To Inv (times)	6.7	4.5	3.8
Assets To Sales (%)	37.7	43.1	51.1
Sales To Nwc (times)	4.9	3.9	3.4
Acct Pay To Sales (%)	2.4	4.3	6.4
PROFITABILITY			
Return On Sales (%)	5.8	3.0	1.6
Return On Assets (%)	11.3	5.7	3.3
Return On Nw (%)	31.5	14.2	4.6

SIC 3714 MTR VHCLE PRTS,ACCS
(NO BREAKDOWN)
2014 (55 Establishments)

	$	%
Cash	25,138,248	11.8
Accounts Receivable	41,755,056	19.6
Notes Receivable	0	0.0
Inventory	46,015,776	21.6
Other Current	13,634,304	6.4
Total Current	**126,543,384**	**59.4**
Fixed Assets	49,637,388	23.3
Other Non-current	36,855,228	17.3
Total Assets	**213,036,000**	**100.0**
Accounts Payable	86,279,580	40.5
Bank Loans	0	0.0
Notes Payable	80,953,680	38.0
Other Current	(15,125,556)	(7.1)
Total Current	**152,107,704**	**71.4**
Other Long Term	88,196,904	41.4
Deferred Credits	426,072	0.2
Net Worth	(27,694,680)	(13.0)
Total Liab & Net Worth	**213,036,000**	**100.0**
Net Sales	309,645,349	100.0
Gross Profit	64,096,587	20.7
Net Profit After Tax	6,502,552	2.1
Working Capital	(25,564,320)	---

RATIOS	UQ	MED	LQ
SOLVENCY			
Quick Ratio (times)	1.8	1.2	0.8
Current Ratio (times)	3.2	2.1	1.5
Curr Liab To Nw (%)	23.3	54.7	106.3
Curr Liab To Inv (%)	87.8	148.9	254.3
Total Liab To Nw (%)	45.2	101.7	241.7
Fixed Assets To Nw (%)	20.7	42.8	78.9
EFFICIENCY			
Coll Period (days)	37.6	46.7	61.0
Sales To Inv (times)	12.8	8.4	5.3
Assets To Sales (%)	50.2	68.8	92.1
Sales To Nwc (times)	6.8	4.6	3.2
Acct Pay To Sales (%)	4.3	8.0	11.9
PROFITABILITY			
Return On Sales (%)	6.7	2.7	0.1
Return On Assets (%)	9.2	4.4	0.1
Return On Nw (%)	23.8	13.0	4.4

SIC 3724 AIRCRFT ENG,ENG PRT
(NO BREAKDOWN)
2014 (10 Establishments)

	$	%
Cash	8,679,771	15.0
Accounts Receivable	9,142,692	15.8
Notes Receivable	0	0.0
Inventory	6,885,951	11.9
Other Current	3,934,829	6.8
Total Current	**28,643,243**	**49.5**
Fixed Assets	13,771,903	23.8
Other Non-current	15,449,991	26.7
Total Assets	**57,865,137**	**100.0**
Accounts Payable	5,439,323	9.4
Bank Loans	0	0.0
Notes Payable	0	0.0
Other Current	8,390,445	14.5
Total Current	**13,829,768**	**23.9**
Other Long Term	14,234,823	24.6
Deferred Credits	0	0.0
Net Worth	29,800,546	51.5
Total Liab & Net Worth	**57,865,137**	**100.0**
Net Sales	53,529,266	100.0
Gross Profit	16,326,426	30.5
Net Profit After Tax	4,978,222	9.3
Working Capital	14,813,475	---

RATIOS	UQ	MED	LQ
SOLVENCY			
Quick Ratio (times)	1.9	1.2	0.9
Current Ratio (times)	2.8	2.5	1.5
Curr Liab To Nw (%)	23.8	38.2	96.6
Curr Liab To Inv (%)	81.2	125.0	335.4
Total Liab To Nw (%)	62.0	106.1	156.8
Fixed Assets To Nw (%)	30.3	46.4	51.0
EFFICIENCY			
Coll Period (days)	47.5	49.3	71.9
Sales To Inv (times)	17.0	6.2	4.7
Assets To Sales (%)	91.7	108.1	119.0
Sales To Nwc (times)	6.1	4.0	3.2
Acct Pay To Sales (%)	4.7	5.3	8.4
PROFITABILITY			
Return On Sales (%)	11.5	7.8	4.1
Return On Assets (%)	9.9	7.5	4.9
Return On Nw (%)	25.4	14.3	7.0

Balance Sheet

	SIC 3728 AIRCRFT PRT,EQP,NEC (NO BREAKDOWN) 2014 (40 Establishments) $	%	SIC 3732 BOATBLDING,REPAIRNG (NO BREAKDOWN) 2014 (13 Establishments) $	%	SIC 38 INSTRUMENTS RLTD PDTS (NO BREAKDOWN) 2014 (407 Establishments) $	%	SIC 3812 SEARCH,NVGTN EQPMNT (NO BREAKDOWN) 2014 (25 Establishments) $	%
Cash	1,379,148	19.5	974,392	7.8	4,039,320	24.6	4,041,704	22.2
Accounts Receivable	1,280,132	18.1	712,056	5.7	2,479,420	15.1	2,785,499	15.3
Notes Receivable	49,508	0.7	0	0.0	32,840	0.2	0	0.0
Inventory	1,739,848	24.6	4,547,163	36.4	3,004,860	18.3	3,550,145	19.5
Other Current	346,554	4.9	1,274,204	10.2	1,871,880	11.4	1,693,146	9.3
Total Current	**4,795,190**	**67.8**	**7,507,815**	**60.1**	**11,428,320**	**69.6**	**12,070,494**	**66.3**
Fixed Assets	1,365,003	19.3	3,897,568	31.2	1,986,820	12.1	2,985,763	16.4
Other Non-current	912,359	12.9	1,086,822	8.7	3,004,860	18.3	3,149,617	17.3
Total Assets	**7,072,552**	**100.0**	**12,492,205**	**100.0**	**16,420,000**	**100.0**	**18,205,874**	**100.0**
Accounts Payable	1,011,375	14.3	1,399,127	11.2	6,994,920	42.6	37,558,718	206.3
Bank Loans	0	0.0	149,906	1.2	49,260	0.3	127,441	0.7
Notes Payable	169,741	2.4	49,969	0.4	1,871,880	11.4	7,373,379	40.5
Other Current	3,380,680	47.8	7,795,136	62.4	12,594,140	76.7	(6,626,938)	(36.4)
Total Current	**4,561,796**	**64.5**	**9,394,138**	**75.2**	**21,510,200**	**131.0**	**38,432,600**	**211.1**
Other Long Term	1,485,236	21.0	4,284,826	34.3	6,141,080	37.4	31,842,074	174.9
Deferred Credits	0	0.0	0	0.0	164,200	1.0	18,206	0.1
Net Worth	1,025,520	14.5	(1,186,759)	(9.5)	(11,395,480)	(69.4)	(52,087,006)	(286.1)
Total Liab & Net Worth	**7,072,552**	**100.0**	**12,492,205**	**100.0**	**16,420,000**	**100.0**	**18,205,874**	**100.0**
Net Sales	10,355,127	100.0	28,135,597	100.0	15,403,377	100.0	18,334,213	100.0
Gross Profit	3,593,229	34.7	8,862,713	31.5	7,409,024	48.1	7,517,027	41.0
Net Profit After Tax	631,663	6.1	1,237,966	4.4	0	0.0	1,686,748	9.2
Working Capital	233,394	---	(1,886,323)	---	(10,081,880)	---	(26,362,106)	---

RATIOS

	SIC 3728 UQ	MED	LQ	SIC 3732 UQ	MED	LQ	SIC 38 UQ	MED	LQ	SIC 3812 UQ	MED	LQ
SOLVENCY												
Quick Ratio (times)	2.9	1.5	0.9	0.8	0.4	0.2	3.0	1.6	0.9	2.0	1.2	0.7
Current Ratio (times)	5.8	3.0	1.7	3.5	2.1	0.8	5.3	3.1	1.6	4.4	2.2	1.4
Curr Liab To Nw (%)	16.5	38.6	98.5	19.5	30.8	76.7	15.3	27.3	61.5	19.1	53.6	70.9
Curr Liab To Inv (%)	49.5	71.8	125.1	45.8	91.9	333.3	77.6	132.7	274.3	97.1	128.4	196.7
Total Liab To Nw (%)	28.8	91.4	193.1	34.0	80.4	175.3	20.2	50.4	116.6	34.6	65.7	167.0
Fixed Assets To Nw (%)	17.6	33.8	64.1	15.0	62.1	100.4	6.6	14.8	31.3	15.2	20.2	47.4
EFFICIENCY												
Coll Period (days)	33.2	46.7	66.1	6.6	11.2	17.0	37.2	53.1	70.1	33.8	47.3	69.0
Sales To Inv (times)	9.0	5.3	3.9	14.8	6.0	5.2	9.6	6.6	4.2	9.0	5.0	3.9
Assets To Sales (%)	44.2	68.3	102.5	27.1	44.4	91.5	62.2	106.6	168.5	64.1	99.3	141.9
Sales To Nwc (times)	5.4	3.5	2.2	8.5	5.6	3.0	4.6	2.3	1.4	7.7	3.2	1.5
Acct Pay To Sales (%)	2.7	5.6	8.4	3.2	3.8	4.1	3.2	5.7	10.5	1.0	5.0	6.4
PROFITABILITY												
Return On Sales (%)	7.9	5.2	1.2	8.4	2.2	(0.6)	8.9	1.7	(20.4)	12.4	9.1	3.5
Return On Assets (%)	10.0	4.9	2.4	14.8	4.9	(1.4)	8.1	1.4	(28.7)	14.5	8.6	3.1
Return On Nw (%)	23.7	11.5	4.9	31.4	13.4	3.1	15.8	5.0	(12.4)	42.8	23.7	9.8

SIC 3823 PROC CNTL INSTRMNTS (NO BREAKDOWN) 2014 (32 Establishments)
SIC 3825 INSTRMNTS MEAS ELEC (NO BREAKDOWN) 2014 (29 Establishments)
SIC 3826 ANALYTCL INSTRMNTS (NO BREAKDOWN) 2014 (33 Establishments)
SIC 3827 OPTCL INSTRMNTS,LNS (NO BREAKDOWN) 2014 (16 Establishments)

	SIC 3823 $	%	SIC 3825 $	%	SIC 3826 $	%	SIC 3827 $	%
Cash	946,661	22.4	2,606,133	23.8	7,373,070	30.5	2,099,494	21.6
Accounts Receivable	845,233	20.0	2,102,426	19.2	2,659,140	11.0	1,448,262	14.9
Notes Receivable	0	0.0	0	0.0	0	0.0	0	0.0
Inventory	1,043,863	24.7	1,773,922	16.2	3,432,708	14.2	2,439,690	25.1
Other Current	380,355	9.0	1,127,864	10.3	4,085,406	16.9	1,244,145	12.8
Total Current	**3,216,112**	**76.1**	**7,610,345**	**69.5**	**17,550,324**	**72.6**	**7,231,591**	**74.4**
Fixed Assets	414,164	9.8	1,215,465	11.1	2,030,616	8.4	1,195,545	12.3
Other Non-current	595,889	14.1	2,124,327	19.4	4,593,060	19.0	1,292,744	13.3
Total Assets	**4,226,165**	**100.0**	**10,950,137**	**100.0**	**24,174,000**	**100.0**	**9,719,880**	**100.0**
Accounts Payable	477,557	11.3	1,511,119	13.8	6,019,326	24.9	748,431	7.7
Bank Loans	42,262	1.0	0	0.0	0	0.0	0	0.0
Notes Payable	16,905	0.4	952,662	8.7	1,643,832	6.8	0	0.0
Other Current	879,041	20.8	5,190,365	47.4	10,757,430	44.5	1,370,503	14.1
Total Current	**1,415,765**	**33.5**	**7,654,146**	**69.9**	**18,420,588**	**76.2**	**2,118,934**	**21.8**
Other Long Term	414,164	9.8	2,485,681	22.7	4,399,668	18.2	2,536,889	26.1
Deferred Credits	0	0.0	21,900	0.2	193,392	0.8	0	0.0
Net Worth	2,396,236	56.7	788,410	7.2	1,160,352	4.8	5,064,057	52.1
Total Liab & Net Worth	**4,226,165**	**100.0**	**10,950,137**	**100.0**	**24,174,000**	**100.0**	**9,719,880**	**100.0**
Net Sales	7,427,355	100.0	11,005,163	100.0	15,656,736	100.0	11,328,531	100.0
Gross Profit	3,342,310	45.0	5,469,566	49.7	7,468,263	47.7	4,270,856	37.7
Net Profit After Tax	653,607	8.8	308,145	2.8	(281,821)	(1.8)	(33,986)	(0.3)
Working Capital	1,800,347	--	(43,801)	--	(870,264)	--	5,112,657	--

RATIOS	SIC 3823 UQ	MED	LQ	SIC 3825 UQ	MED	LQ	SIC 3826 UQ	MED	LQ	SIC 3827 UQ	MED	LQ
SOLVENCY												
Quick Ratio (times)	3.1	1.7	1.1	2.6	1.6	0.9	2.3	1.5	0.9	3.7	1.4	1.0
Current Ratio (times)	6.9	3.0	1.9	4.4	3.2	1.3	4.8	3.2	1.5	6.7	3.6	1.9
Curr Liab To Nw (%)	13.5	40.6	70.8	16.5	31.5	75.3	19.5	27.9	57.3	21.2	33.9	51.8
Curr Liab To Inv (%)	57.8	92.5	197.8	77.4	125.2	402.9	88.4	183.8	318.1	54.7	81.4	130.2
Total Liab To Nw (%)	20.8	51.6	96.6	22.1	59.5	104.3	24.3	65.8	141.6	35.1	48.3	81.0
Fixed Assets To Nw (%)	4.7	8.3	25.6	6.7	12.8	22.3	8.4	13.1	18.9	3.5	8.4	43.5
EFFICIENCY												
Coll Period (days)	36.5	49.6	68.6	37.5	50.4	75.0	24.1	57.9	76.7	27.7	49.1	73.0
Sales To Inv (times)	11.4	6.7	4.4	13.1	7.1	4.7	9.1	7.4	4.6	8.2	4.8	3.7
Assets To Sales (%)	41.9	56.9	107.7	57.1	99.5	165.7	103.8	154.4	227.7	60.3	85.8	128.4
Sales To Nwc (times)	4.9	3.2	2.1	6.1	2.4	1.7	2.6	1.5	0.9	5.1	2.0	1.4
Acct Pay To Sales (%)	1.8	3.9	6.3	3.2	7.5	11.2	4.4	8.8	16.2	1.4	3.5	7.7
PROFITABILITY												
Return On Sales (%)	16.3	6.8	2.0	7.3	3.4	(9.0)	6.2	(2.9)	(143.7)	4.5	1.5	(4.2)
Return On Assets (%)	14.8	7.9	2.3	8.5	3.4	(9.5)	5.2	(4.4)	(66.3)	5.0	2.6	(4.5)
Return On Nw (%)	31.9	10.7	4.5	18.9	6.8	0.8	9.2	(1.4)	(46.9)	10.9	4.5	(4.3)

	SIC 3829 MEAS,CTLNG DVCS,NEC (NO BREAKDOWN) 2014 (38 Establishments) $	%	SIC 3841 SRGL,MDCL INSTRMNTS (NO BREAKDOWN) 2014 (113 Establishments) $	%	SIC 3842 SRGCL APPL,SUPPLS (NO BREAKDOWN) 2014 (27 Establishments) $	%	SIC 3845 ELECTROMDCL EQPT (NO BREAKDOWN) 2014 (37 Establishments) $	%
Cash	1,661,021	26.9	7,303,020	26.8	18,252,770	14.7	4,672,685	23.2
Accounts Receivable	1,173,212	19.0	3,297,259	12.1	17,507,759	14.1	2,779,442	13.8
Notes Receivable	24,699	0.4	136,250	0.5	0	0.0	0	0.0
Inventory	1,234,960	20.0	4,278,261	15.7	27,441,239	22.1	3,162,119	15.7
Other Current	623,655	10.1	3,542,510	13.0	11,175,164	9.0	2,900,288	14.4
Total Current	**4,717,547**	**76.4**	**18,557,300**	**68.1**	**74,376,932**	**59.9**	**13,514,534**	**67.1**
Fixed Assets	703,927	11.4	3,569,760	13.1	18,749,444	15.1	2,356,484	11.7
Other Non-current	753,326	12.2	5,123,013	18.8	31,042,124	25.0	4,269,867	21.2
Total Assets	**6,174,800**	**100.0**	**27,250,073**	**100.0**	**124,168,500**	**100.0**	**20,140,885**	**100.0**
Accounts Payable	456,935	7.4	18,966,051	69.6	50,660,748	40.8	2,900,287	14.4
Bank Loans	0	0.0	109,000	0.4	745,011	0.6	0	0.0
Notes Payable	80,272	1.3	6,839,768	25.1	1,241,685	1.0	886,199	4.4
Other Current	1,055,891	17.1	48,750,381	178.9	163,281,578	131.5	7,512,550	37.3
Total Current	**1,593,098**	**25.8**	**74,665,200**	**274.0**	**215,929,022**	**173.9**	**11,299,036**	**56.1**
Other Long Term	475,460	7.7	13,625,036	50.0	27,565,406	22.2	5,075,503	25.2
Deferred Credits	6,175	0.1	190,751	0.7	124,169	0.1	543,804	2.7
Net Worth	4,100,067	66.4	(61,230,914)	(224.7)	(119,450,097)	(96.2)	3,222,542	16.0
Total Liab & Net Worth	**6,174,800**	**100.0**	**27,250,073**	**100.0**	**124,168,500**	**100.0**	**20,140,885**	**100.0**
Net Sales	8,470,233	100.0	18,537,465	100.0	111,561,995	100.0	17,347,877	100.0
Gross Profit	4,158,884	49.1	9,231,658	49.8	56,896,617	51.0	8,830,069	50.9
Net Profit After Tax	525,154	6.2	(259,525)	(1.4)	(7,028,406)	(6.3)	(2,220,528)	(12.8)
Working Capital	3,124,449	--	(56,107,900)	--	(141,552,090)	--	2,215,498	--

RATIOS	SIC 3829 UQ	MED	LQ	SIC 3841 UQ	MED	LQ	SIC 3842 UQ	MED	LQ	SIC 3845 UQ	MED	LQ
SOLVENCY												
Quick Ratio (times)	4.3	2.6	1.4	2.9	1.5	0.9	2.4	1.5	0.8	2.7	1.5	0.5
Current Ratio (times)	8.1	5.0	2.3	4.9	2.7	1.6	5.5	2.9	2.0	4.3	2.7	1.2
Curr Liab To Nw (%)	12.2	20.7	45.2	15.3	30.7	75.0	13.9	24.2	52.9	18.9	25.4	50.9
Curr Liab To Inv (%)	54.8	89.2	177.5	96.5	168.0	281.1	67.0	114.5	188.3	114.2	210.0	464.4
Total Liab To Nw (%)	12.5	24.6	59.4	19.5	67.0	135.1	22.9	57.7	103.3	26.6	42.6	108.1
Fixed Assets To Nw (%)	3.3	11.6	27.6	9.1	17.5	31.2	9.5	24.6	40.8	9.5	15.3	27.0
EFFICIENCY												
Coll Period (days)	33.1	48.4	64.6	44.4	55.0	71.2	40.5	52.2	68.8	39.1	53.3	73.0
Sales To Inv (times)	9.5	7.2	5.7	8.8	5.6	3.9	7.8	5.9	3.5	10.6	6.9	4.7
Assets To Sales (%)	53.2	72.9	105.2	87.0	147.0	215.2	60.5	111.3	166.3	91.9	116.1	183.3
Sales To Nwc (times)	4.6	2.4	1.6	3.9	2.0	1.1	4.9	3.1	1.8	3.6	2.3	1.5
Acct Pay To Sales (%)	2.2	3.6	5.3	4.0	7.0	18.0	3.6	6.0	9.0	3.8	6.9	10.1
PROFITABILITY												
Return On Sales (%)	9.5	5.5	1.7	6.5	(6.6)	(133.2)	7.7	(11.0)	(7.3)	4.2	(11.0)	(71.1)
Return On Assets (%)	13.1	6.4	1.9	4.9	(7.9)	(70.5)	6.8	(9.3)	(7.1)	3.6	(9.3)	(84.2)
Return On Nw (%)	17.5	9.9	3.6	12.0	(6.0)	(74.5)	16.3	(4.5)	(6.1)	9.0	(4.5)	(24.5)

SIC 3861 PHTGRPH EQPT.SUPPLS
(NO BREAKDOWN)
2014 (13 Establishments)

	$	%
Cash	4,286,448	27.2
Accounts Receivable	2,742,066	17.4
Notes Receivable	0	0.0
Inventory	2,679,030	17.0
Other Current	1,213,443	7.7
Total Current	**10,920,987**	**69.3**
Fixed Assets	3,057,246	19.4
Other Non-current	1,780,767	11.3
Total Assets	**15,759,000**	**100.0**
Accounts Payable	4,097,340	26.0
Bank Loans	0	0.0
Notes Payable	126,072	0.8
Other Current	21,384,963	135.7
Total Current	**25,608,375**	**162.5**
Other Long Term	3,167,559	20.1
Deferred Credits	1,355,274	8.6
Net Worth	(14,372,208)	(91.2)
Total Liab & Net Worth	**15,759,000**	**100.0**
Net Sales	16,381,497	100.0
Gross Profit	6,798,321	41.5
Net Profit After Tax	(1,490,716)	(9.1)
Working Capital	(14,687,388)	—

RATIOS	UQ	MED	LQ
SOLVENCY			
Quick Ratio (times)	5.7	2.1	1.1
Current Ratio (times)	11.9	3.2	1.6
Curr Liab To Nw (%)	4.9	17.3	40.4
Curr Liab To Inv (%)	51.0	169.1	309.5
Total Liab To Nw (%)	4.9	17.4	43.1
Fixed Assets To Nw (%)	6.5	15.8	40.6
EFFICIENCY			
Coll Period (days)	39.5	63.2	69.2
Sales To Inv (times)	10.3	7.0	6.4
Assets To Sales (%)	72.5	96.2	104.4
Sales To Nwc (times)	2.5	2.2	2.1
Acct Pay To Sales (%)	3.2	8.7	9.8
PROFITABILITY			
Return On Sales (%)	2.5	(2.9)	(23.9)
Return On Assets (%)	3.2	(2.6)	(28.7)
Return On Nw (%)	2.5	(2.5)	(39.5)

SIC 39 MISC MANUFACTURING
(NO BREAKDOWN)
2014 (101 Establishments)

	$	%
Cash	789,114	16.1
Accounts Receivable	1,097,897	22.4
Notes Receivable	14,704	0.3
Inventory	1,235,135	25.2
Other Current	431,317	8.8
Total Current	**3,568,167**	**72.8**
Fixed Assets	740,101	15.1
Other Non-current	593,060	12.1
Total Assets	**4,901,328**	**100.0**
Accounts Payable	926,351	18.9
Bank Loans	24,507	0.5
Notes Payable	93,125	1.9
Other Current	2,230,104	45.5
Total Current	**3,274,087**	**66.8**
Other Long Term	1,436,090	29.3
Deferred Credits	19,605	0.4
Net Worth	171,546	3.5
Total Liab & Net Worth	**4,901,328**	**100.0**
Net Sales	9,648,283	100.0
Gross Profit	3,174,285	32.9
Net Profit After Tax	96,483	1.0
Working Capital	294,080	—

RATIOS	UQ	MED	LQ
SOLVENCY			
Quick Ratio (times)	2.2	1.1	0.6
Current Ratio (times)	4.1	2.1	1.3
Curr Liab To Nw (%)	23.6	51.5	127.0
Curr Liab To Inv (%)	64.1	159.8	300.4
Total Liab To Nw (%)	33.0	84.3	213.3
Fixed Assets To Nw (%)	7.7	21.4	41.9
EFFICIENCY			
Coll Period (days)	23.4	39.5	67.0
Sales To Inv (times)	14.2	8.0	4.5
Assets To Sales (%)	33.5	50.8	84.3
Sales To Nwc (times)	9.9	4.5	3.1
Acct Pay To Sales (%)	3.3	6.3	12.9
PROFITABILITY			
Return On Sales (%)	6.0	2.7	(0.2)
Return On Assets (%)	11.0	5.0	(0.9)
Return On Nw (%)	28.2	11.0	4.2

SIC 3911 JEWELRY,PREC MTL
(NO BREAKDOWN)
2014 (14 Establishments)

	$	%
Cash	829,662	14.4
Accounts Receivable	1,025,554	17.8
Notes Receivable	0	0.0
Inventory	2,869,247	49.8
Other Current	190,131	3.3
Total Current	**4,914,594**	**85.3**
Fixed Assets	535,823	9.3
Other Non-current	311,123	5.4
Total Assets	**5,761,540**	**100.0**
Accounts Payable	985,223	17.1
Bank Loans	28,808	0.5
Notes Payable	155,562	2.7
Other Current	1,428,862	24.8
Total Current	**2,598,455**	**45.1**
Other Long Term	190,130	3.3
Deferred Credits	0	0.0
Net Worth	2,972,955	51.6
Total Liab & Net Worth	**5,761,540**	**100.0**
Net Sales	11,928,654	100.0
Gross Profit	3,495,096	29.3
Net Profit After Tax	(214,716)	(1.8)
Working Capital	2,316,139	—

RATIOS	UQ	MED	LQ
SOLVENCY			
Quick Ratio (times)	1.6	0.7	0.5
Current Ratio (times)	4.8	1.7	1.4
Curr Liab To Nw (%)	20.9	96.9	301.6
Curr Liab To Inv (%)	35.9	75.7	105.8
Total Liab To Nw (%)	34.5	107.7	301.6
Fixed Assets To Nw (%)	6.3	15.3	45.2
EFFICIENCY			
Coll Period (days)	8.3	40.5	63.2
Sales To Inv (times)	7.4	3.8	1.9
Assets To Sales (%)	33.8	48.3	119.0
Sales To Nwc (times)	12.2	5.2	2.9
Acct Pay To Sales (%)	1.8	9.6	19.5
PROFITABILITY			
Return On Sales (%)	1.7	1.2	0.4
Return On Assets (%)	5.0	1.6	0.6
Return On Nw (%)	9.8	6.3	1.1

SIC 3944 GMES,TYS,CHLRN VHCL
(NO BREAKDOWN)
2014 (12 Establishments)

	$	%
Cash	2,576,030	20.6
Accounts Receivable	3,551,420	28.4
Notes Receivable	12,505	0.1
Inventory	2,838,635	22.7
Other Current	700,280	5.6
Total Current	**9,678,870**	**77.4**
Fixed Assets	1,150,460	9.2
Other Non-current	1,675,670	13.4
Total Assets	**12,505,000**	**100.0**
Accounts Payable	1,675,670	13.4
Bank Loans	400,160	3.2
Notes Payable	25,010	0.2
Other Current	1,125,450	9.0
Total Current	**3,226,290**	**25.8**
Other Long Term	3,001,200	24.0
Deferred Credits	0	0.0
Net Worth	6,277,510	50.2
Total Liab & Net Worth	**12,505,000**	**100.0**
Net Sales	20,234,628	100.0
Gross Profit	6,717,896	33.2
Net Profit After Tax	(263,050)	(1.3)
Working Capital	6,452,580	—

RATIOS	UQ	MED	LQ
SOLVENCY			
Quick Ratio (times)	2.9	1.8	1.3
Current Ratio (times)	4.7	2.7	2.1
Curr Liab To Nw (%)	31.8	57.2	119.2
Curr Liab To Inv (%)	63.2	168.6	279.7
Total Liab To Nw (%)	31.8	117.2	248.2
Fixed Assets To Nw (%)	5.6	20.6	43.7
EFFICIENCY			
Coll Period (days)	36.4	55.9	79.6
Sales To Inv (times)	11.7	8.1	6.1
Assets To Sales (%)	38.0	61.8	103.4
Sales To Nwc (times)	5.5	3.5	2.8
Acct Pay To Sales (%)	3.1	5.2	7.1
PROFITABILITY			
Return On Sales (%)	9.0	4.4	1.5
Return On Assets (%)	13.4	7.4	2.1
Return On Nw (%)	24.4	16.9	10.2

SIC 3993 SIGNS, ADVT SPCLTIES
(NO BREAKDOWN)
2014 (30 Establishments)

	$	%
Cash	536,135	16.9
Accounts Receivable	923,168	29.1
Notes Receivable	25,379	0.8
Inventory	529,791	16.7
Other Current	434,619	13.7
Total Current	**2,449,092**	**77.2**
Fixed Assets	479,032	15.1
Other Non-current	244,275	7.7
Total Assets	**3,172,399**	**100.0**
Accounts Payable	564,687	17.8
Bank Loans	0	0.0
Notes Payable	60,276	1.9
Other Current	980,271	30.9
Total Current	**1,605,234**	**50.6**
Other Long Term	555,170	17.5
Deferred Credits	25,379	0.8
Net Worth	986,616	31.1
Total Liab & Net Worth	**3,172,399**	**100.0**
Net Sales	8,348,418	100.0
Gross Profit	3,022,127	36.2
Net Profit After Tax	358,982	4.3
Working Capital	843,858	--

RATIOS	UQ	MED	LQ
SOLVENCY			
Quick Ratio (times)	1.9	1.0	0.8
Current Ratio (times)	2.7	1.7	1.2
Curr Liab To Nw (%)	39.8	88.4	239.5
Curr Liab To Inv (%)	150.2	257.7	592.4
Total Liab To Nw (%)	65.0	125.2	266.5
Fixed Assets To Nw (%)	12.0	22.6	39.3
EFFICIENCY			
Coll Period (days)	34.0	43.4	69.0
Sales To Inv (times)	35.7	13.5	8.8
Assets To Sales (%)	30.3	38.0	60.0
Sales To Nwc (times)	16.1	7.3	4.1
Acct Pay To Sales (%)	3.3	5.9	8.3
PROFITABILITY			
Return On Sales (%)	6.3	3.4	1.3
Return On Assets (%)	22.2	10.0	2.9
Return On Nw (%)	82.7	25.8	9.3

SIC 3999 MFG INDUSTRIES, NEC
(NO BREAKDOWN)
2014 (17 Establishments)

	$	%
Cash	486,723	12.4
Accounts Receivable	820,363	20.9
Notes Receivable	0	0.0
Inventory	773,261	19.7
Other Current	294,389	7.5
Total Current	**2,374,736**	**60.5**
Fixed Assets	832,139	21.2
Other Non-current	718,309	18.3
Total Assets	**3,925,184**	**100.0**
Accounts Payable	451,396	11.5
Bank Loans	0	0.0
Notes Payable	0	0.0
Other Current	867,466	22.1
Total Current	**1,318,862**	**33.6**
Other Long Term	3,556,217	90.6
Deferred Credits	47,102	1.2
Net Worth	(996,997)	(25.4)
Total Liab & Net Worth	**3,925,184**	**100.0**
Net Sales	7,188,982	100.0
Gross Profit	2,875,593	40.0
Net Profit After Tax	(186,914)	(2.6)
Working Capital	1,055,874	--

RATIOS	UQ	MED	LQ
SOLVENCY			
Quick Ratio (times)	4.2	1.5	0.6
Current Ratio (times)	5.1	2.6	1.6
Curr Liab To Nw (%)	10.0	29.6	51.5
Curr Liab To Inv (%)	59.9	197.0	281.1
Total Liab To Nw (%)	31.1	74.4	183.6
Fixed Assets To Nw (%)	7.9	20.3	98.9
EFFICIENCY			
Coll Period (days)	22.6	34.7	67.9
Sales To Inv (times)	27.2	8.8	6.0
Assets To Sales (%)	31.0	54.6	101.4
Sales To Nwc (times)	16.2	5.4	3.0
Acct Pay To Sales (%)	3.3	4.4	6.5
PROFITABILITY			
Return On Sales (%)	3.4	1.3	(8.1)
Return On Assets (%)	9.0	2.9	(7.4)
Return On Nw (%)	34.4	3.4	(13.1)

SIC 41 LOCAL PASSENGER TRAN
(NO BREAKDOWN)
2014 (36 Establishments)

	$	%
Cash	635,396	19.1
Accounts Receivable	409,182	12.3
Notes Receivable	3,327	0.1
Inventory	33,267	1.0
Other Current	292,746	8.8
Total Current	**1,373,918**	**41.3**
Fixed Assets	1,779,773	53.5
Other Non-current	172,988	5.2
Total Assets	**3,326,679**	**100.0**
Accounts Payable	216,234	6.5
Bank Loans	99,800	3.0
Notes Payable	73,187	2.2
Other Current	592,149	17.8
Total Current	**981,370**	**29.5**
Other Long Term	878,244	26.4
Deferred Credits	19,960	0.6
Net Worth	1,447,105	43.5
Total Liab & Net Worth	**3,326,679**	**100.0**
Net Sales	5,331,216	100.0
Gross Profit	1,290,154	24.2
Net Profit After Tax	357,191	6.7
Working Capital	392,548	--

RATIOS	UQ	MED	LQ
SOLVENCY			
Quick Ratio (times)	3.5	1.4	0.9
Current Ratio (times)	5.2	2.6	1.2
Curr Liab To Nw (%)	13.3	26.5	75.9
Curr Liab To Inv (%)	608.7	999.9	999.9
Total Liab To Nw (%)	27.7	71.1	137.3
Fixed Assets To Nw (%)	61.5	95.9	147.2
EFFICIENCY			
Coll Period (days)	15.0	29.6	48.6
Sales To Inv (times)	153.7	65.9	13.8
Assets To Sales (%)	34.1	62.4	451.0
Sales To Nwc (times)	19.8	7.2	2.0
Acct Pay To Sales (%)	1.8	3.4	9.6
PROFITABILITY			
Return On Sales (%)	7.5	2.5	(2.7)
Return On Assets (%)	9.4	3.2	(1.6)
Return On Nw (%)	24.6	6.3	(7.1)

SIC 4111 LCL SUBURBAN TRANS
(NO BREAKDOWN)
2014 (11 Establishments)

	$	%
Cash	5,372,867	13.2
Accounts Receivable	3,459,800	8.5
Notes Receivable	0	0.0
Inventory	447,739	1.1
Other Current	5,087,942	12.5
Total Current	**14,368,348**	**35.3**
Fixed Assets	24,259,307	59.6
Other Non-current	2,075,880	5.1
Total Assets	**40,703,535**	**100.0**
Accounts Payable	4,518,092	11.1
Bank Loans	2,238,694	5.5
Notes Payable	569,849	1.4
Other Current	14,409,053	35.4
Total Current	**21,735,688**	**53.4**
Other Long Term	11,356,286	27.9
Deferred Credits	0	0.0
Net Worth	7,611,561	18.7
Total Liab & Net Worth	**40,703,535**	**100.0**
Net Sales	6,745,697	100.0
Gross Profit	1,760,627	26.1
Net Profit After Tax	1,059,074	15.7
Working Capital	(7,367,340)	--

RATIOS	UQ	MED	LQ
SOLVENCY			
Quick Ratio (times)	1.1	0.6	0.2
Current Ratio (times)	2.8	1.1	1.0
Curr Liab To Nw (%)	21.0	28.2	97.0
Curr Liab To Inv (%)	939.5	999.9	999.9
Total Liab To Nw (%)	27.7	30.9	97.4
Fixed Assets To Nw (%)	74.5	97.3	100.8
EFFICIENCY			
Coll Period (days)	8.4	17.9	31.4
Sales To Inv (times)	40.6	13.8	11.5
Assets To Sales (%)	66.1	603.4	999.9
Sales To Nwc (times)	85.4	0.3	0.2
Acct Pay To Sales (%)	4.5	12.9	22.3
PROFITABILITY			
Return On Sales (%)	22.9	1.1	(32.6)
Return On Assets (%)	6.9	0.3	(3.9)
Return On Nw (%)	20.6	2.6	(7.1)

Balance Sheet

	SIC 4119 LCL PASS TRANS NEC (17 Establishments) $	%	SIC 42 TRUCKING & WAREHSNG (223 Establishments) $	%	SIC 4212 LCL TRCKG W/O STRGE (60 Establishments) $	%	SIC 4213 TRCKG, EXCEPT LOCAL (103 Establishments) $	%
Cash	399,843	20.0	581,221	14.7	265,783	12.5	701,763	14.6
Accounts Receivable	303,881	15.2	1,008,240	25.5	537,945	25.3	1,264,134	26.3
Notes Receivable	0	0.0	19,769	0.5	6,379	0.3	33,646	0.7
Inventory	23,991	1.2	102,801	2.6	51,030	2.4	91,325	1.9
Other Current	117,953	5.9	308,403	7.8	174,355	8.2	360,495	7.5
Total Current	**845,668**	**42.3**	**2,020,434**	**51.1**	**1,035,492**	**48.7**	**2,451,363**	**51.0**
Fixed Assets	1,039,591	52.0	1,648,769	41.7	950,441	44.7	2,095,675	43.6
Other Non-current	113,955	5.7	284,680	7.2	140,333	6.6	259,557	5.4
Total Assets	**1,999,214**	**100.0**	**3,953,883**	**100.0**	**2,126,266**	**100.0**	**4,806,595**	**100.0**
Accounts Payable	73,971	3.7	308,403	7.8	159,470	7.5	418,174	8.7
Bank Loans	53,979	2.7	15,816	0.4	8,505	0.4	14,420	0.3
Notes Payable	7,997	0.4	75,124	1.9	21,263	1.0	67,292	1.4
Other Current	209,917	10.5	755,191	19.1	369,970	17.4	951,706	19.8
Total Current	**345,864**	**17.3**	**1,154,534**	**29.2**	**559,208**	**26.3**	**1,451,592**	**30.2**
Other Long Term	429,831	21.5	917,301	23.2	597,481	28.1	1,100,710	22.9
Deferred Credits	0	0.0	3,954	0.1	2,126	0.1	4,807	0.1
Net Worth	1,223,519	61.2	1,878,094	47.5	967,451	45.5	2,249,486	46.8
Total Liab & Net Worth	**1,999,214**	**100.0**	**3,953,883**	**100.0**	**2,126,266**	**100.0**	**4,806,595**	**100.0**
Net Sales	4,533,365	100.0	10,112,233	100.0	5,670,043	100.0	13,096,989	100.0
Gross Profit	752,539	16.6	3,215,690	31.8	2,222,657	39.2	3,444,508	26.3
Net Profit After Tax	122,401	2.7	364,040	3.6	175,771	3.1	471,492	3.6
Working Capital	499,804	---	865,900	---	476,284	---	999,771	---

RATIOS

	SIC 4119 UQ	MED	LQ	SIC 42 UQ	MED	LQ	SIC 4212 UQ	MED	LQ	SIC 4213 UQ	MED	LQ
SOLVENCY												
Quick Ratio (times)	4.7	2.5	1.5	2.6	1.4	0.9	3.1	1.7	0.8	2.3	1.3	0.9
Current Ratio (times)	5.1	3.1	1.7	3.5	1.7	1.2	4.0	1.8	1.1	3.0	1.7	1.2
Curr Liab To Nw (%)	13.3	15.1	69.2	21.4	40.4	86.5	16.1	37.3	90.1	22.4	47.6	85.2
Curr Liab To Inv (%)	494.7	948.5	999.9	266.2	943.3	999.9	255.4	474.8	999.9	380.8	999.9	999.9
Total Liab To Nw (%)	31.4	66.5	106.2	35.2	78.6	180.3	33.8	90.8	171.7	40.6	79.2	182.0
Fixed Assets To Nw (%)	55.9	88.3	102.8	34.0	78.9	153.1	35.6	92.8	161.6	34.9	89.0	153.3
EFFICIENCY												
Coll Period (days)	31.6	39.5	60.1	23.7	34.7	45.1	23.7	35.8	50.7	23.7	33.2	40.8
Sales To Inv (times)	182.3	140.0	65.9	376.7	123.0	33.0	376.7	142.0	50.9	625.2	154.1	56.4
Assets To Sales (%)	35.3	44.1	86.5	24.8	39.1	64.0	25.2	37.5	58.8	23.9	36.7	68.7
Sales To Nwc (times)	16.5	7.1	3.5	24.4	11.8	5.7	20.4	10.9	6.1	29.9	12.5	5.5
Acct Pay To Sales (%)	1.5	2.1	3.4	1.3	2.4	4.3	1.7	2.6	5.3	1.0	2.3	3.8
PROFITABILITY												
Return On Sales (%)	7.5	0.2	(5.2)	5.7	3.2	0.7	4.5	2.4	0.7	5.5	3.4	0.9
Return On Assets (%)	10.2	0.8	(5.7)	14.3	7.3	2.1	13.7	5.9	1.7	15.0	7.8	3.2
Return On Nw (%)	16.2	1.4	(15.7)	28.2	16.3	5.8	31.4	15.4	4.9	28.8	18.3	7.7

SIC 4214 LCL TRCKG WTH STRGE
(NO BREAKDOWN)
2014 (18 Establishments)

	$	%
Cash	547,127	18.0
Accounts Receivable	820,691	27.0
Notes Receivable	33,436	1.1
Inventory	3,040	0.1
Other Current	224,929	7.4
Total Current	**1,629,223**	**53.6**
Fixed Assets	1,167,204	38.4
Other Non-current	243,168	8.0
Total Assets	**3,039,595**	**100.0**
Accounts Payable	170,217	5.6
Bank Loans	27,356	0.9
Notes Payable	75,990	2.5
Other Current	458,979	15.1
Total Current	**732,542**	**24.1**
Other Long Term	501,534	16.5
Deferred Credits	0	0.0
Net Worth	1,805,519	59.4
Total Liab & Net Worth	**3,039,595**	**100.0**
Net Sales	7,754,069	100.0
Gross Profit	3,070,611	39.6
Net Profit After Tax	317,917	4.1
Working Capital	896,681	—

RATIOS	UQ	MED	LQ
SOLVENCY			
Quick Ratio (times)	2.1	1.5	1.2
Current Ratio (times)	2.5	1.7	1.4
Curr Liab To Nw (%)	26.0	44.0	61.7
Curr Liab To Inv (%)	999.9	999.9	999.9
Total Liab To Nw (%)	39.6	64.2	80.6
Fixed Assets To Nw (%)	20.8	53.0	121.8
EFFICIENCY			
Coll Period (days)	27.2	37.6	51.7
Sales To Inv (times)	794.4	590.6	386.7
Assets To Sales (%)	32.1	39.2	45.7
Sales To Nwc (times)	16.6	11.0	6.3
Acct Pay To Sales (%)	1.0	2.1	2.9
PROFITABILITY			
Return On Sales (%)	8.6	3.2	(0.1)
Return On Assets (%)	17.4	8.9	0.5
Return On Nw (%)	31.6	20.8	0.9

SIC 4225 GNRL WRHSG,STRGE
(NO BREAKDOWN)
2014 (14 Establishments)

	$	%
Cash	1,001,413	17.3
Accounts Receivable	1,742,342	30.1
Notes Receivable	0	0.0
Inventory	266,272	4.6
Other Current	393,618	6.8
Total Current	**3,403,645**	**58.8**
Fixed Assets	1,771,285	30.6
Other Non-current	613,582	10.6
Total Assets	**5,788,512**	**100.0**
Accounts Payable	422,561	7.3
Bank Loans	63,674	1.1
Notes Payable	0	0.0
Other Current	2,089,653	36.1
Total Current	**2,575,888**	**44.5**
Other Long Term	908,796	15.7
Deferred Credits	0	0.0
Net Worth	2,303,828	39.8
Total Liab & Net Worth	**5,788,512**	**100.0**
Net Sales	14,617,455	100.0
Gross Profit	4,604,498	31.5
Net Profit After Tax	643,168	4.4
Working Capital	827,757	—

RATIOS	UQ	MED	LQ
Quick Ratio (times)	4.8	1.5	0.9
Current Ratio (times)	5.9	1.9	1.5
Curr Liab To Nw (%)	12.0	42.9	82.3
Curr Liab To Inv (%)	157.8	837.0	999.9
Total Liab To Nw (%)	22.6	68.0	148.8
Fixed Assets To Nw (%)	38.1	60.1	90.2
Coll Period (days)	34.7	50.0	65.7
Sales To Inv (times)	147.5	85.1	26.5
Assets To Sales (%)	34.3	39.6	58.9
Sales To Nwc (times)	15.0	11.6	3.4
Acct Pay To Sales (%)	2.4	2.7	4.5
Return On Sales (%)	7.4	4.0	1.6
Return On Assets (%)	18.2	10.5	1.6
Return On Nw (%)	20.8	12.4	4.4

SIC 4226 SPCL WRHSG,STRG,NEC
(NO BREAKDOWN)
2014 (13 Establishments)

	$	%
Cash	3,090,840	24.3
Accounts Receivable	2,187,755	17.2
Notes Receivable	12,720	0.1
Inventory	317,988	2.5
Other Current	1,271,949	10.0
Total Current	**6,881,252**	**54.1**
Fixed Assets	3,510,583	27.6
Other Non-current	2,327,670	18.3
Total Assets	**12,719,505**	**100.0**
Accounts Payable	953,963	7.5
Bank Loans	0	0.0
Notes Payable	356,146	2.8
Other Current	2,073,279	16.3
Total Current	**3,383,388**	**26.6**
Other Long Term	2,620,218	20.6
Deferred Credits	0	0.0
Net Worth	6,715,899	52.8
Total Liab & Net Worth	**12,719,505**	**100.0**
Net Sales	15,781,024	100.0
Gross Profit	6,596,468	41.8
Net Profit After Tax	1,514,978	9.6
Working Capital	3,497,864	—

RATIOS	UQ	MED	LQ
Quick Ratio (times)	3.8	1.8	1.1
Current Ratio (times)	4.1	2.0	1.8
Curr Liab To Nw (%)	12.8	33.7	98.5
Curr Liab To Inv (%)	317.9	999.9	999.9
Total Liab To Nw (%)	28.6	75.5	529.3
Fixed Assets To Nw (%)	35.5	62.6	99.8
Coll Period (days)	23.7	38.4	69.4
Sales To Inv (times)	484.2	244.8	18.5
Assets To Sales (%)	54.1	80.6	96.9
Sales To Nwc (times)	13.2	5.3	4.1
Acct Pay To Sales (%)	3.5	4.9	7.6
Return On Sales (%)	10.5	6.7	0.7
Return On Assets (%)	11.8	8.2	2.9
Return On Nw (%)	34.5	17.9	5.8

SIC 44 WATER TRANSPORTATION
(NO BREAKDOWN)
2014 (40 Establishments)

	$	%
Cash	22,666,856	12.0
Accounts Receivable	8,877,852	4.7
Notes Receivable	0	0.0
Inventory	9,822,304	5.2
Other Current	22,477,964	11.9
Total Current	**63,844,976**	**33.8**
Fixed Assets	108,989,797	57.7
Other Non-current	16,055,690	8.5
Total Assets	**188,890,463**	**100.0**
Accounts Payable	5,855,604	3.1
Bank Loans	0	0.0
Notes Payable	944,452	0.5
Other Current	21,911,294	11.6
Total Current	**28,711,350**	**15.2**
Other Long Term	55,722,687	29.5
Deferred Credits	944,452	0.5
Net Worth	103,511,974	54.8
Total Liab & Net Worth	**188,890,463**	**100.0**
Net Sales	73,641,506	100.0
Gross Profit	41,312,885	56.1
Net Profit After Tax	5,375,830	7.3
Working Capital	35,133,626	—

RATIOS	UQ	MED	LQ
Quick Ratio (times)	2.4	0.8	0.4
Current Ratio (times)	5.8	2.6	1.4
Curr Liab To Nw (%)	6.2	15.7	38.5
Curr Liab To Inv (%)	306.5	725.4	999.9
Total Liab To Nw (%)	26.9	75.5	150.0
Fixed Assets To Nw (%)	67.8	122.8	162.7
Coll Period (days)	13.9	39.5	59.9
Sales To Inv (times)	55.3	26.1	12.7
Assets To Sales (%)	138.5	256.5	945.6
Sales To Nwc (times)	3.9	2.0	0.9
Acct Pay To Sales (%)	2.8	5.0	8.7
Return On Sales (%)	11.0	8.3	(5.0)
Return On Assets (%)	4.8	3.1	(1.3)
Return On Nw (%)	9.1	5.2	(1.7)

	SIC 45 TRANS BY AIR (NO BREAKDOWN) 2014 (42 Establishments)		SIC 4522 AIR TRANS,NONSCHED (NO BREAKDOWN) 2014 (10 Establishments)		SIC 4581 ARPTS,FLY FLDS,SVCS (NO BREAKDOWN) 2014 (17 Establishments)		SIC 47 TRANSPORTATION SVS (NO BREAKDOWN) 2014 (152 Establishments)	
	$	%	$	%	$	%	$	%
Cash	5,157,787	15.4	1,522,830	24.5	2,508,327	17.1	494,797	18.5
Accounts Receivable	4,286,991	12.8	963,423	15.5	2,185,618	14.9	1,136,696	42.5
Notes Receivable	0	0.0	0	0.0	14,669	0.1	8,024	0.3
Inventory	1,272,701	3.8	198,900	3.2	704,092	4.8	34,770	1.3
Other Current	3,114,767	9.3	540,761	8.7	997,463	6.8	323,624	12.1
Total Current	**13,832,246**	**41.3**	**3,225,914**	**51.9**	**6,410,169**	**43.7**	**1,997,911**	**74.7**
Fixed Assets	15,540,344	46.4	2,243,844	36.1	7,422,301	50.6	425,258	15.9
Other Non-current	4,119,531	12.3	745,875	12.0	836,109	5.7	251,410	9.4
Total Assets	**33,492,121**	**100.0**	**6,215,633**	**100.0**	**14,668,579**	**100.0**	**2,674,579**	**100.0**
Accounts Payable	7,401,759	22.1	478,604	7.7	762,766	5.2	628,526	23.5
Bank Loans	0	0.0	0	0.0	0	0.0	0	0.0
Notes Payable	301,429	0.9	149,175	2.4	102,680	0.7	56,166	2.1
Other Current	51,276,437	153.1	1,255,558	20.2	6,982,244	47.6	989,594	37.0
Total Current	**58,979,625**	**176.1**	**1,883,337**	**30.3**	**7,847,690**	**53.5**	**1,674,286**	**62.6**
Other Long Term	8,808,428	26.3	1,690,652	27.2	1,892,246	12.9	278,157	10.4
Deferred Credits	200,953	0.6	0	0.0	44,006	0.3	10,698	0.4
Net Worth	(34,496,885)	(103.0)	2,641,644	42.5	4,884,637	33.3	711,438	26.6
Total Liab & Net Worth	**33,492,121**	**100.0**	**6,215,633**	**100.0**	**14,668,579**	**100.0**	**2,674,579**	**100.0**
Net Sales	34,175,634	100.0	16,487,090	100.0	16,631,042	100.0	12,920,671	100.0
Gross Profit	12,166,526	35.6	5,688,046	34.5	6,070,330	36.5	3,527,343	27.3
Net Profit After Tax	2,802,402	8.2	544,074	3.3	2,145,404	12.9	555,589	4.3
Working Capital	(45,147,379)	---	1,342,577	---	(1,437,521)	---	323,625	---

RATIOS	UQ	MED	LQ	UQ	MED	LQ	UQ	MED	LQ	UQ	MED	LQ
SOLVENCY												
Quick Ratio (times)	1.8	1.0	0.3	1.8	1.1	0.7	5.2	1.8	1.1	2.6	1.4	1.0
Current Ratio (times)	3.3	1.6	0.8	2.7	1.6	1.3	7.3	3.7	1.9	3.3	1.8	1.1
Curr Liab To Nw (%)	12.4	44.5	112.8	42.6	65.5	100.9	3.1	11.9	34.0	27.5	77.0	183.7
Curr Liab To Inv (%)	354.0	999.9	999.9	354.0	817.3	999.9	136.1	507.0	999.9	419.0	999.9	999.9
Total Liab To Nw (%)	36.0	104.3	205.0	93.5	125.4	189.3	11.4	21.9	81.4	37.9	107.4	238.0
Fixed Assets To Nw (%)	41.6	100.6	206.6	44.4	92.9	166.6	18.1	77.7	110.1	5.6	17.9	47.2
EFFICIENCY												
Coll Period (days)	7.5	16.3	35.8	6.4	31.1	43.5	7.1	17.9	39.3	24.5	41.3	55.5
Sales To Inv (times)	70.3	56.3	30.5	62.8	58.7	30.5	102.7	33.4	18.3	396.2	137.8	29.2
Assets To Sales (%)	36.8	98.0	155.2	27.3	37.7	122.9	28.6	88.2	891.4	12.5	20.7	41.3
Sales To Nwc (times)	14.5	6.4	3.0	14.8	8.8	6.3	11.0	3.0	1.1	31.6	11.8	5.6
Acct Pay To Sales (%)	1.2	4.7	6.5	1.2	5.4	5.4	1.4	4.9	14.1	2.4	4.8	7.9
PROFITABILITY												
Return On Sales (%)	8.0	3.3	1.6	5.7	1.7	0.7	22.7	3.4	0.6	5.7	2.1	0.6
Return On Assets (%)	7.0	3.9	2.0	6.5	3.0	1.4	8.8	3.5	0.3	22.3	7.7	1.8
Return On Nw (%)	22.5	8.3	4.1	10.7	7.8	3.1	16.5	4.6	2.0	51.1	22.8	6.6

	SIC 4724 TRAVEL AGENCIES (NO BREAKDOWN) 2014 (17 Establishments) $	%	SIC 4731 FRGT TRANS ARNGMNT (NO BREAKDOWN) 2014 (105 Establishments) $	%	SIC 4789 TRANS SRVCS, NEC (NO BREAKDOWN) 2014 (14 Establishments) $	%	SIC 48 COMMUNICATION (NO BREAKDOWN) 2014 (201 Establishments) $	%
Cash	5,357,422	30.4	427,078	16.6	184,841	13.8	10,360,966	15.4
Accounts Receivable	1,533,210	8.7	1,317,253	51.2	360,306	26.9	9,149,944	13.6
Notes Receivable	52,869	0.3	10,291	0.4	0	0.0	538,232	0.8
Inventory	35,246	0.2	25,728	1.0	16,073	1.2	2,220,207	3.3
Other Current	2,255,757	12.8	298,440	11.6	156,713	11.7	5,315,041	7.9
Total Current	**9,234,504**	**52.4**	**2,078,790**	**80.8**	**717,933**	**53.6**	**27,584,390**	**41.0**
Fixed Assets	1,938,541	11.0	342,177	13.3	507,643	37.9	19,578,189	29.1
Other Non-current	6,450,055	36.6	151,793	5.9	113,851	8.5	20,116,421	29.9
Total Assets	**17,623,100**	**100.0**	**2,572,760**	**100.0**	**1,339,427**	**100.0**	**67,279,000**	**100.0**
Accounts Payable	1,850,426	10.5	689,500	26.8	200,914	15.0	14,868,659	22.1
Bank Loans	0	0.0	0	0.0	0	0.0	67,279	0.1
Notes Payable	370,085	2.1	59,173	2.3	20,091	1.5	1,816,533	2.7
Other Current	6,573,416	37.3	885,030	34.4	269,225	20.1	57,658,103	85.7
Total Current	**8,793,927**	**49.9**	**1,633,703**	**63.5**	**490,230**	**36.6**	**74,410,574**	**110.6**
Other Long Term	5,956,608	33.8	192,957	7.5	30,807	2.3	23,345,813	34.7
Deferred Credits	0	0.0	0	0.0	12,055	0.9	1,143,743	1.7
Net Worth	2,872,565	16.3	746,100	29.0	806,335	60.2	(31,621,130)	(47.0)
Total Liab & Net Worth	**17,623,100**	**100.0**	**2,572,760**	**100.0**	**1,339,427**	**100.0**	**67,279,000**	**100.0**
Net Sales	20,326,528	100.0	13,399,792	100.0	4,525,091	100.0	40,602,897	100.0
Gross Profit	9,878,693	48.6	2,787,157	20.8	2,217,295	49.0	19,367,582	47.7
Net Profit After Tax	1,361,877	6.7	468,993	3.5	4,525	0.1	1,258,690	3.1
Working Capital	440,577	---	445,087	---	227,703	---	(46,826,184)	---

RATIOS	UQ	MED	LQ	UQ	MED	LQ	UQ	MED	LQ	UQ	MED	LQ
SOLVENCY												
Quick Ratio (times)	2.7	1.2	0.5	2.5	1.4	1.1	2.6	0.9	0.4	1.8	1.1	0.4
Current Ratio (times)	3.0	1.7	0.9	3.2	1.7	1.2	2.8	1.5	0.6	2.9	1.5	0.8
Curr Liab To Nw (%)	26.9	74.9	266.6	33.8	93.9	193.2	27.5	33.3	39.2	17.3	36.7	71.6
Curr Liab To Inv (%)	999.9	999.9	999.9	428.3	999.9	999.9	175.3	587.6	999.9	316.9	766.5	999.9
Total Liab To Nw (%)	62.0	124.7	358.9	39.2	108.0	207.0	32.3	44.4	113.9	42.8	107.7	261.7
Fixed Assets To Nw (%)	7.8	23.3	75.0	4.5	12.0	39.4	38.6	48.6	115.7	14.2	58.4	121.9
EFFICIENCY												
Coll Period (days)	0.6	22.8	47.7	26.9	41.6	55.9	35.0	55.1	60.2	20.8	38.6	65.0
Sales To Inv (times)	999.9	607.8	215.7	396.2	135.5	29.2	156.5	83.6	10.6	77.2	28.5	13.8
Assets To Sales (%)	6.2	86.7	177.0	11.0	19.2	33.9	21.4	29.6	209.2	59.3	165.7	272.4
Sales To Nwc (times)	56.0	4.9	2.8	34.1	13.3	7.6	10.0	5.8	3.9	9.4	4.4	2.1
Acct Pay To Sales (%)	1.1	3.3	6.7	2.7	5.5	8.6	3.4	5.1	7.1	2.4	5.3	10.1
PROFITABILITY												
Return On Sales (%)	11.8	1.9	0.2	4.7	2.1	0.7	4.7	(0.4)	(4.8)	10.4	3.0	(5.1)
Return On Assets (%)	25.1	4.9	1.5	22.3	7.9	3.0	11.6	(0.9)	(16.4)	7.4	2.9	(4.2)
Return On Nw (%)	50.8	31.4	20.0	49.3	22.0	7.6	22.5	0.1	(14.4)	21.4	7.5	(1.5)

	SIC 4812 RDIO TELPHON COMM (NO BREAKDOWN) 2014 (14 Establishments) $	%	SIC 4813 TEL COMM.EXC RDIO (NO BREAKDOWN) 2014 (114 Establishments) $	%	SIC 4832 RAD BRDCSTG STNS (NO BREAKDOWN) 2014 (15 Establishments) $	%	SIC 4899 COMMNCTN SVCS.NEC (NO BREAKDOWN) 2014 (17 Establishments) $	%
Cash	664,085	11.0	6,041,637	14.9	27,108,780	6.0	4,975,520	22.0
Accounts Receivable	1,316,096	21.8	5,757,802	14.2	39,307,731	8.7	4,930,288	21.8
Notes Receivable	0	0.0	567,671	1.4	0	0.0	0	0.0
Inventory	682,196	11.3	892,054	2.2	0	0.0	1,515,272	6.7
Other Current	301,857	5.0	3,162,735	7.8	45,181,300	10.0	2,058,056	9.1
Total Current	**2,964,234**	**49.1**	**16,421,899**	**40.5**	**111,597,811**	**24.7**	**13,479,136**	**59.6**
Fixed Assets	1,992,255	33.0	13,421,354	33.1	78,163,649	17.3	5,269,528	23.3
Other Non-current	1,080,648	17.9	10,704,645	26.4	262,051,540	58.0	3,867,336	17.1
Total Assets	**6,037,137**	**100.0**	**40,547,898**	**100.0**	**451,813,000**	**100.0**	**22,616,000**	**100.0**
Accounts Payable	1,014,239	16.8	7,541,909	18.6	36,145,040	8.0	20,377,016	90.1
Bank Loans	0	0.0	121,644	0.3	0	0.0	0	0.0
Notes Payable	368,265	6.1	1,500,272	3.7	4,066,317	0.9	0	0.0
Other Current	2,372,595	39.3	20,476,688	50.5	90,362,600	20.0	28,270,000	125.0
Total Current	**3,755,099**	**62.2**	**29,640,513**	**73.1**	**130,573,957**	**28.9**	**48,647,016**	**215.1**
Other Long Term	1,110,833	18.4	13,015,876	32.1	228,617,378	50.6	7,101,424	31.4
Deferred Credits	0	0.0	1,013,697	2.5	451,813	0.1	452,320	2.0
Net Worth	1,171,205	19.4	(3,122,188)	(7.7)	92,169,852	20.4	(33,584,760)	(148.5)
Total Liab & Net Worth	**6,037,137**	**100.0**	**40,547,898**	**100.0**	**451,813,000**	**100.0**	**22,616,000**	**100.0**
Net Sales	9,816,483	100.0	22,639,809	100.0	203,336,184	100.0	33,604,755	100.0
Gross Profit	4,780,627	48.7	10,323,753	45.6	106,548,160	52.4	14,987,721	44.6
Net Profit After Tax	78,532	0.8	362,237	1.6	18,300,257	9.0	(672,095)	(2.0)
Working Capital	(790,865)	---	(13,218,614)	---	(18,976,146)	---	(35,167,880)	---

RATIOS	UQ	MED	LQ	UQ	MED	LQ	UQ	MED	LQ	UQ	MED	LQ
SOLVENCY												
Quick Ratio (times)	2.5	1.0	0.5	1.7	1.0	0.4	2.3	1.5	0.4	2.8	1.6	0.8
Current Ratio (times)	3.1	2.0	1.0	2.9	1.3	0.8	2.5	1.6	0.7	3.1	1.9	1.5
Curr Liab To Nw (%)	18.0	23.9	41.5	16.7	37.4	78.5	16.7	27.0	45.1	11.2	38.7	66.4
Curr Liab To Inv (%)	148.8	318.9	605.9	378.6	808.8	999.9	999.9	999.9	999.9	179.6	610.5	999.9
Total Liab To Nw (%)	31.4	40.3	80.0	45.1	124.9	281.3	53.9	158.8	528.5	45.3	77.1	128.7
Fixed Assets To Nw (%)	34.3	80.9	93.5	14.4	79.0	157.1	17.8	39.8	50.9	15.3	29.6	58.5
EFFICIENCY												
Coll Period (days)	40.9	45.3	62.4	17.2	32.5	51.8	56.2	63.2	80.3	23.7	43.1	78.5
Sales To Inv (times)	38.1	16.5	6.9	79.4	34.8	17.9	231.3	223.5	215.6	50.7	23.6	10.6
Assets To Sales (%)	43.5	61.5	166.7	49.7	179.1	302.6	132.4	222.2	312.9	31.7	67.3	237.3
Sales To Nwc (times)	7.3	5.3	2.4	15.2	4.4	1.7	9.3	5.9	3.2	12.8	4.5	2.8
Acct Pay To Sales (%)	1.4	4.6	13.6	2.9	5.4	9.8	1.7	2.1	11.7	2.2	3.6	8.5
PROFITABILITY												
Return On Sales (%)	6.5	0.2	(6.7)	7.7	2.5	(9.1)	11.7	1.8	(7.1)	5.6	0.2	(6.7)
Return On Assets (%)	14.2	1.8	(4.5)	7.3	2.2	(4.4)	7.8	1.5	(3.6)	8.5	0.2	(7.3)
Return On Nw (%)	18.6	7.4	(5.2)	19.6	5.3	(3.5)	34.2	11.4	(1.6)	20.3	7.7	(0.9)

SIC 49 — ELEC,GAS,SANITARY SV (NO BREAKDOWN) 2014 (464 Establishments)

	$	%
Cash	13,991,224	5.9
Accounts Receivable	13,754,084	5.8
Notes Receivable	237,139	0.1
Inventory	4,742,788	2.0
Other Current	13,042,666	5.5
Total Current	**45,767,901**	**19.3**
Fixed Assets	154,377,738	65.1
Other Non-current	36,993,743	15.6
Total Assets	**237,139,382**	**100.0**
Accounts Payable	22,053,963	9.3
Bank Loans	0	0.0
Notes Payable	4,742,788	2.0
Other Current	38,416,579	16.2
Total Current	**65,213,330**	**27.5**
Other Long Term	99,598,541	42.0
Deferred Credits	3,319,951	1.4
Net Worth	69,007,560	29.1
Total Liab & Net Worth	**237,139,382**	**100.0**
Net Sales	85,301,936	100.0
Gross Profit	37,106,342	43.5
Net Profit After Tax	6,653,551	7.8
Working Capital	(19,445,429)	—

RATIOS	UQ	MED	LQ
SOLVENCY			
Quick Ratio (times)	1.3	0.6	0.4
Current Ratio (times)	2.1	1.3	0.9
Curr Liab To Nw (%)	11.9	23.7	39.0
Curr Liab To Inv (%)	382.5	720.3	999.9
Total Liab To Nw (%)	71.1	153.6	231.1
Fixed Assets To Nw (%)	108.6	174.7	240.0
EFFICIENCY			
Coll Period (days)	24.5	33.2	44.5
Sales To Inv (times)	54.3	27.6	14.0
Assets To Sales (%)	188.7	278.0	408.7
Sales To Nwc (times)	17.0	7.7	3.2
Acct Pay To Sales (%)	5.2	7.4	10.1
PROFITABILITY			
Return On Sales (%)	11.1	7.7	3.9
Return On Assets (%)	3.8	2.7	1.5
Return On Nw (%)	10.7	7.5	3.9

SIC 4911 — ELECTRIC SERVICES (NO BREAKDOWN) 2014 (244 Establishments)

	$	%
Cash	11,130,081	4.4
Accounts Receivable	11,888,950	4.7
Notes Receivable	252,956	0.1
Inventory	4,553,215	1.8
Other Current	12,900,777	5.1
Total Current	**40,725,979**	**16.1**
Fixed Assets	171,251,478	67.7
Other Non-current	40,978,936	16.2
Total Assets	**252,956,393**	**100.0**
Accounts Payable	26,813,378	10.6
Bank Loans	0	0.0
Notes Payable	4,300,259	1.7
Other Current	32,125,461	12.7
Total Current	**63,239,098**	**25.0**
Other Long Term	123,695,676	48.9
Deferred Credits	3,035,477	1.2
Net Worth	62,986,142	24.9
Total Liab & Net Worth	**252,956,393**	**100.0**
Net Sales	96,364,340	100.0
Gross Profit	40,376,658	41.9
Net Profit After Tax	6,841,868	7.1
Working Capital	(22,513,119)	—

RATIOS	UQ	MED	LQ
SOLVENCY			
Quick Ratio (times)	0.9	0.6	0.3
Current Ratio (times)	1.7	1.2	0.8
Curr Liab To Nw (%)	17.7	25.8	36.5
Curr Liab To Inv (%)	381.4	708.6	999.9
Total Liab To Nw (%)	118.3	175.2	244.0
Fixed Assets To Nw (%)	143.0	191.9	250.6
EFFICIENCY			
Coll Period (days)	24.1	33.1	42.0
Sales To Inv (times)	56.1	24.4	13.7
Assets To Sales (%)	197.6	262.5	356.1
Sales To Nwc (times)	20.7	11.7	4.7
Acct Pay To Sales (%)	6.0	7.6	9.8
PROFITABILITY			
Return On Sales (%)	10.6	7.5	4.5
Return On Assets (%)	3.6	2.7	1.9
Return On Nw (%)	10.4	7.7	5.2

SIC 4924 — NTRL GAS DIST (NO BREAKDOWN) 2014 (27 Establishments)

	$	%
Cash	54,268,140	6.0
Accounts Receivable	79,593,272	8.8
Notes Receivable	904,469	0.1
Inventory	25,325,132	2.8
Other Current	70,548,582	7.8
Total Current	**230,639,595**	**25.5**
Fixed Assets	541,776,931	59.9
Other Non-current	132,052,474	14.6
Total Assets	**904,469,000**	**100.0**
Accounts Payable	52,459,202	5.8
Bank Loans	0	0.0
Notes Payable	6,331,283	0.7
Other Current	107,631,811	11.9
Total Current	**166,422,296**	**18.4**
Other Long Term	259,582,603	28.7
Deferred Credits	67,835,175	7.5
Net Worth	410,628,926	45.4
Total Liab & Net Worth	**904,469,000**	**100.0**
Net Sales	487,059,235	100.0
Gross Profit	194,823,694	40.0
Net Profit After Tax	27,762,376	5.7
Working Capital	64,217,299	—

RATIOS	UQ	MED	LQ
SOLVENCY			
Quick Ratio (times)	1.2	0.4	0.2
Current Ratio (times)	2.2	1.0	0.8
Curr Liab To Nw (%)	23.1	47.5	64.2
Curr Liab To Inv (%)	299.5	603.1	999.9
Total Liab To Nw (%)	85.0	178.5	266.7
Fixed Assets To Nw (%)	78.1	173.5	249.1
EFFICIENCY			
Coll Period (days)	25.2	31.3	38.7
Sales To Inv (times)	30.6	17.4	11.4
Assets To Sales (%)	145.0	185.7	271.0
Sales To Nwc (times)	28.1	5.0	3.2
Acct Pay To Sales (%)	6.2	8.3	11.1
PROFITABILITY			
Return On Sales (%)	8.6	6.4	4.5
Return On Assets (%)	4.2	3.3	2.5
Return On Nw (%)	12.2	9.1	6.2

SIC 4941 — WATER SUPPLY (NO BREAKDOWN) 2014 (54 Establishments)

	$	%
Cash	6,710,999	9.0
Accounts Receivable	1,342,200	1.8
Notes Receivable	0	0.0
Inventory	298,267	0.4
Other Current	3,131,799	4.2
Total Current	**11,483,265**	**15.4**
Fixed Assets	54,955,623	73.7
Other Non-current	8,127,765	10.9
Total Assets	**74,566,653**	**100.0**
Accounts Payable	1,043,933	1.4
Bank Loans	0	0.0
Notes Payable	74,567	0.1
Other Current	2,311,566	3.1
Total Current	**3,430,066**	**4.6**
Other Long Term	26,993,128	36.2
Deferred Credits	74,567	0.1
Net Worth	44,068,892	59.1
Total Liab & Net Worth	**74,566,653**	**100.0**
Net Sales	11,335,764	100.0
Gross Profit	8,003,049	70.6
Net Profit After Tax	1,496,321	13.2
Working Capital	8,053,199	—

RATIOS	UQ	MED	LQ
SOLVENCY			
Quick Ratio (times)	3.1	1.3	0.8
Current Ratio (times)	5.7	2.3	1.6
Curr Liab To Nw (%)	3.9	6.2	13.6
Curr Liab To Inv (%)	607.4	999.9	999.9
Total Liab To Nw (%)	20.5	65.6	186.3
Fixed Assets To Nw (%)	100.6	133.3	204.3
EFFICIENCY			
Coll Period (days)	27.0	36.5	51.8
Sales To Inv (times)	59.5	42.1	31.4
Assets To Sales (%)	402.8	657.8	885.9
Sales To Nwc (times)	5.8	3.0	1.3
Acct Pay To Sales (%)	2.4	5.8	10.3
PROFITABILITY			
Return On Sales (%)	18.3	12.2	4.2
Return On Assets (%)	3.8	1.7	0.6
Return On Nw (%)	8.9	2.7	1.2

SIC 4952 SEWERAGE SYSTEMS (NO BREAKDOWN) 2014 (20 Establishments)

	$	%
Cash	6,623,565	8.3
Accounts Receivable	1,117,228	1.4
Notes Receivable	0	0.0
Inventory	159,604	0.2
Other Current	6,064,951	7.6
Total Current	**13,965,348**	**17.5**
Fixed Assets	60,090,895	75.3
Other Non-current	5,745,743	7.2
Total Assets	**79,801,986**	**100.0**
Accounts Payable	1,516,238	1.9
Bank Loans	0	0.0
Notes Payable	1,276,832	1.6
Other Current	3,271,881	4.1
Total Current	**6,064,951**	**7.6**
Other Long Term	25,297,229	31.7
Deferred Credits	0	0.0
Net Worth	48,439,806	60.7
Total Liab & Net Worth	**79,801,986**	**100.0**
Net Sales	10,749,190	100.0
Gross Profit	3,869,708	36.0
Net Profit After Tax	1,300,652	12.1
Working Capital	7,900,397	—

RATIOS	UQ	MED	LQ
SOLVENCY			
Quick Ratio (times)	4.3	1.6	0.8
Current Ratio (times)	6.3	2.4	1.4
Curr Liab To Nw (%)	3.9	6.1	9.8
Curr Liab To Inv (%)	952.3	999.9	999.9
Total Liab To Nw (%)	31.6	67.7	119.7
Fixed Assets To Nw (%)	102.7	138.1	152.6
EFFICIENCY			
Coll Period (days)	23.4	32.0	38.7
Sales To Inv (times)	121.6	72.4	40.9
Assets To Sales (%)	553.7	742.4	999.9
Sales To Nwc (times)	7.5	1.7	1.1
Acct Pay To Sales (%)	2.3	3.5	8.1
PROFITABILITY			
Return On Sales (%)	16.6	12.4	5.7
Return On Assets (%)	2.8	1.9	0.9
Return On Nw (%)	4.4	2.8	1.5

SIC 4953 REFUSE SYSTEMS (NO BREAKDOWN) 2014 (29 Establishments)

	$	%
Cash	4,939,260	11.5
Accounts Receivable	7,086,764	16.5
Notes Receivable	85,900	0.2
Inventory	2,018,654	4.7
Other Current	3,221,257	7.5
Total Current	**17,351,835**	**40.4**
Fixed Assets	13,314,527	31.0
Other Non-current	12,283,724	28.6
Total Assets	**42,950,086**	**100.0**
Accounts Payable	15,161,380	35.3
Bank Loans	0	0.0
Notes Payable	6,442,513	15.0
Other Current	44,882,840	104.5
Total Current	**66,486,733**	**154.8**
Other Long Term	13,744,028	32.0
Deferred Credits	42,950	0.1
Net Worth	(37,323,625)	(86.9)
Total Liab & Net Worth	**42,950,086**	**100.0**
Net Sales	32,886,743	100.0
Gross Profit	11,576,134	35.2
Net Profit After Tax	(822,169)	(2.5)
Working Capital	(49,134,898)	—

RATIOS	UQ	MED	LQ
Quick Ratio (times)	1.5	1.0	0.6
Current Ratio (times)	2.0	1.3	0.8
Curr Liab To Nw (%)	23.9	40.6	61.8
Curr Liab To Inv (%)	339.4	999.9	999.9
Total Liab To Nw (%)	42.0	141.9	264.8
Fixed Assets To Nw (%)	17.6	85.5	120.2
Coll Period (days)	32.9	45.6	61.7
Sales To Inv (times)	121.0	58.6	19.6
Assets To Sales (%)	48.9	130.6	218.2
Sales To Nwc (times)	33.1	12.9	5.9
Acct Pay To Sales (%)	5.8	7.7	12.5
Return On Sales (%)	7.4	(0.1)	(5.5)
Return On Assets (%)	5.0	(0.3)	(3.6)
Return On Nw (%)	15.2	3.7	(2.9)

SIC 4959 SANITARY SVCS,NEC (NO BREAKDOWN) 2014 (13 Establishments)

	$	%
Cash	881,877	20.4
Accounts Receivable	1,193,128	27.6
Notes Receivable	0	0.0
Inventory	363,126	8.4
Other Current	350,157	8.1
Total Current	**2,788,288**	**64.5**
Fixed Assets	1,288,232	29.8
Other Non-current	246,407	5.7
Total Assets	**4,322,927**	**100.0**
Accounts Payable	440,939	10.2
Bank Loans	30,260	0.7
Notes Payable	8,646	0.2
Other Current	782,450	18.1
Total Current	**1,262,295**	**29.2**
Other Long Term	393,386	9.1
Deferred Credits	0	0.0
Net Worth	2,667,246	61.7
Total Liab & Net Worth	**4,322,927**	**100.0**
Net Sales	9,276,667	100.0
Gross Profit	3,450,920	37.2
Net Profit After Tax	732,857	7.9
Working Capital	1,525,993	—

RATIOS	UQ	MED	LQ
Quick Ratio (times)	4.6	2.3	1.1
Current Ratio (times)	5.0	3.2	1.7
Curr Liab To Nw (%)	14.8	37.2	70.5
Curr Liab To Inv (%)	124.9	252.7	565.8
Total Liab To Nw (%)	15.7	56.9	162.9
Fixed Assets To Nw (%)	23.1	48.2	62.5
Coll Period (days)	31.0	39.8	65.3
Sales To Inv (times)	115.5	19.3	6.2
Assets To Sales (%)	31.2	46.6	73.4
Sales To Nwc (times)	13.1	7.9	4.9
Acct Pay To Sales (%)	1.3	6.7	8.8
Return On Sales (%)	11.1	8.4	4.4
Return On Assets (%)	25.4	15.2	6.1
Return On Nw (%)	53.2	23.2	19.4

SIC 50 WHOLESALE TRADE (NO BREAKDOWN) 2014 (1765 Establishments)

	$	%
Cash	531,491	14.5
Accounts Receivable	1,026,327	28.0
Notes Receivable	14,662	0.4
Inventory	1,249,920	34.1
Other Current	227,259	6.2
Total Current	**3,049,659**	**83.2**
Fixed Assets	384,873	10.5
Other Non-current	230,923	6.3
Total Assets	**3,665,455**	**100.0**
Accounts Payable	912,698	24.9
Bank Loans	21,993	0.6
Notes Payable	124,625	3.4
Other Current	1,125,295	30.7
Total Current	**2,184,611**	**59.6**
Other Long Term	318,895	8.7
Deferred Credits	3,665	0.1
Net Worth	1,158,284	31.6
Total Liab & Net Worth	**3,665,455**	**100.0**
Net Sales	9,826,957	100.0
Gross Profit	2,790,856	28.4
Net Profit After Tax	294,809	3.0
Working Capital	865,048	—

RATIOS	UQ	MED	LQ
Quick Ratio (times)	2.1	1.1	0.6
Current Ratio (times)	4.1	2.1	1.4
Curr Liab To Nw (%)	26.1	69.9	161.9
Curr Liab To Inv (%)	55.8	102.2	204.1
Total Liab To Nw (%)	33.5	90.8	203.3
Fixed Assets To Nw (%)	5.1	14.0	31.4
Coll Period (days)	22.8	34.7	50.0
Sales To Inv (times)	16.5	8.1	4.6
Assets To Sales (%)	26.2	37.3	53.9
Sales To Nwc (times)	11.9	6.4	3.6
Acct Pay To Sales (%)	2.8	5.3	8.8
Return On Sales (%)	4.9	2.0	0.5
Return On Assets (%)	12.5	5.1	1.5
Return On Nw (%)	27.1	11.2	3.7

SIC 5012 AUTO,OTHR MTR VHCLS (NO BREAKDOWN) 2014 (30 Establishments)

	$	%
Cash	640,278	15.2
Accounts Receivable	636,065	15.1
Notes Receivable	16,849	0.4
Inventory	1,786,037	42.4
Other Current	235,892	5.6
Total Current	**3,315,121**	**78.7**
Fixed Assets	534,969	12.7
Other Non-current	362,262	8.6
Total Assets	**4,212,352**	**100.0**
Accounts Payable	471,783	11.2
Bank Loans	96,884	2.3
Notes Payable	328,563	7.8
Other Current	1,069,938	25.4
Total Current	**1,967,168**	**46.7**
Other Long Term	273,803	6.5
Deferred Credits	0	0.0
Net Worth	1,971,381	46.8
Total Liab & Net Worth	**4,212,352**	**100.0**
Net Sales	11,799,305	100.0
Gross Profit	3,327,404	28.2
Net Profit After Tax	165,190	1.4
Working Capital	1,347,953	---

RATIOS	UQ	MED	LQ
SOLVENCY			
Quick Ratio (times)	1.4	0.5	0.3
Current Ratio (times)	2.7	1.7	1.2
Curr Liab To Nw (%)	35.2	103.7	191.5
Curr Liab To Inv (%)	53.4	102.4	133.7
Total Liab To Nw (%)	50.2	132.4	252.5
Fixed Assets To Nw (%)	10.6	18.4	55.4
EFFICIENCY			
Coll Period (days)	9.5	14.6	23.6
Sales To Inv (times)	10.1	6.0	4.2
Assets To Sales (%)	28.7	35.7	53.1
Sales To Nwc (times)	15.8	7.2	4.8
Acct Pay To Sales (%)	1.7	3.0	6.2
PROFITABILITY			
Return On Sales (%)	4.5	1.4	0.8
Return On Assets (%)	12.6	3.2	2.3
Return On Nw (%)	27.5	14.0	6.7

SIC 5013 MTR VHCL SPLS, PRTS (NO BREAKDOWN) 2014 (50 Establishments)

	$	%
Cash	724,862	13.1
Accounts Receivable	1,272,659	23.0
Notes Receivable	0	0.0
Inventory	2,412,518	43.6
Other Current	265,598	4.8
Total Current	**4,675,637**	**84.5**
Fixed Assets	564,396	10.2
Other Non-current	293,265	5.3
Total Assets	**5,533,298**	**100.0**
Accounts Payable	1,001,527	18.1
Bank Loans	0	0.0
Notes Payable	44,266	0.8
Other Current	1,029,194	18.6
Total Current	**2,074,987**	**37.5**
Other Long Term	453,730	8.2
Deferred Credits	5,533	0.1
Net Worth	2,999,048	54.2
Total Liab & Net Worth	**5,533,298**	**100.0**
Net Sales	13,463,012	100.0
Gross Profit	3,621,550	26.9
Net Profit After Tax	417,353	3.1
Working Capital	2,600,650	---

RATIOS	UQ	MED	LQ
SOLVENCY			
Quick Ratio (times)	1.6	0.8	0.5
Current Ratio (times)	4.2	2.2	1.6
Curr Liab To Nw (%)	34.3	62.1	122.5
Curr Liab To Inv (%)	45.2	75.5	125.6
Total Liab To Nw (%)	41.2	76.4	149.0
Fixed Assets To Nw (%)	5.2	14.1	20.9
EFFICIENCY			
Coll Period (days)	23.0	29.6	38.0
Sales To Inv (times)	8.6	6.0	3.7
Assets To Sales (%)	30.6	41.1	62.9
Sales To Nwc (times)	8.6	5.5	3.4
Acct Pay To Sales (%)	4.7	6.2	10.2
PROFITABILITY			
Return On Sales (%)	4.6	2.0	0.9
Return On Assets (%)	12.3	5.1	2.2
Return On Nw (%)	22.2	9.4	3.5

SIC 5014 TIRES AND TUBES (NO BREAKDOWN) 2014 (16 Establishments)

	$	%
Cash	474,657	8.5
Accounts Receivable	1,211,771	21.7
Notes Receivable	39,089	0.7
Inventory	2,591,068	46.4
Other Current	150,773	2.7
Total Current	**4,467,358**	**80.0**
Fixed Assets	720,362	12.9
Other Non-current	396,478	7.1
Total Assets	**5,584,198**	**100.0**
Accounts Payable	1,920,964	34.4
Bank Loans	0	0.0
Notes Payable	167,526	3.0
Other Current	642,183	11.5
Total Current	**2,730,673**	**48.9**
Other Long Term	491,409	8.8
Deferred Credits	55,842	1.0
Net Worth	2,306,274	41.3
Total Liab & Net Worth	**5,584,198**	**100.0**
Net Sales	16,375,947	100.0
Gross Profit	4,126,739	25.2
Net Profit After Tax	327,519	2.0
Working Capital	1,736,685	---

RATIOS	UQ	MED	LQ
SOLVENCY			
Quick Ratio (times)	0.9	0.5	0.4
Current Ratio (times)	2.1	1.6	1.3
Curr Liab To Nw (%)	45.1	112.8	189.1
Curr Liab To Inv (%)	84.1	107.3	132.6
Total Liab To Nw (%)	47.1	126.0	232.9
Fixed Assets To Nw (%)	25.4	29.8	41.1
EFFICIENCY			
Coll Period (days)	23.0	29.0	34.0
Sales To Inv (times)	8.8	7.6	5.6
Assets To Sales (%)	25.7	34.1	38.1
Sales To Nwc (times)	12.7	9.4	7.4
Acct Pay To Sales (%)	7.0	10.6	13.7
PROFITABILITY			
Return On Sales (%)	2.7	0.9	0.5
Return On Assets (%)	7.8	3.3	1.7
Return On Nw (%)	17.4	11.1	4.4

SIC 5021 FURNITURE (NO BREAKDOWN) 2014 (67 Establishments)

	$	%
Cash	441,499	13.7
Accounts Receivable	1,182,702	36.7
Notes Receivable	12,890	0.4
Inventory	857,217	26.6
Other Current	293,258	9.1
Total Current	**2,787,566**	**86.5**
Fixed Assets	286,813	8.9
Other Non-current	148,241	4.6
Total Assets	**3,222,620**	**100.0**
Accounts Payable	728,312	22.6
Bank Loans	22,558	0.7
Notes Payable	54,785	1.7
Other Current	844,326	26.2
Total Current	**1,649,981**	**51.2**
Other Long Term	(106,346)	(3.3)
Deferred Credits	3,223	0.1
Net Worth	1,675,762	52.0
Total Liab & Net Worth	**3,222,620**	**100.0**
Net Sales	12,442,548	100.0
Gross Profit	3,508,799	28.2
Net Profit After Tax	472,817	3.8
Working Capital	1,137,585	---

RATIOS	UQ	MED	LQ
SOLVENCY			
Quick Ratio (times)	1.5	0.9	0.6
Current Ratio (times)	2.3	1.6	1.3
Curr Liab To Nw (%)	45.8	115.2	260.3
Curr Liab To Inv (%)	85.4	174.3	610.8
Total Liab To Nw (%)	67.2	132.8	285.6
Fixed Assets To Nw (%)	4.5	19.3	39.1
EFFICIENCY			
Coll Period (days)	21.5	37.2	54.0
Sales To Inv (times)	38.1	14.9	8.6
Assets To Sales (%)	18.4	25.9	39.9
Sales To Nwc (times)	23.9	12.1	6.5
Acct Pay To Sales (%)	2.5	5.2	10.2
PROFITABILITY			
Return On Sales (%)	4.4	1.7	0.6
Return On Assets (%)	20.3	7.0	2.6
Return On Nw (%)	40.7	19.3	6.1

SIC 5023 HOMEFURNISHINGS (NO BREAKDOWN) 2014 (49 Establishments)

	$	%
Cash	316,707	14.4
Accounts Receivable	738,983	33.6
Notes Receivable	0	0.0
Inventory	741,182	33.7
Other Current	112,166	5.1
Total Current	**1,909,038**	**86.8**
Fixed Assets	241,929	11.0
Other Non-current	48,386	2.2
Total Assets	**2,199,353**	**100.0**
Accounts Payable	422,276	19.2
Bank Loans	19,794	0.9
Notes Payable	59,383	2.7
Other Current	837,953	38.1
Total Current	**1,339,406**	**60.9**
Other Long Term	151,755	6.9
Deferred Credits	0	0.0
Net Worth	708,192	32.2
Total Liab & Net Worth	**2,199,353**	**100.0**
Net Sales	6,356,512	100.0
Gross Profit	1,792,536	28.2
Net Profit After Tax	222,478	3.5
Working Capital	569,632	---

RATIOS	UQ	MED	LQ
SOLVENCY			
Quick Ratio (times)	2.9	1.1	0.5
Current Ratio (times)	5.7	2.1	1.4
Curr Liab To Nw (%)	19.5	93.4	175.5
Curr Liab To Inv (%)	58.3	103.2	187.2
Total Liab To Nw (%)	25.3	105.5	206.4
Fixed Assets To Nw (%)	4.9	14.1	35.1
EFFICIENCY			
Coll Period (days)	31.4	40.2	74.1
Sales To Inv (times)	20.5	7.0	4.5
Assets To Sales (%)	26.5	34.6	66.6
Sales To Nwc (times)	10.0	5.6	3.6
Acct Pay To Sales (%)	2.3	4.2	13.7
PROFITABILITY			
Return On Sales (%)	4.9	2.2	0.4
Return On Assets (%)	14.9	4.3	0.9
Return On Nw (%)	28.1	15.9	5.2

SIC 5031 LBR,PLYWD,MILLWRK (NO BREAKDOWN) 2014 (108 Establishments)

	$	%
Cash	393,012	9.8
Accounts Receivable	1,287,314	32.1
Notes Receivable	8,021	0.2
Inventory	1,383,562	34.5
Other Current	124,319	3.1
Total Current	**3,196,228**	**79.7**
Fixed Assets	541,394	13.5
Other Non-current	272,702	6.8
Total Assets	**4,010,324**	**100.0**
Accounts Payable	493,270	12.3
Bank Loans	0	0.0
Notes Payable	88,227	2.2
Other Current	922,375	23.0
Total Current	**1,503,872**	**37.5**
Other Long Term	344,887	8.6
Deferred Credits	0	0.0
Net Worth	2,161,565	53.9
Total Liab & Net Worth	**4,010,324**	**100.0**
Net Sales	12,377,543	100.0
Gross Profit	2,611,662	21.1
Net Profit After Tax	123,775	1.0
Working Capital	1,692,356	---

RATIOS	UQ	MED	LQ
SOLVENCY			
Quick Ratio (times)	2.4	1.2	0.7
Current Ratio (times)	4.6	2.5	1.6
Curr Liab To Nw (%)	18.2	50.7	152.3
Curr Liab To Inv (%)	48.7	95.6	150.9
Total Liab To Nw (%)	23.1	68.7	157.1
Fixed Assets To Nw (%)	6.0	18.2	39.3
EFFICIENCY			
Coll Period (days)	25.0	31.4	44.0
Sales To Inv (times)	13.0	8.5	6.0
Assets To Sales (%)	23.2	32.4	42.4
Sales To Nwc (times)	12.8	6.9	4.4
Acct Pay To Sales (%)	2.0	3.4	5.7
PROFITABILITY			
Return On Sales (%)	2.4	1.0	0.1
Return On Assets (%)	7.5	3.9	0.5
Return On Nw (%)	19.4	7.9	1.3

SIC 5032 BRCK,STN,RLTD MTRLS (NO BREAKDOWN) 2014 (19 Establishments)

	$	%
Cash	371,864	13.3
Accounts Receivable	757,707	27.1
Notes Receivable	44,735	1.6
Inventory	696,196	24.9
Other Current	95,063	3.4
Total Current	**1,965,565**	**70.3**
Fixed Assets	623,501	22.3
Other Non-current	206,901	7.4
Total Assets	**2,795,967**	**100.0**
Accounts Payable	483,702	17.3
Bank Loans	0	0.0
Notes Payable	27,960	1.0
Other Current	640,276	22.9
Total Current	**1,151,938**	**41.2**
Other Long Term	760,503	27.2
Deferred Credits	0	0.0
Net Worth	883,526	31.6
Total Liab & Net Worth	**2,795,967**	**100.0**
Net Sales	6,078,189	100.0
Gross Profit	1,635,033	26.9
Net Profit After Tax	182,346	3.0
Working Capital	813,627	---

RATIOS	UQ	MED	LQ
SOLVENCY			
Quick Ratio (times)	3.2	0.8	0.7
Current Ratio (times)	4.3	2.4	1.1
Curr Liab To Nw (%)	22.4	51.6	185.4
Curr Liab To Inv (%)	72.2	144.0	192.9
Total Liab To Nw (%)	22.8	75.1	284.5
Fixed Assets To Nw (%)	6.4	20.1	38.1
EFFICIENCY			
Coll Period (days)	31.8	36.0	47.0
Sales To Inv (times)	13.9	7.9	5.1
Assets To Sales (%)	30.4	46.0	63.4
Sales To Nwc (times)	17.6	5.0	3.1
Acct Pay To Sales (%)	4.4	5.6	7.5
PROFITABILITY			
Return On Sales (%)	6.7	3.3	1.3
Return On Assets (%)	13.3	5.6	2.4
Return On Nw (%)	30.1	19.8	6.1

SIC 5033 RFNG,SIDNG,INSULTN (NO BREAKDOWN) 2014 (13 Establishments)

	$	%
Cash	499,484	14.9
Accounts Receivable	603,403	18.0
Notes Receivable	103,919	3.1
Inventory	1,387,828	41.4
Other Current	113,977	3.4
Total Current	**2,708,611**	**80.8**
Fixed Assets	321,815	9.6
Other Non-current	321,815	9.6
Total Assets	**3,352,241**	**100.0**
Accounts Payable	673,800	20.1
Bank Loans	0	0.0
Notes Payable	2,507,476	74.8
Other Current	646,983	19.3
Total Current	**3,828,259**	**114.2**
Other Long Term	181,021	5.4
Deferred Credits	0	0.0
Net Worth	(657,039)	(19.6)
Total Liab & Net Worth	**3,352,241**	**100.0**
Net Sales	8,297,626	100.0
Gross Profit	2,132,490	25.7
Net Profit After Tax	190,845	2.3
Working Capital	(1,119,648)	---

RATIOS	UQ	MED	LQ
SOLVENCY			
Quick Ratio (times)	1.6	1.0	0.4
Current Ratio (times)	3.1	2.4	1.7
Curr Liab To Nw (%)	26.2	50.5	96.9
Curr Liab To Inv (%)	45.0	82.6	106.1
Total Liab To Nw (%)	30.5	61.1	107.6
Fixed Assets To Nw (%)	6.5	12.0	35.4
EFFICIENCY			
Coll Period (days)	15.7	25.2	35.2
Sales To Inv (times)	7.7	5.4	4.6
Assets To Sales (%)	32.0	40.4	54.0
Sales To Nwc (times)	8.4	6.5	3.4
Acct Pay To Sales (%)	4.4	7.4	8.5
PROFITABILITY			
Return On Sales (%)	6.1	3.2	1.7
Return On Assets (%)	13.1	9.0	3.4
Return On Nw (%)	24.2	14.7	6.2

	SIC 5039 CONSTR MTRLS, NEC (NO BREAKDOWN) 2014 (15 Establishments)		SIC 5044 OFFICE EQUIPMENT (NO BREAKDOWN) 2014 (24 Establishments)		SIC 5045 CMPTRS,PERIPH SFTWR (NO BREAKDOWN) 2014 (87 Establishments)		SIC 5046 CMMRCL EQUIP, NEC (NO BREAKDOWN) 2014 (18 Establishments)	
	$	%	$	%	$	%	$	%
Cash	330,615	21.4	343,047	11.1	1,279,910	26.8	323,581	20.9
Accounts Receivable	662,776	42.9	896,248	29.0	1,824,350	38.2	481,500	31.1
Notes Receivable	0	0.0	3,091	0.1	4,776	0.1	6,193	0.4
Inventory	126,684	8.2	1,029,140	33.3	611,300	12.8	373,124	24.1
Other Current	185,393	12.0	166,887	5.4	448,924	9.4	143,986	9.3
Total Current	**1,305,468**	**84.5**	**2,438,413**	**78.9**	**4,169,260**	**87.3**	**1,328,384**	**85.8**
Fixed Assets	120,505	7.8	429,581	13.9	248,341	5.2	165,661	10.7
Other Non-current	118,959	7.7	222,517	7.2	358,184	7.5	54,188	3.5
Total Assets	**1,544,932**	**100.0**	**3,090,511**	**100.0**	**4,775,785**	**100.0**	**1,548,233**	**100.0**
Accounts Payable	256,459	16.6	503,753	16.3	5,578,117	116.8	393,251	25.4
Bank Loans	0	0.0	0	0.0	14,327	0.3	0	0.0
Notes Payable	12,359	0.8	27,815	0.9	157,601	3.3	44,899	2.9
Other Current	8,934,342	578.3	924,063	29.9	1,031,570	21.6	320,484	20.7
Total Current	**9,203,160**	**595.7**	**1,455,631**	**47.1**	**6,781,615**	**142.0**	**758,634**	**49.0**
Other Long Term	120,505	7.8	383,223	12.4	234,013	4.9	182,692	11.8
Deferred Credits	0	0.0	12,362	0.4	19,103	0.4	9,289	0.6
Net Worth	(7,778,733)	(503.5)	1,239,295	40.1	(2,258,946)	(47.3)	597,618	38.6
Total Liab & Net Worth	**1,544,932**	**100.0**	**3,090,511**	**100.0**	**4,775,785**	**100.0**	**1,548,233**	**100.0**
Net Sales	5,237,058	100.0	7,170,559	100.0	17,886,835	100.0	5,931,927	100.0
Gross Profit	1,267,368	24.2	2,746,324	38.3	5,222,956	29.2	1,702,463	28.7
Net Profit After Tax	(240,905)	(4.6)	351,357	4.9	465,058	2.6	278,801	4.7
Working Capital	(7,897,692)	---	982,782	---	(2,612,355)	---	569,750	---

RATIOS	UQ	MED	LQ	UQ	MED	LQ	UQ	MED	LQ	UQ	MED	LQ
SOLVENCY												
Quick Ratio (times)	3.7	1.5	0.8	1.7	0.8	0.5	2.3	1.3	0.8	2.8	1.2	0.6
Current Ratio (times)	4.7	1.9	1.6	2.9	1.9	1.1	2.8	1.7	1.2	4.8	1.7	1.3
Curr Liab To Nw (%)	16.1	39.7	102.3	49.7	98.4	231.8	39.3	119.0	285.1	42.5	109.9	233.7
Curr Liab To Inv (%)	93.2	328.0	999.9	91.7	158.0	230.3	155.3	368.1	999.9	109.6	167.0	472.6
Total Liab To Nw (%)	26.5	62.5	135.3	64.1	130.4	272.7	43.7	132.9	313.1	63.3	130.6	250.3
Fixed Assets To Nw (%)	3.1	11.8	24.6	9.5	18.4	72.5	1.1	7.3	14.4	2.9	9.2	25.7
EFFICIENCY												
Coll Period (days)	35.4	57.1	69.2	25.6	32.7	44.0	22.6	41.5	65.4	21.5	37.6	45.6
Sales To Inv (times)	93.6	30.9	18.0	15.4	10.9	5.4	108.3	37.2	14.4	29.6	18.8	8.3
Assets To Sales (%)	24.8	29.5	43.2	22.5	43.1	52.5	19.7	26.7	47.2	22.5	26.1	39.6
Sales To Nwc (times)	11.0	4.9	3.3	21.5	9.1	4.3	18.8	9.3	5.2	15.1	11.9	5.5
Acct Pay To Sales (%)	2.9	5.6	8.5	2.7	3.5	6.2	2.7	6.3	11.7	3.0	4.0	7.7
PROFITABILITY												
Return On Sales (%)	3.1	1.2	(1.3)	8.5	3.7	0.7	4.3	1.7	0.4	4.5	1.9	1.4
Return On Assets (%)	8.0	4.1	(5.0)	19.1	8.2	2.8	12.8	4.8	0.8	17.1	6.7	2.7
Return On Nw (%)	11.1	7.0	(0.6)	47.5	19.4	7.0	40.8	13.1	3.8	34.7	11.7	5.1

	SIC 5047 MEDICAL HOSP EQUIP (NO BREAKDOWN) 2014 (51 Establishments)		SIC 5049 PRFSSNL EQUIP,NEC (NO BREAKDOWN) 2014 (28 Establishments)		SIC 5051 METLS SVC CNTRS,OFF (NO BREAKDOWN) 2014 (80 Establishments)		SIC 5063 ELEC APPRATUS,EQUIP (NO BREAKDOWN) 2014 (145 Establishments)	
	$	%	$	%	$	%	$	%
Cash	285,514	14.6	191,530	17.6	1,345,314	12.1	766,306	16.8
Accounts Receivable	647,295	33.1	341,707	31.4	3,079,769	27.7	1,377,526	30.2
Notes Receivable	9,778	0.5	2,176	0.2	11,118	0.1	9,123	0.2
Inventory	516,271	26.4	225,266	20.7	4,447,320	40.0	1,486,998	32.6
Other Current	132,978	6.8	122,972	11.3	433,614	3.9	291,925	6.4
Total Current	**1,591,836**	**81.4**	**883,651**	**81.2**	**9,317,135**	**83.8**	**3,931,878**	**86.2**
Fixed Assets	207,291	10.6	141,471	13.0	1,178,540	10.6	364,907	8.0
Other Non-current	156,446	8.0	63,118	5.8	622,625	5.6	264,558	5.8
Total Assets	**1,955,573**	**100.0**	**1,088,240**	**100.0**	**11,118,300**	**100.0**	**4,561,343**	**100.0**
Accounts Payable	510,405	26.1	181,736	16.7	1,756,691	15.8	866,655	19.0
Bank Loans	33,245	1.7	3,265	0.3	66,710	0.6	13,684	0.3
Notes Payable	23,467	1.2	2,176	0.2	233,484	2.1	141,402	3.1
Other Current	463,470	23.7	198,060	18.2	1,456,498	13.1	597,536	13.1
Total Current	**1,030,587**	**52.7**	**385,237**	**35.4**	**3,513,383**	**31.6**	**1,619,277**	**35.5**
Other Long Term	230,758	11.8	168,677	15.5	1,100,711	9.9	387,714	8.5
Deferred Credits	0	0.0	0	0.0	0	0.0	18,245	0.4
Net Worth	694,228	35.5	534,326	49.1	6,504,206	58.5	2,536,107	55.6
Total Liab & Net Worth	**1,955,573**	**100.0**	**1,088,240**	**100.0**	**11,118,300**	**100.0**	**4,561,343**	**100.0**
Net Sales	5,962,113	100.0	3,065,465	100.0	22,783,402	100.0	11,374,920	100.0
Gross Profit	2,474,277	41.5	1,008,538	32.9	5,832,551	25.6	3,366,976	29.6
Net Profit After Tax	321,954	5.4	70,506	2.3	1,116,387	4.9	386,747	3.4
Working Capital	561,249	---	498,414	---	5,803,752	---	2,312,601	---

RATIOS	UQ	MED	LQ	UQ	MED	LQ	UQ	MED	LQ	UQ	MED	LQ
SOLVENCY												
Quick Ratio (times)	2.1	0.9	0.7	2.7	1.5	0.9	3.1	1.4	0.8	2.7	1.4	0.9
Current Ratio (times)	3.1	1.7	1.3	5.9	2.2	1.7	7.1	3.7	1.6	4.8	2.7	1.8
Curr Liab To Nw (%)	34.3	78.9	322.3	18.8	61.6	99.5	13.2	39.5	128.8	21.6	47.9	114.1
Curr Liab To Inv (%)	91.6	166.5	411.8	57.5	181.1	520.1	30.0	66.5	126.9	52.5	96.2	171.6
Total Liab To Nw (%)	44.8	103.3	384.4	26.7	79.3	129.4	14.5	65.0	146.3	31.1	63.1	162.8
Fixed Assets To Nw (%)	4.3	21.5	62.6	6.1	16.3	42.6	5.0	12.2	32.9	6.4	12.0	20.2
EFFICIENCY												
Coll Period (days)	28.1	37.2	60.8	21.4	36.0	51.3	31.4	42.3	52.6	30.7	42.9	51.7
Sales To Inv (times)	35.7	11.9	5.2	40.3	16.7	9.1	10.1	5.0	3.4	13.8	7.4	4.7
Assets To Sales (%)	22.9	32.8	50.9	24.5	35.5	44.8	32.8	48.8	65.1	30.0	40.1	54.6
Sales To Nwc (times)	15.7	7.0	3.9	10.4	6.0	4.2	9.5	4.9	2.6	8.0	5.0	3.0
Acct Pay To Sales (%)	3.4	7.4	9.9	2.5	3.8	6.0	2.8	4.5	7.7	3.8	5.9	8.8
PROFITABILITY												
Return On Sales (%)	9.1	4.0	0.8	5.2	2.2	0.7	6.5	2.3	0.7	4.2	2.5	0.8
Return On Assets (%)	24.2	6.7	1.9	16.0	7.4	1.4	15.1	4.8	1.8	10.5	5.8	2.1
Return On Nw (%)	66.4	20.9	3.8	38.9	13.2	2.1	23.6	9.2	4.1	24.2	10.1	3.3

	SIC 5064 ELEC APPL,TEL,RADIO (NO BREAKDOWN) 2014 (19 Establishments)		SIC 5065 ELEC PARTS, EQUIP (NO BREAKDOWN) 2014 (107 Establishments)		SIC 5072 HARDWARE (NO BREAKDOWN) 2014 (51 Establishments)		SIC 5074 PLMBG HDRNC,HTG SUP (NO BREAKDOWN) 2014 (83 Establishments)	
	$	%	$	%	$	%	$	%
Cash	373,018	9.0	646,089	18.6	417,649	11.6	374,807	13.4
Accounts Receivable	1,073,462	25.9	1,021,238	29.4	936,109	26.0	640,529	22.9
Notes Receivable	4,145	0.1	10,421	0.3	61,207	1.7	22,377	0.8
Inventory	1,512,794	36.5	962,187	27.7	1,382,562	38.4	1,102,045	39.4
Other Current	480,778	11.6	225,783	6.5	176,421	4.9	201,389	7.2
Total Current	**3,444,197**	**83.1**	**2,865,718**	**82.5**	**2,973,948**	**82.6**	**2,341,147**	**83.7**
Fixed Assets	455,911	11.0	354,307	10.2	352,841	9.8	257,330	9.2
Other Non-current	244,533	5.9	253,573	7.3	273,632	7.6	198,592	7.1
Total Assets	**4,144,641**	**100.0**	**3,473,598**	**100.0**	**3,600,421**	**100.0**	**2,797,069**	**100.0**
Accounts Payable	886,953	21.4	930,924	26.8	435,651	12.1	399,981	14.3
Bank Loans	20,723	0.5	17,368	0.5	46,805	1.3	27,971	1.0
Notes Payable	4,145	0.1	38,210	1.1	75,609	2.1	33,565	1.2
Other Current	849,651	20.5	1,035,132	29.8	504,059	14.0	458,719	16.4
Total Current	**1,761,472**	**42.5**	**2,021,634**	**58.2**	**1,062,124**	**29.5**	**920,236**	**32.9**
Other Long Term	621,697	15.0	267,467	7.7	457,254	12.7	246,142	8.8
Deferred Credits	0	0.0	24,315	0.7	0	0.0	0	0.0
Net Worth	1,761,472	42.5	1,160,182	33.4	2,081,043	57.8	1,630,691	58.3
Total Liab & Net Worth	**4,144,641**	**100.0**	**3,473,598**	**100.0**	**3,600,421**	**100.0**	**2,797,069**	**100.0**
Net Sales	11,449,285	100.0	9,362,798	100.0	8,868,032	100.0	6,707,600	100.0
Gross Profit	2,713,481	23.7	2,780,751	29.7	2,935,319	33.1	2,025,695	30.2
Net Profit After Tax	(228,986)	(2.0)	205,982	2.2	354,721	4.0	160,982	2.4
Working Capital	1,682,725	---	844,084	---	1,911,824	---	1,420,911	---

RATIOS	UQ	MED	LQ	UQ	MED	LQ	UQ	MED	LQ	UQ	MED	LQ
SOLVENCY												
Quick Ratio (times)	1.7	1.1	0.6	2.0	1.2	0.6	2.8	1.3	1.0	2.7	1.2	0.6
Current Ratio (times)	3.6	1.8	1.3	3.5	1.9	1.2	5.0	3.2	2.2	7.2	2.7	1.7
Curr Liab To Nw (%)	32.4	46.0	267.5	33.2	79.6	164.4	20.6	48.6	94.8	15.5	56.6	114.3
Curr Liab To Inv (%)	73.2	99.3	135.6	80.1	168.4	307.2	40.7	68.4	106.5	28.3	71.5	139.4
Total Liab To Nw (%)	44.7	71.7	293.5	49.2	101.1	191.7	20.7	65.8	158.7	25.3	76.3	145.6
Fixed Assets To Nw (%)	3.8	13.3	48.2	5.4	13.2	27.3	4.7	12.3	22.7	4.6	14.6	27.2
EFFICIENCY												
Coll Period (days)	18.5	30.7	38.7	28.3	38.0	59.1	22.7	36.1	49.7	24.1	34.7	44.9
Sales To Inv (times)	9.4	6.5	5.6	24.6	11.4	6.3	8.6	6.7	4.7	9.4	5.5	3.5
Assets To Sales (%)	22.3	36.2	43.8	24.5	37.1	56.5	31.5	40.6	56.0	31.7	41.7	61.4
Sales To Nwc (times)	17.7	10.0	5.1	15.0	6.9	4.1	7.1	5.2	3.5	8.8	5.0	2.6
Acct Pay To Sales (%)	2.8	4.7	6.9	3.7	6.1	9.7	2.4	4.3	6.6	2.9	5.9	7.7
PROFITABILITY												
Return On Sales (%)	4.0	1.2	0.6	6.4	1.6	0.3	5.3	2.0	0.7	4.0	1.8	0.3
Return On Assets (%)	11.5	6.2	1.9	13.4	4.8	1.0	14.1	5.4	1.2	10.7	3.2	0.6
Return On Nw (%)	23.9	13.6	4.4	34.8	13.4	4.0	25.6	11.3	2.5	21.4	6.5	1.0

	SIC 5075 WRM AIR HTG,AC (NO BREAKDOWN) 2014 (46 Establishments)		SIC 5078 RFGTN EQUIP,SPPLS (NO BREAKDOWN) 2014 (11 Establishments)		SIC 5082 CONSTR, MINNG MACH (NO BREAKDOWN) 2014 (38 Establishments)		SIC 5083 FARM,GRDN MACH (NO BREAKDOWN) 2014 (96 Establishments)	
	$	%	$	%	$	%	$	%
Cash	365,296	10.4	1,460,677	22.3	799,269	8.1	388,744	6.7
Accounts Receivable	1,260,975	35.9	2,181,191	33.3	1,716,947	17.4	568,610	9.8
Notes Receivable	17,562	0.5	26,200	0.4	246,688	2.5	17,406	0.3
Inventory	1,236,388	35.2	1,310,024	20.0	4,548,923	46.1	3,962,864	68.3
Other Current	256,411	7.3	569,861	8.7	601,918	6.1	255,295	4.4
Total Current	**3,136,632**	**89.3**	**5,547,953**	**84.7**	**7,913,745**	**80.2**	**5,192,919**	**89.5**
Fixed Assets	245,873	7.0	799,115	12.2	1,440,657	14.6	469,974	8.1
Other Non-current	129,961	3.7	203,054	3.1	513,111	5.2	139,251	2.4
Total Assets	**3,512,466**	**100.0**	**6,550,122**	**100.0**	**9,867,513**	**100.0**	**5,802,144**	**100.0**
Accounts Payable	772,743	22.0	12,949,591	197.7	1,134,764	11.5	818,102	14.1
Bank Loans	0	0.0	0	0.0	108,543	1.1	11,604	0.2
Notes Payable	49,175	1.4	72,051	1.1	700,593	7.1	603,423	10.4
Other Current	681,417	19.4	15,091,482	230.4	2,526,083	25.6	1,647,809	28.4
Total Current	**1,503,335**	**42.8**	**28,113,124**	**429.2**	**4,469,983**	**45.3**	**3,080,938**	**53.1**
Other Long Term	302,073	8.6	917,017	14.0	799,269	8.1	400,348	6.9
Deferred Credits	3,512	0.1	0	0.0	0	0.0	0	0.0
Net Worth	1,703,546	48.5	(22,480,019)	(343.2)	4,598,261	46.6	2,320,858	40.0
Total Liab & Net Worth	**3,512,466**	**100.0**	**6,550,122**	**100.0**	**9,867,513**	**100.0**	**5,802,144**	**100.0**
Net Sales	10,676,188	100.0	15,232,842	100.0	19,234,918	100.0	13,038,526	100.0
Gross Profit	2,935,952	27.5	3,701,581	24.3	5,251,133	27.3	2,685,936	20.6
Net Profit After Tax	320,286	3.0	1,020,600	6.7	807,867	4.2	247,732	1.9
Working Capital	1,633,297	---	(22,565,171)	---	3,443,762	---	2,111,981	---

RATIOS	UQ	MED	LQ	UQ	MED	LQ	UQ	MED	LQ	UQ	MED	LQ
SOLVENCY												
Quick Ratio (times)	1.9	1.1	0.7	2.2	1.2	0.8	1.0	0.5	0.3	0.7	0.2	0.1
Current Ratio (times)	3.5	2.1	1.5	3.1	1.6	1.4	2.8	1.8	1.3	2.5	1.5	1.3
Curr Liab To Nw (%)	37.0	85.1	169.7	44.0	79.2	187.6	41.6	89.6	203.9	62.2	161.1	277.2
Curr Liab To Inv (%)	60.1	105.2	278.3	102.8	286.7	781.5	64.5	87.9	158.1	58.5	79.3	91.3
Total Liab To Nw (%)	44.9	103.5	198.5	44.8	99.2	194.7	41.8	107.9	249.7	88.1	185.1	290.7
Fixed Assets To Nw (%)	4.5	8.6	18.9	5.2	27.0	61.1	9.2	18.5	68.5	8.2	14.9	30.7
EFFICIENCY												
Coll Period (days)	27.0	41.1	62.8	28.1	32.0	62.1	24.1	33.6	44.4	5.1	12.8	18.6
Sales To Inv (times)	19.6	9.2	5.2	12.5	8.1	6.1	7.6	4.2	2.4	5.1	3.0	2.2
Assets To Sales (%)	25.9	32.9	41.5	28.6	43.0	62.7	40.4	51.3	74.5	35.0	44.5	54.2
Sales To Nwc (times)	11.4	7.0	4.7	11.2	6.0	5.1	8.1	4.8	3.5	11.0	7.4	4.4
Acct Pay To Sales (%)	4.0	6.5	11.2	7.8	11.0	25.7	1.7	3.5	7.5	1.2	3.2	8.6
PROFITABILITY												
Return On Sales (%)	4.4	2.6	0.8	6.7	2.6	1.3	6.1	3.0	2.1	3.0	1.7	0.6
Return On Assets (%)	12.4	7.1	2.6	10.6	6.6	4.2	12.7	6.7	3.6	7.2	3.6	1.4
Return On Nw (%)	33.3	12.4	5.0	26.7	22.6	6.3	24.9	16.1	9.0	21.4	11.0	3.7

SIC 5084 INDL MCHNRY.EQPT — SIC 5085 INDUSTRIAL SUPPLIES — SIC 5087 SVC ESTBLSHMNT EQPT — SIC 5088 TRNSPRTN EQPT.SUPPL
(NO BREAKDOWN) 2014

	SIC 5084 (218 Est.) $	%	SIC 5085 (123 Est.) $	%	SIC 5087 (31 Est.) $	%	SIC 5088 (23 Est.) $	%
Cash	547,782	16.8	400,190	13.1	239,736	13.9	818,429	16.2
Accounts Receivable	974,922	29.9	858,423	28.1	500,170	29.0	1,020,511	20.2
Notes Receivable	9,782	0.3	9,165	0.3	1,725	0.1	0	0.0
Inventory	880,364	27.0	1,099,759	36.0	534,664	31.0	2,187,530	43.3
Other Current	140,207	4.3	226,060	7.4	87,961	5.1	338,487	6.7
Total Current	**2,553,057**	**78.3**	**2,593,597**	**84.9**	**1,364,256**	**79.1**	**4,364,957**	**86.4**
Fixed Assets	436,922	13.4	302,434	9.9	175,922	10.2	399,111	7.9
Other Non-current	270,630	8.3	158,854	5.2	184,545	10.7	287,965	5.7
Total Assets	**3,260,609**	**100.0**	**3,054,885**	**100.0**	**1,724,723**	**100.0**	**5,052,033**	**100.0**
Accounts Payable	629,298	19.3	479,617	15.7	315,624	18.3	853,794	16.9
Bank Loans	9,782	0.3	45,823	1.5	37,944	2.2	20,208	0.4
Notes Payable	104,339	3.2	79,427	2.6	58,641	3.4	70,728	1.4
Other Current	857,540	26.3	494,892	16.2	270,781	15.7	1,358,997	26.9
Total Current	**1,600,959**	**49.1**	**1,099,759**	**36.0**	**682,990**	**39.6**	**2,303,727**	**45.6**
Other Long Term	342,364	10.5	238,281	7.8	198,343	11.5	242,498	4.8
Deferred Credits	3,261	0.1	0	0.0	0	0.0	5,052	0.1
Net Worth	1,314,025	40.3	1,716,845	56.2	843,390	48.9	2,500,756	49.5
Total Liab & Net Worth	**3,260,609**	**100.0**	**3,054,885**	**100.0**	**1,724,723**	**100.0**	**5,052,033**	**100.0**
Net Sales	8,625,950	100.0	7,580,360	100.0	6,116,039	100.0	13,728,351	100.0
Gross Profit	2,561,907	29.7	2,327,171	30.7	2,030,525	33.2	4,846,108	35.3
Net Profit After Tax	353,664	4.1	265,313	3.5	281,338	4.6	247,110	1.8
Working Capital	952,098	—	1,493,838	—	681,266	—	2,061,230	—

RATIOS	5084 UQ	MED	LQ	5085 UQ	MED	LQ	5087 UQ	MED	LQ	5088 UQ	MED	LQ
SOLVENCY												
Quick Ratio (times)	2.1	1.1	0.8	2.8	1.5	0.8	1.3	1.0	0.7	2.3	0.6	0.4
Current Ratio (times)	3.6	2.0	1.5	6.5	3.0	1.8	2.9	1.9	1.5	4.4	1.9	1.4
Curr Liab To Nw (%)	25.6	69.3	133.4	16.0	37.0	93.5	34.6	95.3	163.9	20.9	86.5	204.1
Curr Liab To Inv (%)	72.0	124.6	236.2	33.5	75.5	145.9	55.9	117.3	196.3	55.8	92.2	114.9
Total Liab To Nw (%)	32.9	80.7	187.2	18.0	45.7	123.9	52.6	120.5	191.5	23.9	95.0	204.1
Fixed Assets To Nw (%)	7.5	18.5	40.7	4.5	9.7	26.1	12.6	22.1	53.7	3.2	19.5	38.1
EFFICIENCY												
Coll Period (days)	26.5	38.3	50.0	29.0	39.1	49.3	21.5	28.3	41.6	12.6	22.1	43.8
Sales To Inv (times)	17.4	9.8	5.9	12.8	6.9	4.4	14.0	9.8	8.0	8.2	6.8	4.4
Assets To Sales (%)	26.2	37.8	52.4	29.9	40.3	51.9	22.7	28.2	44.5	27.2	36.8	71.2
Sales To Nwc (times)	11.1	6.7	4.3	8.1	4.6	3.0	14.2	8.3	5.2	12.4	4.8	2.3
Acct Pay To Sales (%)	3.2	5.7	8.7	2.8	4.8	7.3	3.2	5.5	7.8	3.2	4.9	7.3
PROFITABILITY												
Return On Sales (%)	5.8	2.5	0.6	6.5	2.9	1.0	5.4	1.5	0.6	3.8	2.2	0.6
Return On Assets (%)	14.5	5.7	2.1	16.2	7.2	2.2	11.2	5.8	2.5	9.3	4.1	1.6
Return On Nw (%)	29.3	11.3	4.8	25.7	14.0	4.2	27.1	11.8	5.1	23.5	5.9	4.7

SIC 5091 — SPTG.RECRTNL GOODS (NO BREAKDOWN) 2014 (27 Establishments)

	$	%
Cash	223,459	11.5
Accounts Receivable	433,317	22.3
Notes Receivable	3,886	0.2
Inventory	942,416	48.5
Other Current	93,271	4.8
Total Current	**1,696,349**	**87.3**
Fixed Assets	124,360	6.4
Other Non-current	122,417	6.3
Total Assets	**1,943,126**	**100.0**
Accounts Payable	394,455	20.3
Bank Loans	0	0.0
Notes Payable	0	0.0
Other Current	371,137	19.1
Total Current	**765,592**	**39.4**
Other Long Term	205,971	10.6
Deferred Credits	0	0.0
Net Worth	971,563	50.0
Total Liab & Net Worth	**1,943,126**	**100.0**
Net Sales	4,995,183	100.0
Gross Profit	1,368,680	27.4
Net Profit After Tax	74,928	1.5
Working Capital	930,757	---

RATIOS	UQ	MED	LQ
SOLVENCY			
Quick Ratio (times)	1.1	0.7	0.5
Current Ratio (times)	3.9	2.4	1.6
Curr Liab To Nw (%)	33.3	89.0	143.0
Curr Liab To Inv (%)	49.2	64.5	166.5
Total Liab To Nw (%)	45.4	92.6	293.0
Fixed Assets To Nw (%)	4.0	16.2	28.6
EFFICIENCY			
Coll Period (days)	18.3	23.9	41.3
Sales To Inv (times)	9.8	6.3	3.9
Assets To Sales (%)	24.7	38.9	55.2
Sales To Nwc (times)	12.4	4.8	3.1
Acct Pay To Sales (%)	6.1	7.9	12.3
PROFITABILITY			
Return On Sales (%)	4.6	2.0	0.3
Return On Assets (%)	8.6	5.4	1.6
Return On Nw (%)	33.0	7.5	2.3

SIC 5092 — TOYS,HBBY GDS,SUPPL (NO BREAKDOWN) 2014 (16 Establishments)

	$	%
Cash	281,561	11.3
Accounts Receivable	508,305	20.4
Notes Receivable	39,867	1.6
Inventory	1,081,395	43.4
Other Current	216,778	8.7
Total Current	**2,127,906**	**85.4**
Fixed Assets	137,043	5.5
Other Non-current	226,744	9.1
Total Assets	**2,491,693**	**100.0**
Accounts Payable	1,791,527	71.9
Bank Loans	0	0.0
Notes Payable	0	0.0
Other Current	8,274,913	332.1
Total Current	**10,066,440**	**404.0**
Other Long Term	318,936	12.8
Deferred Credits	0	0.0
Net Worth	(7,893,683)	(316.8)
Total Liab & Net Worth	**2,491,693**	**100.0**
Net Sales	4,288,628	100.0
Gross Profit	1,706,874	39.8
Net Profit After Tax	68,618	1.6
Working Capital	(7,938,534)	---

RATIOS	UQ	MED	LQ
SOLVENCY			
Quick Ratio (times)	2.2	0.8	0.4
Current Ratio (times)	4.7	2.6	1.4
Curr Liab To Nw (%)	33.5	112.6	146.6
Curr Liab To Inv (%)	37.5	56.4	140.9
Total Liab To Nw (%)	41.8	112.6	208.4
Fixed Assets To Nw (%)	1.8	7.8	27.5
EFFICIENCY			
Coll Period (days)	12.4	39.1	86.1
Sales To Inv (times)	5.6	4.3	3.3
Assets To Sales (%)	34.0	58.1	79.9
Sales To Nwc (times)	8.0	5.6	2.9
Acct Pay To Sales (%)	3.0	11.4	20.6
PROFITABILITY			
Return On Sales (%)	4.6	0.8	(1.1)
Return On Assets (%)	5.7	1.9	(1.2)
Return On Nw (%)	26.8	3.1	1.0

SIC 5093 — SCRAP,WASTE MTRLS (NO BREAKDOWN) 2014 (23 Establishments)

	$	%
Cash	1,009,109	9.4
Accounts Receivable	2,973,650	27.7
Notes Receivable	10,735	0.1
Inventory	1,803,514	16.8
Other Current	493,819	4.6
Total Current	**6,290,827**	**58.6**
Fixed Assets	3,005,856	28.0
Other Non-current	1,438,517	13.4
Total Assets	**10,735,200**	**100.0**
Accounts Payable	1,674,691	15.6
Bank Loans	236,174	2.2
Notes Payable	268,380	2.5
Other Current	1,792,779	16.7
Total Current	**3,972,024**	**37.0**
Other Long Term	1,674,691	15.6
Deferred Credits	0	0.0
Net Worth	5,088,485	47.4
Total Liab & Net Worth	**10,735,200**	**100.0**
Net Sales	36,638,908	100.0
Gross Profit	5,459,197	14.9
Net Profit After Tax	219,833	0.6
Working Capital	2,318,803	---

RATIOS	UQ	MED	LQ
SOLVENCY			
Quick Ratio (times)	2.1	1.0	0.5
Current Ratio (times)	2.9	1.5	1.0
Curr Liab To Nw (%)	27.4	66.2	189.2
Curr Liab To Inv (%)	111.5	169.2	314.1
Total Liab To Nw (%)	54.0	129.0	236.1
Fixed Assets To Nw (%)	8.9	44.2	136.1
EFFICIENCY			
Coll Period (days)	13.5	25.8	32.5
Sales To Inv (times)	60.2	21.3	12.9
Assets To Sales (%)	20.6	29.3	39.8
Sales To Nwc (times)	32.0	9.1	6.5
Acct Pay To Sales (%)	1.7	3.8	5.9
PROFITABILITY			
Return On Sales (%)	1.2	0.6	(0.5)
Return On Assets (%)	6.8	2.5	(2.1)
Return On Nw (%)	17.1	5.3	(2.2)

SIC 5094 — JWLRY,PRCIOUS STNS (NO BREAKDOWN) 2014 (16 Establishments)

	$	%
Cash	701,171	7.4
Accounts Receivable	2,046,660	21.6
Notes Receivable	0	0.0
Inventory	4,538,659	47.9
Other Current	1,487,618	15.7
Total Current	**8,774,108**	**92.6**
Fixed Assets	236,882	2.5
Other Non-current	464,289	4.9
Total Assets	**9,475,279**	**100.0**
Accounts Payable	3,363,724	35.5
Bank Loans	236,882	2.5
Notes Payable	104,228	1.1
Other Current	1,440,242	15.2
Total Current	**5,145,076**	**54.3**
Other Long Term	540,091	5.7
Deferred Credits	0	0.0
Net Worth	3,790,112	40.0
Total Liab & Net Worth	**9,475,279**	**100.0**
Net Sales	16,920,141	100.0
Gross Profit	3,637,830	21.5
Net Profit After Tax	287,642	1.7
Working Capital	3,629,032	---

RATIOS	UQ	MED	LQ
SOLVENCY			
Quick Ratio (times)	1.3	0.6	0.3
Current Ratio (times)	5.6	1.7	1.1
Curr Liab To Nw (%)	22.1	169.9	898.4
Curr Liab To Inv (%)	31.1	109.8	255.3
Total Liab To Nw (%)	39.0	198.4	902.5
Fixed Assets To Nw (%)	1.6	4.3	9.6
EFFICIENCY			
Coll Period (days)	17.5	24.1	54.8
Sales To Inv (times)	7.5	4.2	2.6
Assets To Sales (%)	30.6	56.0	81.1
Sales To Nwc (times)	22.9	9.2	3.0
Acct Pay To Sales (%)	4.4	9.7	19.6
PROFITABILITY			
Return On Sales (%)	4.0	0.8	0.1
Return On Assets (%)	6.7	1.8	0.3
Return On Nw (%)	17.6	13.2	5.4

	SIC 5099 DURABLE GOODS, NEC (NO BREAKDOWN) 2014 (27 Establishments)		SIC 51 WHLE TRD NONDURBL GDS (NO BREAKDOWN) 2014 (1171 Establishments)		SIC 5112 STNRY,OFFC SUPPL (NO BREAKDOWN) 2014 (23 Establishments)		SIC 5113 INDL,PRSNL SVC PPR (NO BREAKDOWN) 2014 (32 Establishments)	
	$	%	$	%	$	%	$	%
Cash	457,370	21.2	914,775	14.5	442,930	21.1	527,252	16.7
Accounts Receivable	591,130	27.4	1,722,301	27.3	741,016	35.3	1,022,932	32.4
Notes Receivable	0	0.0	25,235	0.4	0	0.0	0	0.0
Inventory	560,926	26.0	1,589,817	25.2	354,764	16.9	915,587	29.0
Other Current	297,722	13.8	466,851	7.4	81,869	3.9	110,502	3.5
Total Current	**1,907,148**	**88.4**	**4,718,979**	**74.8**	**1,620,579**	**77.2**	**2,576,273**	**81.6**
Fixed Assets	133,759	6.2	1,072,495	17.0	245,606	11.7	419,907	13.3
Other Non-current	116,500	5.4	517,322	8.2	233,011	11.1	161,017	5.1
Total Assets	**2,157,407**	**100.0**	**6,308,796**	**100.0**	**2,099,196**	**100.0**	**3,157,197**	**100.0**
Accounts Payable	332,241	15.4	1,299,612	20.6	417,740	19.9	457,794	14.5
Bank Loans	0	0.0	18,926	0.3	0	0.0	0	0.0
Notes Payable	0	0.0	428,998	6.8	12,595	0.6	271,519	8.6
Other Current	610,546	28.3	1,476,259	23.4	295,987	14.1	454,636	14.4
Total Current	**942,787**	**43.7**	**3,223,795**	**51.1**	**726,322**	**34.6**	**1,183,949**	**37.5**
Other Long Term	97,084	4.5	706,584	11.2	193,126	9.2	419,907	13.3
Deferred Credits	2,157	0.1	12,618	0.2	44,083	2.1	0	0.0
Net Worth	1,115,379	51.7	2,365,799	37.5	1,135,665	54.1	1,553,341	49.2
Total Liab & Net Worth	**2,157,407**	**100.0**	**6,308,796**	**100.0**	**2,099,196**	**100.0**	**3,157,197**	**100.0**
Net Sales	6,478,700	100.0	23,628,449	100.0	6,974,073	100.0	12,479,040	100.0
Gross Profit	1,969,525	30.4	4,394,892	18.6	2,154,989	30.9	3,606,443	28.9
Net Profit After Tax	265,627	4.1	637,968	2.7	174,352	2.5	411,808	3.3
Working Capital	964,361	---	1,495,184	---	894,257	---	1,392,324	---

RATIOS	UQ	MED	LQ	UQ	MED	LQ	UQ	MED	LQ	UQ	MED	LQ
SOLVENCY												
Quick Ratio (times)	1.8	1.2	0.8	1.8	1.0	0.6	2.6	1.5	1.0	4.4	1.8	1.0
Current Ratio (times)	3.2	2.2	1.7	3.2	1.8	1.3	4.3	2.4	1.5	6.0	3.7	1.7
Curr Liab To Nw (%)	38.2	61.9	135.7	31.4	74.9	169.3	29.8	57.5	155.9	14.1	25.2	112.1
Curr Liab To Inv (%)	75.4	108.5	315.0	86.6	147.7	308.8	88.8	326.0	488.2	54.2	90.6	152.5
Total Liab To Nw (%)	42.5	75.8	144.0	45.3	103.1	214.7	36.2	57.5	191.9	14.1	43.7	137.1
Fixed Assets To Nw (%)	2.9	8.4	22.3	9.1	29.8	59.7	4.1	24.1	55.6	9.0	19.9	30.8
EFFICIENCY												
Coll Period (days)	20.8	37.8	59.7	12.1	22.6	37.2	28.5	34.2	48.2	21.6	28.1	35.8
Sales To Inv (times)	19.9	11.1	5.3	41.1	15.2	7.6	58.3	28.4	9.8	19.0	14.0	8.6
Assets To Sales (%)	27.4	33.3	56.7	15.2	26.7	44.3	21.7	30.1	44.3	19.6	25.3	35.9
Sales To Nwc (times)	8.4	5.2	3.5	25.8	12.5	6.7	13.1	8.9	5.3	13.2	8.1	5.0
Acct Pay To Sales (%)	3.2	4.9	9.7	2.0	3.7	7.0	3.7	6.0	9.1	2.3	3.1	5.5
PROFITABILITY												
Return On Sales (%)	6.0	1.7	0.4	3.6	1.3	0.4	4.7	1.9	0.2	3.8	1.7	0.3
Return On Assets (%)	17.3	7.1	1.3	10.8	5.0	1.8	7.0	5.0	1.7	16.1	7.1	1.1
Return On Nw (%)	35.7	9.7	3.5	25.6	11.6	4.6	15.5	6.4	5.0	28.7	12.0	3.6

	SIC 5122 DRGS,PRPRTRS,SNDRS (NO BREAKDOWN) 2014 (50 Establishments)		SIC 5131 PCE GDS,NOTIONS (NO BREAKDOWN) 2014 (21 Establishments)		SIC 5136 MENS,BOYS CLOTHING (NO BREAKDOWN) 2014 (15 Establishments)		SIC 5137 WMNS,CLDRNS CLTHNG (NO BREAKDOWN) 2014 (21 Establishments)	
	$	%	$	%	$	%	$	%
Cash	1,867,330	24.3	231,498	13.3	275,912	12.8	190,934	8.2
Accounts Receivable	1,836,592	23.9	335,933	19.3	493,624	22.9	705,526	30.3
Notes Receivable	30,738	0.4	40,033	2.3	2,156	0.1	0	0.0
Inventory	2,297,662	29.9	905,105	52.0	784,625	36.4	938,372	40.3
Other Current	338,118	4.4	78,327	4.5	306,089	14.2	153,679	6.6
Total Current	**6,370,440**	**82.9**	**1,590,896**	**91.4**	**1,862,406**	**86.4**	**1,988,511**	**85.4**
Fixed Assets	630,128	8.2	74,845	4.3	198,312	9.2	158,336	6.8
Other Non-current	683,919	8.9	74,845	4.3	94,844	4.4	181,620	7.8
Total Assets	**7,684,487**	**100.0**	**1,740,586**	**100.0**	**2,155,562**	**100.0**	**2,328,467**	**100.0**
Accounts Payable	1,798,170	23.4	226,276	13.0	295,312	13.7	922,073	39.6
Bank Loans	30,738	0.4	41,774	2.4	0	0.0	2,328	0.1
Notes Payable	7,792,070	101.4	5,222	0.3	68,978	3.2	6,985	0.3
Other Current	1,721,325	22.4	240,201	13.8	411,712	19.1	3,339,022	143.4
Total Current	**11,342,303**	**147.6**	**513,473**	**29.5**	**776,002**	**36.0**	**4,270,408**	**183.4**
Other Long Term	722,342	9.4	40,033	2.3	215,557	10.0	69,854	3.0
Deferred Credits	7,684	0.1	0	0.0	0	0.0	0	0.0
Net Worth	(4,387,842)	(57.1)	1,187,080	68.2	1,164,003	54.0	(2,011,795)	(86.4)
Total Liab & Net Worth	**7,684,487**	**100.0**	**1,740,586**	**100.0**	**2,155,562**	**100.0**	**2,328,467**	**100.0**
Net Sales	21,169,386	100.0	5,030,595	100.0	4,665,719	100.0	6,749,180	100.0
Gross Profit	6,117,953	28.9	1,438,750	28.6	1,292,404	27.7	1,943,764	28.8
Net Profit After Tax	931,453	4.4	115,704	2.3	359,260	7.7	269,967	4.0
Working Capital	(4,971,863)	---	1,077,423	---	1,086,404	---	(2,281,897)	---

RATIOS	UQ	MED	LQ	UQ	MED	LQ	UQ	MED	LQ	UQ	MED	LQ
SOLVENCY												
Quick Ratio (times)	2.2	0.9	0.5	2.8	1.2	0.4	4.3	1.0	0.5	2.1	0.7	0.4
Current Ratio (times)	3.9	2.0	1.3	7.8	3.5	2.0	7.5	2.8	1.9	4.4	2.0	1.1
Curr Liab To Nw (%)	30.4	85.8	207.2	16.5	26.0	77.8	10.7	58.1	97.4	27.2	49.9	120.5
Curr Liab To Inv (%)	72.1	122.5	190.9	23.7	41.4	74.5	45.2	73.4	139.4	46.0	129.0	260.9
Total Liab To Nw (%)	40.7	123.0	302.3	16.5	33.9	77.8	15.8	90.2	145.2	29.2	57.7	141.7
Fixed Assets To Nw (%)	2.1	12.9	27.4	3.0	6.8	9.0	9.5	14.7	18.2	1.9	5.2	7.6
EFFICIENCY												
Coll Period (days)	23.4	35.4	53.7	15.4	21.8	47.6	26.8	42.0	58.4	22.6	39.8	54.0
Sales To Inv (times)	12.5	8.1	5.4	7.4	5.6	3.9	11.9	7.8	4.9	11.2	8.6	5.3
Assets To Sales (%)	25.2	36.3	56.6	22.6	34.6	42.5	39.1	46.2	64.3	23.5	34.5	37.4
Sales To Nwc (times)	13.9	9.2	3.4	9.3	5.7	3.3	7.8	3.1	2.2	7.2	5.8	4.0
Acct Pay To Sales (%)	3.5	6.6	10.6	1.3	4.0	5.1	2.8	3.9	5.9	3.3	5.2	10.9
PROFITABILITY												
Return On Sales (%)	4.2	1.5	0.5	4.0	1.5	0.8	1.9	1.2	0.8	6.7	2.2	0.4
Return On Assets (%)	11.0	3.3	(0.6)	14.6	5.6	1.7	5.3	2.4	1.3	23.2	7.9	1.0
Return On Nw (%)	31.5	12.4	0.5	24.9	10.4	4.7	15.2	5.4	3.0	43.3	10.9	4.1

	SIC 5139 FOOTWEAR (NO BREAKDOWN) 2014 (10 Establishments)		SIC 5141 GROCERIES,GNRL LNE (NO BREAKDOWN) 2014 (58 Establishments)		SIC 5142 PCKGD FROZEN GOODS (NO BREAKDOWN) 2014 (12 Establishments)		SIC 5143 DRY EXC DRIED,CNND (NO BREAKDOWN) 2014 (11 Establishments)	
	$	%	$	%	$	%	$	%
Cash	1,024,911	17.0	737,279	12.5	2,521,564	17.7	361,808	8.9
Accounts Receivable	1,820,725	30.2	2,058,483	34.9	4,031,653	28.3	1,865,953	45.9
Notes Receivable	0	0.0	17,695	0.3	0	0.0	28,457	0.7
Inventory	1,754,407	29.1	1,563,032	26.5	4,074,392	28.6	845,573	20.8
Other Current	639,062	10.6	336,199	5.7	925,998	6.5	101,632	2.5
Total Current	**5,239,105**	**86.9**	**4,712,688**	**79.9**	**11,553,607**	**81.1**	**3,203,423**	**78.8**
Fixed Assets	391,878	6.5	719,584	12.2	1,894,735	13.3	707,355	17.4
Other Non-current	397,907	6.6	465,961	7.9	797,783	5.6	154,479	3.8
Total Assets	**6,028,890**	**100.0**	**5,898,233**	**100.0**	**14,246,125**	**100.0**	**4,065,257**	**100.0**
Accounts Payable	1,338,414	22.2	1,592,523	27.0	3,362,086	23.6	1,512,276	37.2
Bank Loans	0	0.0	11,796	0.2	356,153	2.5	0	0.0
Notes Payable	42,202	0.7	58,982	1.0	0	0.0	117,892	2.9
Other Current	813,900	13.5	872,939	14.8	2,065,688	14.5	634,180	15.6
Total Current	**2,194,516**	**36.4**	**2,536,240**	**43.0**	**5,783,927**	**40.6**	**2,264,348**	**55.7**
Other Long Term	639,062	10.6	589,824	10.0	2,749,502	19.3	808,986	19.9
Deferred Credits	0	0.0	5,898	0.1	0	0.0	0	0.0
Net Worth	3,195,312	53.0	2,766,271	46.9	5,712,696	40.1	991,923	24.4
Total Liab & Net Worth	**6,028,890**	**100.0**	**5,898,233**	**100.0**	**14,246,125**	**100.0**	**4,065,257**	**100.0**
Net Sales	13,367,827	100.0	32,407,874	100.0	48,788,099	100.0	33,597,165	100.0
Gross Profit	5,400,602	40.4	4,407,471	13.6	8,537,917	17.5	5,106,769	15.2
Net Profit After Tax	1,163,001	8.7	518,526	1.6	439,093	0.9	369,569	1.1
Working Capital	3,044,589	---	2,176,448	---	5,769,680	---	939,075	---

RATIOS	UQ	MED	LQ	UQ	MED	LQ	UQ	MED	LQ	UQ	MED	LQ
SOLVENCY												
Quick Ratio (times)	4.7	1.7	0.6	2.5	1.2	0.7	1.9	1.2	0.7	1.1	0.9	0.7
Current Ratio (times)	9.1	3.5	1.8	4.1	1.7	1.3	3.4	1.9	1.5	1.5	1.4	1.3
Curr Liab To Nw (%)	13.2	22.0	95.8	25.8	97.2	238.5	44.8	103.7	310.3	147.7	245.1	556.7
Curr Liab To Inv (%)	54.7	135.1	148.4	70.4	142.2	265.0	59.8	109.4	159.5	158.7	252.1	546.6
Total Liab To Nw (%)	25.8	40.2	95.8	37.8	113.3	249.9	103.8	131.5	455.1	147.7	261.0	698.0
Fixed Assets To Nw (%)	4.6	6.5	14.0	6.6	18.8	45.9	7.8	12.1	76.1	14.6	32.3	105.2
EFFICIENCY												
Coll Period (days)	22.3	38.4	75.2	11.7	19.7	31.4	16.3	21.9	40.5	19.9	21.5	24.3
Sales To Inv (times)	14.2	7.6	5.0	30.8	19.6	11.8	20.5	11.7	7.7	84.6	24.5	18.2
Assets To Sales (%)	26.2	45.1	49.7	12.9	18.2	26.8	23.3	29.2	42.9	10.9	12.1	18.5
Sales To Nwc (times)	8.8	5.9	2.9	28.4	13.6	7.7	12.7	9.6	6.4	43.7	33.6	27.0
Acct Pay To Sales (%)	2.4	4.1	7.6	2.1	3.8	7.0	3.7	6.4	13.7	4.4	5.8	6.6
PROFITABILITY												
Return On Sales (%)	11.1	9.3	5.1	1.8	0.7	0.1	1.3	1.1	0.3	1.7	0.5	0.1
Return On Assets (%)	50.8	19.7	7.9	7.9	3.6	1.0	4.3	2.9	1.2	10.1	3.9	1.3
Return On Nw (%)	82.9	42.5	22.3	20.1	9.3	3.5	10.4	5.8	2.8	44.3	14.7	(1.5)

	SIC 5146 FISH AND SEAFOODS (NO BREAKDOWN) 2014 (16 Establishments)		SIC 5147 MEATS,MEAT PRDTS (NO BREAKDOWN) 2014 (37 Establishments)		SIC 5148 FRSH FRTS,VGTBLES (NO BREAKDOWN) 2014 (108 Establishments)		SIC 5149 GRCRS,RLTD PRDS,NEC (NO BREAKDOWN) 2014 (58 Establishments)	
	$	%	$	%	$	%	$	%
Cash	255,563	3.1	920,853	20.5	970,935	17.5	404,817	11.0
Accounts Receivable	2,695,772	32.7	1,441,921	32.1	2,252,569	40.6	927,400	25.2
Notes Receivable	16,488	0.2	13,476	0.3	5,548	0.1	25,761	0.7
Inventory	2,901,871	35.2	916,361	20.4	332,892	6.0	1,129,809	30.7
Other Current	667,760	8.1	157,219	3.5	693,525	12.5	246,571	6.7
Total Current	**6,537,454**	**79.3**	**3,449,830**	**76.8**	**4,255,469**	**76.7**	**2,734,358**	**74.3**
Fixed Assets	1,376,740	16.7	839,998	18.7	926,549	16.7	644,028	17.5
Other Non-current	329,758	4.0	202,138	4.5	366,181	6.6	301,773	8.2
Total Assets	**8,243,952**	**100.0**	**4,491,966**	**100.0**	**5,548,199**	**100.0**	**3,680,159**	**100.0**
Accounts Payable	2,522,649	30.6	754,650	16.8	1,664,460	30.0	938,441	25.5
Bank Loans	189,611	2.3	13,476	0.3	5,548	0.1	22,081	0.6
Notes Payable	131,903	1.6	85,347	1.9	61,030	1.1	246,571	6.7
Other Current	1,920,841	23.3	844,490	18.8	876,616	15.8	1,185,010	32.2
Total Current	**4,765,004**	**57.8**	**1,697,963**	**37.8**	**2,607,654**	**47.0**	**2,392,103**	**65.0**
Other Long Term	469,905	5.7	471,657	10.5	410,567	7.4	651,389	17.7
Deferred Credits	49,464	0.6	0	0.0	11,096	0.2	3,680	0.1
Net Worth	2,959,579	35.9	2,322,346	51.7	2,518,882	45.4	632,987	17.2
Total Liab & Net Worth	**8,243,952**	**100.0**	**4,491,966**	**100.0**	**5,548,199**	**100.0**	**3,680,159**	**100.0**
Net Sales	44,561,903	100.0	25,668,377	100.0	36,262,739	100.0	13,004,095	100.0
Gross Profit	5,525,676	12.4	3,978,598	15.5	6,237,191	17.2	3,316,044	25.5
Net Profit After Tax	935,800	2.1	539,036	2.1	652,729	1.8	260,082	2.0
Working Capital	1,772,450	---	1,751,867	---	1,647,815	---	342,255	---

RATIOS	UQ	MED	LQ	UQ	MED	LQ	UQ	MED	LQ	UQ	MED	LQ
SOLVENCY												
Quick Ratio (times)	0.7	0.6	0.4	4.7	1.4	0.8	1.7	1.2	0.9	1.7	1.1	0.5
Current Ratio (times)	1.7	1.2	1.1	5.1	2.2	1.3	2.3	1.6	1.2	3.4	2.1	1.3
Curr Liab To Nw (%)	62.5	203.9	456.7	15.7	40.5	242.4	56.1	114.5	214.2	23.6	69.7	147.7
Curr Liab To Inv (%)	119.2	147.5	182.9	54.7	158.1	252.6	326.1	552.8	999.9	60.9	127.6	261.6
Total Liab To Nw (%)	78.7	217.6	469.8	20.5	95.5	243.6	68.8	144.8	266.1	30.4	84.8	231.6
Fixed Assets To Nw (%)	3.3	31.1	92.5	3.1	22.0	62.3	4.8	27.4	65.7	3.2	22.2	67.1
EFFICIENCY												
Coll Period (days)	19.7	33.4	39.4	13.5	20.1	25.2	18.6	25.9	32.1	19.4	24.1	34.3
Sales To Inv (times)	23.1	14.5	5.7	51.6	25.7	15.2	166.2	81.1	55.4	17.5	11.3	7.1
Assets To Sales (%)	14.1	18.5	51.0	13.3	17.5	25.8	11.0	15.3	25.2	17.8	28.3	56.5
Sales To Nwc (times)	83.4	32.6	10.3	33.9	17.4	8.4	57.9	21.6	12.9	18.4	8.8	5.5
Acct Pay To Sales (%)	4.0	5.5	10.3	1.2	2.1	3.2	2.8	5.0	7.3	3.0	5.6	9.7
PROFITABILITY												
Return On Sales (%)	3.7	0.9	0.5	3.4	0.6	0.2	3.5	1.0	0.3	4.0	1.7	(0.7)
Return On Assets (%)	8.3	5.0	2.5	14.5	5.7	1.1	13.3	6.3	1.9	18.8	5.6	(1.8)
Return On Nw (%)	49.2	19.8	15.5	32.0	11.5	2.7	38.7	16.9	5.6	36.7	10.1	(1.9)

Balance Sheet

	SIC 5153 GRAIN,FIELD BEANS (109 Est.) $	%	SIC 5162 PLSTCS MTRLS,B SHPS (12 Est.) $	%	SIC 5169 CHEM,ALLD PRDTS,NEC (57 Est.) $	%	SIC 5171 PETRO BLK STNS,TMNL (75 Est.) $	%
Cash	2,216,533	10.1	767,801	13.6	890,722	12.2	1,031,274	15.6
Accounts Receivable	2,238,479	10.2	2,252,592	39.9	2,540,748	34.8	1,969,998	29.8
Notes Receivable	21,946	0.1	0	0.0	7,301	0.1	72,718	1.1
Inventory	6,474,033	29.5	1,546,892	27.4	1,671,929	22.9	912,281	13.8
Other Current	2,962,692	13.5	225,823	4.0	350,448	4.8	310,705	4.7
Total Current	**13,913,683**	**63.4**	**4,793,108**	**84.9**	**5,461,148**	**74.8**	**4,296,976**	**65.0**
Fixed Assets	5,574,252	25.4	429,065	7.6	1,146,257	15.7	1,732,012	26.2
Other Non-current	2,457,938	11.2	423,420	7.5	693,595	9.5	581,744	8.8
Total Assets	**21,945,873**	**100.0**	**5,645,593**	**100.0**	**7,301,000**	**100.0**	**6,610,732**	**100.0**
Accounts Payable	1,799,562	8.2	1,513,019	26.8	1,445,598	19.8	1,388,254	21.0
Bank Loans	0	0.0	0	0.0	43,806	0.6	33,054	0.5
Notes Payable	1,228,969	5.6	350,027	6.2	175,224	2.4	85,940	1.3
Other Current	6,122,898	27.9	1,061,371	18.8	1,168,160	16.0	978,387	14.8
Total Current	**9,151,429**	**41.7**	**2,924,417**	**51.8**	**2,832,788**	**38.8**	**2,485,635**	**37.6**
Other Long Term	2,765,180	12.6	937,168	16.6	759,304	10.4	773,456	11.7
Deferred Credits	0	0.0	5,646	0.1	14,602	0.2	13,221	0.2
Net Worth	10,029,264	45.7	1,778,362	31.5	3,694,306	50.6	3,338,420	50.5
Total Liab & Net Worth	**21,945,873**	**100.0**	**5,645,593**	**100.0**	**7,301,000**	**100.0**	**6,610,732**	**100.0**
Net Sales	55,279,277	100.0	13,905,401	100.0	17,635,266	100.0	55,552,370	100.0
Gross Profit	4,311,784	7.8	2,391,729	17.2	5,290,580	30.0	4,944,161	8.9
Net Profit After Tax	1,437,261	2.6	431,067	3.1	864,128	4.9	944,390	1.7
Working Capital	4,762,254	---	1,868,691	---	2,628,360	---	1,811,341	---

Ratios

RATIOS	5153 UQ	MED	LQ	5162 UQ	MED	LQ	5169 UQ	MED	LQ	5171 UQ	MED	LQ
SOLVENCY												
Quick Ratio (times)	0.8	0.4	0.2	1.9	0.9	0.7	2.0	1.3	0.9	1.8	1.0	0.8
Current Ratio (times)	1.9	1.4	1.2	3.1	1.9	1.1	2.8	1.9	1.5	2.4	1.8	1.3
Curr Liab To Nw (%)	53.8	82.5	163.1	31.2	92.4	226.0	27.6	73.4	150.4	43.2	76.3	122.5
Curr Liab To Inv (%)	103.0	132.6	203.6	101.1	117.9	366.7	98.4	141.0	215.1	152.9	280.0	565.1
Total Liab To Nw (%)	77.9	113.2	194.0	63.5	96.6	229.1	34.7	101.6	195.6	57.3	95.4	182.1
Fixed Assets To Nw (%)	37.1	55.5	69.9	1.5	3.5	10.3	5.9	28.1	49.6	27.0	48.4	81.0
EFFICIENCY												
Coll Period (days)	6.4	11.0	19.0	48.0	55.1	58.1	31.4	39.8	51.1	7.7	12.4	18.6
Sales To Inv (times)	17.2	8.2	5.6	18.3	7.9	6.7	17.9	12.6	7.1	108.7	59.3	39.3
Assets To Sales (%)	27.3	39.7	52.7	28.7	40.6	49.1	27.4	41.4	61.9	8.2	11.9	17.1
Sales To Nwc (times)	22.2	13.5	9.6	25.5	8.0	6.2	14.3	7.7	4.5	74.0	27.9	13.3
Acct Pay To Sales (%)	1.2	2.4	4.7	4.7	8.2	10.6	3.5	6.0	9.3	1.7	2.4	3.1
PROFITABILITY												
Return On Sales (%)	3.3	2.0	1.0	4.6	2.1	1.8	6.9	3.6	0.5	1.5	0.6	0.2
Return On Assets (%)	7.5	4.8	3.0	12.6	6.7	3.7	23.4	7.5	1.4	8.8	4.7	1.6
Return On Nw (%)	15.4	10.8	7.0	21.4	14.3	6.5	43.5	17.0	3.7	18.2	9.4	4.5

	SIC 5172 PETRO PRDTS,NEC (NO BREAKDOWN) 2014 (112 Establishments)		SIC 5181 BEER AND ALE (NO BREAKDOWN) 2014 (15 Establishments)		SIC 5191 FARM SUPPLIES (NO BREAKDOWN) 2014 (128 Establishments)		SIC 5193 FLWRS,FLRSTS SPPLS (NO BREAKDOWN) 2014 (20 Establishments)	
	$	%	$	%	$	%	$	%
Cash	1,381,970	13.9	1,694,017	10.7	1,374,289	14.2	495,703	10.1
Accounts Receivable	2,823,593	28.4	1,393,211	8.8	1,432,357	14.8	1,128,829	23.0
Notes Receivable	119,307	1.2	0	0.0	38,712	0.4	4,908	0.1
Inventory	1,531,103	15.4	3,514,690	22.2	3,213,126	33.2	1,712,875	34.9
Other Current	646,245	6.5	664,942	4.2	735,535	7.6	299,384	6.1
Total Current	**6,502,218**	**65.4**	**7,266,860**	**45.9**	**6,794,019**	**70.2**	**3,641,699**	**74.2**
Fixed Assets	2,346,366	23.6	2,358,959	14.9	1,993,687	20.6	863,799	17.6
Other Non-current	1,093,646	11.0	6,206,119	39.2	890,384	9.2	402,452	8.2
Total Assets	**9,942,230**	**100.0**	**15,831,938**	**100.0**	**9,678,090**	**100.0**	**4,907,950**	**100.0**
Accounts Payable	2,028,215	20.4	1,646,522	10.4	977,487	10.1	942,326	19.2
Bank Loans	9,942	0.1	0	0.0	48,390	0.5	93,251	1.9
Notes Payable	149,133	1.5	174,151	1.1	406,480	4.2	63,803	1.3
Other Current	1,590,757	16.0	2,723,093	17.2	2,458,235	25.4	652,758	13.3
Total Current	**3,778,047**	**38.0**	**4,543,766**	**28.7**	**3,890,592**	**40.2**	**1,752,138**	**35.7**
Other Long Term	1,550,988	15.6	3,134,724	19.8	977,487	10.1	426,992	8.7
Deferred Credits	39,769	0.4	0	0.0	0	0.0	9,816	0.2
Net Worth	4,573,426	46.0	8,153,448	51.5	4,810,011	49.7	2,719,004	55.4
Total Liab & Net Worth	**9,942,230**	**100.0**	**15,831,938**	**100.0**	**9,678,090**	**100.0**	**4,907,950**	**100.0**
Net Sales	73,104,632	100.0	54,972,007	100.0	24,316,809	100.0	13,446,438	100.0
Gross Profit	7,675,986	10.5	14,457,638	26.3	4,304,075	17.7	4,168,396	31.0
Net Profit After Tax	1,096,569	1.5	1,924,020	3.5	705,187	2.9	389,947	2.9
Working Capital	2,724,171	---	2,723,094	---	2,903,427	---	1,889,561	---

RATIOS	UQ	MED	LQ	UQ	MED	LQ	UQ	MED	LQ	UQ	MED	LQ
SOLVENCY												
Quick Ratio (times)	1.8	1.1	0.6	1.0	0.9	0.5	1.1	0.7	0.4	1.5	1.1	0.3
Current Ratio (times)	2.6	1.6	1.3	2.4	1.7	1.2	2.1	1.6	1.3	3.3	2.1	1.5
Curr Liab To Nw (%)	36.8	72.4	169.6	24.7	48.1	81.6	40.6	80.7	163.7	35.5	59.9	121.8
Curr Liab To Inv (%)	135.0	266.1	512.1	76.9	134.4	207.4	99.1	134.8	177.1	48.8	66.5	155.6
Total Liab To Nw (%)	61.9	106.4	216.0	51.7	84.3	218.4	54.6	104.1	203.0	36.2	91.2	192.0
Fixed Assets To Nw (%)	20.4	51.1	80.6	9.6	24.4	36.5	21.1	34.7	69.9	17.0	36.2	57.2
EFFICIENCY												
Coll Period (days)	7.5	13.9	24.9	1.8	2.8	26.3	13.7	23.4	40.9	10.2	24.7	46.4
Sales To Inv (times)	116.2	51.5	26.0	24.4	20.5	14.9	14.3	9.0	5.3	15.3	4.0	2.9
Assets To Sales (%)	8.3	13.6	25.3	18.2	28.8	42.7	31.1	39.8	52.0	21.3	36.5	62.9
Sales To Nwc (times)	64.3	25.3	12.4	24.3	18.3	11.6	17.2	11.4	6.0	12.9	6.8	3.0
Acct Pay To Sales (%)	1.6	2.3	3.7	1.8	2.8	3.1	2.5	4.6	8.6	4.9	7.3	9.6
PROFITABILITY												
Return On Sales (%)	1.6	0.7	0.3	5.6	2.8	1.4	3.9	2.3	0.9	5.8	3.9	(0.3)
Return On Assets (%)	10.7	5.4	2.3	20.1	9.3	4.8	8.6	4.8	2.0	14.6	5.6	(0.7)
Return On Nw (%)	24.0	13.2	6.0	32.4	19.5	12.9	16.7	9.7	6.1	37.6	16.6	(1.4)

SIC 5194 TBCCO,TBCCO PRDTS
(NO BREAKDOWN)
2014 (27 Establishments)

	$	%
Cash	554,776	9.7
Accounts Receivable	2,098,997	36.7
Notes Receivable	5,719	0.1
Inventory	2,036,084	35.6
Other Current	291,687	5.1
Total Current	**4,987,263**	**87.2**
Fixed Assets	629,127	11.0
Other Non-current	102,948	1.8
Total Assets	**5,719,338**	**100.0**
Accounts Payable	629,127	11.0
Bank Loans	0	0.0
Notes Payable	74,351	1.3
Other Current	926,533	16.2
Total Current	**1,630,011**	**28.5**
Other Long Term	623,408	10.9
Deferred Credits	0	0.0
Net Worth	3,465,919	60.6
Total Liab & Net Worth	**5,719,338**	**100.0**
Net Sales	48,883,231	100.0
Gross Profit	3,177,410	6.5
Net Profit After Tax	195,533	0.4
Working Capital	3,357,252	---

RATIOS	UQ	MED	LQ
SOLVENCY			
Quick Ratio (times)	2.9	1.6	1.1
Current Ratio (times)	5.2	3.5	2.1
Curr Liab To Nw (%)	19.3	50.3	110.5
Curr Liab To Inv (%)	40.3	78.2	120.6
Total Liab To Nw (%)	16.8	82.2	137.2
Fixed Assets To Nw (%)	8.0	13.2	22.7
EFFICIENCY			
Coll Period (days)	9.5	13.0	22.3
Sales To Inv (times)	30.3	23.3	16.0
Assets To Sales (%)	8.2	11.7	18.6
Sales To Nwc (times)	25.6	16.2	10.2
Acct Pay To Sales (%)	0.8	1.3	1.6
PROFITABILITY			
Return On Sales (%)	0.7	0.4	0.2
Return On Assets (%)	4.8	3.6	2.0
Return On Nw (%)	11.5	6.5	3.8

SIC 5198 PNTS,VRNSHS,SUPPL
(NO BREAKDOWN)
2014 (10 Establishments)

	$	%
Cash	204,342	12.8
Accounts Receivable	335,248	21.0
Notes Receivable	0	0.0
Inventory	783,843	49.1
Other Current	68,646	4.3
Total Current	**1,392,079**	**87.2**
Fixed Assets	183,588	11.5
Other Non-current	20,754	1.3
Total Assets	**1,596,421**	**100.0**
Accounts Payable	312,899	19.6
Bank Loans	0	0.0
Notes Payable	4,789	0.3
Other Current	164,431	10.3
Total Current	**482,119**	**30.2**
Other Long Term	98,978	6.2
Deferred Credits	0	0.0
Net Worth	1,015,324	63.6
Total Liab & Net Worth	**1,596,421**	**100.0**
Net Sales	5,485,983	100.0
Gross Profit	1,931,066	35.2
Net Profit After Tax	213,953	3.9
Working Capital	909,960	---

RATIOS	UQ	MED	LQ
SOLVENCY			
Quick Ratio (times)	1.9	1.4	0.9
Current Ratio (times)	6.2	3.9	2.1
Curr Liab To Nw (%)	15.8	40.3	72.2
Curr Liab To Inv (%)	23.0	62.0	114.3
Total Liab To Nw (%)	22.7	50.1	94.8
Fixed Assets To Nw (%)	2.4	11.3	26.9
EFFICIENCY			
Coll Period (days)	13.4	21.5	31.6
Sales To Inv (times)	11.1	7.1	4.8
Assets To Sales (%)	21.8	29.1	38.1
Sales To Nwc (times)	7.9	7.4	5.4
Acct Pay To Sales (%)	1.2	3.8	5.5
PROFITABILITY			
Return On Sales (%)	7.5	1.9	0.2
Return On Assets (%)	19.1	6.7	0.6
Return On Nw (%)	50.2	20.0	0.8

SIC 5199 NNDRBL GDS,NEC
(NO BREAKDOWN)
2014 (81 Establishments)

	$	%
Cash	305,249	17.4
Accounts Receivable	535,063	30.5
Notes Receivable	1,754	0.1
Inventory	477,171	27.2
Other Current	163,151	9.3
Total Current	**1,482,388**	**84.5**
Fixed Assets	178,939	10.2
Other Non-current	92,978	5.3
Total Assets	**1,754,305**	**100.0**
Accounts Payable	347,352	19.8
Bank Loans	(14,034)	(0.8)
Notes Payable	7,017	0.4
Other Current	384,193	21.9
Total Current	**724,528**	**41.3**
Other Long Term	194,728	11.1
Deferred Credits	0	0.0
Net Worth	835,049	47.6
Total Liab & Net Worth	**1,754,305**	**100.0**
Net Sales	5,677,362	100.0
Gross Profit	1,555,597	27.4
Net Profit After Tax	181,676	3.2
Working Capital	757,860	---

RATIOS	UQ	MED	LQ
SOLVENCY			
Quick Ratio (times)	2.7	1.1	0.6
Current Ratio (times)	4.7	2.2	1.4
Curr Liab To Nw (%)	25.3	55.0	198.7
Curr Liab To Inv (%)	53.0	133.5	272.6
Total Liab To Nw (%)	42.5	102.6	233.2
Fixed Assets To Nw (%)	5.2	14.0	30.7
EFFICIENCY			
Coll Period (days)	21.4	39.6	52.0
Sales To Inv (times)	23.2	9.4	6.3
Assets To Sales (%)	19.5	30.9	43.8
Sales To Nwc (times)	10.8	7.1	4.3
Acct Pay To Sales (%)	2.1	4.4	9.1
PROFITABILITY			
Return On Sales (%)	5.3	2.2	0.6
Return On Assets (%)	15.8	6.5	1.9
Return On Nw (%)	47.9	13.4	5.8

SIC 52 BLD MTLS HDW GDN SUP
(NO BREAKDOWN)
2014 (409 Establishments)

	$	%
Cash	307,860	12.0
Accounts Receivable	443,832	17.3
Notes Receivable	7,697	0.3
Inventory	1,039,028	40.5
Other Current	123,144	4.8
Total Current	**1,921,561**	**74.9**
Fixed Assets	420,742	16.4
Other Non-current	223,199	8.7
Total Assets	**2,565,502**	**100.0**
Accounts Payable	300,164	11.7
Bank Loans	5,131	0.2
Notes Payable	51,310	2.0
Other Current	461,790	18.0
Total Current	**818,395**	**31.9**
Other Long Term	248,854	9.7
Deferred Credits	0	0.0
Net Worth	1,498,253	58.4
Total Liab & Net Worth	**2,565,502**	**100.0**
Net Sales	6,397,761	100.0
Gross Profit	1,906,533	29.8
Net Profit After Tax	153,546	2.4
Working Capital	1,103,166	---

RATIOS	UQ	MED	LQ
SOLVENCY			
Quick Ratio (times)	2.3	1.1	0.5
Current Ratio (times)	5.8	2.8	1.8
Curr Liab To Nw (%)	14.7	41.2	84.1
Curr Liab To Inv (%)	34.5	64.0	102.3
Total Liab To Nw (%)	18.4	52.9	137.0
Fixed Assets To Nw (%)	6.8	20.6	47.6
EFFICIENCY			
Coll Period (days)	12.8	25.4	36.5
Sales To Inv (times)	9.5	6.2	4.3
Assets To Sales (%)	30.0	40.1	55.6
Sales To Nwc (times)	8.9	5.2	3.5
Acct Pay To Sales (%)	2.5	4.0	5.8
PROFITABILITY			
Return On Sales (%)	3.7	1.7	0.5
Return On Assets (%)	8.2	4.2	1.2
Return On Nw (%)	15.6	6.8	2.3

	SIC 5211 LMBR.BLDNG MTRLS (NO BREAKDOWN) 2014 (227 Establishments) $	%	SIC 5251 HARDWARE STORES (NO BREAKDOWN) 2014 (124 Establishments) $	%	SIC 5261 RET NSRS,GDN STRS (NO BREAKDOWN) 2014 (44 Establishments) $	%	SIC 53 GEN MERCHANDISE (NO BREAKDOWN) 2014 (84 Establishments) $	%
Cash	369,307	11.6	191,931	12.2	209,985	10.5	763,298	15.0
Accounts Receivable	713,144	22.4	155,747	9.9	207,986	10.4	274,787	5.4
Notes Receivable	6,367	0.2	9,439	0.6	0	0.0	0	0.0
Inventory	1,155,676	36.3	720,526	45.8	1,009,930	50.5	2,203,388	43.3
Other Current	165,552	5.2	61,355	3.9	93,993	4.7	218,812	4.3
Total Current	**2,410,046**	**75.7**	**1,138,998**	**72.4**	**1,521,894**	**76.1**	**3,460,285**	**68.0**
Fixed Assets	531,675	16.7	235,980	15.0	391,973	19.6	1,221,277	24.0
Other Non-current	241,959	7.6	198,223	12.6	85,994	4.3	407,093	8.0
Total Assets	**3,183,680**	**100.0**	**1,573,201**	**100.0**	**1,999,861**	**100.0**	**5,088,655**	**100.0**
Accounts Payable	378,858	11.9	165,186	10.5	319,978	16.0	702,234	13.8
Bank Loans	3,184	0.1	11,012	0.7	0	0.0	0	0.0
Notes Payable	76,408	2.4	11,012	0.7	75,995	3.8	50,887	1.0
Other Current	553,960	17.4	239,127	15.2	517,963	25.9	666,614	13.1
Total Current	**1,012,410**	**31.8**	**426,337**	**27.1**	**913,936**	**45.7**	**1,419,735**	**27.9**
Other Long Term	315,185	9.9	158,894	10.1	179,988	9.0	1,501,153	29.5
Deferred Credits	0	0.0	0	0.0	0	0.0	5,089	0.1
Net Worth	1,856,085	58.3	987,970	62.8	905,937	45.3	2,162,678	42.5
Total Liab & Net Worth	**3,183,680**	**100.0**	**1,573,201**	**100.0**	**1,999,861**	**100.0**	**5,088,655**	**100.0**
Net Sales	8,163,282	100.0	3,600,002	100.0	5,539,781	100.0	9,336,982	100.0
Gross Profit	2,122,453	26.0	1,267,201	35.2	1,722,872	31.1	3,258,607	34.9
Net Profit After Tax	179,592	2.2	93,600	2.6	127,415	2.3	364,142	3.9
Working Capital	1,397,636	---	712,661	---	607,958	---	2,040,550	---

RATIOS	UQ	MED	LQ	UQ	MED	LQ	UQ	MED	LQ	UQ	MED	LQ
SOLVENCY												
Quick Ratio (times)	2.8	1.4	0.7	1.7	0.9	0.4	1.0	0.4	0.2	1.6	0.6	0.2
Current Ratio (times)	6.3	3.0	1.8	6.6	3.2	2.1	2.4	1.6	1.3	5.4	2.5	1.7
Curr Liab To Nw (%)	14.2	34.9	71.7	12.4	33.9	63.4	51.9	90.3	177.9	19.0	43.2	68.2
Curr Liab To Inv (%)	37.2	67.7	106.9	24.5	50.2	78.3	65.7	93.4	121.3	36.6	64.1	106.4
Total Liab To Nw (%)	17.2	47.3	101.6	14.6	48.6	111.9	59.4	141.5	227.9	27.4	67.0	136.8
Fixed Assets To Nw (%)	8.9	21.0	41.4	5.2	15.6	45.4	6.8	34.9	81.4	4.7	32.1	89.4
EFFICIENCY												
Coll Period (days)	20.8	32.1	40.2	6.6	14.8	25.9	2.6	9.5	17.2	1.7	4.3	10.8
Sales To Inv (times)	10.6	6.8	4.8	7.2	5.0	3.7	11.1	6.7	3.6	6.9	4.3	3.0
Assets To Sales (%)	29.9	39.0	55.5	34.3	43.7	57.8	27.3	36.1	55.7	36.8	54.5	70.5
Sales To Nwc (times)	8.7	5.1	3.4	7.1	4.8	3.3	17.2	10.1	6.4	7.8	3.5	2.6
Acct Pay To Sales (%)	2.8	4.0	5.9	2.4	4.3	5.8	2.4	3.2	5.9	1.6	6.5	10.0
PROFITABILITY												
Return On Sales (%)	3.4	1.7	0.8	4.0	1.8	0.4	2.6	1.0	0.4	5.9	2.9	0.7
Return On Assets (%)	7.6	4.6	1.5	9.4	3.8	0.9	6.7	3.4	0.8	10.0	5.1	2.2
Return On Nw (%)	14.2	6.5	2.8	15.7	7.3	1.8	19.8	7.4	2.2	18.1	9.2	3.2

	SIC 5311 DEPARTMENT STORES (NO BREAKDOWN) 2014 (48 Establishments) $	%	SIC 5331 VARIETY STORES (NO BREAKDOWN) 2014 (17 Establishments) $	%	SIC 5399 MISC GNRL MRCH STRS (NO BREAKDOWN) 2014 (19 Establishments) $	%	SIC 54 FOOD STORES (NO BREAKDOWN) 2014 (104 Establishments) $	%
Cash	913,450	13.4	496,896	17.9	594,361	16.3	1,221,462	19.4
Accounts Receivable	293,122	4.3	55,519	2.0	404,749	11.1	522,584	8.3
Notes Receivable	0	0.0	0	0.0	0	0.0	50,370	0.8
Inventory	2,978,939	43.7	1,265,835	45.6	1,465,848	40.2	1,385,163	22.0
Other Current	354,474	5.2	183,214	6.6	3,647	0.1	384,068	6.1
Total Current	**4,539,985**	**66.6**	**2,001,464**	**72.1**	**2,468,605**	**67.7**	**3,563,647**	**56.6**
Fixed Assets	1,799,634	26.4	433,049	15.6	922,536	25.3	1,907,747	30.3
Other Non-current	477,175	7.0	341,442	12.3	255,248	7.0	824,802	13.1
Total Assets	**6,816,794**	**100.0**	**2,775,955**	**100.0**	**3,646,389**	**100.0**	**6,296,196**	**100.0**
Accounts Payable	961,168	14.1	408,065	14.7	448,506	12.3	862,579	13.7
Bank Loans	0	0.0	0	0.0	0	0.0	31,481	0.5
Notes Payable	102,252	1.5	16,656	0.6	3,646	0.1	69,258	1.1
Other Current	790,748	11.6	366,426	13.2	601,654	16.5	812,209	12.9
Total Current	**1,854,168**	**27.2**	**791,147**	**28.5**	**1,053,806**	**28.9**	**1,775,527**	**28.2**
Other Long Term	2,808,519	41.2	233,180	8.4	696,461	19.1	1,385,163	22.0
Deferred Credits	6,817	0.1	8,328	0.3	0	0.0	0	0.0
Net Worth	2,147,290	31.5	1,743,300	62.8	1,896,122	52.0	3,135,506	49.8
Total Liab & Net Worth	**6,816,794**	**100.0**	**2,775,955**	**100.0**	**3,646,389**	**100.0**	**6,296,196**	**100.0**
Net Sales	11,632,754	100.0	7,210,273	100.0	6,932,298	100.0	27,494,306	100.0
Gross Profit	4,187,791	36.0	2,768,745	38.4	2,003,434	28.9	7,725,900	28.1
Net Profit After Tax	418,779	3.6	223,518	3.1	374,344	5.4	769,841	2.8
Working Capital	2,685,817	—	1,210,317	—	1,414,799	—	1,788,120	—

RATIOS	UQ	MED	LQ	UQ	MED	LQ	UQ	MED	LQ	UQ	MED	LQ
SOLVENCY												
Quick Ratio (times)	1.6	0.6	0.3	1.1	0.5	0.2	2.0	0.5	0.3	1.9	0.8	0.4
Current Ratio (times)	4.5	2.6	1.7	6.8	2.0	1.8	6.9	2.6	1.4	3.7	2.2	1.2
Curr Liab To Nw (%)	20.5	43.2	67.5	16.9	43.5	66.1	23.4	41.8	98.4	19.6	40.3	75.2
Curr Liab To Inv (%)	38.1	58.1	113.1	46.9	66.3	83.9	18.5	84.3	109.7	60.1	107.9	216.3
Total Liab To Nw (%)	27.1	62.9	107.9	17.8	66.1	101.2	38.7	114.9	213.2	27.8	67.1	198.2
Fixed Assets To Nw (%)	6.9	34.7	96.1	2.7	19.4	69.0	6.1	32.0	88.6	22.3	51.1	106.8
EFFICIENCY												
Coll Period (days)	2.4	4.8	10.8	0.4	0.9	6.6	2.2	4.4	19.4	1.5	4.4	9.5
Sales To Inv (times)	5.5	3.8	2.6	8.5	6.3	4.7	12.1	4.0	3.6	45.8	23.3	12.2
Assets To Sales (%)	49.6	58.6	70.5	34.8	38.5	54.6	24.8	52.6	74.6	16.3	22.9	42.5
Sales To Nwc (times)	7.5	3.2	2.7	11.5	7.5	2.6	7.3	4.6	1.8	30.0	13.6	6.7
Acct Pay To Sales (%)	4.9	7.2	10.6	1.8	5.3	6.9	1.1	1.7	10.0	1.8	2.8	4.1
PROFITABILITY												
Return On Sales (%)	4.9	3.0	0.4	5.1	2.8	1.6	9.4	2.6	0.7	4.0	1.4	0.5
Return On Assets (%)	8.1	5.0	0.6	9.8	6.4	3.4	15.8	5.0	2.3	11.3	6.3	2.8
Return On Nw (%)	14.4	9.2	2.6	23.3	9.1	4.7	31.3	9.8	4.3	26.6	14.3	6.4

	SIC 5411 GROCERY STORES (NO BREAKDOWN) 2014 (83 Establishments) $	%	SIC 55 AUTO DEALER SVC STATN (NO BREAKDOWN) 2014 (354 Establishments) $	%	SIC 5511 NEW/USED CAR DLRS (NO BREAKDOWN) 2014 (162 Establishments) $	%	SIC 5531 AUTO.HOME SPPL STRS (NO BREAKDOWN) 2014 (62 Establishments) $	%
Cash	1,423,318	17.3	1,074,601	13.0	1,382,398	10.7	296,984	13.6
Accounts Receivable	559,455	6.8	653,027	7.9	762,257	5.9	307,903	14.1
Notes Receivable	82,273	1.0	16,532	0.2	12,920	0.1	2,184	0.1
Inventory	2,015,682	24.5	4,050,420	49.0	7,661,326	59.3	936,811	42.9
Other Current	477,182	5.8	471,172	5.7	956,050	7.4	63,327	2.9
Total Current	**4,557,910**	**55.4**	**6,265,752**	**75.8**	**10,774,951**	**83.4**	**1,607,209**	**73.6**
Fixed Assets	2,690,319	32.7	1,413,514	17.1	1,408,237	10.9	417,088	19.1
Other Non-current	979,045	11.9	586,898	7.1	736,417	5.7	159,411	7.3
Total Assets	**8,227,274**	**100.0**	**8,266,164**	**100.0**	**12,919,605**	**100.0**	**2,183,708**	**100.0**
Accounts Payable	1,127,137	13.7	768,753	9.3	478,025	3.7	486,967	22.3
Bank Loans	49,364	0.6	66,129	0.8	64,598	0.5	30,572	1.4
Notes Payable	90,500	1.1	1,066,335	12.9	2,919,831	22.6	28,388	1.3
Other Current	921,454	11.2	2,322,793	28.1	4,948,209	38.3	262,045	12.0
Total Current	**2,188,455**	**26.6**	**4,224,010**	**51.1**	**8,410,663**	**65.1**	**807,972**	**37.0**
Other Long Term	1,629,000	19.8	859,681	10.4	1,136,925	8.8	242,392	11.1
Deferred Credits	0	0.0	8,266	0.1	0	0.0	6,551	0.3
Net Worth	4,409,819	53.6	3,174,207	38.4	3,372,017	26.1	1,126,793	51.6
Total Liab & Net Worth	**8,227,274**	**100.0**	**8,266,164**	**100.0**	**12,919,605**	**100.0**	**2,183,708**	**100.0**
Net Sales	39,177,495	100.0	25,994,226	100.0	43,795,271	100.0	6,577,434	100.0
Gross Profit	8,854,114	22.6	5,094,868	19.6	5,780,976	13.2	2,229,750	33.9
Net Profit After Tax	1,253,680	3.2	623,861	2.4	744,520	1.7	157,858	2.4
Working Capital	2,369,455	---	2,041,742	---	2,364,288	---	799,237	---

RATIOS	UQ	MED	LQ	UQ	MED	LQ	UQ	MED	LQ	UQ	MED	LQ
SOLVENCY												
Quick Ratio (times)	1.7	0.7	0.4	0.9	0.3	0.2	0.4	0.3	0.2	1.9	0.9	0.3
Current Ratio (times)	3.5	2.1	1.3	2.1	1.4	1.2	1.5	1.2	1.1	4.5	2.1	1.5
Curr Liab To Nw (%)	20.0	41.9	76.7	48.1	147.9	337.4	147.9	258.0	541.6	21.7	51.1	141.5
Curr Liab To Inv (%)	60.1	104.2	184.9	84.4	107.6	131.0	96.1	110.5	125.6	46.2	93.1	124.9
Total Liab To Nw (%)	27.5	67.0	195.5	72.7	201.4	399.6	177.3	328.5	585.2	30.5	78.4	189.6
Fixed Assets To Nw (%)	22.7	53.9	121.6	13.5	34.4	79.6	11.8	35.1	85.7	7.3	20.7	49.8
EFFICIENCY												
Coll Period (days)	1.5	3.5	6.6	2.6	6.8	13.9	2.9	6.6	11.5	7.7	17.2	28.3
Sales To Inv (times)	41.2	23.3	13.7	11.6	6.4	4.2	7.1	5.9	4.7	12.0	8.5	5.0
Assets To Sales (%)	14.7	21.0	39.0	22.8	31.8	44.0	24.3	29.5	36.7	20.0	33.2	45.8
Sales To Nwc (times)	30.2	18.4	8.3	29.6	14.4	6.6	35.8	20.1	12.2	14.2	7.3	4.1
Acct Pay To Sales (%)	1.9	2.8	4.1	0.6	1.4	3.3	0.5	0.8	1.3	2.9	6.3	10.3
PROFITABILITY												
Return On Sales (%)	2.7	1.3	0.5	3.2	1.5	0.7	2.3	1.5	0.7	3.7	1.4	0.5
Return On Assets (%)	11.0	5.9	2.7	9.4	4.8	2.1	7.8	4.4	2.5	11.9	3.9	1.5
Return On Nw (%)	21.8	13.7	6.0	27.8	14.9	5.3	32.9	21.6	9.9	21.8	8.6	3.2

SIC 5541 GASLNE SVC STATIONS
(NO BREAKDOWN)
2014 (61 Establishments)

	$	%
Cash	1,782,235	17.1
Accounts Receivable	1,146,467	11.0
Notes Receivable	10,422	0.1
Inventory	1,490,407	14.3
Other Current	541,967	5.2
Total Current	**4,971,498**	**47.7**
Fixed Assets	4,179,393	40.1
Other Non-current	1,271,536	12.2
Total Assets	**10,422,427**	**100.0**
Accounts Payable	1,334,071	12.8
Bank Loans	83,379	0.8
Notes Payable	72,957	0.7
Other Current	1,500,830	14.4
Total Current	**2,991,237**	**28.7**
Other Long Term	1,584,209	15.2
Deferred Credits	10,422	0.1
Net Worth	5,836,559	56.0
Total Liab & Net Worth	**10,422,427**	**100.0**
Net Sales	50,107,822	100.0
Gross Profit	7,917,036	15.8
Net Profit After Tax	1,503,235	3.0
Working Capital	1,980,261	---

RATIOS	UQ	MED	LQ
SOLVENCY			
Quick Ratio (times)	2.2	1.0	0.5
Current Ratio (times)	3.3	1.7	1.2
Curr Liab To Nw (%)	22.8	43.2	78.6
Curr Liab To Inv (%)	106.4	197.6	315.2
Total Liab To Nw (%)	35.5	70.5	151.3
Fixed Assets To Nw (%)	36.0	73.1	133.7
EFFICIENCY			
Coll Period (days)	2.2	4.8	13.0
Sales To Inv (times)	81.8	50.6	30.3
Assets To Sales (%)	10.2	20.8	31.6
Sales To Nwc (times)	48.4	29.6	11.7
Acct Pay To Sales (%)	1.3	2.1	3.1
PROFITABILITY			
Return On Sales (%)	2.8	1.3	0.6
Return On Assets (%)	11.1	7.8	2.5
Return On Nw (%)	22.0	12.2	3.9

SIC 5551 BOAT DEALERS
(NO BREAKDOWN)
2014 (17 Establishments)

	$	%
Cash	408,037	11.1
Accounts Receivable	183,801	5.0
Notes Receivable	0	0.0
Inventory	2,135,762	58.1
Other Current	139,688	3.8
Total Current	**2,867,288**	**78.0**
Fixed Assets	466,853	12.7
Other Non-current	341,869	9.3
Total Assets	**3,676,010**	**100.0**
Accounts Payable	466,853	12.7
Bank Loans	0	0.0
Notes Payable	257,321	7.0
Other Current	1,088,099	29.6
Total Current	**1,812,273**	**49.3**
Other Long Term	341,869	9.3
Deferred Credits	0	0.0
Net Worth	1,521,868	41.4
Total Liab & Net Worth	**3,676,010**	**100.0**
Net Sales	6,449,140	100.0
Gross Profit	1,786,412	27.7
Net Profit After Tax	219,271	3.4
Working Capital	1,055,015	---

RATIOS	UQ	MED	LQ
SOLVENCY			
Quick Ratio (times)	0.4	0.2	0.1
Current Ratio (times)	3.2	1.5	1.3
Curr Liab To Nw (%)	41.1	164.2	291.8
Curr Liab To Inv (%)	43.4	81.0	95.8
Total Liab To Nw (%)	68.3	225.0	309.4
Fixed Assets To Nw (%)	20.5	25.7	42.6
EFFICIENCY			
Coll Period (days)	2.2	7.3	14.3
Sales To Inv (times)	3.9	2.8	2.5
Assets To Sales (%)	40.2	57.0	67.3
Sales To Nwc (times)	13.4	5.7	3.9
Acct Pay To Sales (%)	1.4	2.8	8.1
PROFITABILITY			
Return On Sales (%)	4.8	3.4	1.2
Return On Assets (%)	7.4	5.2	2.1
Return On Nw (%)	29.0	8.2	5.7

SIC 5561 RCRTNL VHCLE DLRS
(NO BREAKDOWN)
2014 (16 Establishments)

	$	%
Cash	686,465	15.1
Accounts Receivable	40,915	0.9
Notes Receivable	0	0.0
Inventory	3,136,827	69.0
Other Current	127,292	2.8
Total Current	**3,991,499**	**87.8**
Fixed Assets	436,428	9.6
Other Non-current	118,199	2.6
Total Assets	**4,546,126**	**100.0**
Accounts Payable	77,284	1.7
Bank Loans	127,292	2.8
Notes Payable	1,031,971	22.7
Other Current	1,409,298	31.0
Total Current	**2,645,845**	**58.2**
Other Long Term	413,698	9.1
Deferred Credits	0	0.0
Net Worth	1,486,583	32.7
Total Liab & Net Worth	**4,546,126**	**100.0**
Net Sales	9,002,230	100.0
Gross Profit	2,061,511	22.9
Net Profit After Tax	396,098	4.4
Working Capital	1,345,654	---

RATIOS	UQ	MED	LQ
SOLVENCY			
Quick Ratio (times)	0.8	0.1	0.0
Current Ratio (times)	1.9	1.3	1.2
Curr Liab To Nw (%)	92.2	304.5	392.1
Curr Liab To Inv (%)	76.3	90.2	104.7
Total Liab To Nw (%)	107.0	322.3	434.5
Fixed Assets To Nw (%)	28.6	34.6	37.7
EFFICIENCY			
Coll Period (days)	0.6	0.7	1.7
Sales To Inv (times)	3.8	2.6	2.4
Assets To Sales (%)	41.4	50.5	57.5
Sales To Nwc (times)	13.0	8.2	3.8
Acct Pay To Sales (%)	0.2	0.5	1.0
PROFITABILITY			
Return On Sales (%)	4.3	2.5	1.4
Return On Assets (%)	8.3	6.4	3.0
Return On Nw (%)	26.0	15.0	12.2

SIC 5571 MOTORCYCLE DEALERS
(NO BREAKDOWN)
2014 (19 Establishments)

	$	%
Cash	567,201	16.8
Accounts Receivable	114,791	3.4
Notes Receivable	23,633	0.7
Inventory	2,251,923	66.7
Other Current	175,562	5.2
Total Current	**3,133,110**	**92.8**
Fixed Assets	165,434	4.9
Other Non-current	77,652	2.3
Total Assets	**3,376,196**	**100.0**
Accounts Payable	290,353	8.6
Bank Loans	0	0.0
Notes Payable	347,748	10.3
Other Current	1,134,402	33.6
Total Current	**1,772,503**	**52.5**
Other Long Term	327,491	9.7
Deferred Credits	0	0.0
Net Worth	1,276,202	37.8
Total Liab & Net Worth	**3,376,196**	**100.0**
Net Sales	6,918,434	100.0
Gross Profit	1,404,442	20.3
Net Profit After Tax	172,961	2.5
Working Capital	1,360,607	---

RATIOS	UQ	MED	LQ
SOLVENCY			
Quick Ratio (times)	0.9	0.2	0.1
Current Ratio (times)	4.5	1.4	1.2
Curr Liab To Nw (%)	30.6	170.5	396.1
Curr Liab To Inv (%)	58.7	86.2	91.2
Total Liab To Nw (%)	57.7	223.8	506.3
Fixed Assets To Nw (%)	3.8	11.7	26.2
EFFICIENCY			
Coll Period (days)	1.1	3.7	5.5
Sales To Inv (times)	5.1	3.3	2.0
Assets To Sales (%)	34.5	48.8	68.7
Sales To Nwc (times)	14.0	10.4	3.0
Acct Pay To Sales (%)	0.9	1.4	1.8
PROFITABILITY			
Return On Sales (%)	4.0	1.0	0.2
Return On Assets (%)	6.1	2.2	0.3
Return On Nw (%)	23.4	7.0	2.0

	SIC 5599 ATMTVE DLRS,NEC (NO BREAKDOWN) 2014 (11 Establishments)		SIC 56 APPAREL ACCES STORES (NO BREAKDOWN) 2014 (257 Establishments)		SIC 5611 MNS,BYS CLTHNG STRS (NO BREAKDOWN) 2014 (67 Establishments)		SIC 5621 WOMENS CLTHNG STRS (NO BREAKDOWN) 2014 (60 Establishments)	
	$	%	$	%	$	%	$	%
Cash	399,665	11.8	163,719	17.1	111,879	16.8	204,845	20.4
Accounts Receivable	433,535	12.8	54,573	5.7	43,287	6.5	43,178	4.3
Notes Receivable	50,805	1.5	3,830	0.4	1,998	0.3	0	0.0
Inventory	1,761,237	52.0	470,095	49.1	350,955	52.7	440,819	43.9
Other Current	142,254	4.2	46,914	4.9	29,967	4.5	79,328	7.9
Total Current	**2,787,496**	**82.3**	**739,131**	**77.2**	**538,086**	**80.8**	**768,170**	**76.5**
Fixed Assets	298,055	8.8	147,443	15.4	74,586	11.2	174,721	17.4
Other Non-current	301,443	8.9	70,849	7.4	53,276	8.0	61,253	6.1
Total Assets	**3,386,994**	**100.0**	**957,423**	**100.0**	**665,948**	**100.0**	**1,004,144**	**100.0**
Accounts Payable	379,343	11.2	125,422	13.1	87,905	13.2	148,613	14.8
Bank Loans	0	0.0	957	0.1	1,998	0.3	2,008	0.2
Notes Payable	37,257	1.1	10,532	1.1	12,653	1.9	5,021	0.5
Other Current	1,066,903	31.5	153,188	16.0	108,550	16.3	103,427	10.3
Total Current	**1,483,503**	**43.8**	**290,099**	**30.3**	**211,106**	**31.7**	**259,069**	**25.8**
Other Long Term	169,350	5.0	88,083	9.2	41,954	6.3	83,344	8.3
Deferred Credits	6,774	0.2	1,915	0.2	666	0.1	2,008	0.2
Net Worth	1,727,367	51.0	577,326	60.3	412,222	61.9	659,723	65.7
Total Liab & Net Worth	**3,386,994**	**100.0**	**957,423**	**100.0**	**665,948**	**100.0**	**1,004,144**	**100.0**
Net Sales	8,820,297	100.0	2,067,868	100.0	1,348,073	100.0	2,425,469	100.0
Gross Profit	1,878,723	21.3	872,640	42.2	628,202	46.6	1,013,846	41.8
Net Profit After Tax	255,789	2.9	62,036	3.0	49,879	3.7	60,637	2.5
Working Capital	1,303,993	—	449,032	—	326,980	—	509,101	—

RATIOS	UQ	MED	LQ	UQ	MED	LQ	UQ	MED	LQ	UQ	MED	LQ
SOLVENCY												
Quick Ratio (times)	1.9	1.0	0.1	2.0	0.7	0.2	2.0	0.9	0.3	3.7	0.8	0.4
Current Ratio (times)	3.9	2.2	1.4	6.9	2.9	1.8	6.6	3.6	2.2	7.8	3.1	1.7
Curr Liab To Nw (%)	30.4	84.7	321.9	13.0	32.8	82.8	14.3	29.9	70.6	13.7	32.9	80.1
Curr Liab To Inv (%)	73.8	83.9	91.6	25.4	48.4	97.3	24.7	45.0	75.3	24.5	48.1	114.5
Total Liab To Nw (%)	35.6	95.1	326.1	17.0	45.3	108.4	16.3	32.7	85.8	15.2	46.3	115.9
Fixed Assets To Nw (%)	8.4	11.9	28.5	5.4	16.9	45.0	4.5	10.8	27.4	5.1	15.1	54.7
EFFICIENCY												
Coll Period (days)	1.5	8.8	23.4	1.5	5.8	17.4	1.5	6.8	22.5	1.5	3.5	9.5
Sales To Inv (times)	14.3	5.3	3.0	8.2	5.0	3.2	6.2	4.0	2.7	10.9	7.8	4.6
Assets To Sales (%)	29.0	38.4	51.6	31.6	46.3	64.1	34.4	49.4	71.1	30.2	41.4	60.0
Sales To Nwc (times)	12.4	8.1	5.6	8.4	4.9	2.8	5.7	3.9	2.4	15.3	6.7	3.0
Acct Pay To Sales (%)	1.3	2.0	3.3	2.6	5.1	8.1	3.2	5.5	9.0	2.7	5.0	6.6
PROFITABILITY												
Return On Sales (%)	4.9	2.8	1.4	5.1	2.1	0.2	5.7	2.2	(0.1)	4.1	1.8	0.5
Return On Assets (%)	11.6	7.3	5.6	11.1	4.4	0.6	11.8	4.1	0.0	9.9	4.8	2.0
Return On Nw (%)	26.1	13.4	10.0	18.0	7.4	1.7	18.2	5.7	0.5	15.0	7.5	3.0

	SIC 5632 WMNS ACCY.SPCTY STR (NO BREAKDOWN) 2014 (10 Establishments)		SIC 5651 FMLY CLTHNG STRS (NO BREAKDOWN) 2014 (31 Establishments)		SIC 5661 SHOE STORES (NO BREAKDOWN) 2014 (47 Establishments)		SIC 5699 MISC APPRL.ACCY STR (NO BREAKDOWN) 2014 (36 Establishments)	
	$	%	$	%	$	%	$	%
Cash	184,152	6.7	173,999	14.7	136,893	16.9	175,846	17.0
Accounts Receivable	123,684	4.5	65,102	5.5	21,060	2.6	96,198	9.3
Notes Receivable	0	0.0	1,184	0.1	0	0.0	22,757	2.2
Inventory	1,176,372	42.8	561,057	47.4	488,439	60.3	437,547	42.3
Other Current	382,045	13.9	39,060	3.3	25,110	3.1	25,859	2.5
Total Current	**1,866,253**	**67.9**	**840,402**	**71.0**	**671,502**	**82.9**	**758,207**	**73.3**
Fixed Assets	340,818	12.4	254,488	21.5	81,002	10.0	232,738	22.5
Other Non-current	541,461	19.7	88,775	7.5	57,511	7.1	43,444	4.2
Total Assets	**2,748,532**	**100.0**	**1,183,665**	**100.0**	**810,015**	**100.0**	**1,034,389**	**100.0**
Accounts Payable	310,584	11.3	92,326	7.8	106,112	13.1	162,399	15.7
Bank Loans	0	0.0	0	0.0	810	0.1	0	0.0
Notes Payable	85,204	3.1	0	0.0	6,480	0.8	15,516	1.5
Other Current	972,981	35.4	197,672	16.7	149,043	18.4	175,846	17.0
Total Current	**1,368,769**	**49.8**	**289,998**	**24.5**	**262,445**	**32.4**	**353,761**	**34.2**
Other Long Term	824,560	30.0	147,958	12.5	42,121	5.2	122,058	11.8
Deferred Credits	32,982	1.2	0	0.0	810	0.1	2,069	0.2
Net Worth	522,221	19.0	745,709	63.0	504,639	62.3	556,501	53.8
Total Liab & Net Worth	**2,748,532**	**100.0**	**1,183,665**	**100.0**	**810,015**	**100.0**	**1,034,389**	**100.0**
Net Sales	5,137,443	100.0	2,386,421	100.0	1,656,472	100.0	2,672,840	100.0
Gross Profit	2,034,427	39.6	925,931	38.8	650,993	39.3	1,114,574	41.7
Net Profit After Tax	(303,109)	(5.9)	107,389	4.5	62,946	3.8	77,512	2.9
Working Capital	497,484	—	550,404	—	409,057	—	404,446	—

RATIOS	UQ	MED	LQ	UQ	MED	LQ	UQ	MED	LQ	UQ	MED	LQ
SOLVENCY												
Quick Ratio (times)	0.6	0.2	0.1	2.7	0.7	0.1	1.6	0.6	0.2	1.9	0.8	0.3
Current Ratio (times)	1.8	1.6	1.1	11.1	2.9	2.0	6.8	3.3	2.2	5.5	2.1	1.6
Curr Liab To Nw (%)	117.8	152.6	212.3	7.8	26.9	88.7	15.6	28.5	63.6	23.7	46.7	79.5
Curr Liab To Inv (%)	77.3	112.9	140.4	17.3	42.5	83.5	25.2	44.4	70.7	35.5	81.4	104.1
Total Liab To Nw (%)	185.7	234.2	402.6	9.3	37.8	156.3	22.2	39.7	75.3	26.5	51.8	128.7
Fixed Assets To Nw (%)	22.6	40.6	50.5	7.8	39.9	80.6	5.5	12.6	27.1	14.2	34.0	78.0
EFFICIENCY												
Coll Period (days)	4.4	18.3	39.6	2.2	6.2	14.2	0.7	3.0	8.4	1.8	12.1	26.0
Sales To Inv (times)	8.5	6.2	3.1	7.5	3.8	2.5	6.0	4.6	2.4	8.8	6.3	4.3
Assets To Sales (%)	51.5	53.5	143.8	33.0	49.6	78.5	34.9	48.9	63.7	26.7	38.7	52.7
Sales To Nwc (times)	8.1	8.0	6.1	10.8	4.8	3.2	5.3	3.9	2.1	9.5	6.8	5.0
Acct Pay To Sales (%)	5.2	5.6	8.3	1.7	3.1	7.2	2.3	4.9	7.4	2.6	5.7	8.7
PROFITABILITY												
Return On Sales (%)	0.4	(1.3)	(9.5)	5.8	2.4	1.1	5.2	1.8	0.5	7.4	2.5	0.8
Return On Assets (%)	1.4	(2.4)	(6.6)	8.8	7.8	2.1	10.6	4.2	1.0	17.0	6.8	1.7
Return On Nw (%)	4.5	(4.0)	(81.7)	32.5	10.7	4.0	13.5	7.3	1.8	46.1	14.3	3.7

	SIC 57 FURN.HOME FURNISHGS (NO BREAKDOWN) 2014 (428 Establishments) $	%	SIC 5712 FURNITURE STORES (NO BREAKDOWN) 2014 (204 Establishments) $	%	SIC 5713 FLR CVRNG STRS (NO BREAKDOWN) 2014 (72 Establishments) $	%	SIC 5719 MISC HMFRNSHNGS STR (NO BREAKDOWN) 2014 (26 Establishments) $	%
Cash	246,387	18.5	212,420	16.0	210,510	16.2	235,330	28.3
Accounts Receivable	211,759	15.9	188,523	14.2	270,284	20.8	34,094	4.1
Notes Receivable	7,991	0.6	7,966	0.6	20,791	1.6	0	0.0
Inventory	520,742	39.1	582,829	43.9	426,217	32.8	360,064	43.3
Other Current	79,909	6.0	73,020	5.5	93,560	7.2	22,452	2.7
Total Current	**1,066,788**	**80.1**	**1,064,758**	**80.2**	**1,021,362**	**78.6**	**651,940**	**78.4**
Fixed Assets	197,109	14.8	200,472	15.1	205,312	15.8	127,228	15.3
Other Non-current	67,923	5.1	62,398	4.7	72,769	5.6	52,388	6.3
Total Assets	**1,331,820**	**100.0**	**1,327,628**	**100.0**	**1,299,443**	**100.0**	**831,556**	**100.0**
Accounts Payable	193,114	14.5	152,677	11.5	193,617	14.9	108,102	13.0
Bank Loans	7,991	0.6	3,983	0.3	0	0.0	0	0.0
Notes Payable	17,314	1.3	13,276	1.0	23,390	1.8	0	0.0
Other Current	296,995	22.3	269,509	20.3	255,990	19.7	182,943	22.0
Total Current	**515,414**	**38.7**	**439,445**	**33.1**	**472,997**	**36.4**	**291,045**	**35.0**
Other Long Term	130,519	9.8	116,831	8.8	165,030	12.7	78,997	9.5
Deferred Credits	1,332	0.1	1,328	0.1	1,299	0.1	0	0.0
Net Worth	684,555	51.4	770,024	58.0	660,117	50.8	461,514	55.5
Total Liab & Net Worth	**1,331,820**	**100.0**	**1,327,628**	**100.0**	**1,299,443**	**100.0**	**831,556**	**100.0**
Net Sales	3,730,588	100.0	2,970,085	100.0	3,833,165	100.0	2,726,413	100.0
Gross Profit	1,406,432	37.7	1,235,555	41.6	1,280,277	33.4	1,155,999	42.4
Net Profit After Tax	89,534	2.4	86,132	2.9	99,662	2.6	95,424	3.5
Working Capital	551,374	---	625,313	---	548,365	---	360,895	---

RATIOS	UQ	MED	LQ	UQ	MED	LQ	UQ	MED	LQ	UQ	MED	LQ
SOLVENCY												
Quick Ratio (times)	2.1	0.9	0.4	2.3	0.8	0.3	2.1	1.1	0.6	2.1	0.8	0.5
Current Ratio (times)	4.4	2.5	1.5	5.3	2.6	1.6	3.8	2.7	1.5	4.5	2.9	1.6
Curr Liab To Nw (%)	22.0	47.4	114.5	18.9	39.6	100.7	27.9	50.4	113.9	22.3	44.1	69.4
Curr Liab To Inv (%)	46.7	82.7	144.9	34.3	67.6	108.1	56.4	96.6	156.2	44.1	71.3	100.2
Total Liab To Nw (%)	26.5	61.0	154.3	22.7	52.6	133.5	30.4	59.3	163.6	26.7	44.1	116.5
Fixed Assets To Nw (%)	6.6	20.2	45.8	6.6	20.1	41.4	6.8	21.5	56.7	6.9	14.5	56.2
EFFICIENCY												
Coll Period (days)	4.8	15.3	34.0	3.9	12.4	35.8	12.1	26.7	35.0	2.2	9.9	26.9
Sales To Inv (times)	13.2	6.9	4.1	8.1	4.9	3.6	20.6	10.3	6.4	12.2	6.9	4.5
Assets To Sales (%)	22.9	35.7	53.8	30.5	44.7	60.8	24.2	33.9	42.8	21.3	30.5	53.3
Sales To Nwc (times)	12.0	5.9	3.5	10.4	4.5	2.8	9.9	5.6	4.2	7.9	5.6	4.6
Acct Pay To Sales (%)	2.5	4.3	6.4	2.6	4.0	5.9	2.9	4.4	6.3	2.1	3.2	6.7
PROFITABILITY												
Return On Sales (%)	4.4	1.7	0.3	4.8	2.2	0.5	5.2	1.8	0.4	6.4	2.4	1.1
Return On Assets (%)	11.4	4.7	1.0	10.4	4.6	1.1	12.4	4.2	1.2	19.1	9.8	5.0
Return On Nw (%)	25.6	8.8	2.2	22.7	7.3	1.9	28.0	9.2	3.1	50.6	21.8	5.2

SIC 5722 HSHLD APPLNCE STRS
(NO BREAKDOWN)
2014 (29 Establishments)

	$	%
Cash	276,444	15.1
Accounts Receivable	172,091	9.4
Notes Receivable	0	0.0
Inventory	1,016,068	55.5
Other Current	60,415	3.3
Total Current	**1,525,018**	**83.3**
Fixed Assets	236,167	12.9
Other Non-current	69,569	3.8
Total Assets	**1,830,754**	**100.0**
Accounts Payable	311,228	17.0
Bank Loans	0	0.0
Notes Payable	40,277	2.2
Other Current	470,504	25.7
Total Current	**822,009**	**44.9**
Other Long Term	219,690	12.0
Deferred Credits	0	0.0
Net Worth	789,055	43.1
Total Liab & Net Worth	**1,830,754**	**100.0**
Net Sales	6,805,777	100.0
Gross Profit	2,096,179	30.8
Net Profit After Tax	102,087	1.5
Working Capital	703,009	---

RATIOS	UQ	MED	LQ
SOLVENCY			
Quick Ratio (times)	1.3	0.7	0.3
Current Ratio (times)	4.2	2.1	1.3
Curr Liab To Nw (%)	27.2	65.1	237.0
Curr Liab To Inv (%)	46.5	84.5	114.4
Total Liab To Nw (%)	41.1	100.8	266.1
Fixed Assets To Nw (%)	8.1	16.1	54.4
EFFICIENCY			
Coll Period (days)	4.1	5.5	13.7
Sales To Inv (times)	8.1	6.7	5.3
Assets To Sales (%)	21.4	26.9	38.0
Sales To Nwc (times)	16.3	9.6	3.8
Acct Pay To Sales (%)	2.2	4.6	7.8
PROFITABILITY			
Return On Sales (%)	2.8	0.9	0.2
Return On Assets (%)	7.9	2.5	1.0
Return On Nw (%)	16.3	8.5	1.9

SIC 5731 RDO,TV,ELECTRNC STR
(NO BREAKDOWN)
2014 (29 Establishments)

	$	%
Cash	294,221	23.0
Accounts Receivable	222,584	17.4
Notes Receivable	0	0.0
Inventory	377,370	29.5
Other Current	80,591	6.3
Total Current	**974,766**	**76.2**
Fixed Assets	193,162	15.1
Other Non-current	111,292	8.7
Total Assets	**1,279,220**	**100.0**
Accounts Payable	246,889	19.3
Bank Loans	0	0.0
Notes Payable	10,234	0.8
Other Current	258,403	20.2
Total Current	**515,526**	**40.3**
Other Long Term	101,058	7.9
Deferred Credits	12,792	1.0
Net Worth	649,844	50.8
Total Liab & Net Worth	**1,279,220**	**100.0**
Net Sales	3,985,109	100.0
Gross Profit	1,323,056	33.2
Net Profit After Tax	107,598	2.7
Working Capital	459,240	---

RATIOS	UQ	MED	LQ
Quick Ratio (times)	2.6	1.1	0.5
Current Ratio (times)	3.6	2.3	1.7
Curr Liab To Nw (%)	20.6	43.8	101.4
Curr Liab To Inv (%)	82.0	106.4	172.4
Total Liab To Nw (%)	30.5	53.7	107.1
Fixed Assets To Nw (%)	12.8	21.0	45.5
Coll Period (days)	11.7	24.7	42.0
Sales To Inv (times)	18.5	9.2	6.3
Assets To Sales (%)	20.6	32.1	53.8
Sales To Nwc (times)	13.5	8.1	5.0
Acct Pay To Sales (%)	3.5	5.0	8.7
Return On Sales (%)	4.6	2.7	0.0
Return On Assets (%)	21.3	5.2	0.0
Return On Nw (%)	41.9	14.7	0.7

SIC 5734 COMPTR,SOFTWRE STRS
(NO BREAKDOWN)
2014 (52 Establishments)

	$	%
Cash	494,864	26.5
Accounts Receivable	509,803	27.3
Notes Receivable	14,939	0.8
Inventory	382,819	20.5
Other Current	154,995	8.3
Total Current	**1,557,420**	**83.4**
Fixed Assets	220,354	11.8
Other Non-current	89,636	4.8
Total Assets	**1,867,410**	**100.0**
Accounts Payable	442,576	23.7
Bank Loans	24,276	1.3
Notes Payable	33,613	1.8
Other Current	616,246	33.0
Total Current	**1,116,711**	**59.8**
Other Long Term	138,188	7.4
Deferred Credits	3,735	0.2
Net Worth	608,776	32.6
Total Liab & Net Worth	**1,867,410**	**100.0**
Net Sales	7,946,426	100.0
Gross Profit	2,407,767	30.3
Net Profit After Tax	63,571	0.8
Working Capital	440,709	---

RATIOS	UQ	MED	LQ
Quick Ratio (times)	2.2	1.2	0.7
Current Ratio (times)	3.9	1.8	1.1
Curr Liab To Nw (%)	39.0	68.9	161.0
Curr Liab To Inv (%)	118.2	201.1	504.6
Total Liab To Nw (%)	48.1	132.8	188.2
Fixed Assets To Nw (%)	3.1	18.9	47.1
Coll Period (days)	10.8	23.4	40.8
Sales To Inv (times)	59.3	22.5	10.4
Assets To Sales (%)	16.1	23.5	33.1
Sales To Nwc (times)	28.3	10.6	5.8
Acct Pay To Sales (%)	2.3	4.3	10.4
Return On Sales (%)	2.9	1.1	0.1
Return On Assets (%)	10.7	6.9	1.0
Return On Nw (%)	38.7	17.3	2.6

SIC 58 EATING,DRINKG PLACES
(NO BREAKDOWN)
2014 (110 Establishments)

	$	%
Cash	3,839,632	15.7
Accounts Receivable	1,271,725	5.2
Notes Receivable	48,913	0.2
Inventory	1,222,813	5.0
Other Current	1,565,200	6.4
Total Current	**7,948,283**	**32.5**
Fixed Assets	10,907,489	44.6
Other Non-current	5,600,482	22.9
Total Assets	**24,456,254**	**100.0**
Accounts Payable	2,298,888	9.4
Bank Loans	24,456	0.1
Notes Payable	513,581	2.1
Other Current	6,089,608	24.9
Total Current	**8,926,533**	**36.5**
Other Long Term	8,070,564	33.0
Deferred Credits	122,281	0.5
Net Worth	7,336,876	30.0
Total Liab & Net Worth	**24,456,254**	**100.0**
Net Sales	39,005,190	100.0
Gross Profit	21,335,839	54.7
Net Profit After Tax	1,482,197	3.8
Working Capital	(978,250)	---

RATIOS	UQ	MED	LQ
Quick Ratio (times)	1.4	0.6	0.3
Current Ratio (times)	1.8	1.2	0.7
Curr Liab To Nw (%)	20.4	40.1	81.1
Curr Liab To Inv (%)	436.0	822.4	999.9
Total Liab To Nw (%)	45.9	84.8	239.2
Fixed Assets To Nw (%)	52.1	87.3	156.2
Coll Period (days)	2.6	6.2	21.4
Sales To Inv (times)	123.5	84.7	43.7
Assets To Sales (%)	44.6	62.7	97.3
Sales To Nwc (times)	27.8	12.5	6.0
Acct Pay To Sales (%)	1.9	3.1	5.0
Return On Sales (%)	8.0	4.6	0.5
Return On Assets (%)	13.9	5.4	0.6
Return On Nw (%)	33.3	14.8	4.5

	SIC 5812 EATING PLACES (NO BREAKDOWN) 2014 (106 Establishments) $	%	SIC 59 MISC RETAIL STORES (NO BREAKDOWN) 2014 (587 Establishments) $	%	SIC 5912 DRG STRS,PRPRTRY ST (NO BREAKDOWN) 2014 (43 Establishments) $	%	SIC 5932 USED MERCH STRES (NO BREAKDOWN) 2014 (15 Establishments) $	%
Cash	4,109,865	15.2	408,065	19.1	264,398	21.8	682,114	21.6
Accounts Receivable	1,297,852	4.8	301,242	14.1	162,520	13.4	271,582	8.6
Notes Receivable	54,077	0.2	4,273	0.2	1,213	0.1	0	0.0
Inventory	1,351,929	5.0	799,039	37.4	469,368	38.7	442,111	14.0
Other Current	1,703,432	6.3	126,051	5.9	81,260	6.7	432,638	13.7
Total Current	**8,517,155**	**31.5**	**1,638,670**	**76.7**	**978,759**	**80.7**	**1,828,445**	**57.9**
Fixed Assets	12,248,479	45.3	314,061	14.7	145,540	12.0	956,855	30.3
Other Non-current	6,272,952	23.2	183,736	8.6	88,537	7.3	372,636	11.8
Total Assets	**27,038,586**	**100.0**	**2,136,467**	**100.0**	**1,212,836**	**100.0**	**3,157,936**	**100.0**
Accounts Payable	2,568,666	9.5	337,562	15.8	263,185	21.7	192,634	6.1
Bank Loans	0	0.0	6,409	0.3	0	0.0	0	0.0
Notes Payable	567,810	2.1	59,821	2.8	30,321	2.5	66,317	2.1
Other Current	6,759,646	25.0	484,978	22.7	217,098	17.9	154,739	4.9
Total Current	**9,896,122**	**36.6**	**888,770**	**41.6**	**510,604**	**42.1**	**413,690**	**13.1**
Other Long Term	8,598,271	31.8	329,017	15.4	110,368	9.1	524,217	16.6
Deferred Credits	135,193	0.5	2,136	0.1	4,851	0.4	3,158	0.1
Net Worth	8,409,000	31.1	916,544	42.9	587,013	48.4	2,216,871	70.2
Total Liab & Net Worth	**27,038,586**	**100.0**	**2,136,467**	**100.0**	**1,212,836**	**100.0**	**3,157,936**	**100.0**
Net Sales	43,055,073	100.0	5,622,282	100.0	5,011,719	100.0	8,160,041	100.0
Gross Profit	23,335,850	54.2	1,928,443	34.3	1,453,399	29.0	3,655,698	44.8
Net Profit After Tax	1,377,762	3.2	140,557	2.5	35,082	0.7	244,801	3.0
Working Capital	(1,378,967)	---	749,900	---	468,155	---	1,414,755	---

RATIOS	UQ	MED	LQ	UQ	MED	LQ	UQ	MED	LQ	UQ	MED	LQ
SOLVENCY												
Quick Ratio (times)	1.3	0.6	0.3	2.1	0.8	0.3	3.2	1.0	0.5	3.9	1.4	1.1
Current Ratio (times)	1.8	1.2	0.7	4.4	2.2	1.4	6.8	2.8	1.5	6.9	5.0	2.6
Curr Liab To Nw (%)	20.2	40.1	82.1	20.9	48.5	132.9	16.4	43.2	109.8	10.0	16.7	23.2
Curr Liab To Inv (%)	436.0	832.6	999.9	44.9	88.5	188.0	33.5	72.8	174.1	34.3	131.5	233.6
Total Liab To Nw (%)	47.6	85.6	246.7	27.0	67.3	164.4	17.8	52.5	127.0	17.5	34.3	64.3
Fixed Assets To Nw (%)	53.2	87.3	156.8	6.9	18.8	43.9	3.5	8.3	27.6	13.1	31.2	79.3
EFFICIENCY												
Coll Period (days)	2.6	6.2	21.2	4.8	14.6	28.5	3.1	6.6	20.9	5.5	8.8	32.7
Sales To Inv (times)	124.1	87.6	43.3	19.7	8.5	3.9	16.3	11.6	8.7	40.1	25.6	9.3
Assets To Sales (%)	47.0	62.8	94.5	24.1	38.0	59.6	15.9	24.2	29.6	29.7	38.7	101.7
Sales To Nwc (times)	28.3	13.1	6.3	12.9	6.8	3.7	14.4	9.3	4.9	14.1	4.4	2.5
Acct Pay To Sales (%)	2.0	3.1	4.9	2.1	4.2	8.0	1.8	3.9	6.8	1.4	2.3	6.8
PROFITABILITY												
Return On Sales (%)	7.4	4.5	0.4	4.4	1.7	0.2	2.7	1.3	0.0	6.3	2.4	(1.2)
Return On Assets (%)	13.5	5.3	0.3	11.5	4.3	0.5	13.2	4.0	(0.4)	11.8	1.2	(4.5)
Return On Nw (%)	33.1	14.8	4.0	22.5	8.6	1.2	24.9	7.0	0.0	15.8	1.4	(4.5)

SIC 5941 SPTG GDS,BCYLE SHPS (NO BREAKDOWN) 2014 (60 Establishments)

	$	%
Cash	301,096	19.0
Accounts Receivable	120,438	7.6
Notes Receivable	6,339	0.4
Inventory	862,084	54.4
Other Current	55,465	3.5
Total Current	**1,345,422**	**84.9**
Fixed Assets	188,581	11.9
Other Non-current	50,711	3.2
Total Assets	**1,584,714**	**100.0**
Accounts Payable	318,528	20.1
Bank Loans	12,678	0.8
Notes Payable	14,262	0.9
Other Current	288,418	18.2
Total Current	**633,886**	**40.0**
Other Long Term	129,946	8.2
Deferred Credits	0	0.0
Net Worth	820,882	51.8
Total Liab & Net Worth	**1,584,714**	**100.0**
Net Sales	4,052,977	100.0
Gross Profit	1,442,860	35.6
Net Profit After Tax	105,377	2.6
Working Capital	711,536	---

RATIOS	UQ	MED	LQ
SOLVENCY			
Quick Ratio (times)	1.7	0.4	0.3
Current Ratio (times)	3.7	2.4	1.6
Curr Liab To Nw (%)	23.0	52.2	131.9
Curr Liab To Inv (%)	40.4	67.8	101.1
Total Liab To Nw (%)	30.9	56.4	141.0
Fixed Assets To Nw (%)	5.3	17.0	43.2
EFFICIENCY			
Coll Period (days)	1.5	5.8	21.5
Sales To Inv (times)	7.9	4.4	3.3
Assets To Sales (%)	30.0	39.1	48.9
Sales To Nwc (times)	9.9	6.0	3.5
Acct Pay To Sales (%)	4.2	7.3	9.5
PROFITABILITY			
Return On Sales (%)	4.3	1.8	0.5
Return On Assets (%)	9.8	4.5	1.7
Return On Nw (%)	19.6	7.8	3.9

SIC 5942 BOOK STORES (NO BREAKDOWN) 2014 (23 Establishments)

	$	%
Cash	2,188,126	29.2
Accounts Receivable	292,250	3.9
Notes Receivable	14,987	0.2
Inventory	1,993,293	26.6
Other Current	577,005	7.7
Total Current	**5,065,661**	**67.6**
Fixed Assets	1,461,248	19.5
Other Non-current	966,672	12.9
Total Assets	**7,493,581**	**100.0**
Accounts Payable	839,281	11.2
Bank Loans	0	0.0
Notes Payable	22,481	0.3
Other Current	899,230	12.0
Total Current	**1,760,992**	**23.5**
Other Long Term	1,064,088	14.2
Deferred Credits	0	0.0
Net Worth	4,668,501	62.3
Total Liab & Net Worth	**7,493,581**	**100.0**
Net Sales	12,386,084	100.0
Gross Profit	4,458,990	36.0
Net Profit After Tax	408,741	3.3
Working Capital	3,304,669	---

RATIOS	UQ	MED	LQ
SOLVENCY			
Quick Ratio (times)	3.3	1.4	0.4
Current Ratio (times)	6.3	3.7	1.6
Curr Liab To Nw (%)	11.2	25.9	66.7
Curr Liab To Inv (%)	29.6	56.3	109.4
Total Liab To Nw (%)	21.3	41.7	102.0
Fixed Assets To Nw (%)	7.4	29.3	72.9
EFFICIENCY			
Coll Period (days)	1.8	2.9	8.8
Sales To Inv (times)	6.5	5.0	4.0
Assets To Sales (%)	43.9	60.5	87.0
Sales To Nwc (times)	8.2	4.3	2.0
Acct Pay To Sales (%)	2.0	4.6	10.2
PROFITABILITY			
Return On Sales (%)	5.0	2.1	(0.2)
Return On Assets (%)	10.1	3.5	(0.2)
Return On Nw (%)	12.6	5.6	(0.3)

SIC 5943 STATIONERY STORES (NO BREAKDOWN) 2014 (25 Establishments)

	$	%
Cash	185,521	18.3
Accounts Receivable	344,684	34.0
Notes Receivable	0	0.0
Inventory	241,279	23.8
Other Current	23,317	2.3
Total Current	**794,801**	**78.4**
Fixed Assets	172,342	17.0
Other Non-current	46,634	4.6
Total Assets	**1,013,777**	**100.0**
Accounts Payable	279,802	27.6
Bank Loans	0	0.0
Notes Payable	11,152	1.1
Other Current	179,439	17.7
Total Current	**470,393**	**46.4**
Other Long Term	52,716	5.2
Deferred Credits	0	0.0
Net Worth	490,668	48.4
Total Liab & Net Worth	**1,013,777**	**100.0**
Net Sales	4,022,925	100.0
Gross Profit	1,259,176	31.3
Net Profit After Tax	28,160	0.7
Working Capital	324,408	---

RATIOS	UQ	MED	LQ
SOLVENCY			
Quick Ratio (times)	1.6	1.2	0.8
Current Ratio (times)	2.3	1.6	1.5
Curr Liab To Nw (%)	34.5	102.3	177.2
Curr Liab To Inv (%)	108.1	201.6	334.5
Total Liab To Nw (%)	48.6	120.9	177.2
Fixed Assets To Nw (%)	11.1	20.4	41.8
EFFICIENCY			
Coll Period (days)	20.4	27.1	35.3
Sales To Inv (times)	38.9	22.9	9.9
Assets To Sales (%)	16.3	25.2	35.9
Sales To Nwc (times)	21.7	13.4	5.9
Acct Pay To Sales (%)	4.3	5.4	6.9
PROFITABILITY			
Return On Sales (%)	2.0	0.4	(0.2)
Return On Assets (%)	5.8	2.2	(0.5)
Return On Nw (%)	12.5	4.5	(0.6)

SIC 5944 JEWELRY STORES (NO BREAKDOWN) 2014 (53 Establishments)

	$	%
Cash	230,167	11.5
Accounts Receivable	196,143	9.8
Notes Receivable	4,003	0.2
Inventory	1,230,895	61.5
Other Current	78,057	3.9
Total Current	**1,739,265**	**86.9**
Fixed Assets	154,112	7.7
Other Non-current	108,079	5.4
Total Assets	**2,001,456**	**100.0**
Accounts Payable	302,220	15.1
Bank Loans	2,001	0.1
Notes Payable	68,050	3.4
Other Current	278,202	13.9
Total Current	**650,473**	**32.5**
Other Long Term	148,108	7.4
Deferred Credits	4,003	0.2
Net Worth	1,198,872	59.9
Total Liab & Net Worth	**2,001,456**	**100.0**
Net Sales	3,027,921	100.0
Gross Profit	1,274,755	42.1
Net Profit After Tax	121,117	4.0
Working Capital	1,088,792	---

RATIOS	UQ	MED	LQ
SOLVENCY			
Quick Ratio (times)	1.5	0.5	0.2
Current Ratio (times)	6.2	3.3	1.8
Curr Liab To Nw (%)	14.7	32.0	98.2
Curr Liab To Inv (%)	21.4	42.5	70.2
Total Liab To Nw (%)	14.7	42.0	110.3
Fixed Assets To Nw (%)	2.6	7.0	20.2
EFFICIENCY			
Coll Period (days)	4.6	18.6	33.4
Sales To Inv (times)	3.5	2.4	1.7
Assets To Sales (%)	42.8	66.1	99.5
Sales To Nwc (times)	4.1	2.4	1.6
Acct Pay To Sales (%)	2.8	7.9	10.9
PROFITABILITY			
Return On Sales (%)	5.8	2.1	0.0
Return On Assets (%)	7.0	2.2	0.1
Return On Nw (%)	14.7	6.0	0.2

SIC 5947 GFT,NVLTY,SVENR SHP
(NO BREAKDOWN)
2014 (14 Establishments)

	$	%
Cash	378,957	27.2
Accounts Receivable	11,146	0.8
Notes Receivable	0	0.0
Inventory	709,152	50.9
Other Current	91,952	6.6
Total Current	**1,191,207**	**85.5**
Fixed Assets	188,085	13.5
Other Non-current	13,933	1.0
Total Assets	**1,393,225**	**100.0**
Accounts Payable	242,421	17.4
Bank Loans	0	0.0
Notes Payable	0	0.0
Other Current	192,265	13.8
Total Current	**434,686**	**31.2**
Other Long Term	37,617	2.7
Deferred Credits	0	0.0
Net Worth	920,922	66.1
Total Liab & Net Worth	**1,393,225**	**100.0**
Net Sales	3,902,591	100.0
Gross Profit	1,771,776	45.4
Net Profit After Tax	148,298	3.8
Working Capital	756,521	---

RATIOS	UQ	MED	LQ
SOLVENCY			
Quick Ratio (times)	1.4	0.7	0.4
Current Ratio (times)	4.3	2.1	1.8
Curr Liab To Nw (%)	18.2	53.8	122.4
Curr Liab To Inv (%)	46.3	57.8	91.9
Total Liab To Nw (%)	29.8	57.7	122.4
Fixed Assets To Nw (%)	8.2	18.9	28.9
EFFICIENCY			
Coll Period (days)	0.0	0.8	1.8
Sales To Inv (times)	10.3	6.3	4.2
Assets To Sales (%)	25.3	35.7	40.5
Sales To Nwc (times)	9.3	6.8	4.0
Acct Pay To Sales (%)	2.9	3.5	11.8
PROFITABILITY			
Return On Sales (%)	5.0	0.0	(1.2)
Return On Assets (%)	15.8	0.1	(2.9)
Return On Nw (%)	26.9	0.2	(5.0)

SIC 5961 CTLG,ML-ORDER HSES
(NO BREAKDOWN)
2014 (50 Establishments)

	$	%
Cash	1,308,620	19.8
Accounts Receivable	733,620	11.1
Notes Receivable	72,701	1.1
Inventory	2,240,516	33.9
Other Current	733,622	11.1
Total Current	**5,089,079**	**77.0**
Fixed Assets	601,437	9.1
Other Non-current	918,677	13.9
Total Assets	**6,609,193**	**100.0**
Accounts Payable	1,064,080	16.1
Bank Loans	39,655	0.6
Notes Payable	46,264	0.7
Other Current	2,425,574	36.7
Total Current	**3,575,573**	**54.1**
Other Long Term	588,219	8.9
Deferred Credits	13,218	0.2
Net Worth	2,432,183	36.8
Total Liab & Net Worth	**6,609,193**	**100.0**
Net Sales	17,256,379	100.0
Gross Profit	7,075,115	41.0
Net Profit After Tax	811,050	4.7
Working Capital	1,513,506	---

RATIOS	UQ	MED	LQ
SOLVENCY			
Quick Ratio (times)	2.1	0.8	0.4
Current Ratio (times)	4.7	1.9	1.4
Curr Liab To Nw (%)	13.0	69.9	142.2
Curr Liab To Inv (%)	37.5	114.7	185.7
Total Liab To Nw (%)	17.9	102.6	198.9
Fixed Assets To Nw (%)	3.9	15.5	34.6
EFFICIENCY			
Coll Period (days)	5.5	15.3	40.4
Sales To Inv (times)	14.1	8.9	5.5
Assets To Sales (%)	25.6	38.3	107.2
Sales To Nwc (times)	16.5	7.8	3.1
Acct Pay To Sales (%)	3.0	6.7	9.3
PROFITABILITY			
Return On Sales (%)	5.1	1.6	(0.8)
Return On Assets (%)	12.9	2.7	(4.2)
Return On Nw (%)	27.5	6.8	(1.4)

SIC 5963 DRCT SLLNG ESTBMNTS
(NO BREAKDOWN)
2014 (10 Establishments)

	$	%
Cash	121,326	26.4
Accounts Receivable	38,604	8.4
Notes Receivable	0	0.0
Inventory	110,297	24.0
Other Current	23,897	5.2
Total Current	**294,124**	**64.0**
Fixed Assets	101,565	22.1
Other Non-current	63,880	13.9
Total Assets	**459,569**	**100.0**
Accounts Payable	39,063	8.5
Bank Loans	0	0.0
Notes Payable	0	0.0
Other Current	107,080	23.3
Total Current	**146,143**	**31.8**
Other Long Term	121,327	26.4
Deferred Credits	(30,332)	(6.6)
Net Worth	222,431	48.4
Total Liab & Net Worth	**459,569**	**100.0**
Net Sales	897,596	100.0
Gross Profit	383,273	42.7
Net Profit After Tax	(88,862)	(9.9)
Working Capital	147,981	---

RATIOS	UQ	MED	LQ
SOLVENCY			
Quick Ratio (times)	2.3	1.9	0.9
Current Ratio (times)	5.2	2.3	1.3
Curr Liab To Nw (%)	22.1	33.8	94.2
Curr Liab To Inv (%)	37.0	231.2	247.2
Total Liab To Nw (%)	22.1	94.2	207.3
Fixed Assets To Nw (%)	9.4	59.7	92.9
EFFICIENCY			
Coll Period (days)	14.8	19.7	25.6
Sales To Inv (times)	14.1	8.5	4.9
Assets To Sales (%)	36.1	51.2	68.4
Sales To Nwc (times)	30.1	4.9	2.4
Acct Pay To Sales (%)	2.1	4.2	35.5
PROFITABILITY			
Return On Sales (%)	6.7	0.8	(36.7)
Return On Assets (%)	20.3	12.0	(28.3)
Return On Nw (%)	83.5	26.8	(118.9)

SIC 5983 FUEL OIL DEALERS
(NO BREAKDOWN)
2014 (41 Establishments)

	$	%
Cash	934,191	27.5
Accounts Receivable	805,103	23.7
Notes Receivable	3,397	0.1
Inventory	434,824	12.8
Other Current	152,867	4.5
Total Current	**2,330,382**	**68.6**
Fixed Assets	699,794	20.6
Other Non-current	366,883	10.8
Total Assets	**3,397,059**	**100.0**
Accounts Payable	462,000	13.6
Bank Loans	0	0.0
Notes Payable	115,500	3.4
Other Current	655,632	19.3
Total Current	**1,233,132**	**36.3**
Other Long Term	295,544	8.7
Deferred Credits	37,368	1.1
Net Worth	1,831,015	53.9
Total Liab & Net Worth	**3,397,059**	**100.0**
Net Sales	18,872,550	100.0
Gross Profit	2,981,863	15.8
Net Profit After Tax	301,961	1.6
Working Capital	1,097,250	---

RATIOS	UQ	MED	LQ
SOLVENCY			
Quick Ratio (times)	2.4	1.2	0.8
Current Ratio (times)	3.2	1.8	1.3
Curr Liab To Nw (%)	35.3	63.5	159.3
Curr Liab To Inv (%)	174.6	407.7	770.0
Total Liab To Nw (%)	39.9	84.0	164.3
Fixed Assets To Nw (%)	14.3	29.8	62.7
EFFICIENCY			
Coll Period (days)	9.4	16.3	25.8
Sales To Inv (times)	106.4	63.9	31.6
Assets To Sales (%)	14.2	18.0	27.8
Sales To Nwc (times)	21.5	14.1	9.6
Acct Pay To Sales (%)	1.9	2.4	3.4
PROFITABILITY			
Return On Sales (%)	2.1	1.2	0.1
Return On Assets (%)	11.6	5.0	0.9
Return On Nw (%)	26.3	11.8	2.2

	SIC 5984 LQFD PETRO GAS DLRS (NO BREAKDOWN) 2014 (25 Establishments)		SIC 5999 MISC RTL STRS,NEC (NO BREAKDOWN) 2014 (192 Establishments)		SIC 61 CREDIT AGENC EX BANK (NO BREAKDOWN) 2014 (25 Establishments)		SIC 62 SEC,COM BROKERS,SVS (NO BREAKDOWN) 2014 (23 Establishments)	
	$	%	$	%	$	%	$	%
Cash	634,557	21.7	373,678	15.9	3,228,168	18.9	67,338,864	21.6
Accounts Receivable	482,497	16.5	411,280	17.5	1,759,266	10.3	32,422,416	10.4
Notes Receivable	2,924	0.1	2,350	0.1	85,401	0.5	0	0.0
Inventory	394,771	13.5	925,969	39.4	0	0.0	19,328,748	6.2
Other Current	195,923	6.7	143,360	6.1	5,260,717	30.8	41,463,282	13.3
Total Current	**1,710,672**	**58.5**	**1,856,637**	**79.0**	**10,333,552**	**60.5**	**160,553,310**	**51.5**
Fixed Assets	725,208	24.8	317,273	13.5	836,932	4.9	48,945,378	15.7
Other Non-current	488,346	16.7	176,264	7.5	5,909,768	34.6	102,255,312	32.8
Total Assets	**2,924,226**	**100.0**	**2,350,174**	**100.0**	**17,080,252**	**100.0**	**311,754,000**	**100.0**
Accounts Payable	298,271	10.2	361,927	15.4	2,066,710	12.1	22,446,288	7.2
Bank Loans	0	0.0	14,101	0.6	0	0.0	2,182,278	0.7
Notes Payable	20,470	0.7	126,909	5.4	683,210	4.0	0	0.0
Other Current	467,876	16.0	676,850	28.8	20,837,908	122.0	57,362,736	18.4
Total Current	**786,617**	**26.9**	**1,179,787**	**50.2**	**23,587,828**	**138.1**	**81,991,302**	**26.3**
Other Long Term	549,754	18.8	606,345	25.8	2,476,637	14.5	73,573,944	23.6
Deferred Credits	0	0.0	9,401	0.4	0	0.0	311,754	0.1
Net Worth	1,587,855	54.3	554,641	23.6	(8,984,213)	(52.6)	155,877,000	50.0
Total Liab & Net Worth	**2,924,226**	**100.0**	**2,350,174**	**100.0**	**17,080,252**	**100.0**	**311,754,000**	**100.0**
Net Sales	8,970,018	100.0	5,817,262	100.0	2,756,213	100.0	197,939,048	100.0
Gross Profit	2,448,815	27.3	1,942,966	33.4	1,689,559	61.3	103,522,122	52.3
Net Profit After Tax	322,921	3.6	151,249	2.6	214,985	7.8	18,012,453	9.1
Working Capital	924,055	---	676,850	---	(13,254,276)	---	78,562,008	---

RATIOS	UQ	MED	LQ	UQ	MED	LQ	UQ	MED	LQ	UQ	MED	LQ
SOLVENCY												
Quick Ratio (times)	3.3	0.9	0.7	2.1	0.7	0.3	2.6	1.1	0.1	2.5	1.4	0.9
Current Ratio (times)	4.7	2.1	1.2	3.8	2.1	1.3	3.1	1.5	1.1	6.1	2.6	1.4
Curr Liab To Nw (%)	17.4	45.4	134.8	24.4	54.5	173.4	12.0	91.2	504.7	12.5	19.3	58.9
Curr Liab To Inv (%)	121.4	241.9	489.8	58.4	87.4	151.9	999.9	999.9	999.9	57.9	109.6	158.9
Total Liab To Nw (%)	21.0	112.1	172.1	31.6	76.0	218.2	53.1	167.2	604.0	29.4	87.1	165.0
Fixed Assets To Nw (%)	23.0	42.7	112.5	9.4	19.2	39.3	0.5	3.2	7.5	3.8	7.1	21.7
EFFICIENCY												
Coll Period (days)	10.6	19.4	25.6	5.1	16.1	36.0	3.7	15.3	29.6	11.7	49.7	58.4
Sales To Inv (times)	54.4	28.3	19.4	15.2	7.3	3.4	999.9	999.9	999.9	26.1	7.0	4.9
Assets To Sales (%)	25.2	32.6	49.6	26.2	40.4	56.1	107.3	619.7	855.2	59.0	157.5	330.9
Sales To Nwc (times)	34.7	14.3	5.3	10.7	6.7	4.5	2.9	1.1	0.5	7.9	4.5	1.7
Acct Pay To Sales (%)	1.8	2.8	4.7	1.7	4.0	6.6	1.2	6.3	13.6	1.6	4.3	6.3
PROFITABILITY												
Return On Sales (%)	5.2	2.3	0.8	4.8	2.2	0.6	21.9	6.0	(2.3)	17.4	10.3	(1.8)
Return On Assets (%)	14.8	8.2	2.8	12.1	5.1	1.6	5.1	1.0	(0.8)	13.1	7.7	(0.4)
Return On Nw (%)	23.2	19.2	8.5	26.0	10.0	4.1	12.8	10.5	0.0	25.5	14.1	4.4

SIC 6211 SECURITY BRKRS.DLRS (NO BREAKDOWN) 2014 (12 Establishments) | SIC 65 REAL ESTATE (NO BREAKDOWN) 2014 (140 Establishments) | SIC 6512 NRSDNTL BLDG OPRTRS (NO BREAKDOWN) 2014 (27 Establishments) | SIC 6513 APMNT BLDG OPRTRS (NO BREAKDOWN) 2014 (27 Establishments)

	SIC 6211 $	%	SIC 65 $	%	SIC 6512 $	%	SIC 6513 $	%
Cash	36,583,590	19.7	1,024,114	17.0	2,761,828	13.1	421,379	12.1
Accounts Receivable	30,641,078	16.5	337,355	5.6	1,960,687	9.3	62,684	1.8
Notes Receivable	0	0.0	36,145	0.6	126,496	0.6	17,412	0.5
Inventory	12,070,728	6.5	108,436	1.8	252,992	1.2	3,482	0.1
Other Current	27,669,820	14.9	753,025	12.5	1,370,372	6.5	271,634	7.8
Total Current	**106,965,216**	**57.6**	**2,259,075**	**37.5**	**6,472,375**	**30.7**	**776,591**	**22.3**
Fixed Assets	35,469,369	19.1	2,656,672	44.1	11,679,791	55.4	2,009,385	57.7
Other Non-current	43,268,915	23.3	1,108,453	18.4	2,930,490	13.9	696,494	20.0
Total Assets	**185,703,500**	**100.0**	**6,024,200**	**100.0**	**21,082,656**	**100.0**	**3,482,470**	**100.0**
Accounts Payable	18,570,350	10.0	385,549	6.4	1,496,869	7.1	160,194	4.6
Bank Loans	2,599,849	1.4	0	0.0	0	0.0	6,965	0.2
Notes Payable	0	0.0	481,936	8.0	885,472	4.2	52,237	1.5
Other Current	32,683,816	17.6	3,132,584	52.0	1,897,438	9.0	546,747	15.7
Total Current	**53,854,015**	**29.0**	**4,000,069**	**66.4**	**4,279,779**	**20.3**	**766,143**	**22.0**
Other Long Term	36,954,996	19.9	1,692,800	28.1	4,743,598	22.5	1,828,297	52.5
Deferred Credits	0	0.0	42,169	0.7	358,405	1.7	52,237	1.5
Net Worth	94,894,489	51.1	289,162	4.8	11,700,874	55.5	835,793	24.0
Total Liab & Net Worth	**185,703,500**	**100.0**	**6,024,200**	**100.0**	**21,082,656**	**100.0**	**3,482,470**	**100.0**
Net Sales	196,719,809	100.0	2,760,862	100.0	8,333,066	100.0	1,278,440	100.0
Gross Profit	109,179,494	55.5	1,247,910	45.2	991,635	11.9	755,558	59.1
Net Profit After Tax	28,721,092	14.6	292,651	10.6	599,981	7.2	(29,404)	(2.3)
Working Capital	53,111,201	—	(1,740,994)	—	2,192,596	—	10,448	—

RATIOS	SIC 6211 UQ	MED	LQ	SIC 65 UQ	MED	LQ	SIC 6512 UQ	MED	LQ	SIC 6513 UQ	MED	LQ
SOLVENCY												
Quick Ratio (times)	1.7	1.3	1.0	3.1	1.0	0.2	3.1	1.0	0.3	2.9	1.0	0.6
Current Ratio (times)	5.4	2.5	1.5	5.1	1.8	0.7	4.8	1.6	1.1	3.9	1.5	0.7
Curr Liab To Nw (%)	9.3	19.1	107.3	5.9	20.6	99.4	8.5	18.2	83.9	2.5	11.9	61.2
Curr Liab To Inv (%)	23.5	127.0	190.8	223.4	895.7	999.9	204.1	625.4	999.9	813.6	999.9	999.9
Total Liab To Nw (%)	25.7	91.4	170.8	13.8	65.9	199.4	16.7	38.7	157.7	12.8	36.3	531.2
Fixed Assets To Nw (%)	5.8	13.0	85.1	21.8	70.0	150.5	53.3	82.3	125.6	44.8	98.6	228.1
EFFICIENCY												
Coll Period (days)	10.6	49.3	58.4	6.6	20.8	38.7	11.0	24.8	38.7	2.2	6.9	14.6
Sales To Inv (times)	43.4	8.8	5.2	105.4	22.6	4.1	102.9	36.8	6.0	105.4	105.4	105.4
Assets To Sales (%)	37.2	94.4	241.9	80.7	218.2	465.6	88.6	253.0	416.1	159.1	272.4	473.4
Sales To Nwc (times)	8.2	5.5	2.1	12.0	3.0	1.2	17.5	2.6	1.2	14.0	7.6	3.2
Acct Pay To Sales (%)	1.8	4.6	6.3	1.3	3.2	10.1	2.0	3.2	11.6	2.1	7.9	10.3
PROFITABILITY												
Return On Sales (%)	26.8	10.8	3.7	18.0	5.4	(0.7)	7.9	3.8	0.5	8.7	1.8	(7.2)
Return On Assets (%)	18.8	11.3	2.2	14.1	2.6	(1.0)	3.5	1.8	0.4	7.8	0.6	(1.9)
Return On Nw (%)	26.3	18.3	14.1	41.5	8.6	1.2	12.4	3.3	1.0	88.7	24.8	5.0

	SIC 6531 RL ESTE AGNTS,MGRS (NO BREAKDOWN) 2014 (50 Establishments) $	%	SIC 6552 SBDVDRS,DVLPRS,NEC (NO BREAKDOWN) 2014 (22 Establishments) $	%	SIC 67 HOLDG,RE INVESTM COS (NO BREAKDOWN) 2014 (158 Establishments) $	%	SIC 6719 HOLDING COS,NEC (NO BREAKDOWN) 2014 (21 Establishments) $	%
Cash	1,405,863	20.9	3,044,584	16.3	636,067	43.6	1,066,439	18.5
Accounts Receivable	396,870	5.9	1,083,349	5.8	72,944	5.0	674,451	11.7
Notes Receivable	67,266	1.0	0	0.0	10,212	0.7	23,058	0.4
Inventory	208,525	3.1	373,569	2.0	40,848	2.8	634,099	11.0
Other Current	1,123,346	16.7	2,745,729	14.7	166,311	11.4	1,245,139	21.6
Total Current	**3,201,870**	**47.6**	**7,247,231**	**38.8**	**926,382**	**63.5**	**3,643,186**	**63.2**
Fixed Assets	2,307,230	34.3	7,284,588	39.0	179,441	12.3	1,550,660	26.9
Other Non-current	1,217,518	18.1	4,146,612	22.2	353,047	24.2	570,689	9.9
Total Assets	**6,726,618**	**100.0**	**18,678,431**	**100.0**	**1,458,870**	**100.0**	**5,764,535**	**100.0**
Accounts Payable	544,856	8.1	1,139,384	6.1	4,715,068	323.2	1,683,244	29.2
Bank Loans	0	0.0	0	0.0	523,734	35.9	0	0.0
Notes Payable	565,036	8.4	4,632,251	24.8	3,396,249	232.8	357,401	6.2
Other Current	7,419,460	110.3	6,780,271	36.3	6,426,323	440.5	1,510,309	26.2
Total Current	**8,529,352**	**126.8**	**12,551,906**	**67.2**	**15,061,374**	**32.4**	**3,550,954**	**61.6**
Other Long Term	1,506,762	22.4	4,744,321	25.4	1,285,264	88.1	1,054,909	18.3
Deferred Credits	6,727	0.1	56,035	0.3	2,918	0.2	0	0.0
Net Worth	(3,316,223)	(49.3)	1,326,169	7.1	(14,890,686)	(20.7)	1,158,672	20.1
Total Liab & Net Worth	**6,726,618**	**100.0**	**18,678,431**	**100.0**	**1,458,870**	**100.0**	**5,764,535**	**100.0**
Net Sales	3,634,045	100.0	6,340,268	100.0	856,647	100.0	9,575,640	100.0
Gross Profit	1,780,682	49.0	2,764,357	43.6	404,337	47.2	2,690,755	28.1
Net Profit After Tax	403,379	11.1	1,451,921	22.9	92,518	10.8	603,265	6.3
Working Capital	(5,327,482)	---	(5,304,675)	---	(14,134,992)	---	92,232	---

RATIOS	6531 UQ	MED	LQ	6552 UQ	MED	LQ	67 UQ	MED	LQ	6719 UQ	MED	LQ
SOLVENCY												
Quick Ratio (times)	2.3	0.9	0.2	2.2	0.7	0.2	2.3	0.6	0.0	1.4	0.7	0.2
Current Ratio (times)	3.8	1.5	0.5	5.9	2.3	0.2	3.6	1.0	0.1	2.3	1.8	0.7
Curr Liab To Nw (%)	10.6	57.5	122.1	5.5	19.7	53.7	4.5	19.5	72.4	18.6	62.2	166.1
Curr Liab To Inv (%)	333.0	999.9	999.9	46.6	791.4	999.9	192.4	586.3	999.9	159.4	411.3	999.9
Total Liab To Nw (%)	34.1	108.0	220.9	15.1	53.7	167.1	10.6	71.8	324.8	21.8	110.0	229.8
Fixed Assets To Nw (%)	10.7	53.3	138.9	1.1	67.7	206.9	0.8	15.3	88.9	18.3	59.1	75.6
EFFICIENCY												
Coll Period (days)	6.3	19.7	39.1	6.8	26.5	65.5	9.9	30.7	60.6	13.9	46.6	54.8
Sales To Inv (times)	215.7	22.6	2.5	46.4	24.1	1.7	201.3	28.9	5.2	48.8	18.4	5.1
Assets To Sales (%)	61.4	185.1	385.1	92.4	294.6	967.6	54.3	170.3	407.5	36.2	60.2	407.5
Sales To Nwc (times)	10.6	3.7	1.0	7.1	3.0	0.9	11.9	3.4	0.8	9.7	6.7	3.3
Acct Pay To Sales (%)	1.0	2.9	9.4	1.3	4.5	10.5	2.3	5.2	18.2	3.2	6.2	22.3
PROFITABILITY												
Return On Sales (%)	17.4	5.6	(1.2)	21.1	8.9	(12.5)	14.3	2.0	(50.9)	4.8	1.7	(68.9)
Return On Assets (%)	23.0	3.0	(0.9)	15.0	4.4	(15.4)	1.0	(26.0)	(640.2)	6.2	0.7	(48.0)
Return On Nw (%)	42.0	9.4	1.1	45.9	27.8	10.3	9.5	(4.0)	(42.5)	16.2	4.7	(36.9)

Balance Sheet

	SIC 6794 PATENT OWNERS,LESSO (NO BREAKDOWN) 2014 (27 Establishments) $	%	SIC 6799 INVESTORS, NEC (NO BREAKDOWN) 2014 (90 Establishments) $	%	SIC 70 HOTELS,RE LODGG PLA (NO BREAKDOWN) 2014 (56 Establishments) $	%	SIC 7011 HOTELS AND MOTELS (NO BREAKDOWN) 2014 (51 Establishments) $	%
Cash	4,110,663	24.8	45,612	61.2	5,913,054	11.1	9,396,131	10.1
Accounts Receivable	1,160,268	7.0	2,087	2.8	2,450,455	4.6	4,465,488	4.8
Notes Receivable	0	0.0	820	1.1	0	0.0	0	0.0
Inventory	464,107	2.8	224	0.3	692,520	1.3	1,209,403	1.3
Other Current	2,867,519	17.3	6,335	8.5	4,581,284	8.6	8,093,697	8.7
Total Current	**8,602,557**	**51.9**	**55,078**	**73.9**	**13,637,313**	**25.6**	**23,164,719**	**24.9**
Fixed Assets	1,276,295	7.7	4,397	5.9	28,872,749	54.2	49,492,492	53.2
Other Non-current	6,696,402	40.4	15,055	20.2	10,760,693	20.2	20,373,789	21.9
Total Assets	**16,575,254**	**100.0**	**74,530**	**100.0**	**53,270,755**	**100.0**	**93,031,000**	**100.0**
Accounts Payable	1,740,402	10.5	415,207	557.1	3,675,682	6.9	6,884,294	7.4
Bank Loans	0	0.0	46,954	63.0	0	0.0	0	0.0
Notes Payable	1,790,127	10.8	300,878	403.7	1,491,581	2.8	2,790,930	3.0
Other Current	5,668,737	34.2	562,030	754.1	10,014,902	18.8	17,582,859	18.9
Total Current	**9,199,266**	**55.5**	**1,325,069**	**777.9**	**15,182,165**	**28.5**	**27,258,083**	**29.3**
Other Long Term	2,154,783	13.0	104,715	140.5	33,081,139	62.1	35,723,904	38.4
Deferred Credits	232,054	1.4	0	0.0	53,271	0.1	93,031	0.1
Net Worth	4,989,151	30.1	(1,355,254)	(818.4)	4,954,180	9.3	29,955,982	32.2
Total Liab & Net Worth	**16,575,254**	**100.0**	**74,530**	**100.0**	**53,270,755**	**100.0**	**93,031,000**	**100.0**
Net Sales	6,999,685	100.0	62,160	100.0	37,942,133	100.0	66,261,396	100.0
Gross Profit	4,808,784	68.7	27,226	43.8	25,003,866	65.9	40,883,281	61.7
Net Profit After Tax	636,971	9.1	1,368	2.2	2,731,834	7.2	4,041,945	6.1
Working Capital	(596,709)	—	(1,269,991)	—	(1,544,852)	—	(4,093,364)	—

RATIOS

	SIC 6794 UQ	MED	LQ	SIC 6799 UQ	MED	LQ	SIC 70 UQ	MED	LQ	SIC 7011 UQ	MED	LQ
SOLVENCY												
Quick Ratio (times)	2.8	0.9	0.2	1.4	0.1	0.0	1.4	0.8	0.4	1.1	0.7	0.4
Current Ratio (times)	5.3	2.2	0.6	2.6	0.1	0.0	1.9	1.2	0.7	1.6	1.2	0.7
Curr Liab To Nw (%)	8.8	19.1	84.5	3.9	12.9	53.9	16.3	44.7	153.6	18.6	47.9	153.6
Curr Liab To Inv (%)	206.7	681.3	999.9	328.6	999.9	999.9	630.5	999.9	999.9	630.5	999.9	999.9
Total Liab To Nw (%)	11.7	20.1	142.2	12.2	158.7	999.9	43.8	191.8	303.1	59.0	195.5	303.1
Fixed Assets To Nw (%)	0.7	1.5	9.1	0.4	50.0	187.5	75.0	168.1	231.9	94.6	171.4	231.9
EFFICIENCY												
Coll Period (days)	5.8	24.3	48.9	0.7	72.3	89.8	7.3	15.9	28.3	7.3	15.9	28.8
Sales To Inv (times)	574.3	56.0	26.7	999.9	28.9	14.1	166.6	67.8	26.0	149.0	66.0	25.7
Assets To Sales (%)	91.2	236.8	409.6	26.3	119.9	231.1	58.7	140.4	214.6	55.0	140.4	220.2
Sales To Nwc (times)	4.3	0.8	0.5	15.0	7.0	2.7	30.8	12.3	6.6	31.4	12.8	8.3
Acct Pay To Sales (%)	3.1	9.1	17.4	0.6	11.5	19.9	1.7	2.9	7.5	1.7	3.0	7.7
PROFITABILITY												
Return On Sales (%)	22.0	(5.0)	(145.2)	2.9	1.0	(181.7)	20.2	7.8	0.5	20.2	7.4	(0.8)
Return On Assets (%)	24.6	(7.7)	(55.0)	(4.9)	(335.1)	(999.9)	21.0	5.5	0.5	21.0	4.5	0.3
Return On Nw (%)	31.5	(1.7)	(44.4)	(4.1)	(14.8)	(56.3)	71.3	14.5	1.7	71.3	14.5	1.4

Balance Sheet

	SIC 72 PERSONAL SERVICES (NO BREAKDOWN) 2014 (54 Establishments) $	%	SIC 7299 MISC PRSNL SVCS,NEC (NO BREAKDOWN) 2014 (19 Establishments) $	%	SIC 73 MISC BUSINESS SVS (NO BREAKDOWN) 2014 (1510 Establishments) $	%	SIC 7311 ADVRTSNG AGENCIES (NO BREAKDOWN) 2014 (62 Establishments) $	%
Cash	691,216	18.3	1,675,537	22.4	972,358	26.6	882,058	27.7
Accounts Receivable	562,793	14.9	964,930	12.9	1,023,534	28.0	1,235,518	38.8
Notes Receivable	22,663	0.6	0	0.0	18,277	0.5	0	0.0
Inventory	385,268	10.2	291,723	3.9	127,942	3.5	60,502	1.9
Other Current	434,370	11.5	1,383,815	18.5	391,137	10.7	238,825	7.5
Total Current	**2,096,310**	**55.5**	**4,316,005**	**57.7**	**2,533,248**	**69.3**	**2,416,903**	**75.9**
Fixed Assets	921,621	24.4	1,578,296	21.1	471,557	12.9	296,142	9.3
Other Non-current	759,205	20.1	1,585,777	21.2	650,675	17.8	471,280	14.8
Total Assets	**3,777,136**	**100.0**	**7,480,078**	**100.0**	**3,655,480**	**100.0**	**3,184,325**	**100.0**
Accounts Payable	596,787	15.8	1,742,858	23.3	1,400,049	38.3	1,745,010	54.8
Bank Loans	11,331	0.3	0	0.0	25,588	0.7	35,028	1.1
Notes Payable	101,983	2.7	172,042	2.3	413,069	11.3	19,106	0.6
Other Current	751,651	19.9	2,004,661	26.8	3,253,378	89.0	2,416,902	75.9
Total Current	**1,461,752**	**38.7**	**3,919,561**	**52.4**	**5,092,084**	**139.3**	**4,216,046**	**132.4**
Other Long Term	1,004,718	26.6	1,376,334	18.4	1,188,031	32.5	576,363	18.1
Deferred Credits	7,554	0.2	22,440	0.3	32,899	0.9	3,184	0.1
Net Worth	1,303,112	34.5	2,161,743	28.9	(2,657,534)	(72.7)	(1,611,268)	(50.6)
Total Liab & Net Worth	**3,777,136**	**100.0**	**7,480,078**	**100.0**	**3,655,480**	**100.0**	**3,184,325**	**100.0**
Net Sales	7,377,219	100.0	9,842,208	100.0	7,711,983	100.0	8,082,043	100.0
Gross Profit	3,496,802	47.4	4,281,360	43.5	3,670,904	47.6	3,507,607	43.4
Net Profit After Tax	612,309	8.3	629,901	6.4	177,376	2.3	(307,118)	(3.8)
Working Capital	634,558	—	396,444	—	(2,558,836)	—	(1,799,143)	—

RATIOS

	SIC 72 UQ	MED	LQ	SIC 7299 UQ	MED	LQ	SIC 73 UQ	MED	LQ	SIC 7311 UQ	MED	LQ
SOLVENCY												
Quick Ratio (times)	2.2	1.1	0.6	2.7	1.1	0.6	2.8	1.4	0.8	2.0	1.1	0.8
Current Ratio (times)	4.0	2.1	1.1	4.0	1.3	1.0	3.5	1.8	1.1	2.7	1.4	0.9
Curr Liab To Nw (%)	19.0	32.8	73.6	20.1	26.8	79.2	20.8	53.6	130.8	43.1	119.9	261.8
Curr Liab To Inv (%)	141.4	388.6	905.1	233.6	911.6	999.9	187.2	617.0	999.9	387.0	717.3	999.9
Total Liab To Nw (%)	26.4	76.5	155.4	24.6	58.0	187.0	30.2	78.9	185.5	62.4	143.9	390.5
Fixed Assets To Nw (%)	21.5	37.4	79.7	14.0	27.7	73.3	4.4	12.3	37.4	4.3	16.4	26.5
EFFICIENCY												
Coll Period (days)	8.8	24.5	40.5	7.7	31.0	68.6	29.6	49.6	70.7	36.2	56.1	102.1
Sales To Inv (times)	100.2	29.1	8.3	177.1	69.0	5.1	133.5	34.2	10.6	49.2	17.1	8.4
Assets To Sales (%)	25.3	51.2	118.3	34.4	76.0	154.0	25.2	47.4	118.4	22.1	39.4	121.1
Sales To Nwc (times)	13.3	6.8	3.7	17.5	5.6	3.5	13.4	6.2	2.9	28.2	9.8	3.4
Acct Pay To Sales (%)	2.1	4.1	8.9	2.2	6.0	8.3	1.7	3.8	8.9	2.7	6.9	19.7
PROFITABILITY												
Return On Sales (%)	9.2	4.7	0.3	8.6	2.0	(1.0)	8.6	2.8	(1.6)	4.4	1.0	(12.9)
Return On Assets (%)	24.4	5.8	0.8	10.4	3.5	(1.8)	18.2	5.2	(3.0)	11.0	2.9	(22.3)
Return On Nw (%)	60.0	13.0	4.4	30.3	9.0	4.2	43.8	13.6	0.4	64.8	11.9	(35.2)

SIC 7319 ADVERTISING, NEC
(NO BREAKDOWN)
2014 (11 Establishments)

	$	%
Cash	690,929	30.8
Accounts Receivable	538,386	24.0
Notes Receivable	13,460	0.6
Inventory	47,109	2.1
Other Current	394,816	17.6
Total Current	**1,684,700**	**75.1**
Fixed Assets	318,545	14.2
Other Non-current	240,030	10.7
Total Assets	**2,243,275**	**100.0**
Accounts Payable	5,428,726	242.0
Bank Loans	0	0.0
Notes Payable	42,622	1.9
Other Current	(2,214,113)	(98.7)
Total Current	**3,257,235**	**145.2**
Other Long Term	76,272	3.4
Deferred Credits	0	0.0
Net Worth	(1,090,232)	(48.6)
Total Liab & Net Worth	**2,243,275**	**100.0**
Net Sales	6,923,688	100.0
Gross Profit	2,991,033	43.2
Net Profit After Tax	(387,727)	(5.6)
Working Capital	(1,572,535)	—

RATIOS	UQ	MED	LQ
SOLVENCY			
Quick Ratio (times)	1.3	0.9	0.8
Current Ratio (times)	1.8	1.3	1.0
Curr Liab To Nw (%)	48.4	76.1	251.4
Curr Liab To Inv (%)	182.3	999.9	999.9
Total Liab To Nw (%)	57.9	81.0	255.6
Fixed Assets To Nw (%)	10.3	14.0	29.7
EFFICIENCY			
Coll Period (days)	36.9	52.6	62.3
Sales To Inv (times)	162.3	113.5	9.7
Assets To Sales (%)	27.3	32.4	149.6
Sales To Nwc (times)	25.5	5.2	4.1
Acct Pay To Sales (%)	4.3	8.2	43.9
PROFITABILITY			
Return On Sales (%)	5.5	(0.7)	(12.9)
Return On Assets (%)	9.0	(2.1)	(8.2)
Return On Nw (%)	23.4	14.2	(5.6)

SIC 7322 ADJSTMNT,CLCTN SVCS
(NO BREAKDOWN)
2014 (10 Establishments)

	$	%
Cash	396,419	19.7
Accounts Receivable	432,640	21.5
Notes Receivable	0	0.0
Inventory	0	0.0
Other Current	342,087	17.0
Total Current	**1,171,146**	**58.2**
Fixed Assets	392,394	19.5
Other Non-current	448,738	22.3
Total Assets	**2,012,278**	**100.0**
Accounts Payable	6,173,669	306.8
Bank Loans	12,074	0.6
Notes Payable	774,727	38.5
Other Current	2,960,061	147.1
Total Current	**9,920,531**	**493.0**
Other Long Term	3,940,040	195.8
Deferred Credits	0	0.0
Net Worth	(11,848,293)	(588.8)
Total Liab & Net Worth	**2,012,278**	**100.0**
Net Sales	5,186,284	100.0
Gross Profit	1,955,229	37.7
Net Profit After Tax	217,824	4.2
Working Capital	(8,749,385)	—

RATIOS	UQ	MED	LQ
SOLVENCY			
Quick Ratio (times)	1.6	0.9	0.6
Current Ratio (times)	2.9	1.1	0.7
Curr Liab To Nw (%)	37.5	91.3	211.5
Curr Liab To Inv (%)	—	—	—
Total Liab To Nw (%)	65.0	95.8	342.3
Fixed Assets To Nw (%)	19.7	64.3	121.9
EFFICIENCY			
Coll Period (days)	23.0	29.2	53.3
Sales To Inv (times)	—	—	—
Assets To Sales (%)	30.0	38.8	75.1
Sales To Nwc (times)	13.4	3.4	2.1
Acct Pay To Sales (%)	2.0	5.7	13.1
PROFITABILITY			
Return On Sales (%)	3.1	1.9	1.1
Return On Assets (%)	6.6	4.0	1.6
Return On Nw (%)	32.5	9.7	3.1

SIC 7336 COMMRCL ART,GR DSGN
(NO BREAKDOWN)
2014 (24 Establishments)

	$	%
Cash	308,557	31.6
Accounts Receivable	349,567	35.8
Notes Receivable	0	0.0
Inventory	42,964	4.4
Other Current	39,057	4.0
Total Current	**740,145**	**75.8**
Fixed Assets	195,289	20.0
Other Non-current	41,011	4.2
Total Assets	**976,445**	**100.0**
Accounts Payable	136,702	14.0
Bank Loans	5,859	0.6
Notes Payable	976	0.1
Other Current	228,489	23.4
Total Current	**372,026**	**38.1**
Other Long Term	106,432	10.9
Deferred Credits	7,812	0.8
Net Worth	490,175	50.2
Total Liab & Net Worth	**976,445**	**100.0**
Net Sales	3,160,016	100.0
Gross Profit	1,608,448	50.9
Net Profit After Tax	287,561	9.1
Working Capital	368,119	—

RATIOS	UQ	MED	LQ
SOLVENCY			
Quick Ratio (times)	4.2	2.2	1.3
Current Ratio (times)	4.3	2.4	1.4
Curr Liab To Nw (%)	23.5	54.5	124.7
Curr Liab To Inv (%)	214.8	999.9	999.9
Total Liab To Nw (%)	32.7	64.7	145.8
Fixed Assets To Nw (%)	7.9	23.0	52.2
EFFICIENCY			
Coll Period (days)	32.1	57.7	62.4
Sales To Inv (times)	255.8	78.0	30.4
Assets To Sales (%)	19.6	30.9	45.1
Sales To Nwc (times)	13.9	7.7	5.2
Acct Pay To Sales (%)	2.8	4.2	8.4
PROFITABILITY			
Return On Sales (%)	15.1	3.2	1.6
Return On Assets (%)	70.5	12.9	4.5
Return On Nw (%)	93.3	29.8	15.4

SIC 7342 DSNFCTNG,PST CNTRL
(NO BREAKDOWN)
2014 (16 Establishments)

	$	%
Cash	471,278	24.5
Accounts Receivable	313,544	16.3
Notes Receivable	0	0.0
Inventory	82,714	4.3
Other Current	117,340	6.1
Total Current	**984,876**	**51.2**
Fixed Assets	546,298	28.4
Other Non-current	392,411	20.4
Total Assets	**1,923,585**	**100.0**
Accounts Payable	123,109	6.4
Bank Loans	0	0.0
Notes Payable	96,179	5.0
Other Current	544,375	28.3
Total Current	**763,663**	**39.7**
Other Long Term	432,807	22.5
Deferred Credits	0	0.0
Net Worth	727,115	37.8
Total Liab & Net Worth	**1,923,585**	**100.0**
Net Sales	5,157,064	100.0
Gross Profit	3,393,348	65.8
Net Profit After Tax	366,152	7.1
Working Capital	221,213	—

RATIOS	UQ	MED	LQ
SOLVENCY			
Quick Ratio (times)	1.7	1.1	0.5
Current Ratio (times)	2.5	1.3	0.7
Curr Liab To Nw (%)	46.2	97.8	139.3
Curr Liab To Inv (%)	314.2	699.2	999.9
Total Liab To Nw (%)	74.7	97.8	317.9
Fixed Assets To Nw (%)	25.6	37.9	63.1
EFFICIENCY			
Coll Period (days)	20.1	22.6	30.3
Sales To Inv (times)	99.4	76.3	28.1
Assets To Sales (%)	24.2	37.3	56.1
Sales To Nwc (times)	22.2	11.4	6.0
Acct Pay To Sales (%)	1.6	3.4	4.3
PROFITABILITY			
Return On Sales (%)	14.5	3.7	0.1
Return On Assets (%)	27.6	11.1	1.5
Return On Nw (%)	55.2	19.8	8.8

SIC 7349 — BLDNG MAINT SVC,NEC (NO BREAKDOWN) 2014 (40 Establishments)

	$	%
Cash	656,579	25.5
Accounts Receivable	947,534	36.8
Notes Receivable	5,150	0.2
Inventory	41,197	1.6
Other Current	185,387	7.2
Total Current	**1,835,847**	**71.3**
Fixed Assets	345,026	13.4
Other Non-current	393,948	15.3
Total Assets	**2,574,821**	**100.0**
Accounts Payable	262,632	10.2
Bank Loans	15,449	0.6
Notes Payable	121,017	4.7
Other Current	512,389	19.9
Total Current	**911,487**	**35.4**
Other Long Term	314,128	12.2
Deferred Credits	2,575	0.1
Net Worth	1,346,631	52.3
Total Liab & Net Worth	**2,574,821**	**100.0**
Net Sales	9,066,271	100.0
Gross Profit	3,535,846	39.0
Net Profit After Tax	317,319	3.5
Working Capital	924,360	—

RATIOS	UQ	MED	LQ
SOLVENCY			
Quick Ratio (times)	3.0	1.6	1.3
Current Ratio (times)	3.5	1.9	1.4
Curr Liab To Nw (%)	31.8	65.0	137.6
Curr Liab To Inv (%)	425.8	999.9	999.9
Total Liab To Nw (%)	45.6	99.5	164.9
Fixed Assets To Nw (%)	5.9	17.8	49.3
EFFICIENCY			
Coll Period (days)	27.6	45.7	65.7
Sales To Inv (times)	585.3	371.9	91.0
Assets To Sales (%)	18.7	28.4	43.3
Sales To Nwc (times)	17.6	11.2	5.8
Acct Pay To Sales (%)	1.4	2.7	4.5
PROFITABILITY			
Return On Sales (%)	3.9	1.8	0.4
Return On Assets (%)	16.0	7.0	1.0
Return On Nw (%)	57.5	18.1	1.7

SIC 7352 — MEDCL EQPT RNTL (NO BREAKDOWN) 2014 (14 Establishments)

	$	%
Cash	285,911	17.0
Accounts Receivable	393,548	23.4
Notes Receivable	10,091	0.6
Inventory	168,183	10.0
Other Current	87,455	5.2
Total Current	**945,188**	**56.2**
Fixed Assets	588,641	35.0
Other Non-current	148,001	8.8
Total Assets	**1,681,830**	**100.0**
Accounts Payable	173,228	10.3
Bank Loans	8,409	0.5
Notes Payable	45,409	2.7
Other Current	243,866	14.5
Total Current	**470,912**	**28.0**
Other Long Term	385,139	22.9
Deferred Credits	1,682	0.1
Net Worth	824,097	49.0
Total Liab & Net Worth	**1,681,830**	**100.0**
Net Sales	4,082,112	100.0
Gross Profit	2,506,417	61.4
Net Profit After Tax	265,337	6.5
Working Capital	474,276	—

RATIOS	UQ	MED	LQ
SOLVENCY			
Quick Ratio (times)	2.8	1.1	0.8
Current Ratio (times)	4.8	1.4	1.0
Curr Liab To Nw (%)	13.0	32.8	67.0
Curr Liab To Inv (%)	146.0	360.0	640.5
Total Liab To Nw (%)	13.8	56.8	123.8
Fixed Assets To Nw (%)	37.5	49.2	102.9
EFFICIENCY			
Coll Period (days)	39.8	54.0	62.1
Sales To Inv (times)	44.7	25.5	18.0
Assets To Sales (%)	23.7	41.2	62.1
Sales To Nwc (times)	17.0	15.4	3.8
Acct Pay To Sales (%)	1.6	4.4	9.0
PROFITABILITY			
Return On Sales (%)	11.5	6.5	2.7
Return On Assets (%)	34.8	16.4	7.2
Return On Nw (%)	58.7	36.9	10.8

SIC 7353 — HVY CONST EQPT RNTL (NO BREAKDOWN) 2014 (22 Establishments)

	$	%
Cash	1,569,911	11.7
Accounts Receivable	2,267,649	16.9
Notes Receivable	134,180	1.0
Inventory	1,247,878	9.3
Other Current	536,721	4.0
Total Current	**5,756,339**	**42.9**
Fixed Assets	6,776,110	50.5
Other Non-current	885,590	6.6
Total Assets	**13,418,039**	**100.0**
Accounts Payable	751,410	5.6
Bank Loans	0	0.0
Notes Payable	939,263	7.0
Other Current	1,247,878	9.3
Total Current	**2,938,551**	**21.9**
Other Long Term	6,601,675	49.2
Deferred Credits	53,672	0.4
Net Worth	3,824,141	28.5
Total Liab & Net Worth	**13,418,039**	**100.0**
Net Sales	12,143,022	100.0
Gross Profit	4,529,347	37.3
Net Profit After Tax	789,296	6.5
Working Capital	2,817,788	—

RATIOS	UQ	MED	LQ
SOLVENCY			
Quick Ratio (times)	2.2	1.5	0.9
Current Ratio (times)	4.0	2.2	1.4
Curr Liab To Nw (%)	16.5	46.8	69.6
Curr Liab To Inv (%)	109.5	365.2	992.8
Total Liab To Nw (%)	37.8	80.8	376.1
Fixed Assets To Nw (%)	46.8	80.9	166.1
EFFICIENCY			
Coll Period (days)	36.2	63.2	84.0
Sales To Inv (times)	82.6	9.6	6.9
Assets To Sales (%)	61.9	110.5	209.3
Sales To Nwc (times)	7.8	4.2	2.6
Acct Pay To Sales (%)	2.4	4.5	7.9
PROFITABILITY			
Return On Sales (%)	12.6	6.1	1.3
Return On Assets (%)	11.8	5.1	3.4
Return On Nw (%)	21.2	14.7	5.9

SIC 7359 — EQPT RNTL,LSING,NEC (NO BREAKDOWN) 2014 (58 Establishments)

	$	%
Cash	563,260	13.2
Accounts Receivable	490,719	11.5
Notes Receivable	34,137	0.8
Inventory	537,657	12.6
Other Current	482,183	11.3
Total Current	**2,107,956**	**49.4**
Fixed Assets	1,877,532	44.0
Other Non-current	281,630	6.6
Total Assets	**4,267,118**	**100.0**
Accounts Payable	294,431	6.9
Bank Loans	0	0.0
Notes Payable	93,877	2.2
Other Current	849,156	19.9
Total Current	**1,237,464**	**29.0**
Other Long Term	921,698	21.6
Deferred Credits	4,267	0.1
Net Worth	2,103,689	49.3
Total Liab & Net Worth	**4,267,118**	**100.0**
Net Sales	5,918,333	100.0
Gross Profit	3,184,063	53.8
Net Profit After Tax	331,427	5.6
Working Capital	870,492	—

RATIOS	UQ	MED	LQ
SOLVENCY			
Quick Ratio (times)	2.5	0.9	0.4
Current Ratio (times)	5.0	1.7	1.1
Curr Liab To Nw (%)	15.1	33.8	134.0
Curr Liab To Inv (%)	84.0	200.0	530.1
Total Liab To Nw (%)	21.3	86.5	222.5
Fixed Assets To Nw (%)	22.7	91.7	161.1
EFFICIENCY			
Coll Period (days)	12.4	31.8	52.9
Sales To Inv (times)	39.7	12.9	8.9
Assets To Sales (%)	41.1	72.1	219.3
Sales To Nwc (times)	21.1	6.1	2.3
Acct Pay To Sales (%)	1.6	3.5	7.1
PROFITABILITY			
Return On Sales (%)	7.3	4.0	1.3
Return On Assets (%)	12.0	4.1	2.0
Return On Nw (%)	22.8	12.4	4.8

SIC 7361 EMPLOYMENT AGENCIES — SIC 7363 HELP SUPPLY SVCS — SIC 7371 CSTM CMPTR PRGMG SV — SIC 7372 PREPACKAGED SFTWARE
(NO BREAKDOWN) 2014

	SIC 7361 EMPLOYMENT AGENCIES (39 Establishments)		SIC 7363 HELP SUPPLY SVCS (43 Establishments)		SIC 7371 CSTM CMPTR PRGMG SV (235 Establishments)		SIC 7372 PREPACKAGED SFTWARE (196 Establishments)	
	$	%	$	%	$	%	$	%
Cash	815,472	28.0	1,926,233	15.6	1,117,015	36.8	11,498,081	28.7
Accounts Receivable	1,007,690	34.6	5,420,617	43.9	901,504	29.7	6,329,954	15.8
Notes Receivable	0	0.0	12,348	0.1	6,071	0.2	160,252	0.4
Inventory	0	0.0	37,043	0.3	30,354	1.0	440,693	1.1
Other Current	332,013	11.4	1,074,246	8.7	282,289	9.3	5,648,883	14.1
Total Current	**2,155,175**	**74.0**	**8,470,487**	**68.6**	**2,337,233**	**77.0**	**24,077,863**	**60.1**
Fixed Assets	133,970	4.6	1,395,284	11.3	267,112	8.8	2,884,536	7.2
Other Non-current	623,254	21.4	2,481,877	20.1	431,022	14.2	13,100,601	32.7
Total Assets	**2,912,399**	**100.0**	**12,347,648**	**100.0**	**3,035,367**	**100.0**	**40,063,000**	**100.0**
Accounts Payable	742,662	25.5	1,012,507	8.2	346,032	11.4	29,766,809	74.3
Bank Loans	0	0.0	135,824	1.1	15,177	0.5	0	0.0
Notes Payable	49,511	1.7	234,605	1.9	36,424	1.2	25,640,320	64.0
Other Current	3,669,622	126.0	3,543,776	28.7	2,385,799	78.6	101,119,012	252.4
Total Current	**4,461,795**	**153.2**	**4,926,712**	**39.9**	**2,783,432**	**91.7**	**156,526,141**	**390.7**
Other Long Term	288,328	9.9	2,000,318	16.2	613,144	20.2	30,247,565	75.5
Deferred Credits	0	0.0	86,434	0.7	36,424	1.2	1,081,701	2.7
Net Worth	(1,837,724)	(63.1)	5,334,184	43.2	(397,633)	(13.1)	(147,792,407)	(368.9)
Total Liab & Net Worth	**2,912,399**	**100.0**	**12,347,648**	**100.0**	**3,035,367**	**100.0**	**40,063,000**	**100.0**
Net Sales	11,936,061	100.0	43,785,986	100.0	6,821,049	100.0	27,899,025	100.0
Gross Profit	3,521,138	29.5	10,902,711	24.9	3,703,830	54.3	17,185,799	61.6
Net Profit After Tax	680,355	5.7	656,790	1.5	375,158	5.5	(1,590,244)	(5.7)
Working Capital	(2,306,620)	---	3,543,775	---	(446,199)	---	(132,448,278)	---

RATIOS	UQ	MED	LQ	UQ	MED	LQ	UQ	MED	LQ	UQ	MED	LQ
SOLVENCY												
Quick Ratio (times)	4.6	1.5	0.6	3.2	1.5	1.0	4.2	1.8	1.1	1.9	1.0	0.3
Current Ratio (times)	4.8	1.8	0.9	3.4	1.6	1.2	4.8	2.3	1.3	2.4	1.3	0.6
Curr Liab To Nw (%)	16.8	52.2	231.3	25.3	67.6	147.2	17.6	45.9	109.0	28.0	58.6	98.7
Curr Liab To Inv (%)	400.9	400.9	400.9	428.6	999.9	999.9	196.5	999.9	999.9	966.0	999.9	999.9
Total Liab To Nw (%)	33.1	68.0	231.3	42.9	127.3	209.8	25.4	61.4	152.4	38.8	83.9	157.6
Fixed Assets To Nw (%)	0.8	5.7	14.5	4.3	7.4	24.4	3.3	8.1	20.2	5.3	10.9	24.6
EFFICIENCY												
Coll Period (days)	35.0	45.3	52.2	39.4	46.9	60.4	36.5	54.4	76.3	39.8	61.3	87.2
Sales To Inv (times)	84.0	84.0	84.0	999.9	304.8	19.6	405.9	66.1	17.5	243.1	53.5	15.4
Assets To Sales (%)	16.5	24.4	70.5	16.0	28.2	47.9	24.2	44.5	100.9	72.8	143.6	211.5
Sales To Nwc (times)	17.3	8.8	6.4	36.3	16.5	8.9	10.1	5.8	2.5	7.6	2.9	1.5
Acct Pay To Sales (%)	0.5	0.8	4.6	0.4	1.4	5.1	1.6	3.4	7.7	1.9	4.1	10.9
PROFITABILITY												
Return On Sales (%)	7.7	3.2	0.1	4.6	2.4	0.4	14.0	(7.3)	0.5	6.7	(7.3)	(47.6)
Return On Assets (%)	32.4	14.5	0.7	18.6	6.2	1.9	28.1	(7.2)	0.4	4.0	(7.2)	(55.0)
Return On Nw (%)	58.9	38.7	2.8	38.7	14.5	9.5	57.3	(1.4)	2.9	11.6	1.4	(29.1)

SIC 7373 CPTR INTGTD SYS DGN
(NO BREAKDOWN)
2014 (139 Establishments)

	$	%
Cash	1,552,133	25.8
Accounts Receivable	2,177,799	36.2
Notes Receivable	72,192	1.2
Inventory	228,609	3.8
Other Current	487,297	8.1
Total Current	**4,518,030**	**75.1**
Fixed Assets	529,410	8.8
Other Non-current	968,578	16.1
Total Assets	**6,016,018**	**100.0**
Accounts Payable	998,659	16.6
Bank Loans	114,304	1.9
Notes Payable	66,176	1.1
Other Current	2,653,064	44.1
Total Current	**3,832,203**	**63.7**
Other Long Term	836,227	13.9
Deferred Credits	36,096	0.6
Net Worth	1,311,492	21.8
Total Liab & Net Worth	**6,016,018**	**100.0**
Net Sales	14,891,134	100.0
Gross Profit	6,581,881	44.2
Net Profit After Tax	148,911	1.0
Working Capital	685,827	---

RATIOS	UQ	MED	LQ
SOLVENCY			
Quick Ratio (times)	2.9	1.6	1.0
Current Ratio (times)	3.4	1.9	1.2
Curr Liab To Nw (%)	22.9	49.3	136.0
Curr Liab To Inv (%)	248.8	955.9	999.9
Total Liab To Nw (%)	33.1	60.6	178.7
Fixed Assets To Nw (%)	3.0	7.7	19.5
EFFICIENCY			
Coll Period (days)	32.1	54.4	71.5
Sales To Inv (times)	150.8	43.6	14.0
Assets To Sales (%)	24.7	40.4	95.2
Sales To Nwc (times)	16.0	4.8	2.7
Acct Pay To Sales (%)	2.3	4.7	8.4
PROFITABILITY			
Return On Sales (%)	6.5	2.4	(1.0)
Return On Assets (%)	17.6	6.4	(1.0)
Return On Nw (%)	41.1	12.7	(1.2)

SIC 7378 COMP MAINT,REPAIR
(NO BREAKDOWN)
2014 (10 Establishments)

	$	%
Cash	304,725	31.9
Accounts Receivable	167,169	17.5
Notes Receivable	0	0.0
Inventory	117,496	12.3
Other Current	46,807	4.9
Total Current	**636,197**	**66.6**
Fixed Assets	198,692	20.8
Other Non-current	120,361	12.6
Total Assets	**955,250**	**100.0**
Accounts Payable	155,706	16.3
Bank Loans	0	0.0
Notes Payable	0	0.0
Other Current	541,627	56.7
Total Current	**697,333**	**73.0**
Other Long Term	61,136	6.4
Deferred Credits	(1,911)	(0.2)
Net Worth	198,692	20.8
Total Liab & Net Worth	**955,250**	**100.0**
Net Sales	3,387,411	100.0
Gross Profit	1,700,480	50.2
Net Profit After Tax	44,036	1.3
Working Capital	(61,136)	---

RATIOS	UQ	MED	LQ
SOLVENCY			
Quick Ratio (times)	1.4	1.1	0.6
Current Ratio (times)	1.9	1.6	0.7
Curr Liab To Nw (%)	63.2	106.2	172.9
Curr Liab To Inv (%)	319.7	832.9	999.9
Total Liab To Nw (%)	99.9	110.0	180.9
Fixed Assets To Nw (%)	6.1	18.3	40.7
EFFICIENCY			
Coll Period (days)	9.0	20.3	47.1
Sales To Inv (times)	128.1	76.2	46.9
Assets To Sales (%)	25.6	28.2	35.2
Sales To Nwc (times)	13.5	10.9	6.2
Acct Pay To Sales (%)	2.2	4.6	11.4
PROFITABILITY			
Return On Sales (%)	7.2	2.8	0.6
Return On Assets (%)	24.5	13.3	1.8
Return On Nw (%)	62.3	37.1	(6.1)

SIC 7374 DATA PROC,PRPRTN
(NO BREAKDOWN)
2014 (60 Establishments)

	$	%
Cash	2,211,638	29.0
Accounts Receivable	1,426,125	18.7
Notes Receivable	0	0.0
Inventory	129,648	1.7
Other Current	1,113,445	14.6
Total Current	**4,880,856**	**64.0**
Fixed Assets	938,040	12.3
Other Non-current	1,807,442	23.7
Total Assets	**7,626,338**	**100.0**
Accounts Payable	10,234,546	134.2
Bank Loans	7,626	0.1
Notes Payable	1,098,193	14.4
Other Current	6,040,059	79.2
Total Current	**17,380,424**	**227.9**
Other Long Term	1,311,730	17.2
Deferred Credits	129,648	1.7
Net Worth	(11,195,464)	(146.8)
Total Liab & Net Worth	**7,626,338**	**100.0**
Net Sales	8,656,456	100.0
Gross Profit	4,423,449	51.1
Net Profit After Tax	69,252	0.8
Working Capital	(12,499,568)	---

RATIOS	UQ	MED	LQ
SOLVENCY			
Quick Ratio (times)	2.8	1.6	0.9
Current Ratio (times)	3.5	2.0	1.1
Curr Liab To Nw (%)	21.9	45.2	85.7
Curr Liab To Inv (%)	367.9	718.3	999.9
Total Liab To Nw (%)	29.6	65.7	132.6
Fixed Assets To Nw (%)	4.6	10.6	23.5
EFFICIENCY			
Coll Period (days)	21.9	42.0	64.2
Sales To Inv (times)	138.9	110.8	16.1
Assets To Sales (%)	34.8	88.1	159.8
Sales To Nwc (times)	6.7	4.7	2.3
Acct Pay To Sales (%)	1.6	3.3	6.6
PROFITABILITY			
Return On Sales (%)	7.5	2.1	(8.9)
Return On Assets (%)	11.8	1.5	(17.4)
Return On Nw (%)	22.7	4.4	(21.0)

SIC 7375 INFRMTN RTRVL SVCS
(NO BREAKDOWN)
2014 (34 Establishments)

	$	%
Cash	4,819,027	28.3
Accounts Receivable	2,281,801	13.4
Notes Receivable	442,737	2.6
Inventory	374,624	2.2
Other Current	3,116,192	18.3
Total Current	**11,034,381**	**64.8**
Fixed Assets	1,753,922	10.3
Other Non-current	4,240,062	24.9
Total Assets	**17,028,365**	**100.0**
Accounts Payable	7,867,105	46.2
Bank Loans	0	0.0
Notes Payable	4,120,864	24.2
Other Current	56,687,427	332.9
Total Current	**68,675,396**	**403.3**
Other Long Term	4,904,170	28.8
Deferred Credits	442,737	2.6
Net Worth	(56,993,938)	(334.7)
Total Liab & Net Worth	**17,028,365**	**100.0**
Net Sales	11,583,922	100.0
Gross Profit	6,718,675	58.0
Net Profit After Tax	(127,423)	(1.1)
Working Capital	(57,641,015)	---

RATIOS	UQ	MED	LQ
SOLVENCY			
Quick Ratio (times)	2.1	0.5	0.2
Current Ratio (times)	4.9	1.6	0.5
Curr Liab To Nw (%)	11.7	33.6	95.9
Curr Liab To Inv (%)	256.6	376.7	999.9
Total Liab To Nw (%)	39.1	63.2	128.2
Fixed Assets To Nw (%)	4.8	10.7	30.1
EFFICIENCY			
Coll Period (days)	24.0	46.0	85.5
Sales To Inv (times)	24.0	19.9	17.4
Assets To Sales (%)	82.9	147.0	283.5
Sales To Nwc (times)	4.6	1.9	1.0
Acct Pay To Sales (%)	2.9	5.8	20.7
PROFITABILITY			
Return On Sales (%)	9.3	2.8	(39.3)
Return On Assets (%)	6.6	(0.3)	(140.9)
Return On Nw (%)	26.4	4.9	(6.8)

	SIC 7379 COMP RLTD SVCS.NEC (NO BREAKDOWN) 2014 (145 Establishments) $	%	SIC 7381 DTCTV.ARMRD CAR SVC (NO BREAKDOWN) 2014 (16 Establishments) $	%	SIC 7382 SECURITY SYS SVCS (NO BREAKDOWN) 2014 (39 Establishments) $	%	SIC 7389 BUS SERVICES, NEC (NO BREAKDOWN) 2014 (238 Establishments) $	%
Cash	825,601	29.1	498,325	18.9	398,912	17.2	486,370	22.0
Accounts Receivable	1,106,476	39.0	1,102,116	41.8	862,764	37.2	552,693	25.0
Notes Receivable	22,697	0.8	5,273	0.2	2,319	0.1	13,265	0.6
Inventory	19,860	0.7	0	0.0	185,541	8.0	168,019	7.6
Other Current	357,476	12.6	242,572	9.2	229,607	9.9	276,346	12.5
Total Current	**2,332,110**	**82.2**	**1,848,286**	**70.1**	**1,679,143**	**72.4**	**1,496,693**	**67.7**
Fixed Assets	229,806	8.1	179,292	6.8	287,588	12.4	340,459	15.4
Other Non-current	275,201	9.7	609,064	23.1	352,527	15.2	373,620	16.9
Total Assets	**2,837,117**	**100.0**	**2,636,642**	**100.0**	**2,319,258**	**100.0**	**2,210,772**	**100.0**
Accounts Payable	1,010,014	35.6	179,292	6.8	693,458	29.9	855,569	38.7
Bank Loans	34,045	1.2	68,553	2.6	13,916	0.6	22,108	1.0
Notes Payable	102,136	3.6	63,279	2.4	169,306	7.3	24,318	1.1
Other Current	1,659,714	58.5	6,599,515	250.3	6,280,550	270.8	302,876	13.7
Total Current	**2,805,909**	**98.9**	**6,910,639**	**262.1**	**7,157,230**	**308.6**	**1,204,871**	**54.5**
Other Long Term	712,116	25.1	590,608	22.4	2,553,503	110.1	762,716	34.5
Deferred Credits	2,837	0.1	13,183	0.5	34,789	1.5	4,422	0.2
Net Worth	(683,745)	(24.1)	(4,877,788)	(185.0)	(7,426,264)	(320.2)	238,763	10.8
Total Liab & Net Worth	**2,837,117**	**100.0**	**2,636,642**	**100.0**	**2,319,258**	**100.0**	**2,210,772**	**100.0**
Net Sales	10,625,906	100.0	10,063,519	100.0	6,841,469	100.0	4,644,479	100.0
Gross Profit	4,027,218	37.9	2,918,421	29.0	2,893,941	42.3	2,006,415	43.2
Net Profit After Tax	414,410	3.9	(422,668)	(4.2)	82,098	1.2	204,357	4.4
Working Capital	(473,799)	---	(5,062,353)	---	(5,478,087)	---	291,822	---

RATIOS	UQ	MED	LQ	UQ	MED	LQ	UQ	MED	LQ	UQ	MED	LQ
SOLVENCY												
Quick Ratio (times)	3.1	1.6	1.0	3.7	1.5	0.8	2.1	1.2	0.6	2.8	1.3	0.8
Current Ratio (times)	3.6	1.9	1.3	4.0	2.1	1.1	2.5	1.6	1.1	4.0	1.9	1.3
Curr Liab To Nw (%)	28.8	71.9	147.8	16.5	29.3	85.2	44.5	89.8	130.1	14.8	44.0	123.0
Curr Liab To Inv (%)	368.6	999.9	999.9	931.6	931.6	931.6	379.8	518.7	717.6	124.3	338.4	999.9
Total Liab To Nw (%)	30.6	98.7	182.4	19.1	32.6	172.8	50.7	123.6	183.7	23.4	70.6	168.9
Fixed Assets To Nw (%)	2.1	9.7	24.3	5.9	12.5	19.9	8.6	19.4	34.2	6.5	19.0	55.6
EFFICIENCY												
Coll Period (days)	35.8	49.5	63.5	30.3	41.8	58.8	21.9	53.9	63.2	21.0	42.5	60.4
Sales To Inv (times)	640.6	101.5	13.7	44.8	44.8	44.8	36.2	24.2	13.1	96.6	25.4	9.0
Assets To Sales (%)	19.1	26.7	45.0	22.3	26.2	46.7	24.2	33.9	60.2	26.8	47.6	98.7
Sales To Nwc (times)	15.7	7.9	4.6	11.6	9.1	5.8	18.5	7.9	5.4	13.8	6.2	3.2
Acct Pay To Sales (%)	1.5	3.3	5.8	0.8	3.2	5.8	2.8	4.7	10.4	1.8	4.1	8.2
PROFITABILITY												
Return On Sales (%)	7.6	4.0	0.9	8.7	2.9	0.9	6.5	1.9	(1.3)	8.6	3.5	0.1
Return On Assets (%)	29.3	10.3	3.3	40.5	10.0	2.5	16.1	4.0	(2.9)	19.3	5.5	0.1
Return On Nw (%)	66.0	29.8	7.6	46.9	26.9	5.9	40.1	10.2	1.6	42.1	13.0	2.6

	SIC 75 AUTO REPAIR,SVS,GAR (NO BREAKDOWN) 2014 (100 Establishments)		SIC 7532 TP,BDY RPR,PNT SHPS (NO BREAKDOWN) 2014 (13 Establishments)		SIC 7538 GNRL ATMTVE RPR SHP (NO BREAKDOWN) 2014 (29 Establishments)		SIC 7539 ATMTVE RPR SHPS,NEC (NO BREAKDOWN) 2014 (13 Establishments)	
	$	%	$	%	$	%	$	%
Cash	228,739	19.0	200,566	18.2	182,899	22.7	119,050	26.0
Accounts Receivable	190,215	15.8	191,750	17.4	114,413	14.2	91,577	20.0
Notes Receivable	2,408	0.2	0	0.0	0	0.0	0	0.0
Inventory	226,331	18.8	309,666	28.1	185,316	23.0	75,551	16.5
Other Current	69,825	5.8	44,081	4.0	61,234	7.6	16,942	3.7
Total Current	**717,518**	**59.6**	**746,063**	**67.7**	**543,862**	**67.5**	**303,120**	**66.2**
Fixed Assets	378,021	31.4	217,097	19.7	244,939	30.4	83,335	18.2
Other Non-current	108,351	9.0	138,853	12.6	16,921	2.1	71,430	15.6
Total Assets	**1,203,890**	**100.0**	**1,102,013**	**100.0**	**805,722**	**100.0**	**457,885**	**100.0**
Accounts Payable	160,117	13.3	263,381	23.9	90,241	11.2	77,383	16.9
Bank Loans	4,816	0.4	9,918	0.9	2,417	0.3	6,410	1.4
Notes Payable	37,321	3.1	39,672	3.6	(2,417)	(0.3)	8,700	1.9
Other Current	255,224	21.2	224,811	20.4	151,476	18.8	116,303	25.4
Total Current	**457,478**	**38.0**	**537,782**	**48.8**	**241,717**	**30.0**	**208,796**	**45.6**
Other Long Term	286,526	23.8	249,055	22.6	130,527	16.2	82,419	18.0
Deferred Credits	2,408	0.2	17,632	1.6	0	0.0	0	0.0
Net Worth	457,478	38.0	297,544	27.0	433,478	53.8	166,670	36.4
Total Liab & Net Worth	**1,203,890**	**100.0**	**1,102,013**	**100.0**	**805,722**	**100.0**	**457,885**	**100.0**
Net Sales	4,224,175	100.0	4,479,728	100.0	3,098,931	100.0	2,062,545	100.0
Gross Profit	1,774,154	42.0	1,603,743	35.8	1,276,760	41.2	688,890	33.4
Net Profit After Tax	143,622	3.4	125,432	2.8	127,056	4.1	88,689	4.3
Working Capital	260,040	---	208,281	---	302,145	---	94,324	---

RATIOS	UQ	MED	LQ	UQ	MED	LQ	UQ	MED	LQ	UQ	MED	LQ
SOLVENCY												
Quick Ratio (times)	2.1	0.9	0.4	1.8	0.8	0.5	2.4	1.6	0.6	2.9	1.1	0.6
Current Ratio (times)	3.3	1.7	1.1	2.3	1.7	1.2	4.2	2.7	1.4	4.2	1.9	1.1
Curr Liab To Nw (%)	22.0	46.7	133.0	37.4	82.9	141.3	16.5	34.6	71.0	17.0	28.2	107.5
Curr Liab To Inv (%)	75.2	155.7	423.4	120.4	168.7	219.1	49.3	75.8	141.9	84.3	174.3	999.9
Total Liab To Nw (%)	36.7	72.9	247.7	48.2	98.3	155.8	31.7	49.4	143.0	22.2	49.4	107.5
Fixed Assets To Nw (%)	18.6	46.0	110.2	15.2	40.7	44.5	14.0	25.8	99.9	10.3	22.1	55.3
EFFICIENCY												
Coll Period (days)	6.4	16.5	27.6	9.9	17.5	21.2	5.5	13.0	27.0	9.9	19.7	25.6
Sales To Inv (times)	46.2	20.2	8.4	35.2	18.7	7.6	24.7	13.9	8.1	62.7	25.4	12.8
Assets To Sales (%)	18.0	28.5	43.0	17.0	24.6	29.6	22.3	26.0	35.1	16.0	22.2	41.3
Sales To Nwc (times)	24.3	9.2	5.5	18.9	11.9	7.2	22.6	7.6	4.5	26.5	14.7	4.9
Acct Pay To Sales (%)	1.6	3.3	5.5	3.0	4.1	6.9	1.6	3.1	5.0	1.6	3.3	6.3
PROFITABILITY												
Return On Sales (%)	6.7	3.0	0.6	5.1	1.9	0.6	7.8	3.6	0.6	6.6	5.8	1.4
Return On Assets (%)	21.1	9.4	2.5	22.1	11.4	4.6	26.1	12.3	2.7	26.2	11.9	3.8
Return On Nw (%)	44.5	18.9	7.4	48.4	20.9	3.1	37.9	24.3	4.0	81.7	14.3	8.9

SIC 7549 ATMTVE SVCS.NEC (NO BREAKDOWN) 2014 (13 Establishments)

	$	%
Cash	150,102	18.6
Accounts Receivable	185,610	23.0
Notes Receivable	3,228	0.4
Inventory	150,102	18.6
Other Current	65,367	8.1
Total Current	**554,409**	**68.7**
Fixed Assets	149,295	18.5
Other Non-current	103,296	12.8
Total Assets	**807,000**	**100.0**
Accounts Payable	142,839	17.7
Bank Loans	0	0.0
Notes Payable	20,982	2.6
Other Current	263,082	32.6
Total Current	**426,903**	**52.9**
Other Long Term	424,482	52.6
Deferred Credits	0	0.0
Net Worth	(44,385)	(5.5)
Total Liab & Net Worth	**807,000**	**100.0**
Net Sales	3,140,078	100.0
Gross Profit	1,372,214	43.7
Net Profit After Tax	53,381	1.7
Working Capital	127,506	---

RATIOS	UQ	MED	LQ
SOLVENCY			
Quick Ratio (times)	1.1	0.8	0.5
Current Ratio (times)	2.4	1.4	1.2
Curr Liab To Nw (%)	50.6	65.9	177.7
Curr Liab To Inv (%)	77.0	149.8	351.5
Total Liab To Nw (%)	58.0	143.8	214.9
Fixed Assets To Nw (%)	25.2	44.2	64.9
EFFICIENCY			
Coll Period (days)	10.1	19.2	55.3
Sales To Inv (times)	46.2	10.1	7.4
Assets To Sales (%)	14.9	25.7	45.2
Sales To Nwc (times)	24.1	9.2	7.0
Acct Pay To Sales (%)	1.3	3.2	3.7
PROFITABILITY			
Return On Sales (%)	6.8	2.5	0.6
Return On Assets (%)	20.7	10.0	5.1
Return On Nw (%)	64.4	15.4	12.8

SIC 76 MISC REPAIR SERVICE (NO BREAKDOWN) 2014 (161 Establishments)

	$	%
Cash	345,962	22.4
Accounts Receivable	409,285	26.5
Notes Receivable	0	0.0
Inventory	327,428	21.2
Other Current	140,547	9.1
Total Current	**1,223,222**	**79.2**
Fixed Assets	244,027	15.8
Other Non-current	77,223	5.0
Total Assets	**1,544,472**	**100.0**
Accounts Payable	165,259	10.7
Bank Loans	6,178	0.4
Notes Payable	40,156	2.6
Other Current	347,506	22.5
Total Current	**559,099**	**36.2**
Other Long Term	149,814	9.7
Deferred Credits	1,544	0.1
Net Worth	834,015	54.0
Total Liab & Net Worth	**1,544,472**	**100.0**
Net Sales	3,950,056	100.0
Gross Profit	1,591,873	40.3
Net Profit After Tax	221,203	5.6
Working Capital	664,123	---

RATIOS	UQ	MED	LQ
SOLVENCY			
Quick Ratio (times)	4.3	1.8	0.7
Current Ratio (times)	7.0	2.8	1.5
Curr Liab To Nw (%)	14.3	39.5	106.6
Curr Liab To Inv (%)	49.3	118.7	280.2
Total Liab To Nw (%)	16.0	57.1	145.3
Fixed Assets To Nw (%)	6.5	16.9	44.5
EFFICIENCY			
Coll Period (days)	24.5	37.4	55.1
Sales To Inv (times)	36.9	11.0	5.7
Assets To Sales (%)	30.8	39.1	54.9
Sales To Nwc (times)	8.0	4.4	3.0
Acct Pay To Sales (%)	2.2	3.6	5.7
PROFITABILITY			
Return On Sales (%)	7.4	3.1	0.7
Return On Assets (%)	19.9	7.1	1.8
Return On Nw (%)	33.2	13.0	3.1

SIC 7623 RFRGRTN SVC.RPR (NO BREAKDOWN) 2014 (17 Establishments)

	$	%
Cash	349,126	35.4
Accounts Receivable	297,842	30.2
Notes Receivable	0	0.0
Inventory	148,921	15.1
Other Current	41,423	4.2
Total Current	**837,312**	**84.9**
Fixed Assets	134,128	13.6
Other Non-current	14,793	1.5
Total Assets	**986,233**	**100.0**
Accounts Payable	116,375	11.8
Bank Loans	0	0.0
Notes Payable	4,931	0.5
Other Current	179,495	18.2
Total Current	**300,801**	**30.5**
Other Long Term	56,215	5.7
Deferred Credits	0	0.0
Net Worth	629,217	63.8
Total Liab & Net Worth	**986,233**	**100.0**
Net Sales	2,988,585	100.0
Gross Profit	1,072,902	35.9
Net Profit After Tax	74,715	2.5
Working Capital	536,511	---

RATIOS	UQ	MED	LQ
SOLVENCY			
Quick Ratio (times)	3.3	2.3	1.9
Current Ratio (times)	4.8	3.2	2.3
Curr Liab To Nw (%)	23.2	36.3	59.7
Curr Liab To Inv (%)	78.7	168.9	350.4
Total Liab To Nw (%)	36.2	44.8	61.0
Fixed Assets To Nw (%)	12.2	22.1	42.2
EFFICIENCY			
Coll Period (days)	27.2	29.9	35.6
Sales To Inv (times)	52.0	23.9	9.9
Assets To Sales (%)	24.5	33.0	42.2
Sales To Nwc (times)	7.9	5.0	3.1
Acct Pay To Sales (%)	3.2	4.5	5.3
PROFITABILITY			
Return On Sales (%)	4.7	1.7	(0.1)
Return On Assets (%)	11.8	5.0	(0.3)
Return On Nw (%)	15.7	6.7	1.1

SIC 7629 ELECTL RPR SHPS.NEC (NO BREAKDOWN) 2014 (21 Establishments)

	$	%
Cash	255,087	17.6
Accounts Receivable	598,584	41.3
Notes Receivable	0	0.0
Inventory	182,619	12.6
Other Current	92,758	6.4
Total Current	**1,129,048**	**77.9**
Fixed Assets	195,663	13.5
Other Non-current	124,645	8.6
Total Assets	**1,449,356**	**100.0**
Accounts Payable	173,923	12.0
Bank Loans	1,449	0.1
Notes Payable	56,525	3.9
Other Current	402,921	27.8
Total Current	**634,818**	**43.8**
Other Long Term	200,011	13.8
Deferred Credits	7,247	0.5
Net Worth	607,280	41.9
Total Liab & Net Worth	**1,449,356**	**100.0**
Net Sales	4,003,746	100.0
Gross Profit	1,849,731	46.2
Net Profit After Tax	252,236	6.3
Working Capital	494,230	---

RATIOS	UQ	MED	LQ
SOLVENCY			
Quick Ratio (times)	5.5	2.0	0.7
Current Ratio (times)	6.5	2.8	1.2
Curr Liab To Nw (%)	16.6	33.7	61.9
Curr Liab To Inv (%)	167.1	206.5	999.9
Total Liab To Nw (%)	18.6	33.7	87.2
Fixed Assets To Nw (%)	5.6	11.8	53.1
EFFICIENCY			
Coll Period (days)	31.8	55.1	88.7
Sales To Inv (times)	60.7	40.4	17.4
Assets To Sales (%)	30.0	36.2	48.9
Sales To Nwc (times)	5.9	4.0	3.3
Acct Pay To Sales (%)	2.3	4.2	7.6
PROFITABILITY			
Return On Sales (%)	11.6	4.6	0.7
Return On Assets (%)	21.6	14.8	3.7
Return On Nw (%)	57.1	25.2	11.7

SIC 7694 ARMTRE REWNDNG SHPS
(NO BREAKDOWN)
2014 (18 Establishments)

	$	%
Cash	141,121	14.1
Accounts Receivable	238,204	23.8
Notes Receivable	0	0.0
Inventory	275,236	27.5
Other Current	161,138	16.1
Total Current	**815,699**	**81.5**
Fixed Assets	165,142	16.5
Other Non-current	20,017	2.0
Total Assets	**1,000,858**	**100.0**
Accounts Payable	117,100	11.7
Bank Loans	14,012	1.4
Notes Payable	6,005	0.6
Other Current	126,109	12.6
Total Current	**263,226**	**26.3**
Other Long Term	130,111	13.0
Deferred Credits	2,002	0.2
Net Worth	605,519	60.5
Total Liab & Net Worth	**1,000,858**	**100.0**
Net Sales	1,924,727	100.0
Gross Profit	719,848	37.4
Net Profit After Tax	63,516	3.3
Working Capital	552,473	---

RATIOS	UQ	MED	LQ
SOLVENCY			
Quick Ratio (times)	3.3	1.4	0.9
Current Ratio (times)	6.9	3.0	1.7
Curr Liab To Nw (%)	15.9	38.1	63.4
Curr Liab To Inv (%)	43.1	83.8	207.3
Total Liab To Nw (%)	24.4	53.0	111.0
Fixed Assets To Nw (%)	4.4	19.3	55.0
EFFICIENCY			
Coll Period (days)	30.3	39.8	42.0
Sales To Inv (times)	11.9	9.9	6.2
Assets To Sales (%)	37.7	52.0	57.9
Sales To Nwc (times)	5.5	3.1	2.6
Acct Pay To Sales (%)	3.1	4.3	5.1
PROFITABILITY			
Return On Sales (%)	5.0	2.7	0.7
Return On Assets (%)	11.7	5.8	1.4
Return On Nw (%)	32.3	7.7	2.3

SIC 7699 REPAIR SVCS,NEC
(NO BREAKDOWN)
2014 (87 Establishments)

	$	%
Cash	404,040	20.4
Accounts Receivable	475,342	24.0
Notes Receivable	0	0.0
Inventory	441,672	22.3
Other Current	217,864	11.0
Total Current	**1,538,918**	**77.7**
Fixed Assets	326,797	16.5
Other Non-current	114,875	5.8
Total Assets	**1,980,590**	**100.0**
Accounts Payable	205,981	10.4
Bank Loans	7,922	0.4
Notes Payable	69,321	3.5
Other Current	526,837	26.6
Total Current	**810,061**	**40.9**
Other Long Term	194,098	9.8
Deferred Credits	0	0.0
Net Worth	976,431	49.3
Total Liab & Net Worth	**1,980,590**	**100.0**
Net Sales	5,267,527	100.0
Gross Profit	2,159,686	41.0
Net Profit After Tax	363,459	6.9
Working Capital	728,857	---

RATIOS	UQ	MED	LQ
SOLVENCY			
Quick Ratio (times)	3.9	1.4	0.4
Current Ratio (times)	6.6	2.4	1.5
Curr Liab To Nw (%)	14.9	52.4	155.6
Curr Liab To Inv (%)	47.1	96.4	313.2
Total Liab To Nw (%)	15.7	77.8	182.0
Fixed Assets To Nw (%)	6.9	16.2	43.3
EFFICIENCY			
Coll Period (days)	18.3	38.0	58.8
Sales To Inv (times)	34.6	9.9	5.2
Assets To Sales (%)	31.2	37.6	55.5
Sales To Nwc (times)	9.7	4.6	3.3
Acct Pay To Sales (%)	2.2	3.3	5.8
PROFITABILITY			
Return On Sales (%)	8.3	3.3	1.0
Return On Assets (%)	22.5	7.6	2.5
Return On Nw (%)	35.7	15.2	3.5

SIC 78 MOTION PICTURES
(NO BREAKDOWN)
2014 (47 Establishments)

	$	%
Cash	819,351	30.8
Accounts Receivable	305,926	11.5
Notes Receivable	0	0.0
Inventory	45,224	1.7
Other Current	332,528	12.5
Total Current	**1,503,029**	**56.5**
Fixed Assets	686,339	25.8
Other Non-current	470,861	17.7
Total Assets	**2,660,229**	**100.0**
Accounts Payable	4,921,424	185.0
Bank Loans	23,942	0.9
Notes Payable	21,282	0.8
Other Current	6,860,730	257.9
Total Current	**11,827,378**	**444.6**
Other Long Term	3,221,537	121.1
Deferred Credits	18,622	0.7
Net Worth	(12,407,308)	(466.4)
Total Liab & Net Worth	**2,660,229**	**100.0**
Net Sales	3,292,363	100.0
Gross Profit	1,791,045	54.4
Net Profit After Tax	161,326	4.9
Working Capital	(10,324,349)	---

RATIOS	UQ	MED	LQ
SOLVENCY			
Quick Ratio (times)	3.0	0.9	0.3
Current Ratio (times)	3.8	1.7	0.5
Curr Liab To Nw (%)	16.1	37.4	55.5
Curr Liab To Inv (%)	292.0	999.9	999.9
Total Liab To Nw (%)	39.6	85.8	211.3
Fixed Assets To Nw (%)	9.7	41.6	130.5
EFFICIENCY			
Coll Period (days)	13.1	30.3	55.1
Sales To Inv (times)	190.3	111.9	16.4
Assets To Sales (%)	34.4	80.8	172.9
Sales To Nwc (times)	12.7	5.7	1.6
Acct Pay To Sales (%)	1.8	4.3	9.7
PROFITABILITY			
Return On Sales (%)	13.4	2.4	(5.7)
Return On Assets (%)	9.4	1.3	(15.5)
Return On Nw (%)	35.6	8.9	(4.4)

SIC 7812 MTN PCTRE,VDEO PROD
(NO BREAKDOWN)
2014 (31 Establishments)

	$	%
Cash	488,575	35.1
Accounts Receivable	197,657	14.2
Notes Receivable	1,392	0.1
Inventory	29,231	2.1
Other Current	204,617	14.7
Total Current	**921,472**	**66.2**
Fixed Assets	254,727	18.3
Other Non-current	215,753	15.5
Total Assets	**1,391,952**	**100.0**
Accounts Payable	3,685,889	264.8
Bank Loans	2,784	0.2
Notes Payable	2,784	0.2
Other Current	3,012,184	216.4
Total Current	**6,703,641**	**481.6**
Other Long Term	218,536	15.7
Deferred Credits	8,352	0.6
Net Worth	(5,538,577)	(397.9)
Total Liab & Net Worth	**1,391,952**	**100.0**
Net Sales	3,267,493	100.0
Gross Profit	1,744,841	53.4
Net Profit After Tax	238,527	7.3
Working Capital	(5,782,169)	---

RATIOS	UQ	MED	LQ
SOLVENCY			
Quick Ratio (times)	6.6	1.3	0.4
Current Ratio (times)	6.9	2.2	0.6
Curr Liab To Nw (%)	7.0	34.5	55.5
Curr Liab To Inv (%)	82.9	292.0	999.9
Total Liab To Nw (%)	34.5	81.5	141.3
Fixed Assets To Nw (%)	8.7	31.1	55.4
EFFICIENCY			
Coll Period (days)	26.3	37.2	59.9
Sales To Inv (times)	116.5	77.3	9.1
Assets To Sales (%)	30.3	42.6	99.1
Sales To Nwc (times)	11.1	5.7	2.7
Acct Pay To Sales (%)	1.2	2.2	7.5
PROFITABILITY			
Return On Sales (%)	15.2	3.3	(2.8)
Return On Assets (%)	17.1	3.7	(70.1)
Return On Nw (%)	45.3	18.1	(2.9)

	SIC 79 AMUSE RECREATION SVCS (NO BREAKDOWN) 2014 (131 Establishments)		SIC 7922 THTRCL PRDCRS,SVCS (NO BREAKDOWN) 2014 (43 Establishments)		SIC 7929 ENTRS.ENTRTNMNT GRP (NO BREAKDOWN) 2014 (20 Establishments)		SIC 7997 MBRSHP SPT,RCTN CLB (NO BREAKDOWN) 2014 (15 Establishments)	
	$	%	$	%	$	%	$	%
Cash	367,953	24.8	258,723	28.8	208,275	41.2	1,554,549	13.1
Accounts Receivable	69,733	4.7	53,002	5.9	10,110	2.0	403,471	3.4
Notes Receivable	2,967	0.2	0	0.0	0	0.0	11,867	0.1
Inventory	37,092	2.5	8,983	1.0	9,605	1.9	178,002	1.5
Other Current	160,238	10.8	126,667	14.1	62,180	12.3	949,343	8.0
Total Current	**637,983**	**43.0**	**447,375**	**49.8**	**290,170**	**57.4**	**3,097,232**	**26.1**
Fixed Assets	534,126	36.0	226,383	25.2	43,981	8.7	7,986,349	67.3
Other Non-current	311,573	21.0	224,586	25.0	171,372	33.9	783,208	6.6
Total Assets	**1,483,682**	**100.0**	**898,344**	**100.0**	**505,523**	**100.0**	**11,866,789**	**100.0**
Accounts Payable	83,086	5.6	61,986	6.9	21,232	4.2	154,268	1.3
Bank Loans	1,484	0.1	0	0.0	0	0.0	0	0.0
Notes Payable	8,902	0.6	3,593	0.4	0	0.0	47,467	0.4
Other Current	362,018	24.4	295,555	32.9	70,773	14.0	1,068,011	9.0
Total Current	**455,490**	**30.7**	**361,134**	**40.2**	**92,005**	**18.2**	**1,269,746**	**10.7**
Other Long Term	243,324	16.4	79,055	8.8	12,638	2.5	2,361,492	19.9
Deferred Credits	23,739	1.6	0	0.0	32,859	6.5	261,069	2.2
Net Worth	761,129	51.3	458,155	51.0	368,021	72.8	7,974,482	67.2
Total Liab & Net Worth	**1,483,682**	**100.0**	**898,344**	**100.0**	**505,523**	**100.0**	**11,866,789**	**100.0**
Net Sales	1,367,449	100.0	1,235,686	100.0	438,062	100.0	6,666,735	100.0
Gross Profit	976,359	71.4	551,116	44.6	279,045	63.7	5,906,727	88.6
Net Profit After Tax	142,215	10.4	163,111	13.2	76,223	17.4	320,003	4.8
Working Capital	182,493	---	86,241	---	198,165	---	1,827,486	---

RATIOS	UQ	MED	LQ	UQ	MED	LQ	UQ	MED	LQ	UQ	MED	LQ
SOLVENCY												
Quick Ratio (times)	2.7	1.0	0.4	3.1	1.1	0.4	14.6	1.5	0.7	1.8	1.1	0.9
Current Ratio (times)	5.0	1.9	0.8	5.1	1.9	0.7	15.4	3.5	1.4	2.8	1.4	1.2
Curr Liab To Nw (%)	5.6	14.8	40.4	9.7	14.0	38.1	4.2	7.2	50.6	10.8	16.5	21.1
Curr Liab To Inv (%)	282.3	875.2	999.9	974.1	999.9	999.9	184.0	422.9	999.9	487.2	990.3	999.9
Total Liab To Nw (%)	8.5	35.1	90.7	9.9	25.7	51.5	4.4	7.2	58.3	24.6	44.6	90.2
Fixed Assets To Nw (%)	11.0	48.3	107.8	11.0	26.0	57.8	0.8	4.5	13.1	91.1	121.7	152.6
EFFICIENCY												
Coll Period (days)	2.6	11.7	27.0	1.5	12.4	23.4	0.6	4.4	8.4	13.5	22.3	29.6
Sales To Inv (times)	116.5	50.9	22.8	722.3	356.4	72.0	501.1	49.5	7.6	94.9	50.1	32.5
Assets To Sales (%)	48.3	108.5	218.8	27.0	72.7	234.9	38.5	115.4	191.9	115.6	178.0	226.2
Sales To Nwc (times)	14.4	5.4	2.5	15.1	4.3	1.9	9.8	4.2	1.6	53.3	8.0	5.0
Acct Pay To Sales (%)	1.4	2.9	5.4	0.9	3.0	5.2	0.6	1.7	3.1	1.6	2.6	3.3
PROFITABILITY												
Return On Sales (%)	16.3	6.0	(0.1)	26.4	7.4	0.8	27.3	11.7	1.1	5.5	1.5	0.0
Return On Assets (%)	16.6	4.0	(0.1)	29.6	6.5	1.8	40.8	11.7	0.9	1.9	0.6	(0.1)
Return On Nw (%)	36.7	6.5	1.5	48.8	9.3	4.3	62.4	15.8	1.7	4.4	1.5	(0.1)

SIC 7999 AMUSEMENT,RCRTN.NEC
(NO BREAKDOWN)
2014 (28 Establishments)

	$	%
Cash	292,522	22.3
Accounts Receivable	60,341	4.6
Notes Receivable	5,247	0.4
Inventory	80,017	6.1
Other Current	89,201	6.8
Total Current	**527,328**	**40.2**
Fixed Assets	574,551	43.8
Other Non-current	209,881	16.0
Total Assets	**1,311,760**	**100.0**
Accounts Payable	110,188	8.4
Bank Loans	3,935	0.3
Notes Payable	19,676	1.5
Other Current	237,429	18.1
Total Current	**371,228**	**28.3**
Other Long Term	233,494	17.8
Deferred Credits	3,935	0.3
Net Worth	703,103	53.6
Total Liab & Net Worth	**1,311,760**	**100.0**
Net Sales	1,372,134	100.0
Gross Profit	946,772	69.0
Net Profit After Tax	118,004	8.6
Working Capital	156,100	---

RATIOS	UQ	MED	LQ
SOLVENCY			
Quick Ratio (times)	3.1	1.2	0.5
Current Ratio (times)	4.5	2.0	1.1
Curr Liab To Nw (%)	5.3	12.0	35.3
Curr Liab To Inv (%)	155.1	249.7	999.9
Total Liab To Nw (%)	9.8	43.6	97.8
Fixed Assets To Nw (%)	15.0	65.3	122.2
EFFICIENCY			
Coll Period (days)	2.2	5.5	30.5
Sales To Inv (times)	71.3	20.1	7.9
Assets To Sales (%)	66.9	95.6	161.3
Sales To Nwc (times)	11.9	5.2	2.2
Acct Pay To Sales (%)	1.5	3.0	6.0
PROFITABILITY			
Return On Sales (%)	13.2	4.4	(2.4)
Return On Assets (%)	11.4	4.3	(2.3)
Return On Nw (%)	24.0	6.7	(1.4)

SIC 80 HEALTH SERVICES
(NO BREAKDOWN)
2014 (331 Establishments)

	$	%
Cash	4,337,471	14.8
Accounts Receivable	4,308,164	14.7
Notes Receivable	29,307	0.1
Inventory	615,452	2.1
Other Current	3,165,181	10.8
Total Current	**12,455,575**	**42.5**
Fixed Assets	10,609,219	36.2
Other Non-current	6,242,442	21.3
Total Assets	**29,307,236**	**100.0**
Accounts Payable	5,920,062	20.2
Bank Loans	205,151	0.7
Notes Payable	322,380	1.1
Other Current	4,396,084	15.0
Total Current	**10,843,677**	**37.0**
Other Long Term	10,462,684	35.7
Deferred Credits	263,765	0.9
Net Worth	7,737,110	26.4
Total Liab & Net Worth	**29,307,236**	**100.0**
Net Sales	26,546,409	100.0
Gross Profit	12,317,534	46.4
Net Profit After Tax	955,671	3.6
Working Capital	1,611,898	---

RATIOS	UQ	MED	LQ
SOLVENCY			
Quick Ratio (times)	2.5	1.4	0.9
Current Ratio (times)	3.8	2.1	1.3
Curr Liab To Nw (%)	13.5	24.4	49.9
Curr Liab To Inv (%)	485.7	882.8	999.9
Total Liab To Nw (%)	32.2	67.1	139.0
Fixed Assets To Nw (%)	26.1	59.8	106.3
EFFICIENCY			
Coll Period (days)	30.3	43.4	55.1
Sales To Inv (times)	118.2	57.8	37.6
Assets To Sales (%)	69.7	110.4	151.6
Sales To Nwc (times)	9.9	6.1	3.1
Acct Pay To Sales (%)	2.0	3.5	6.0
PROFITABILITY			
Return On Sales (%)	8.0	3.1	(1.8)
Return On Assets (%)	7.0	3.0	(2.1)
Return On Nw (%)	13.7	6.0	(1.3)

SIC 8011 OFCS.CLNS OF MDL DR
(NO BREAKDOWN)
2014 (46 Establishments)

	$	%
Cash	1,843,442	21.2
Accounts Receivable	1,043,458	12.0
Notes Receivable	0	0.0
Inventory	278,255	3.2
Other Current	869,549	10.0
Total Current	**4,034,704**	**46.4**
Fixed Assets	3,069,505	35.3
Other Non-current	1,591,274	18.3
Total Assets	**8,695,483**	**100.0**
Accounts Payable	826,071	9.5
Bank Loans	34,782	0.4
Notes Payable	417,383	4.8
Other Current	1,408,668	16.2
Total Current	**2,686,904**	**30.9**
Other Long Term	2,765,164	31.8
Deferred Credits	0	0.0
Net Worth	3,243,415	37.3
Total Liab & Net Worth	**8,695,483**	**100.0**
Net Sales	10,040,973	100.0
Gross Profit	5,030,527	50.1
Net Profit After Tax	622,540	6.2
Working Capital	1,347,800	---

RATIOS	UQ	MED	LQ
SOLVENCY			
Quick Ratio (times)	4.2	1.8	0.8
Current Ratio (times)	4.9	2.4	1.0
Curr Liab To Nw (%)	10.9	23.9	50.1
Curr Liab To Inv (%)	558.1	999.9	999.9
Total Liab To Nw (%)	25.7	55.0	144.2
Fixed Assets To Nw (%)	33.8	61.2	104.0
EFFICIENCY			
Coll Period (days)	21.2	34.3	49.5
Sales To Inv (times)	248.0	87.4	70.8
Assets To Sales (%)	49.0	86.6	145.3
Sales To Nwc (times)	8.7	5.1	3.1
Acct Pay To Sales (%)	1.3	2.6	5.7
PROFITABILITY			
Return On Sales (%)	14.0	5.0	(2.2)
Return On Assets (%)	11.5	5.3	(9.3)
Return On Nw (%)	29.8	11.0	(2.3)

SIC 8051 SKLLD NRSNG CR FCLT
(NO BREAKDOWN)
2014 (35 Establishments)

	$	%
Cash	1,632,637	6.3
Accounts Receivable	5,208,890	20.1
Notes Receivable	25,915	0.1
Inventory	77,745	0.3
Other Current	2,176,849	8.4
Total Current	**9,122,036**	**35.2**
Fixed Assets	12,620,545	48.7
Other Non-current	4,172,295	16.1
Total Assets	**25,914,876**	**100.0**
Accounts Payable	1,217,999	4.7
Bank Loans	0	0.0
Notes Payable	0	0.0
Other Current	2,513,743	9.7
Total Current	**3,731,742**	**14.4**
Other Long Term	11,894,928	45.9
Deferred Credits	103,660	0.4
Net Worth	10,184,546	39.3
Total Liab & Net Worth	**25,914,876**	**100.0**
Net Sales	15,782,507	100.0
Gross Profit	5,981,570	37.9
Net Profit After Tax	268,303	1.7
Working Capital	5,390,294	---

RATIOS	UQ	MED	LQ
SOLVENCY			
Quick Ratio (times)	2.1	1.4	0.6
Current Ratio (times)	4.7	1.9	1.1
Curr Liab To Nw (%)	10.2	26.0	73.3
Curr Liab To Inv (%)	999.9	999.9	999.9
Total Liab To Nw (%)	19.6	87.4	265.2
Fixed Assets To Nw (%)	47.0	104.3	280.1
EFFICIENCY			
Coll Period (days)	22.5	32.1	45.8
Sales To Inv (times)	191.7	127.4	78.3
Assets To Sales (%)	85.1	164.2	235.7
Sales To Nwc (times)	11.7	8.4	5.5
Acct Pay To Sales (%)	2.0	2.9	4.4
PROFITABILITY			
Return On Sales (%)	5.6	1.0	(3.2)
Return On Assets (%)	3.0	1.0	(1.9)
Return On Nw (%)	12.8	3.0	(2.5)

SIC 8059 NRSNG,PRSNL CRE,NEC (NO BREAKDOWN) 2014 (16 Establishments)
SIC 8062 GNL MDL,SRGL HSPTLS (NO BREAKDOWN) 2014 (96 Establishments)
SIC 8071 MDCL LBRTRS (NO BREAKDOWN) 2014 (25 Establishments)
SIC 8082 HME HLTH CRE SVCS (NO BREAKDOWN) 2014 (21 Establishments)

	SIC 8059 $	%	SIC 8062 $	%	SIC 8071 $	%	SIC 8082 $	%
Cash	4,461,391	8.2	11,332,727	8.6	9,869,968	27.6	976,727	10.1
Accounts Receivable	7,018,530	12.9	16,208,435	12.3	5,042,266	14.1	2,601,383	26.9
Notes Receivable	0	0.0	0	0.0	0	0.0	0	0.0
Inventory	435,258	0.8	2,240,190	1.7	1,895,320	5.3	473,858	4.9
Other Current	4,243,762	7.8	12,255,159	9.3	5,721,721	16.0	647,928	6.7
Total Current	**16,158,941**	**29.7**	**42,036,511**	**31.9**	**22,529,275**	**63.0**	**4,699,896**	**48.6**
Fixed Assets	24,646,466	45.3	53,237,463	40.4	5,757,481	16.1	2,156,536	22.3
Other Non-current	13,601,802	25.0	36,501,924	27.7	7,473,998	20.9	2,814,135	29.1
Total Assets	**54,407,209**	**100.0**	**131,775,898**	**100.0**	**35,760,754**	**100.0**	**9,670,567**	**100.0**
Accounts Payable	3,590,876	6.6	5,666,364	4.3	5,113,788	14.3	319,129	3.3
Bank Loans	0	0.0	0	0.0	0	0.0	0	0.0
Notes Payable	163,222	0.3	395,328	0.3	178,804	0.5	106,376	1.1
Other Current	924,922	1.7	14,495,348	11.0	6,186,610	17.3	2,340,278	24.2
Total Current	**4,679,020**	**8.6**	**20,557,040**	**15.6**	**11,479,202**	**32.1**	**3,694,157**	**38.2**
Other Long Term	20,892,369	38.4	44,672,029	33.9	9,941,489	27.8	2,359,618	24.4
Deferred Credits	2,176,288	4.0	131,776	0.1	750,976	2.1	0	0.0
Net Worth	26,659,532	49.0	66,415,053	50.4	13,589,087	38.0	3,616,792	37.4
Total Liab & Net Worth	**54,407,209**	**100.0**	**131,775,898**	**100.0**	**35,760,754**	**100.0**	**9,670,567**	**100.0**
Net Sales	35,747,181	100.0	116,409,804	100.0	29,432,719	100.0	15,724,499	100.0
Gross Profit	6,648,976	18.6	107,795,479	92.6	14,039,407	47.7	5,755,167	36.6
Net Profit After Tax	1,823,106	5.1	6,053,310	5.2	(294,327)	(1.0)	456,010	2.9
Working Capital	11,479,921	---	21,479,471	---	11,050,073	---	1,005,739	---

RATIOS	8059 UQ	MED	LQ	8062 UQ	MED	LQ	8071 UQ	MED	LQ	8082 UQ	MED	LQ
SOLVENCY												
Quick Ratio (times)	1.6	1.2	0.6	2.1	1.4	1.1	3.2	1.4	1.0	2.0	1.6	0.8
Current Ratio (times)	2.8	1.6	1.1	3.2	2.3	1.6	4.1	2.5	1.6	2.4	2.0	1.2
Curr Liab To Nw (%)	7.8	29.9	58.9	14.3	22.5	33.1	20.9	33.9	59.1	21.5	39.9	77.8
Curr Liab To Inv (%)	436.1	999.9	999.9	521.9	723.8	999.9	121.3	695.3	999.9	187.4	411.1	627.3
Total Liab To Nw (%)	28.6	136.1	278.7	41.3	69.3	120.6	25.9	53.5	122.5	55.7	73.1	166.6
Fixed Assets To Nw (%)	13.7	80.9	258.4	49.0	66.9	98.3	6.4	20.8	26.8	13.3	27.8	74.4
EFFICIENCY												
Coll Period (days)	16.8	28.5	40.5	39.5	49.6	55.5	35.8	50.0	91.6	38.7	51.7	69.7
Sales To Inv (times)	215.1	189.7	36.5	70.3	51.1	39.5	40.0	13.2	10.2	40.8	27.1	19.1
Assets To Sales (%)	119.3	152.2	293.3	89.0	113.2	143.5	67.3	121.5	205.6	36.1	61.5	92.9
Sales To Nwc (times)	10.9	7.9	6.0	9.1	5.6	3.4	7.2	4.1	0.9	11.9	7.9	6.2
Acct Pay To Sales (%)	3.0	3.4	3.9	2.8	4.0	5.8	4.1	8.6	19.4	1.6	2.8	4.2
PROFITABILITY												
Return On Sales (%)	6.3	2.7	(0.4)	8.0	4.7	0.7	6.9	(1.6)	(101.7)	6.4	3.6	(1.3)
Return On Assets (%)	4.0	1.9	(0.1)	6.4	3.4	0.4	6.5	(4.6)	(47.6)	10.1	5.6	(1.3)
Return On Nw (%)	15.6	5.2	(3.0)	10.6	5.7	0.9	20.1	1.9	(58.6)	21.4	10.1	5.9

	SIC 8093 SPTY OTPNT CLNS,NEC (NO BREAKDOWN) 2014 (37 Establishments) $	%	SIC 8099 HLTH,ALLD SVCS,NEC (NO BREAKDOWN) 2014 (22 Establishments) $	%	SIC 81 LEGAL SERVICES (NO BREAKDOWN) 2014 (12 Establishments) $	%	SIC 8111 LEGAL SERVICES (NO BREAKDOWN) 2014 (12 Establishments) $	%
Cash	2,071,115	20.0	1,303,303	20.5	468,976	50.3	468,976	50.3
Accounts Receivable	1,211,603	11.7	1,169,794	18.4	222,833	23.9	222,833	23.9
Notes Receivable	0	0.0	12,715	0.2	0	0.0	0	0.0
Inventory	82,845	0.8	101,721	1.6	22,377	2.4	22,377	2.4
Other Current	1,159,824	11.2	1,004,498	15.8	80,182	8.6	80,182	8.6
Total Current	**4,525,387**	**43.7**	**3,592,031**	**56.5**	**794,368**	**85.2**	**794,368**	**85.2**
Fixed Assets	4,753,210	45.9	1,392,309	21.9	132,395	14.2	132,395	14.2
Other Non-current	1,076,980	10.4	1,373,237	21.6	5,594	0.6	5,594	0.6
Total Assets	**10,355,577**	**100.0**	**6,357,577**	**100.0**	**932,357**	**100.0**	**932,357**	**100.0**
Accounts Payable	12,623,448	121.9	947,279	14.9	49,415	5.3	49,415	5.3
Bank Loans	0	0.0	0	0.0	2,797	0.3	2,797	0.3
Notes Payable	10,356	0.1	0	0.0	0	0.0	0	0.0
Other Current	(165,689)	(1.6)	2,930,843	46.1	757,074	81.2	757,074	81.2
Total Current	**12,468,115**	**120.4**	**3,878,122**	**61.0**	**809,286**	**86.8**	**809,286**	**86.8**
Other Long Term	1,967,560	19.0	1,500,388	23.6	26,106	2.8	26,106	2.8
Deferred Credits	41,422	0.4	267,018	4.2	0	0.0	0	0.0
Net Worth	(4,121,520)	(39.8)	712,049	11.2	96,965	10.4	96,965	10.4
Total Liab & Net Worth	**10,355,577**	**100.0**	**6,357,577**	**100.0**	**932,357**	**100.0**	**932,357**	**100.0**
Net Sales	10,854,903	100.0	6,763,380	100.0	3,027,133	100.0	3,027,133	100.0
Gross Profit	3,592,973	33.1	3,084,101	45.6	1,204,799	39.8	1,204,799	39.8
Net Profit After Tax	911,812	8.4	(588,414)	(8.7)	432,880	14.3	432,880	14.3
Working Capital	(7,942,728)	---	(286,091)	---	(14,918)	---	(14,918)	---

RATIOS	UQ	MED	LQ	UQ	MED	LQ	UQ	MED	LQ	UQ	MED	LQ
SOLVENCY												
Quick Ratio (times)	2.7	1.8	1.1	3.3	1.5	0.7	11.4	1.6	1.0	11.4	1.6	1.0
Current Ratio (times)	4.1	2.7	1.4	4.0	2.1	1.1	12.1	3.1	1.0	12.1	3.1	1.0
Curr Liab To Nw (%)	10.9	17.6	38.1	10.6	23.2	85.3	6.4	16.2	91.0	6.4	16.2	91.0
Curr Liab To Inv (%)	464.2	999.9	999.9	357.3	463.7	867.4	40.8	188.7	336.5	40.8	188.7	336.5
Total Liab To Nw (%)	26.3	43.8	86.1	22.3	42.8	131.9	6.7	24.8	91.0	6.7	24.8	91.0
Fixed Assets To Nw (%)	47.3	70.3	108.1	4.6	24.2	51.9	24.2	54.8	72.1	24.2	54.8	72.1
EFFICIENCY												
Coll Period (days)	19.7	28.3	52.6	31.8	48.2	73.7	8.2	15.7	43.9	8.2	15.7	43.9
Sales To Inv (times)	432.6	411.1	35.0	39.9	33.6	18.3	55.0	30.7	6.4	55.0	30.7	6.4
Assets To Sales (%)	64.6	95.4	132.3	48.4	94.0	169.6	15.7	30.8	68.9	15.7	30.8	68.9
Sales To Nwc (times)	10.2	6.1	2.1	12.4	5.8	2.3	25.0	4.0	1.5	25.0	4.0	1.5
Acct Pay To Sales (%)	1.8	2.2	3.5	1.6	5.7	13.4	0.6	1.0	1.8	0.6	1.0	1.8
PROFITABILITY												
Return On Sales (%)	16.5	3.6	0.2	3.6	.3	(30.7)	21.1	11.6	6.5	21.1	11.6	6.5
Return On Assets (%)	8.1	2.4	(0.2)	5.9	0.2	(37.5)	63.7	22.6	12.8	63.7	22.6	12.8
Return On Nw (%)	11.7	4.2	0.3	8.5	3.0	(37.1)	51.0	24.4	13.2	51.0	24.4	13.2

	SIC 82 EDUCATIONAL SERVICE (NO BREAKDOWN) 2014 (273 Establishments) $	%	SIC 8211 ELMNTRY,SCNDRY SCLS (NO BREAKDOWN) 2014 (103 Establishments) $	%	SIC 8221 COLLEGES,UNVRSTES (NO BREAKDOWN) 2014 (41 Establishments) $	%	SIC 8222 JUNIOR COLLEGES (NO BREAKDOWN) 2014 (29 Establishments) $	%
Cash	3,276,633	24.1	3,681,463	22.9	50,173,845	16.3	7,396,312	11.8
Accounts Receivable	870,143	6.4	723,432	4.5	15,698,565	5.1	2,068,460	3.3
Notes Receivable	13,596	0.1	16,076	0.1	307,815	0.1	62,681	0.1
Inventory	176,748	1.3	48,229	0.3	615,630	0.2	313,403	0.5
Other Current	1,821,863	13.4	1,671,930	10.4	29,242,425	9.5	8,399,202	13.4
Total Current	**6,158,983**	**45.3**	**6,141,130**	**38.2**	**96,038,280**	**31.2**	**18,240,058**	**29.1**
Fixed Assets	5,669,527	41.7	8,729,408	54.3	148,982,460	48.4	32,593,917	52.0
Other Non-current	1,767,478	13.0	1,205,719	7.5	62,794,260	20.4	11,846,635	18.9
Total Assets	**13,595,988**	**100.0**	**16,076,257**	**100.0**	**307,815,000**	**100.0**	**62,680,610**	**100.0**
Accounts Payable	625,415	4.6	434,059	2.7	8,926,635	2.9	1,065,570	1.7
Bank Loans	0	0.0	0	0.0	0	0.0	0	0.0
Notes Payable	135,960	1.0	16,076	0.1	0	0.0	125,361	0.2
Other Current	2,229,742	16.4	2,186,371	13.6	36,322,170	11.8	5,641,255	9.0
Total Current	**2,991,117**	**22.0**	**2,636,506**	**16.4**	**45,248,805**	**14.7**	**6,832,186**	**10.9**
Other Long Term	3,222,249	23.7	5,273,012	32.8	68,950,560	22.4	17,801,293	28.4
Deferred Credits	40,788	0.3	96,458	0.6	0	0.0	62,681	0.1
Net Worth	7,341,834	54.0	8,070,281	50.2	193,615,635	62.9	37,984,450	60.6
Total Liab & Net Worth	**13,595,988**	**100.0**	**16,076,257**	**100.0**	**307,815,000**	**100.0**	**62,680,610**	**100.0**
Net Sales	9,192,690	100.0	9,655,410	100.0	128,096,130	100.0	14,435,884	100.0
Gross Profit	5,212,255	56.7	3,968,374	41.1	77,882,447	60.8	(2,165,383)	(15.0)
Net Profit After Tax	726,223	7.9	299,318	3.1	15,243,439	11.9	1,804,486	12.5
Working Capital	3,167,866	---	3,504,624	---	50,789,475	---	11,407,872	---

RATIOS	UQ	MED	LQ	UQ	MED	LQ	UQ	MED	LQ	UQ	MED	LQ
SOLVENCY												
Quick Ratio (times)	3.7	1.8	0.8	5.0	1.7	0.7	2.4	1.5	0.9	2.6	1.7	0.9
Current Ratio (times)	6.1	2.7	1.4	6.5	2.5	1.4	3.4	2.3	1.8	4.5	2.9	2.0
Curr Liab To Nw (%)	7.0	17.9	43.9	7.6	20.4	42.0	9.1	14.7	31.8	7.1	16.8	27.6
Curr Liab To Inv (%)	985.6	999.9	999.9	999.9	999.9	999.9	999.9	999.9	999.9	921.6	999.9	999.9
Total Liab To Nw (%)	15.3	54.6	146.2	18.6	72.8	214.6	32.8	51.4	72.7	12.7	65.4	114.7
Fixed Assets To Nw (%)	33.5	75.8	129.0	68.5	106.0	189.3	46.5	80.9	97.6	63.8	84.0	129.1
EFFICIENCY												
Coll Period (days)	4.4	14.8	40.2	0.6	5.7	12.8	14.6	26.7	45.6	19.6	31.4	55.2
Sales To Inv (times)	621.3	189.0	44.5	999.9	693.0	339.9	291.9	125.1	52.7	70.1	44.5	20.8
Assets To Sales (%)	62.2	147.9	279.5	90.8	166.5	224.0	103.1	240.3	392.0	279.5	434.2	670.7
Sales To Nwc (times)	8.5	3.6	1.7	9.4	4.3	2.2	5.5	3.2	2.1	2.8	1.6	0.9
Acct Pay To Sales (%)	1.3	3.4	6.7	0.8	1.8	4.0	3.1	4.9	9.2	3.5	5.8	10.1
PROFITABILITY												
Return On Sales (%)	13.3	4.1	(0.6)	6.4	2.2	(3.4)	15.5	8.3	1.2	26.4	8.4	2.5
Return On Assets (%)	10.1	2.9	(0.4)	4.6	0.9	(2.1)	8.8	5.1	1.7	4.2	2.1	0.2
Return On Nw (%)	19.8	6.4	0.0	11.3	3.1	(6.0)	14.7	7.7	2.9	6.6	3.3	0.9

SIC 8231 LIBRARIES (NO BREAKDOWN) 2014 (18 Establishments)

	$	%
Cash	1,376,405	22.2
Accounts Receivable	365,801	5.9
Notes Receivable	0	0.0
Inventory	130,200	2.1
Other Current	1,351,605	21.8
Total Current	**3,224,011**	**52.0**
Fixed Assets	1,568,605	25.3
Other Non-current	1,407,405	22.7
Total Assets	**6,200,021**	**100.0**
Accounts Payable	155,001	2.5
Bank Loans	0	0.0
Notes Payable	6,200	0.1
Other Current	310,001	5.0
Total Current	**471,202**	**7.6**
Other Long Term	694,402	11.2
Deferred Credits	0	0.0
Net Worth	5,034,417	81.2
Total Liab & Net Worth	**6,200,021**	**100.0**
Net Sales	2,044,862	100.0
Gross Profit	1,247,366	61.0
Net Profit After Tax	529,619	25.9
Working Capital	2,752,809	—

RATIOS	UQ	MED	LQ
SOLVENCY			
Quick Ratio (times)	21.3	6.2	2.3
Current Ratio (times)	36.7	15.5	5.9
Curr Liab To Nw (%)	0.7	2.3	12.5
Curr Liab To Inv (%)	20.6	153.3	305.7
Total Liab To Nw (%)	1.0	2.8	57.1
Fixed Assets To Nw (%)	25.4	39.4	112.5
EFFICIENCY			
Coll Period (days)	0.2	35.5	72.3
Sales To Inv (times)	76.9	76.9	76.9
Assets To Sales (%)	92.9	303.2	482.9
Sales To Nwc (times)	10.3	2.4	0.9
Acct Pay To Sales (%)	0.7	1.2	4.4
PROFITABILITY			
Return On Sales (%)	54.0	6.7	(0.5)
Return On Assets (%)	10.6	3.8	(0.3)
Return On Nw (%)	14.4	4.7	(0.5)

SIC 8249 VOCTNL SCHLS, NEC (NO BREAKDOWN) 2014 (11 Establishments)

	$	%
Cash	432,956	14.8
Accounts Receivable	511,941	17.5
Notes Receivable	46,806	1.6
Inventory	84,836	2.9
Other Current	734,270	25.1
Total Current	**1,810,809**	**61.9**
Fixed Assets	880,539	30.1
Other Non-current	234,030	8.0
Total Assets	**2,925,378**	**100.0**
Accounts Payable	266,209	9.1
Bank Loans	0	0.0
Notes Payable	40,955	1.4
Other Current	558,748	19.1
Total Current	**865,912**	**29.6**
Other Long Term	356,896	12.2
Deferred Credits	0	0.0
Net Worth	1,702,570	58.2
Total Liab & Net Worth	**2,925,378**	**100.0**
Net Sales	3,721,855	100.0
Gross Profit	2,251,722	60.5
Net Profit After Tax	163,762	4.4
Working Capital	944,897	—

RATIOS	UQ	MED	LQ
SOLVENCY			
Quick Ratio (times)	2.3	1.8	0.7
Current Ratio (times)	4.2	2.8	1.5
Curr Liab To Nw (%)	24.3	29.2	66.9
Curr Liab To Inv (%)	378.6	697.6	999.9
Total Liab To Nw (%)	28.6	54.8	174.0
Fixed Assets To Nw (%)	14.4	69.1	90.0
EFFICIENCY			
Coll Period (days)	13.5	29.6	40.8
Sales To Inv (times)	283.5	112.8	16.3
Assets To Sales (%)	35.2	78.6	142.4
Sales To Nwc (times)	9.0	5.6	3.7
Acct Pay To Sales (%)	2.2	4.3	6.2
PROFITABILITY			
Return On Sales (%)	5.8	2.8	1.2
Return On Assets (%)	8.1	5.2	2.0
Return On Nw (%)	23.5	13.3	2.9

SIC 8299 SCLS,EDCTL SVCS,NEC (NO BREAKDOWN) 2014 (67 Establishments)

	$	%
Cash	1,094,827	37.7
Accounts Receivable	246,844	8.5
Notes Receivable	0	0.0
Inventory	92,930	3.2
Other Current	487,881	16.8
Total Current	**1,922,482**	**66.2**
Fixed Assets	606,947	20.9
Other Non-current	374,622	12.9
Total Assets	**2,904,051**	**100.0**
Accounts Payable	249,748	8.6
Bank Loans	0	0.0
Notes Payable	104,546	3.6
Other Current	827,655	28.5
Total Current	**1,181,949**	**40.7**
Other Long Term	409,471	14.1
Deferred Credits	5,808	0.2
Net Worth	1,306,823	45.0
Total Liab & Net Worth	**2,904,051**	**100.0**
Net Sales	5,041,755	100.0
Gross Profit	2,979,677	59.1
Net Profit After Tax	292,422	5.8
Working Capital	740,533	—

RATIOS	UQ	MED	LQ
SOLVENCY			
Quick Ratio (times)	4.3	2.0	0.7
Current Ratio (times)	6.3	2.8	1.2
Curr Liab To Nw (%)	5.0	20.2	93.6
Curr Liab To Inv (%)	376.4	992.8	999.9
Total Liab To Nw (%)	10.6	37.1	140.4
Fixed Assets To Nw (%)	5.6	18.5	55.3
EFFICIENCY			
Coll Period (days)	1.5	5.8	33.6
Sales To Inv (times)	345.9	51.3	30.1
Assets To Sales (%)	29.5	57.6	123.6
Sales To Nwc (times)	11.0	4.6	2.2
Acct Pay To Sales (%)	0.7	2.7	6.8
PROFITABILITY			
Return On Sales (%)	16.6	4.1	0.0
Return On Assets (%)	21.6	10.1	0.0
Return On Nw (%)	54.0	24.5	2.4

SIC 83 SOC SEV (NO BREAKDOWN) 2014 (399 Establishments)

	$	%
Cash	573,843	28.5
Accounts Receivable	205,375	10.2
Notes Receivable	4,027	0.2
Inventory	16,108	0.8
Other Current	267,793	13.3
Total Current	**1,067,146**	**53.0**
Fixed Assets	664,449	33.0
Other Non-current	281,888	14.0
Total Assets	**2,013,483**	**100.0**
Accounts Payable	153,025	7.6
Bank Loans	2,013	0.1
Notes Payable	16,108	0.8
Other Current	483,236	24.0
Total Current	**654,382**	**32.5**
Other Long Term	269,807	13.4
Deferred Credits	4,027	0.2
Net Worth	1,085,267	53.9
Total Liab & Net Worth	**2,013,483**	**100.0**
Net Sales	3,050,732	100.0
Gross Profit	1,583,330	51.9
Net Profit After Tax	189,145	6.2
Working Capital	412,764	—

RATIOS	UQ	MED	LQ
SOLVENCY			
Quick Ratio (times)	5.1	1.9	0.8
Current Ratio (times)	8.1	3.2	1.3
Curr Liab To Nw (%)	4.8	14.8	50.2
Curr Liab To Inv (%)	174.4	954.3	999.9
Total Liab To Nw (%)	7.4	27.6	99.8
Fixed Assets To Nw (%)	12.8	48.0	90.5
EFFICIENCY			
Coll Period (days)	5.8	21.9	37.6
Sales To Inv (times)	524.9	112.6	28.7
Assets To Sales (%)	27.0	66.0	151.4
Sales To Nwc (times)	13.4	5.6	2.5
Acct Pay To Sales (%)	1.0	2.2	4.1
PROFITABILITY			
Return On Sales (%)	9.2	3.0	(0.4)
Return On Assets (%)	12.4	4.3	(0.6)
Return On Nw (%)	30.0	9.5	0.3

SIC 8322 INDVDL.FMLY SVCS (NO BREAKDOWN) — 2014 (203 Establishments)
SIC 8331 JOB TRNNG,RLTD SVCS (NO BREAKDOWN) — 2014 (49 Establishments)
SIC 8351 CHILD DAY CARE SVCS (NO BREAKDOWN) — 2014 (29 Establishments)
SIC 8361 RESIDENTIAL CARE (NO BREAKDOWN) — 2014 (49 Establishments)

	SIC 8322 $	SIC 8322 %	SIC 8331 $	SIC 8331 %	SIC 8351 $	SIC 8351 %	SIC 8361 $	SIC 8361 %
Cash	411,934	30.0	917,034	25.8	172,260	34.6	1,112,691	17.4
Accounts Receivable	151,042	11.0	394,538	11.1	62,730	12.6	473,213	7.4
Notes Receivable	4,119	0.3	0	0.0	0	0.0	19,184	0.3
Inventory	6,866	0.5	135,067	3.8	0	0.0	6,395	0.1
Other Current	186,743	13.6	458,517	12.9	68,207	13.7	505,188	7.9
Total Current	**760,704**	**55.4**	**1,905,156**	**53.6**	**303,197**	**60.9**	**2,116,671**	**33.1**
Fixed Assets	444,888	32.4	1,244,038	35.0	144,379	29.0	3,043,913	47.6
Other Non-current	167,520	12.2	405,201	11.4	50,284	10.1	1,234,192	19.3
Total Assets	**1,373,112**	**100.0**	**3,554,395**	**100.0**	**497,860**	**100.0**	**6,394,776**	**100.0**
Accounts Payable	113,968	8.3	177,720	5.0	71,692	14.4	159,869	2.5
Bank Loans	2,746	0.2	0	0.0	0	0.0	0	0.0
Notes Payable	6,866	0.5	21,326	0.6	0	0.0	57,553	0.9
Other Current	366,621	26.7	767,749	21.6	138,903	27.9	722,610	11.3
Total Current	**490,201**	**35.7**	**966,795**	**27.2**	**210,595**	**42.3**	**940,032**	**14.7**
Other Long Term	167,520	12.2	394,538	11.1	76,670	15.4	1,758,563	27.5
Deferred Credits	1,373	0.1	0	0.0	0	0.0	70,343	1.1
Net Worth	714,018	52.0	2,193,062	61.7	210,595	42.3	3,625,838	56.7
Total Liab & Net Worth	**1,373,112**	**100.0**	**3,554,395**	**100.0**	**497,860**	**100.0**	**6,394,776**	**100.0**
Net Sales	2,258,408	100.0	5,562,433	100.0	2,127,607	100.0	4,062,755	100.0
Gross Profit	1,135,979	50.3	2,747,842	49.4	1,036,145	48.7	1,438,215	35.4
Net Profit After Tax	178,414	7.9	250,309	4.5	38,297	1.8	101,569	2.5
Working Capital	270,503	---	938,361	---	92,602	---	1,176,639	---

RATIOS

	SIC 8322 UQ	SIC 8322 MED	SIC 8322 LQ	SIC 8331 UQ	SIC 8331 MED	SIC 8331 LQ	SIC 8351 UQ	SIC 8351 MED	SIC 8351 LQ	SIC 8361 UQ	SIC 8361 MED	SIC 8361 LQ
SOLVENCY												
Quick Ratio (times)	5.9	2.1	0.9	3.9	2.4	1.2	4.1	1.2	0.6	3.3	1.3	0.8
Current Ratio (times)	8.9	3.5	1.2	5.9	3.2	2.2	6.4	1.5	1.2	6.0	2.5	1.2
Curr Liab To Nw (%)	5.0	13.1	46.4	9.0	17.8	46.4	7.9	37.2	81.2	3.2	17.5	42.9
Curr Liab To Inv (%)	175.2	773.6	999.9	131.5	807.4	999.9	---	---	---	63.9	999.9	999.9
Total Liab To Nw (%)	6.3	27.4	94.5	12.6	25.4	80.2	11.0	50.3	206.6	5.8	36.8	197.1
Fixed Assets To Nw (%)	11.5	48.5	95.0	17.2	49.1	73.1	22.4	57.6	89.3	36.3	73.3	154.5
EFFICIENCY												
Coll Period (days)	4.6	21.6	41.1	14.2	30.3	42.0	4.4	22.3	31.8	11.9	22.5	33.8
Sales To Inv (times)	326.3	85.5	45.6	273.5	80.7	13.1	---	---	---	917.4	793.9	489.6
Assets To Sales (%)	28.0	60.8	138.9	33.0	63.9	110.8	14.2	23.4	50.0	87.4	157.4	274.9
Sales To Nwc (times)	13.0	5.3	2.6	11.3	4.9	2.6	37.4	9.2	6.2	11.7	4.5	1.8
Acct Pay To Sales (%)	0.9	2.1	4.2	1.0	1.9	3.6	1.3	3.1	6.9	1.2	2.9	4.2
PROFITABILITY												
Return On Sales (%)	14.3	4.8	(0.5)	6.6	3.3	0.9	5.6	3.2	(0.1)	13.2	4.2	(1.8)
Return On Assets (%)	16.5	4.8	(0.8)	8.6	4.7	1.0	15.5	7.1	(0.4)	6.8	3.4	(1.7)
Return On Nw (%)	37.3	10.1	(0.2)	13.5	5.7	1.8	46.1	14.7	4.0	17.5	7.0	2.1

SIC 8399 SOCIAL SVCS,NEC (NO BREAKDOWN) 2014 (69 Establishments)

	$	%
Cash	1,113,490	31.2
Accounts Receivable	292,648	8.2
Notes Receivable	7,138	0.2
Inventory	24,982	0.7
Other Current	585,295	16.4
Total Current	**2,023,553**	**56.7**
Fixed Assets	892,219	25.0
Other Non-current	653,105	18.3
Total Assets	**3,568,877**	**100.0**
Accounts Payable	299,786	8.4
Bank Loans	0	0.0
Notes Payable	64,240	1.8
Other Current	913,632	25.6
Total Current	**1,277,658**	**35.8**
Other Long Term	267,665	7.5
Deferred Credits	7,138	0.2
Net Worth	2,016,416	56.5
Total Liab & Net Worth	**3,568,877**	**100.0**
Net Sales	6,929,858	100.0
Gross Profit	4,726,163	68.2
Net Profit After Tax	498,950	7.2
Working Capital	745,895	---

RATIOS	UQ	MED	LQ
SOLVENCY			
Quick Ratio (times)	4.2	1.6	0.7
Current Ratio (times)	8.7	3.5	1.1
Curr Liab To Nw (%)	3.3	13.6	73.8
Curr Liab To Inv (%)	660.3	999.9	999.9
Total Liab To Nw (%)	6.7	27.5	93.0
Fixed Assets To Nw (%)	3.6	22.9	70.2
EFFICIENCY			
Coll Period (days)	4.0	13.5	25.4
Sales To Inv (times)	862.0	449.8	57.7
Assets To Sales (%)	23.5	51.5	151.5
Sales To Nwc (times)	22.7	5.1	2.4
Acct Pay To Sales (%)	0.7	2.5	3.9
PROFITABILITY			
Return On Sales (%)	11.2	1.5	(0.7)
Return On Assets (%)	10.8	2.7	(1.9)
Return On Nw (%)	23.3	9.1	0.2

SIC 84 MUSEUM,BOT,ZOO GARD (NO BREAKDOWN) 2014 (43 Establishments)

	$	%
Cash	271,726	19.8
Accounts Receivable	13,724	1.0
Notes Receivable	0	0.0
Inventory	34,309	2.5
Other Current	212,714	15.5
Total Current	**532,473**	**38.8**
Fixed Assets	411,706	30.0
Other Non-current	428,173	31.2
Total Assets	**1,372,352**	**100.0**
Accounts Payable	20,585	1.5
Bank Loans	4,117	0.3
Notes Payable	6,862	0.5
Other Current	104,299	7.6
Total Current	**135,863**	**9.9**
Other Long Term	38,426	2.8
Deferred Credits	20,585	1.5
Net Worth	1,177,478	85.8
Total Liab & Net Worth	**1,372,352**	**100.0**
Net Sales	634,760	100.0
Gross Profit	552,241	87.0
Net Profit After Tax	166,942	26.3
Working Capital	396,610	---

RATIOS	UQ	MED	LQ
SOLVENCY			
Quick Ratio (times)	13.9	2.9	1.0
Current Ratio (times)	29.4	5.0	2.1
Curr Liab To Nw (%)	0.7	2.3	16.9
Curr Liab To Inv (%)	60.1	329.9	894.0
Total Liab To Nw (%)	0.8	3.7	21.7
Fixed Assets To Nw (%)	17.7	32.6	59.5
EFFICIENCY			
Coll Period (days)	1.5	2.6	7.2
Sales To Inv (times)	72.8	32.5	10.5
Assets To Sales (%)	115.3	216.2	436.8
Sales To Nwc (times)	5.0	2.4	1.3
Acct Pay To Sales (%)	0.8	2.1	3.2
PROFITABILITY			
Return On Sales (%)	42.8	21.3	1.6
Return On Assets (%)	22.3	5.9	0.4
Return On Nw (%)	27.8	6.7	0.4

SIC 8412 MUSEUMS,ART GALLRS (NO BREAKDOWN) 2014 (42 Establishments)

	$	%
Cash	334,014	20.0
Accounts Receivable	16,701	1.0
Notes Receivable	0	0.0
Inventory	43,422	2.6
Other Current	265,540	15.9
Total Current	**659,677**	**39.5**
Fixed Assets	507,701	30.4
Other Non-current	502,690	30.1
Total Assets	**1,670,068**	**100.0**
Accounts Payable	25,051	1.5
Bank Loans	5,010	0.3
Notes Payable	8,350	0.5
Other Current	130,266	7.8
Total Current	**168,677**	**10.1**
Other Long Term	48,432	2.9
Deferred Credits	25,051	1.5
Net Worth	1,427,908	85.5
Total Liab & Net Worth	**1,670,068**	**100.0**
Net Sales	760,158	100.0
Gross Profit	661,337	87.0
Net Profit After Tax	194,600	25.6
Working Capital	491,000	---

RATIOS	UQ	MED	LQ
SOLVENCY			
Quick Ratio (times)	15.7	2.8	0.9
Current Ratio (times)	32.8	4.9	2.0
Curr Liab To Nw (%)	0.6	2.5	17.0
Curr Liab To Inv (%)	60.1	329.9	894.0
Total Liab To Nw (%)	0.7	4.3	24.9
Fixed Assets To Nw (%)	19.7	36.1	59.5
EFFICIENCY			
Coll Period (days)	1.5	2.6	7.2
Sales To Inv (times)	72.8	32.5	10.5
Assets To Sales (%)	105.8	219.7	456.3
Sales To Nwc (times)	4.6	2.3	1.3
Acct Pay To Sales (%)	0.8	2.1	3.2
PROFITABILITY			
Return On Sales (%)	42.6	20.9	1.1
Return On Assets (%)	21.5	5.8	0.4
Return On Nw (%)	27.7	6.1	0.4

SIC 86 MEMBERSHIP ORGANIZATI (NO BREAKDOWN) 2014 (217 Establishments)

	$	%
Cash	752,640	33.9
Accounts Receivable	124,330	5.6
Notes Receivable	8,881	0.4
Inventory	26,642	1.2
Other Current	326,366	14.7
Total Current	**1,238,859**	**55.8**
Fixed Assets	557,265	25.1
Other Non-current	424,054	19.1
Total Assets	**2,220,178**	**100.0**
Accounts Payable	321,926	14.5
Bank Loans	0	0.0
Notes Payable	11,101	0.5
Other Current	348,568	15.7
Total Current	**681,595**	**30.7**
Other Long Term	144,311	6.5
Deferred Credits	19,982	0.9
Net Worth	1,374,290	61.9
Total Liab & Net Worth	**2,220,178**	**100.0**
Net Sales	2,038,731	100.0
Gross Profit	1,294,594	63.5
Net Profit After Tax	140,672	6.9
Working Capital	557,264	---

RATIOS	UQ	MED	LQ
SOLVENCY			
Quick Ratio (times)	7.8	2.1	0.9
Current Ratio (times)	14.1	3.5	1.4
Curr Liab To Nw (%)	2.8	12.8	39.6
Curr Liab To Inv (%)	310.4	644.1	999.9
Total Liab To Nw (%)	5.4	23.6	72.5
Fixed Assets To Nw (%)	3.8	20.1	70.6
EFFICIENCY			
Coll Period (days)	1.8	8.8	29.6
Sales To Inv (times)	286.0	60.7	17.2
Assets To Sales (%)	51.3	108.9	179.5
Sales To Nwc (times)	8.8	4.0	1.9
Acct Pay To Sales (%)	1.3	2.7	6.7
PROFITABILITY			
Return On Sales (%)	11.8	5.0	(0.4)
Return On Assets (%)	11.7	6.2	(0.1)
Return On Nw (%)	22.3	8.8	1.0

SIC 8611 BUSINESS ASSNS
(NO BREAKDOWN)
2014 (41 Establishments)

	$	%
Cash	804,004	41.1
Accounts Receivable	183,884	9.4
Notes Receivable	11,737	0.6
Inventory	9,781	0.5
Other Current	293,432	15.0
Total Current	**1,302,838**	**66.6**
Fixed Assets	338,425	17.3
Other Non-current	314,950	16.1
Total Assets	**1,956,213**	**100.0**
Accounts Payable	160,409	8.2
Bank Loans	0	0.0
Notes Payable	0	0.0
Other Current	735,537	37.6
Total Current	**895,946**	**45.8**
Other Long Term	101,723	5.2
Deferred Credits	0	0.0
Net Worth	958,544	49.0
Total Liab & Net Worth	**1,956,213**	**100.0**
Net Sales	1,866,615	100.0
Gross Profit	864,243	46.3
Net Profit After Tax	65,332	3.5
Working Capital	406,892	---

RATIOS	UQ	MED	LQ
SOLVENCY			
Quick Ratio (times)	3.3	2.0	0.9
Current Ratio (times)	4.9	2.5	1.6
Curr Liab To Nw (%)	12.3	25.9	52.9
Curr Liab To Inv (%)	495.3	999.9	999.9
Total Liab To Nw (%)	19.0	38.1	65.7
Fixed Assets To Nw (%)	2.5	17.0	42.7
EFFICIENCY			
Coll Period (days)	3.2	35.4	54.6
Sales To Inv (times)	491.5	55.9	28.9
Assets To Sales (%)	45.2	104.8	152.1
Sales To Nwc (times)	9.2	3.7	1.6
Acct Pay To Sales (%)	2.5	4.7	7.2
PROFITABILITY			
Return On Sales (%)	11.8	3.0	(0.2)
Return On Assets (%)	11.6	4.2	(0.1)
Return On Nw (%)	21.5	8.1	4.4

SIC 8621 PRFSSNL ORGNZTNS
(NO BREAKDOWN)
2014 (34 Establishments)

	$	%
Cash	1,108,211	37.8
Accounts Receivable	181,770	6.2
Notes Receivable	8,795	0.3
Inventory	17,591	0.6
Other Current	554,105	18.9
Total Current	**1,870,472**	**63.8**
Fixed Assets	354,745	12.1
Other Non-current	706,558	24.1
Total Assets	**2,931,775**	**100.0**
Accounts Payable	287,314	9.8
Bank Loans	0	0.0
Notes Payable	0	0.0
Other Current	507,197	17.3
Total Current	**794,511**	**27.1**
Other Long Term	170,043	5.8
Deferred Credits	85,021	2.9
Net Worth	1,882,200	64.2
Total Liab & Net Worth	**2,931,775**	**100.0**
Net Sales	2,667,675	100.0
Gross Profit	1,600,605	60.0
Net Profit After Tax	298,780	11.2
Working Capital	1,075,961	---

RATIOS	UQ	MED	LQ
SOLVENCY			
Quick Ratio (times)	3.6	1.6	0.8
Current Ratio (times)	7.7	2.8	1.1
Curr Liab To Nw (%)	6.5	33.8	75.5
Curr Liab To Inv (%)	772.7	999.9	999.9
Total Liab To Nw (%)	15.0	56.3	114.3
Fixed Assets To Nw (%)	2.1	9.9	50.4
EFFICIENCY			
Coll Period (days)	5.1	15.3	19.7
Sales To Inv (times)	687.0	111.3	68.5
Assets To Sales (%)	53.1	109.9	131.8
Sales To Nwc (times)	8.5	2.7	2.1
Acct Pay To Sales (%)	2.0	4.2	7.2
PROFITABILITY			
Return On Sales (%)	11.7	7.2	0.7
Return On Assets (%)	12.0	6.2	0.8
Return On Nw (%)	22.0	9.0	1.5

SIC 8641 CIVIC,SOCL ASSNS
(NO BREAKDOWN)
2014 (61 Establishments)

	$	%
Cash	401,343	26.8
Accounts Receivable	47,922	3.2
Notes Receivable	0	0.0
Inventory	13,478	0.9
Other Current	215,646	14.4
Total Current	**678,389**	**45.3**
Fixed Assets	501,679	33.5
Other Non-current	317,480	21.2
Total Assets	**1,497,548**	**100.0**
Accounts Payable	106,326	7.1
Bank Loans	0	0.0
Notes Payable	22,463	1.5
Other Current	133,282	8.9
Total Current	**262,071**	**17.5**
Other Long Term	119,803	8.0
Deferred Credits	1,498	0.1
Net Worth	1,114,176	74.4
Total Liab & Net Worth	**1,497,548**	**100.0**
Net Sales	1,660,253	100.0
Gross Profit	889,896	53.6
Net Profit After Tax	106,256	6.4
Working Capital	416,318	---

RATIOS	UQ	MED	LQ
SOLVENCY			
Quick Ratio (times)	13.9	2.4	0.9
Current Ratio (times)	19.4	3.9	1.2
Curr Liab To Nw (%)	1.7	13.7	40.7
Curr Liab To Inv (%)	362.7	452.1	999.9
Total Liab To Nw (%)	4.3	23.0	72.3
Fixed Assets To Nw (%)	6.9	45.7	88.6
EFFICIENCY			
Coll Period (days)	1.1	5.3	29.0
Sales To Inv (times)	268.9	53.4	21.8
Assets To Sales (%)	51.5	90.2	179.4
Sales To Nwc (times)	9.8	5.2	2.3
Acct Pay To Sales (%)	0.8	2.2	4.0
PROFITABILITY			
Return On Sales (%)	9.8	5.8	0.8
Return On Assets (%)	12.7	8.5	0.1
Return On Nw (%)	22.0	12.4	0.1

SIC 8661 RELIGIOUS ORGNZTNS
(NO BREAKDOWN)
2014 (23 Establishments)

	$	%
Cash	929,821	25.4
Accounts Receivable	128,125	3.5
Notes Receivable	87,857	2.4
Inventory	117,143	3.2
Other Current	333,125	9.1
Total Current	**1,596,071**	**43.6**
Fixed Assets	1,760,803	48.1
Other Non-current	303,839	8.3
Total Assets	**3,660,713**	**100.0**
Accounts Payable	2,895,624	79.1
Bank Loans	0	0.0
Notes Payable	10,982	0.3
Other Current	223,304	6.1
Total Current	**3,129,910**	**85.5**
Other Long Term	399,017	10.9
Deferred Credits	0	0.0
Net Worth	131,786	3.6
Total Liab & Net Worth	**3,660,713**	**100.0**
Net Sales	3,599,521	100.0
Gross Profit	3,268,365	90.8
Net Profit After Tax	151,180	4.2
Working Capital	(1,533,839)	---

RATIOS	UQ	MED	LQ
SOLVENCY			
Quick Ratio (times)	6.1	1.7	0.5
Current Ratio (times)	11.0	4.1	1.1
Curr Liab To Nw (%)	6.0	10.2	13.6
Curr Liab To Inv (%)	174.1	276.4	473.1
Total Liab To Nw (%)	7.9	18.6	48.6
Fixed Assets To Nw (%)	20.1	66.2	92.6
EFFICIENCY			
Coll Period (days)	0.0	0.7	3.3
Sales To Inv (times)	90.2	41.8	14.5
Assets To Sales (%)	57.5	101.7	181.6
Sales To Nwc (times)	17.2	6.0	4.7
Acct Pay To Sales (%)	0.8	2.2	4.0
PROFITABILITY			
Return On Sales (%)	12.3	4.5	0.3
Return On Assets (%)	11.8	4.4	(0.6)
Return On Nw (%)	26.3	5.6	1.1

	SIC 8699 MBRSHP ORGNZTNS,NEC (NO BREAKDOWN) 2014 (52 Establishments)		SIC 87 ENGINEERING MGMT SVC (NO BREAKDOWN) 2014 (1101 Establishments)		SIC 8711 ENGINEERING SVCS (NO BREAKDOWN) 2014 (306 Establishments)		SIC 8712 ARCHITECTURAL SVCS (NO BREAKDOWN) 2014 (65 Establishments)	
	$	%	$	%	$	%	$	%
Cash	1,119,707	39.4	866,406	25.7	821,073	23.2	336,541	16.4
Accounts Receivable	184,723	6.5	1,200,158	35.6	1,543,051	43.6	978,842	47.7
Notes Receivable	0	0.0	13,485	0.4	14,156	0.4	0	0.0
Inventory	45,470	1.6	84,281	2.5	95,556	2.7	75,927	3.7
Other Current	392,182	13.8	418,032	12.4	353,911	10.0	188,792	9.2
Total Current	**1,742,082**	**61.3**	**2,582,362**	**76.6**	**2,827,747**	**79.9**	**1,580,102**	**77.0**
Fixed Assets	539,960	19.0	414,661	12.3	399,919	11.3	316,020	15.4
Other Non-current	559,854	19.7	374,207	11.1	311,442	8.8	155,958	7.6
Total Assets	**2,841,896**	**100.0**	**3,371,230**	**100.0**	**3,539,108**	**100.0**	**2,052,080**	**100.0**
Accounts Payable	119,360	4.2	927,088	27.5	410,537	11.6	301,656	14.7
Bank Loans	0	0.0	26,970	0.8	35,391	1.0	28,729	1.4
Notes Payable	0	0.0	205,645	6.1	21,235	0.6	36,937	1.8
Other Current	323,976	11.4	1,749,668	51.9	1,111,279	31.4	707,968	34.5
Total Current	**443,336**	**15.6**	**2,909,371**	**86.3**	**1,578,442**	**44.6**	**1,075,290**	**52.4**
Other Long Term	107,992	3.8	168,562	5.0	353,911	10.0	203,156	9.9
Deferred Credits	5,684	0.2	13,485	0.4	3,539	0.1	6,156	0.3
Net Worth	2,284,884	80.4	279,812	8.3	1,603,216	45.3	767,478	37.4
Total Liab & Net Worth	**2,841,896**	**100.0**	**3,371,230**	**100.0**	**3,539,108**	**100.0**	**2,052,080**	**100.0**
Net Sales	2,138,372	100.0	8,513,207	100.0	8,959,767	100.0	5,561,192	100.0
Gross Profit	1,710,698	80.0	3,737,298	43.9	3,870,619	43.2	2,980,799	53.6
Net Profit After Tax	175,347	8.2	485,253	5.7	474,868	5.3	250,254	4.5
Working Capital	1,298,746	—	(327,009)	—	1,249,305	—	504,812	—

RATIOS	UQ	MED	LQ	UQ	MED	LQ	UQ	MED	LQ	UQ	MED	LQ
SOLVENCY												
Quick Ratio (times)	12.6	2.9	1.0	3.6	1.7	1.0	3.7	1.7	1.1	3.1	1.5	1.1
Current Ratio (times)	18.4	8.9	1.8	4.5	2.1	1.3	4.3	2.2	1.5	3.3	2.0	1.2
Curr Liab To Nw (%)	2.2	7.0	20.5	19.9	50.8	138.4	24.9	55.5	125.1	28.0	67.7	140.9
Curr Liab To Inv (%)	170.9	598.6	999.9	189.1	572.8	999.9	176.4	390.4	999.9	172.9	372.3	999.9
Total Liab To Nw (%)	3.0	8.3	32.2	27.0	71.4	173.6	29.6	75.5	159.4	34.0	77.3	162.2
Fixed Assets To Nw (%)	1.9	10.5	47.6	4.3	13.8	34.5	5.4	15.9	31.1	7.9	26.0	45.8
EFFICIENCY												
Coll Period (days)	4.4	13.0	44.2	36.1	56.6	81.2	46.7	69.2	90.9	55.9	77.8	108.0
Sales To Inv (times)	155.6	15.3	10.6	135.7	34.7	11.0	122.0	35.7	11.9	275.1	25.6	8.0
Assets To Sales (%)	39.1	132.9	245.2	25.5	39.6	66.6	29.3	39.5	55.1	29.2	36.9	47.7
Sales To Nwc (times)	7.2	3.6	0.7	11.5	6.0	3.4	9.5	5.9	3.5	11.4	6.9	4.3
Acct Pay To Sales (%)	1.3	2.7	7.9	1.2	3.7	8.0	1.4	4.2	7.2	2.3	4.4	7.0
PROFITABILITY												
Return On Sales (%)	11.2	3.9	(2.6)	9.3	3.8	0.4	9.2	4.5	0.9	4.5	2.3	0.9
Return On Assets (%)	10.5	3.9	(1.4)	23.5	7.9	0.3	23.2	10.6	1.9	17.3	5.7	1.4
Return On Nw (%)	19.5	6.1	(1.2)	49.8	17.0	3.1	48.6	21.9	4.8	29.6	12.6	3.4

	SIC 8713 SURVEYING SERVICES (NO BREAKDOWN) 2014 (18 Establishments) $	%	SIC 8721 ACCTNG,AUDTNG,BKPNG (NO BREAKDOWN) 2014 (28 Establishments) $	%	SIC 8731 COMMRCL PHYS RSRCH (NO BREAKDOWN) 2014 (100 Establishments) $	%	SIC 8732 COMMRCL NPHYS RSRCH (NO BREAKDOWN) 2014 (26 Establishments) $	%
Cash	654,616	24.3	304,102	19.8	13,902,217	40.2	580,961	24.2
Accounts Receivable	808,168	30.0	519,123	33.8	4,080,750	11.8	825,828	34.4
Notes Receivable	0	0.0	13,823	0.9	34,583	0.1	4,801	0.2
Inventory	0	0.0	26,110	1.7	760,818	2.2	43,212	1.8
Other Current	390,615	14.5	167,409	10.9	6,985,691	20.2	482,534	20.1
Total Current	**1,853,399**	**68.8**	**1,030,567**	**67.1**	**25,764,059**	**74.5**	**1,937,336**	**80.7**
Fixed Assets	630,371	23.4	253,418	16.5	3,977,002	11.5	235,265	9.8
Other Non-current	210,124	7.8	251,882	16.4	4,841,568	14.0	228,063	9.5
Total Assets	**2,693,894**	**100.0**	**1,535,867**	**100.0**	**34,582,629**	**100.0**	**2,400,664**	**100.0**
Accounts Payable	67,347	2.5	201,199	13.1	59,136,296	171.0	158,444	6.6
Bank Loans	0	0.0	39,933	2.6	0	0.0	14,404	0.6
Notes Payable	339,431	12.6	33,789	2.2	11,204,772	32.4	12,003	0.5
Other Current	503,758	18.7	388,574	25.3	32,196,427	93.1	645,779	26.9
Total Current	**910,536**	**33.8**	**663,495**	**43.2**	**102,537,495**	**296.5**	**830,630**	**34.6**
Other Long Term	317,880	11.8	190,447	12.4	(24,242,423)	(70.1)	96,026	4.0
Deferred Credits	0	0.0	15,359	1.0	518,739	1.5	60,017	2.5
Net Worth	1,465,478	54.4	666,566	43.4	(44,231,182)	(127.9)	1,413,991	58.9
Total Liab & Net Worth	**2,693,894**	**100.0**	**1,535,867**	**100.0**	**34,582,629**	**100.0**	**2,400,664**	**100.0**
Net Sales	5,659,441	100.0	3,656,826	100.0	26,912,552	100.0	4,189,640	100.0
Gross Profit	2,761,807	48.8	2,468,358	67.5	11,087,971	41.2	1,935,614	46.2
Net Profit After Tax	503,690	8.9	888,609	24.3	(1,318,715)	(4.9)	477,619	11.4
Working Capital	942,863	—	367,072	—	(76,773,436)	—	1,106,706	—

RATIOS	UQ	MED	LQ	UQ	MED	LQ	UQ	MED	LQ	UQ	MED	LQ
SOLVENCY												
Quick Ratio (times)	9.6	2.1	0.9	3.1	1.5	0.8	3.9	1.8	0.7	2.4	1.8	1.1
Current Ratio (times)	10.2	3.2	1.7	4.2	1.9	1.0	7.5	2.9	1.3	3.3	2.1	1.5
Curr Liab To Nw (%)	6.6	16.0	115.6	6.0	42.8	150.5	10.6	26.6	64.3	18.0	66.3	128.3
Curr Liab To Inv (%)	999.9	999.9	999.9	419.5	999.9	999.9	270.9	999.9	999.9	26.1	89.1	289.8
Total Liab To Nw (%)	11.0	42.7	144.6	10.4	83.3	183.1	20.1	57.2	155.1	31.9	67.2	135.0
Fixed Assets To Nw (%)	15.7	24.7	100.8	13.6	30.0	64.6	1.8	8.8	22.0	3.4	22.7	32.7
EFFICIENCY												
Coll Period (days)	32.7	50.4	72.9	17.9	49.6	84.0	28.8	41.1	76.5	45.9	66.1	79.9
Sales To Inv (times)	999.9	999.9	999.9	774.0	59.0	23.6	80.6	15.7	6.3	44.6	8.2	6.6
Assets To Sales (%)	35.3	47.6	59.8	24.6	42.0	97.4	47.8	128.5	695.9	35.1	57.3	94.2
Sales To Nwc (times)	7.7	4.8	3.1	11.6	6.0	3.0	7.3	2.8	0.2	9.0	5.7	3.0
Acct Pay To Sales (%)	0.4	1.0	2.1	0.6	1.1	2.9	3.4	10.8	42.9	1.0	2.8	4.9
PROFITABILITY												
Return On Sales (%)	16.6	5.5	2.1	36.6	19.3	11.1	3.4	(17.7)	(278.4)	12.4	4.8	2.7
Return On Assets (%)	35.6	9.3	5.5	75.5	45.7	10.0	6.3	(22.9)	(58.4)	22.3	11.4	2.4
Return On Nw (%)	41.4	17.0	8.8	109.2	70.0	20.5	11.8	(22.7)	(69.8)	37.8	19.1	7.5

SIC 8733 — NCMRCL RSCH ORGNZTN (NO BREAKDOWN) 2014 (28 Establishments)

	$	%
Cash	4,086,224	33.7
Accounts Receivable	885,146	7.3
Notes Receivable	0	0.0
Inventory	84,877	0.7
Other Current	1,964,298	16.2
Total Current	**7,020,545**	**57.9**
Fixed Assets	2,679,690	22.1
Other Non-current	2,425,059	20.0
Total Assets	**12,125,294**	**100.0**
Accounts Payable	545,638	4.5
Bank Loans	0	0.0
Notes Payable	24,251	0.2
Other Current	8,305,826	68.5
Total Current	**8,875,715**	**73.2**
Other Long Term	2,134,052	17.6
Deferred Credits	72,752	0.6
Net Worth	1,042,775	8.6
Total Liab & Net Worth	**12,125,294**	**100.0**
Net Sales	8,316,388	100.0
Gross Profit	3,118,646	37.5
Net Profit After Tax	241,175	2.9
Working Capital	(1,855,170)	---

RATIOS	UQ	MED	LQ
SOLVENCY			
Quick Ratio (times)	6.1	1.5	0.9
Current Ratio (times)	10.2	4.6	1.1
Curr Liab To Nw (%)	6.0	17.7	37.7
Curr Liab To Inv (%)	318.8	999.9	999.9
Total Liab To Nw (%)	11.4	27.9	85.5
Fixed Assets To Nw (%)	2.9	8.1	59.6
EFFICIENCY			
Coll Period (days)	2.4	38.6	54.2
Sales To Inv (times)	534.8	38.7	4.1
Assets To Sales (%)	73.2	145.8	466.4
Sales To Nwc (times)	9.4	1.7	0.7
Acct Pay To Sales (%)	2.9	5.6	11.6
PROFITABILITY			
Return On Sales (%)	6.7	(1.8)	(8.8)
Return On Assets (%)	6.4	(1.4)	(9.6)
Return On Nw (%)	12.4	2.3	(10.6)

SIC 8734 — TESTING LABRTRS (NO BREAKDOWN) 2014 (22 Establishments)

	$	%
Cash	802,916	25.9
Accounts Receivable	703,714	22.7
Notes Receivable	49,601	1.6
Inventory	34,101	1.1
Other Current	362,706	11.7
Total Current	**1,953,038**	**63.0**
Fixed Assets	691,314	22.3
Other Non-current	455,709	14.7
Total Assets	**3,100,061**	**100.0**
Accounts Payable	877,317	28.3
Bank Loans	21,700	0.7
Notes Payable	1,621,332	52.3
Other Current	4,693,493	151.4
Total Current	**7,213,842**	**232.7**
Other Long Term	1,026,120	33.1
Deferred Credits	15,500	0.5
Net Worth	(5,155,401)	(166.3)
Total Liab & Net Worth	**3,100,061**	**100.0**
Net Sales	5,184,048	100.0
Gross Profit	2,576,472	49.7
Net Profit After Tax	279,939	5.4
Working Capital	(5,260,804)	---

RATIOS	UQ	MED	LQ
SOLVENCY			
Quick Ratio (times)	4.1	2.2	1.3
Current Ratio (times)	6.5	3.1	1.5
Curr Liab To Nw (%)	9.3	24.2	74.3
Curr Liab To Inv (%)	402.9	614.0	968.8
Total Liab To Nw (%)	15.3	34.3	98.2
Fixed Assets To Nw (%)	22.6	50.1	63.9
EFFICIENCY			
Coll Period (days)	35.0	51.8	72.6
Sales To Inv (times)	305.7	111.6	28.3
Assets To Sales (%)	29.9	59.8	110.8
Sales To Nwc (times)	11.7	5.5	3.6
Acct Pay To Sales (%)	1.7	4.9	7.8
PROFITABILITY			
Return On Sales (%)	8.9	5.4	0.5
Return On Assets (%)	23.3	11.1	(0.2)
Return On Nw (%)	36.4	14.1	1.4

SIC 8741 — MANAGEMENT SERVICES (NO BREAKDOWN) 2014 (81 Establishments)

	$	%
Cash	795,916	20.1
Accounts Receivable	1,421,562	35.9
Notes Receivable	23,759	0.6
Inventory	154,431	3.9
Other Current	554,370	14.0
Total Current	**2,950,038**	**74.5**
Fixed Assets	483,093	12.2
Other Non-current	526,651	13.3
Total Assets	**3,959,782**	**100.0**
Accounts Payable	744,439	18.8
Bank Loans	23,759	0.6
Notes Payable	71,276	1.8
Other Current	1,144,377	28.9
Total Current	**1,983,851**	**50.1**
Other Long Term	780,077	19.7
Deferred Credits	3,960	0.1
Net Worth	1,191,894	30.1
Total Liab & Net Worth	**3,959,782**	**100.0**
Net Sales	9,825,762	100.0
Gross Profit	3,409,539	34.7
Net Profit After Tax	491,288	5.0
Working Capital	966,187	---

RATIOS	UQ	MED	LQ
SOLVENCY			
Quick Ratio (times)	2.0	1.2	0.7
Current Ratio (times)	2.9	1.5	1.2
Curr Liab To Nw (%)	24.9	63.1	212.6
Curr Liab To Inv (%)	106.9	559.0	999.9
Total Liab To Nw (%)	40.7	109.0	280.7
Fixed Assets To Nw (%)	3.3	12.0	34.5
EFFICIENCY			
Coll Period (days)	28.7	47.3	74.8
Sales To Inv (times)	90.7	49.7	7.4
Assets To Sales (%)	23.9	40.3	76.1
Sales To Nwc (times)	13.2	8.7	4.6
Acct Pay To Sales (%)	1.8	5.7	11.9
PROFITABILITY			
Return On Sales (%)	7.6	3.6	0.2
Return On Assets (%)	23.0	6.8	0.2
Return On Nw (%)	59.8	16.1	1.9

SIC 8742 — MNGMNT CNSLTNG SVCS (NO BREAKDOWN) 2014 (208 Establishments)

	$	%
Cash	677,700	28.9
Accounts Receivable	813,709	34.7
Notes Receivable	16,415	0.7
Inventory	49,245	2.1
Other Current	241,534	10.3
Total Current	**1,798,603**	**76.7**
Fixed Assets	229,808	9.8
Other Non-current	316,573	13.5
Total Assets	**2,344,984**	**100.0**
Accounts Payable	335,333	14.3
Bank Loans	23,450	1.0
Notes Payable	98,489	4.2
Other Current	1,177,182	50.2
Total Current	**1,634,454**	**69.7**
Other Long Term	379,887	16.2
Deferred Credits	9,380	0.4
Net Worth	321,263	13.7
Total Liab & Net Worth	**2,344,984**	**100.0**
Net Sales	8,286,163	100.0
Gross Profit	3,571,336	43.1
Net Profit After Tax	480,597	5.8
Working Capital	164,149	---

RATIOS	UQ	MED	LQ
SOLVENCY			
Quick Ratio (times)	3.6	1.7	0.9
Current Ratio (times)	4.1	2.0	1.2
Curr Liab To Nw (%)	22.2	52.5	180.0
Curr Liab To Inv (%)	169.0	784.1	999.9
Total Liab To Nw (%)	26.6	74.0	221.9
Fixed Assets To Nw (%)	3.3	8.9	27.8
EFFICIENCY			
Coll Period (days)	28.5	48.2	65.0
Sales To Inv (times)	251.9	38.0	15.8
Assets To Sales (%)	19.4	28.3	60.1
Sales To Nwc (times)	16.7	6.8	4.0
Acct Pay To Sales (%)	1.1	3.3	6.1
PROFITABILITY			
Return On Sales (%)	9.6	3.8	1.0
Return On Assets (%)	32.5	8.9	2.1
Return On Nw (%)	71.9	25.2	8.0

SIC 8743 PUBLIC RLTNS SVCS (NO BREAKDOWN) 2014 (12 Establishments) — SIC 8744 FCLTS SPPRT SVCS (NO BREAKDOWN) 2014 (25 Establishments) — SIC 8748 BUS CNSLTNG.NEC (NO BREAKDOWN) 2014 (182 Establishments)

	SIC 8743 $	%	SIC 8744 $	%	SIC 8748 $	%
Cash	204,023	18.2	784,262	14.1	557,555	26.0
Accounts Receivable	366,569	32.7	2,241,542	40.3	823,466	38.4
Notes Receivable	0	0.0	0	0.0	8,578	0.4
Inventory	17,936	1.6	0	0.0	66,478	3.1
Other Current	201,782	18.0	1,079,055	19.4	257,334	12.0
Total Current	**790,310**	**70.5**	**4,104,859**	**73.8**	**1,713,411**	**79.9**
Fixed Assets	181,603	16.2	817,635	14.7	240,178	11.2
Other Non-current	149,094	13.3	639,646	11.5	190,855	8.9
Total Assets	**1,121,007**	**100.0**	**5,562,140**	**100.0**	**2,144,444**	**100.0**
Accounts Payable	88,560	7.9	762,013	13.7	283,067	13.2
Bank Loans	12,331	1.1	0	0.0	15,011	0.7
Notes Payable	0	0.0	11,124	0.2	81,489	3.8
Other Current	337,423	30.1	2,931,248	52.7	1,702,688	79.4
Total Current	**438,314**	**39.1**	**3,704,385**	**66.6**	**2,082,255**	**97.1**
Other Long Term	175,998	15.7	645,208	11.6	180,134	8.4
Deferred Credits	0	0.0	38,935	0.7	2,144	0.1
Net Worth	506,695	45.2	1,173,612	21.1	(120,089)	(5.6)
Total Liab & Net Worth	**1,121,007**	**100.0**	**5,562,140**	**100.0**	**2,144,444**	**100.0**
Net Sales	5,287,769	100.0	16,703,123	100.0	5,859,137	100.0
Gross Profit	2,575,144	48.7	5,244,781	31.4	2,619,034	44.7
Net Profit After Tax	153,345	2.9	868,562	5.2	392,562	6.7
Working Capital	351,996	—	400,474	—	(368,844)	—

RATIOS	UQ	MED	LQ	UQ	MED	LQ	UQ	MED	LQ
SOLVENCY									
Quick Ratio (times)	1.7	1.4	1.2	2.2	1.2	0.6	3.8	2.0	1.1
Current Ratio (times)	3.7	1.6	1.3	2.7	1.4	1.0	4.7	2.5	1.4
Curr Liab To Nw (%)	44.2	86.7	135.3	36.6	75.9	428.3	19.5	54.7	141.7
Curr Liab To Inv (%)	159.8	740.9	999.9	999.9	999.9	999.9	200.7	568.0	999.9
Total Liab To Nw (%)	64.3	115.7	359.0	44.0	129.3	449.9	27.8	70.5	152.6
Fixed Assets To Nw (%)	7.8	15.7	50.5	4.6	17.0	71.5	3.7	11.5	26.9
EFFICIENCY									
Coll Period (days)	25.6	39.4	45.6	39.8	58.4	87.5	39.1	58.8	84.3
Sales To Inv (times)	69.6	66.8	14.4	999.9	945.2	890.4	111.4	34.0	11.7
Assets To Sales (%)	18.1	21.2	35.5	22.4	33.3	66.4	23.5	36.6	57.8
Sales To Nwc (times)	25.3	10.4	8.1	21.0	10.1	5.2	11.2	5.9	3.5
Acct Pay To Sales (%)	0.9	2.7	3.6	1.9	3.3	7.8	0.9	3.0	7.6
PROFITABILITY									
Return On Sales (%)	7.0	5.7	(0.3)	8.2	3.7	1.1	9.9	4.1	0.7
Return On Assets (%)	32.1	12.8	(1.5)	25.5	11.5	1.1	27.2	9.9	2.3
Return On Nw (%)	78.8	23.0	(5.2)	93.3	42.3	17.3	51.4	18.1	5.1